THE DARK PAGE

Books That Inspired American Film Noir
[1940-1949]

THE DARK PAGE

Books That Inspired American Film Noir [1940-1949]

Kevin Johnson
FOREWORD BY PAUL SCHRADER

PHOTOGRAPHY BY DAN GREGORY
DESIGN BY JOHN MALLOY

OAK KNOLL PRESS

First Edition published 2007
Reprinted with corrections 2008

Published by
Oak Knoll Press
310 Delaware Street, New Castle, DE 19720
www.oakknoll.com
Publishing Director: Mark S. Parker Miller

Designed and typeset by John Malloy
Photographed by Dan Gregory
Printed and bound by Kwong Fat Offset Printing

ISBN: 978-1-58456-217-7 (standard cloth)
ISBN: 978-1-58456-218-4 (deluxe limited)

Printed in China on acid-free paper meeting the requirements
of ANSI/NISO Z39.48-1992 (Permanence of Paper)

Library of Congress Cataloging-in-Publication Data

Johnson, Kevin 1961-
  Dark page : books that inspired American film noir, 1940-1949 / Kevin Johnson ; foreword by Paul Schrader.
       p. cm.
  Summary: "A guide to first edition published books that provided source material for "film noir" movies made in the United States during the years 1940-
1949. Describes points for identifying first edition copies and offers background information concerning each book and each film that was based on it"--
Provided by publisher.
  Includes bibliographical references and index.
  ISBN 978-1-58456-217-7 (hard cover : alk. paper) -- ISBN 978-1-58456-218-4 (deluxe limited issue : alk. paper) 1. Detective and mystery stories,
American--Bibliography. 2. Detective and mystery stories, English--Bibliography. 3. First editions. 4. Noir fiction, American--Bibliography. 5. Noir fiction,
American--Film and video adaptations. 6. Noir fiction, English--Bibliography. 7. Noir fiction, English--Film and video adaptations. 8. Film noir--United
States--History and criticism. I. Title.
  Z1231.D47J64 2007
  [PS374.D4]
  016.813'087208--dc22
                              2007029750

CONTENTS

FOREWORD

PAUL SCHRADER

What a joy this book is. Finally, a visual and factual look at two worlds that have long been intertwined, but whose relationship has rarely been examined in depth or detail. I've long been a fan and an advocate of film noir, and in recent years have begun collecting first editions. *The Dark Page* brings the two together as both a reference and a visual treat.

In 1971 I programmed and wrote notes for Filmex, the first Los Angeles Film Exposition. The program notes were subsequently published by *Film Comment* as "Notes on Film Noir." At that time, pre-VHS and DVD, films, particularly low-budget films, fell off the radar after release. Although these films were only twenty years old, they had been, for the most part, forgotten. When I contacted Joseph H. Lewis, director of *Gun Crazy*, for an article we wished to run in *Cinema* magazine, he was surprised anyone remembered him or his "old movies."

At that time only one article had been published in English on film noir: Raymond Durgnat's "Family Tree of Film Noir," 1970, in *British Cinema* magazine. The primary source for the films in Durgnat's piece was Raymond Borde and Etienne Chaumeton's "Panorama du film noir Americain" in 1955.

Largely in response to the Durgnat piece, Filmex screened, on a Saturday and Sunday, *Gun Crazy*, *They Live By Night*, *White Heat*, *T-Men*, *Out of the Past*, *Kiss Me Deadly*, and *Pickup on South Street* followed by a panel discussion with Samuel Fuller, Robert Aldrich, and Joseph H. Lewis.

The Filmex series rang a bell which has been reverberating ever since. There are now dozens of books on film noir, film courses and a profitable expanding DVD market. The Castro Theater in San Francisco has for years hosted an annual noir festival that brings in thousands of viewers over a week-long period, and similar festivals have sprung up all over the country. "I see no end in sight," George Feltenstein, head of Warner Brothers Home Video, replied in 2006 when asked about the studio's series of restored film noir DVDs. "People are always asking for more."

Film noir began as "roman noir," the French term for the hard-boiled crime fiction pioneered by Raymond Chandler, Dashiell Hammett, James M. Cain, David Goodis, Cornell Woolrich, and Jim Thompson. In 1946. French publisher Gallimard inaugurated the Serie Noire line of novels; the same year, French cineaste Nino Frank coined the term "film noir."

American crime fiction of the 1930s and 1940s was plot-driven, steeped in atmosphere and foreboding—ideal "underlying material" for movies. The great American novels of this period were diminished by adaptation to the screen. Film could not, for financial reasons as well as aesthetic, capture the complexities of novels like *For Whom the Bell Tolls*, *The Grapes of Wrath*, or *The Fountainhead*. With crime fiction, it was just the opposite. Woolrich and Goodis were made for the screen. Their novels became richer and more complex with addition of lighting, music, acting, set design, and film editing. In a 1970 interview, Francois Truffaut, who adapted both Cornell Woolrich *(The Bride Wore Black* and *Mississippi Mermaid)* and David Goodis *(Down There*, the basis for *Shoot the Piano Player)*, said "Writers like David Goodis and William Irish (pen name for Woolrich) have special value and they have no counterparts in France. Because so many books appear each year in the States, these detective story writers are usually ignored. Ironically, this liberates them. Made humble by their neglect, they are free to experiment because they think no one is paying attention anyway. Not expecting to be analyzed, they put anything into their books they choose." Well, not quite; these writers were slaves to the marketplace, but they were also free in ways highbrow writers weren't. This freedom, however hobbled by commercial constraints, managed the jump straight to the screen. For film noir, like roman noir, the lower the budget, the smaller the target audience, the freer the expression.

After World War II the noir sensibility became commercially successful in films and drew to it many practitioners, some of whom had little feel for the genre. Hollywood can accommodate anything and it easily accommodated the "dark novel." Some of the artists we now associate with film noir had a natural aptitude for its themes and style; for others it was just a job, the "current thing." But all of them had functional lives: they arrived to work on time, got paid, followed instructions, and had a good time.

The literary origins are darker and more tragic. One need only look at the lives of roman noir's two premiere practitioners, Cornell Woolrich and David Goodis, to find the torment that first created these stories. Woolrich began his writing career as an F. Scott Fitzgerald wannabe (evidenced by his early novels, and personal favorites, *Cover Charge, Children of the Ritz, Times Square, A Young Man's Heart, The Time of Her Life,* and *Manhattan Love Song*), but after his wife discovered his homosexual diary —perhaps left out intentionally —his marriage was annulled, and he returned to his mother's Harlem tenement apartment. After eight years of silence he found his métier with *The Bride Wore Black*. Fifteen novels followed in the next ten years, five with "black" in the title, and many of which were made into films. He remained in that tenement with his mother until he died, retreating to another room to write books and stories replete with scathing descriptions of effeminate men, never showing his mother what he had written, drinking and cruising the Manhattan waterfronts.

David Goodis fared little better. He retreated from Hollywood in 1950 to live with his parents and schizophrenic brother in Philadelphia, spending his nights in the bars and dives he wrote about. Like Woolrich, he died of alcoholism. These were not Hollywood lives. They were the real deal.

The greatest treat of *The Dark Page* is, of course, the dust jackets themselves. Although influenced by graphic design trends, deco, dada, futurism, the illustrators of these covers, straitjacketed by the dictates of the marketplace, created an instantly recognizable style. Their names for the most part have been lost in the fog of literary history. It remains left to some future researcher, with access to the archives of the publishing houses, to unearth the names, histories, and styles of these graphic artists.

I'd like to add one addendum to my 1971 article. One factor I hadn't acknowledged in the rise of film noir was technology itself. During World War II, 16-mm cameras—Bell and Howell's Eyemo in the United States, and Bolex in Europe—were adapted to document the war effort, both hand-held in combat and mounted in jet fighters. High speed black-and-white film was developed to shoot this action without the need for artificial lighting. The Office of Strategic Services' Photographic Division enlisted Hollywood's top talent (including directors John Ford, John Huston, Frank Capra, William Wyler, and George Stevens) in this effort. With these directors came present and soon-to-be Hollywood cameramen shooting real action in real locations without lighting or preparation. The lessons these technicians learned during the War served them well on the home front. Shooting real locations in low light was the ideal creative solution to the budgetary constraints of a 10-day schedule of a crime B-film melodrama. In 1945 John Huston shot *The Battle of San Pietro*. Two years later he used many of the same tools to shoot *The Treasure of the Sierra Madre* on location in Mexico; then two years after that, in Los Angeles, *The Asphalt Jungle*. Yet another factor in the rise of film noir.

Paul Schrader
New York City

INTRODUCTION

KEVIN JOHNSON

Welcome to *The Dark Page*, a book about books, a book about American film noir, and a book about the novelists, screenwriters, and directors that make up the fascinating and rarely discussed relationship between the two. Every book you see in the pages that follow has been documented for the same reason—it was the basis for a film in the American film noir cycle during the 1940s. Before going into the criteria for book selection, I'd like to first discuss a few basic ground rules about the films themselves.

A Definition of Film Noir

The first step in understanding the American film noir cycle is to obtain a better grasp of just what "film noir" is and what it is not. I find that film enthusiasts sometimes have a shaky understanding of the term, due mostly to the casual way it is defined in popular culture. Film noir has in fact been the subject of much scholarship since the 1940s, beginning in France and moving later to the United States, and has a well-established critical history that is unknown to the average filmgoer. The collision of this scholarship with the huge popularity of films noir has resulted in some major misconceptions.

The first and most common misconception is that film noir is a genre, when it is in fact a style. The noir thread runs through virtually every genre, including Westerns, melodramas, science fiction, crime, and horror. The 1956 sci-fi classic *Invasion of the Body Snatchers* is a film noir, as is the 1948 Western, *Blood on the Moon*.

The second most common misconception is that a film noir always involves detectives or a crime. While these elements are commonly found in films noir, they do not define the style, nor does the style require their inclusion. Noir protagonists run the gamut from housewives to bankers to journalists, and while a criminous element is typically somewhere to be found, it is often subtle, tangential to the story, or even altogether absent.

The third most common misconception is that film noir is meant to be a broad term, covering everything from a film like *The Maltese Falcon* to Roman Polanski's *Chinatown* to the Coen Brothers' *The Man Who Wasn't There*. The film noir cycle, by critical consensus, did not begin until 1940, and depending on who you ask, ended somewhere between 1959 and 1965. Key crime films before 1940, such as *Little Caesar* or *Beast of the City* are considered *noir antecedents,* with the distinction being that all the elements of noir had not yet come together. Films after 1965 are considered *post-noir* or *neo-noir,* and that dividing line is based on the point at which noir films became "self-aware." In other words, once filmmakers were consciously making films in the noir style, the original cycle had effectively come to an end.

The noir style is defined as a combination of several elements that came together in American film beginning in 1940. Speaking generally, three of those elements are (1) the arrival of German directors and cinematographers in Hollywood during both World Wars, who brought with them the expressionistic style of German films of the 1920s and 1930s, (2) a cultural malaise in America, resulting from both World Wars, that brought about a more cynical outlook and a strong response to darker themes, motivations, and story lines in films, (3) Hollywood's adoption of the "hard-boiled" school of storytelling, which had existed in print since the early 1920s, but did not reach full realization on the screen until 1940. There are other factors as well, such as the rigidly structured Hollywood studio system, which accommodated the aforementioned elements and caused the noir style to flourish once it became popular with audiences.

Recommended Reading on Film Noir

The Dark Page is built on a foundation of existing scholarship on film noir, but is meant only to be an in-depth study of the book sources themselves. The two best pieces I can recommend with regard to a comprehensive definition of film noir are by Paul Schrader and David Spicer. Schrader's seminal 1971 essay, "Notes on Film Noir," which has remained completely relevant and undated over the past thirty-five years, can be found in *Film Noir Reader*, edited by Alain Silver and James Ursini and published by Limelight Editions in 1996. David Spicer's book simply titled, *Film Noir,* published by Longmans in

2002, is the most straightforward and thorough primer on the subject I have encountered, with detailed discussions of everything from the expressionist origins of the noir style to the role of the Hollywood system in its development.

Film Sources

In determining a source list for *The Dark Page*, I used as my template the work of three film writers whose published books on the films in the noir canon I found to be the most deeply rooted in careful research and thought. My primary reference is ***Dark City: The Film Noir* by Spencer Selby** (McFarland,1984). Selby's book is an extraordinarily comprehensive study of American film noir, published well before most of the many American books and articles on the subject that followed it, with a scope that has never been improved upon. Among *Dark City*'s few significant antecedents in English are Raymond Durgnat's "The Family Tree of Film Noir" (*Cinema,* August 1970) and Paul Schrader's essay noted earlier. What makes Selby's book singular is that it attempts to identify all the American films in the noir canon, with an eye for detail and an understanding of the scholarship that preceded it. Selby is at work on his magnum opus, an expanded, comprehensive guide to the American, British and Western European films in the cycle.

My two secondary references are two books that I feel are both complementary to Selby's work, but in different ways. The first is ***Film Noir: An Encyclopedic Reference,* edited by Alain Silver and Elizabeth Ward** (Overlook Press, 1993). Now in its third edition, the Silver and Ward guide is one of the most articulate studies of American film noir, and while it is not as exhaustive or inclusive as Selby's *Dark City*, it stands on its own as an important and detailed study, particularly in the case of films from the major studios. Also, there is no better reference for detailed plot deconstructions of the major films in the cycle.

My other secondary reference is ***Death on the Cheap: The B-Movies of Film Noir* by Arthur Lyons** (Da Capo Press, 2000). Lyons' book focuses almost exclusively on the important films noir that were released outside of the major studios, many of which are today considered classics of the genre. These films were among the first to successfully subvert the Hays Code and have remained the most difficult to locate in any kind of viewable format. Like Selby, Lyons is at work on a revised edition of his book.

Book Sources

The range of literature that constitutes the basis for American film noir is surprisingly broad. While a number of the sources are crime novels as one would expect, many fall well outside that category. Some are romances, some are examples of great western literature, and a few are even nonfiction. The range of authors runs the gamut, starting from the giants of high literature from the past two centuries (Henry James, Aldous Huxley, Ernest Hemingway, Ayn Rand, W. Somerset Maugham, Graham Greene, Robert Louis Stevenson) to its classic crime authors (Wilkie Collins, Raymond Chandler, Dashiell Hammett), to its "cult" authors who never quite received their due (Geoffrey Homes, David Goodis, B. Traven), and finally to the weird and intriguing heap at the bottom, a healthy dose of authors who languish in obscurity, whether deservedly or undeservedly (Robert Du Soe, Martin Goldsmith, Ernst Lothar, John Taintor Foote, and many others).

While it is a strongly held belief among some bibliophiles that a book has an inherently greater legacy than a film, there are more than a few arguments to the contrary. There are numerous cases where a legendary film is based on a book that is completely forgotten or long out of print; and conversely, in the defense of said bibliophiles, cases where a legendary book has been made into a mediocre film. Since opinions on this subject vary widely, I've made an attempt to give every book source and related film in the American noir cycle equal consideration, without attempting to assign rank or relative importance.

A Note about Attribution

The content of the book and film "discussions" found in each entry, sometimes paraphrased and sometimes quoted directly, is drawn almost entirely from other sources. The discussions are meant to be light and factual, and I've made no attempt to shed new critical light on any book or film. Rather, my goal was to include interesting information about authors, screenwriters, and directors that would make for a good accompaniment to the core content of this guide, that being the books themselves.

Credit for the sources used is attributed either at the beginning of a quote, or at the end of a given section. In cases where one source provided content for the entire entry (i.e., both the book section and the film section), the source is credited only once, at the end of the entry.

How to use this book

The entries in this volume are presented in alphabetical order by book author, and within a given author, by the order in which the books were adapted to film. This sometimes results in a sequence that will be unfamiliar to book collectors. For example, Raymond Chandler's second novel, *Farewell, My Lovely* was made into a film before his first novel, *The Big Sleep*; hence, *Farewell, My Lovely* is shown first.

Each entry begins with the book title, author, and publisher of the first edition, followed by a discussion of the book and/or its author. Next are the book points that identify the first edition, which include any information that cannot be clearly seen in the photo to the right of the description. The second part of each entry is devoted to the film made from the book or a short story from the book, beginning with the title and film director, followed by detailed information regarding the screenwriter(s), film studio, cinematographer(s), actors, and composer(s) involved. A discussion of the film follows, ending with a notation of the scholarly reference used to qualify the film for inclusion in the 1940s American film noir cycle.

What is a Contributor?

After each book and film entry, you will see a brief paragraph with information about each "contributor," and where that person's "contribution" fits into the 1940s American film noir cycle. In the context of this book, a "contributor" is defined as an author, a film director, or a screenwriter that had some intersection with a literary source. In a few select cases, film producers are noted as well. For example, if a sentence reads, "John Huston's second of five contributions," it means that the entry you are reading about is the second film in which John Huston was involved, either as a screenwriter or a director, during the 1940s. Since some of the contributors' entries do not involve literary sources (e.g., John Huston's contribution to *Three Strangers* as a screenwriter in 1946), a Selected Filmography of Key Contributors is provided at the end of the book, which shows every contribution by a given individual during the 1940s, including original screenplays. A discussion of this section follows.

Selected Filmography of Key Contributors

Early on in the research process, I found a significant intersection of authors, screenwriters, and directors in the world of 1940s American film noir. Prolific screenwriters like Richard Brooks and Jay Dratler wrote obscure novels, and famous novelists like Ayn Rand, William Faulkner and Raymond Chandler worked as screenwriters in near-anonymity. Many films noir were based on plays, many of which were hits on Broadway, and others that barely made it past opening night. In the case of Ben Hecht, one man functioned as author of the book source, screenwriter, and director. The *Selected Filmography* shows the order of contributions by each writer, director and screenwriter, and the list includes films that were based on books as well as those based on original stories, unpublished plays, or screenplays.

If a contributor to the 1940s American film noir cycle has no intersection with a literary source, that contributor is not discussed in *The Dark Page*. Examples of directors in this category during the 1940s would include Douglas Sirk and Elia Kazan. This certainly does not mean that the contribution or the film was insignificant, it simply means that the contributor's work has no connection in the 1940s to a literary adaptation. For a more complete list of films noir, I recommend the aforementioned guides by Selby, Silver and Ward, and Lyons.

Guidelines for Selection of First Editions

The book types considered in this volume are limited to sources for films noir made between 1940 and 1949, and include the following:

> Novels and plays, published either in hardcover or as paperback originals
> Short stories published in collections
> Nonfiction books used as a film source

The following book types are not considered:

> Novelizations of films (with a few important exceptions)
> Photoplay editions
> Actors' softcover play editions
> Novels or collections of stories that were published long after the release of a film
> Magazine, digest or pulp appearances

In the cases where a film has two book sources (or the book has two significant binding or jacket variants), the primary source is pictured in the Main Bibliography, and the secondary source is discussed in *Appendix A: Secondary Book Sources.*

In the cases where a book has content that is the basis for more than one film, the first produced film adaptation is discussed in the Main Bibliography, and the later film adaptations are discussed in *Appendix B: Secondary Films.*

In the cases where the photo for a rare book source has been reconstructed based on available information, the entry appears in *Appendix C: Reconstructed Book Sources.*

Types of editions

In cases where the trade first edition of a book was preceded by or issued simultaneously with a signed limited edition or presentation edition, preference is given to the trade edition.

American, British and foreign first editions

In the case of first editions in translation (works originally written in a language other than English), the first edition in English is given preference.

Within the scope of English-language editions, a "follow the flag" position is taken in the matter of correct first editions. This means that the country most strongly associated with the author's nationality (typically either the United States or the United Kingdom, but occasionally other countries) is the preferred country of first edition publication.

Book Points

First edition points are provided for each book just below the description of each book source. For those unfamiliar with the terminology used in the description of a book, I recommend John Carter's *ABC for Book Collectors,* published by the Oak Knoll Press. For a more general overview of first editions and book collecting, I recommend *Book Collecting 2000* by Patricia and Allen Ahearn, published by Putnam.

Condition, scarcity and book values

A conscious effort has been made to avoid discussion of condition, scarcity and value of books in this volume, as this information is constantly changing.

Regarding Photographic Reproductions of Books

The books represented in *The Dark Page* came from many sources, including major institutions, personal libraries, and the photographic archives of rare booksellers. Our goal was to reproduce with complete accuracy the first edition of the book described in each entry, with extreme attention to detail regarding color, size, texture, and most of all, the correct representation of the book details. Most of the books you see in the pages that follow are actual photographs of a given book. In the case of a few extremely rare books, however, the book and jacket have been carefully reconstructed from parts that exist in different collections, often located in different parts of the world. In only one instance did we have to make a "guess" at the accuracy of a given representation, and that single volume is in Appendix C (*Reconstructed Books*). It is important to understand that the representation we present is that of a "perfect" copy. That representation may (or may not) have involved digital manipulation, combination of parts, and other techniques.

Future volumes

Two future volumes in this series are envisioned. The second volume will cover the book sources for American films noir released between 1950 and 1965, and the third volume will cover British and European films noir.

A Final Word

The last days of tracking down photographs of the first editions in *The Dark Page* were truly dramatic. After years of effort, two months prior to our deadline, it still appeared that there would be at least a dozen titles we simply weren't going to find. Then, at the eleventh hour, we had one magical break after another, and by the end of July 2007, literally forty-eight hours before submitting our manuscript, the last photo (one of the rarest Haycraft Queen cornerstones, Israel Zangwill's *The Big Bow Mystery*) was inserted. To say the hunt was a thrill would be an understatement at best.

FOR SAM

THE DARK PAGE

BOOKS THAT INSPIRED AMERICAN FILM NOIR
[1940-1949]

JOURNEY INTO FEAR

ERIC AMBLER

Publisher	London: Hodder and Stoughton, 1940

Eric Ambler was born in London on June 28, 1909, to a family of entertainers. After graduating London University he served an apprenticeship with an engineering firm, but he soon found success writing plays and other works. He joined the Royal Artillery at the start of World War II, and ended his service as a Lieutenant Colonel and assistant director of the army film unit. He continued to write novels and worked in the civilian film industry as a screenwriter, earning an Academy Award nomination in 1953 for his gritty adaptation of Nicholas Monsarrat's *The Cruel Sea*.

A recurring theme in Ambler's books is the amateur who finds himself unwillingly in the company of professional criminals. Typically the protagonist is out of his depth and spends much of the book as a bumbling anti-hero, yet eventually manages to surprise himself with a decisive action that outwits his more experienced opponents. Such is the case in his novels, *Journey into Fear, The Light of Day,* and *Dirty Story*.

The author's first of two contributions.

Blue cloth with black titles at the spine, no topstain. "First published 1940" stated on the copyright page. Front flap shows a price of "8/3 net" at the bottom right corner, with a nine-line blurb on Ambler at the top. Rear flap advertises five Ambler novels, beginning with *The Dark Frontier* and ending with *The Mask of Dimitrios*. Rear panel is devoted to a plot summary of the book.

JOURNEY INTO FEAR

NORMAN FOSTER AND ORSON WELLES (UNCREDITED)

Screenwriter	Joseph Cotten, Richard Collins (uncredited), Ben Hecht (uncredited), Orson Welles (uncredited)
Cinematographer	Karl Struss
Composer	Roy Webb, Rex Dunn (uncredited)
Cast	Joseph Cotten, Dolores Del Rio, Orson Welles, Ruth Warrick, Agnes Moorehead, Everett Sloan
Studio	RKO, 1943
Runtime	68 minutes

In the summer of 1941, RKO purchased the rights for *Journey into Fear* from writer Ben Hecht, who owned them at the time. Hecht had already written a screenplay from the book, and there had been fierce competition for the rights, with both Gary Cooper and Charles Boyer eager to play the central character. RKO had slated Orson Welles for the lead role, and though the project was initially separate from Welles' Mercury unit there, he quickly took a personal interest in the project. He abandoned Hecht's version and began working with his writers on a new one. As a result, *Journey into Fear* soon became a Mercury project, with directorial reins handed to Norman Foster (though Welles, as usual, provided no small amount of assistance). The project was filmed in tandem with *The Magnificent Ambersons*, with much of the same cast, shuttling back and forth on the RKO lot between the two sets. The atmosphere was Welles' favorite: one for all and all for one. When Peter Bogdanovich later asked him who was responsible for the penultimate scene in the film—Banat and Graham crawling around the highest ledge of a tall building in a driving rain—he answered, "Whoever was nearest the camera." (Callow)

Welles' first of four contributions, and Ben Hecht's second of twelve.

Reference	Selby, Silver and Ward, Lyons

JOURNEY INTO FEAR

JOURNEY
INTO
FEAR

ERIC
AMBLER

ERIC AMBLER

H&S
HODDER & STOUGHTON

THE MASK OF DIMITRIOS

ERIC AMBLER

Publisher   London: Hodder and Stoughton, 1939

In Eric Ambler's fifth and most famous novel, *The Mask of Dimitrios,* author Charles Latimer becomes obsessed with tracing the history of Dimitrios Makropoulos, whose sudden, squalid death is of interest to many unusual characters. Latimer's curiosity is simultaneously satisfied and intensified as he learns more about the mysterious Greek, whose career has been recorded in police dossiers in every Central European country for two decades. Latimer slowly becomes convinced Dimitrios is still alive and a trans-European chase ensues, bringing into the story a wide array of strange characters and mixed motives. (Penzler)

Ambler's second contribution, and a Haycraft Queen cornerstone.

Red cloth with titles and rule in black at the spine, no topstain. "FIRST PRINTED - - 1939" stated at the top of the copyright page. Front flap shows a price of "7/6 / net" at the bottom right corner, and contains a single blurb about Ambler at the top, ending with the publisher's device. Rear flap is an advertisement for four titles by Ambler, beginning with *The Dark Frontier* and ending with *Cause for Alarm.* Rear panel is another quote about Ambler from Anthony Berkeley, followed by a publisher's note about *The Mask of Dimitrios*, ending with the publisher's device at the bottom right corner.

THE MASK OF DIMITRIOS

JEAN NEGULESCO

Screenwriter   Frank Gruber
Cinematographer   Arthur Edeson
Composer   Adolph Deutsch
Cast   Sydney Greenstreet, Zachary Scott, Faye Emerson, Peter Lorre, George Tobias
Studio   Warner Brothers, 1944
Runtime   95 minutes

In his autobiography, *Here Lies,* Eric Ambler notes that his preferred title for his novel had always been A *Coffin for Dimitrios,* and while his friend Alfred A. Knopf was good enough to keep it, his UK publisher had other ideas. Ambler: "They did not like the title, and I never knew exactly why. But I have never found the second senses of higher authorities worth challenging unless one is prepared for a fight to the finish and to shed blood. It is only fair to mention that when Warner Brothers came to make a film of the book two years later, they too preferred *The Mask of Dimitrios*. Another second sense at work."

The first of six contributions by Negulesco, and the first of three by novelist-screenwriter Frank Gruber.

Reference   Selby, Silver and Ward

The mask of Dimitrios

ERIC AMBLER

Berlow

ERIC AMBLER

HODDER &
STOUGHTON

THIEVES LIKE US

EDWARD ANDERSON

Publisher   New York: Frederick A. Stokes, 1937

Born in 1905 and raised in Texas and Oklahoma, Edward Anderson knocked around the Southwest as a young man, working as a journalist at several newspapers. He soon turned to fiction, getting invaluable tips from his neighbor, pulp writer John Knox. Anderson sold his first piece, a prizefight story, "The Little Spic," to a sports pulp magazine, but after that he hit the road, taking Depression-era hard knocks and hoboing his way across the US.

Anderson's colorful write-what-you-know experiences informed much of his first novel, 1935's *Hungry Men*. His second and final novel, *Thieves Like Us,* about a bank robbery binge running through Texas and Oklahoma, stands as an underrated American classic. The novel is written in the *Bonnie and Clyde* mold, but with a proletarian bent at odds with the author's own downward-spiraling later life, in which he courted Nazi sympathies, anti-Semitism, and crackpot religion. (Hauptfleisch)

The author's only contribution.

Light brown cloth with titles in black at the front board and spine, no topstain. Title page shows a date of MCMXXXVII, with no statement of edition or later printing on the copyright page. Front flap shows a price of $2.50, followed by a plot summary. Rear flap contains an advertisement for *Forty Centuries Look Down* by F. Britten Austin. Rear panel begins with an illustration of the author, followed by a biography reprinted from *WINGS*, the Literary Guild magazine. At least three printings have been noted.

THEY LIVE BY NIGHT

NICHOLAS RAY

Screenwriter   Charles Schnee
Cinematographer   George E. Diskant
Composer   Leigh Harline
Cast   Cathy O'Donnell, Farley Granger, Howard da Silva, Jay C. Flippen, Helen Craig
Studio   RKO, 1948
Alternate Titles   The Twisted Road (UK), Your Red Wagon (working title)
Runtime   95 minutes

After purchasing the film rights to *Thieves Like Us* from Edward Anderson for a reported $500, producers Dore Schary and John Houseman assigned first-time director Nicholas Ray to the project. Ray, who had studied architecture with Frank Lloyd Wright and worked in the New York theater with Houseman and Elia Kazan, had made an impression as a Broadway director and with the short films he had made for the Office of War Information during World War II. He brought a strong sense of style to the low-budget project, which predicted the highly individual work that would follow in the next two decades. (Smiley)

In a 1977 interview with Robert Porfirio, producer Dore Schary ruminates about how *They Live by Night* has a more realistic tone than its more successful protege, *Bonnie and Clyde:* "I am not saying that *Bonnie and Clyde* wasn't high class, but when they suddenly gave you that violent and shocking ending, it almost had a comic effect. I remember being in the theater watching with an audience, and it didn't shock—it got laughs, nervous laughter, not gasps. In *They Live by Night,* when the kid dies, there is a sense of sadness, no shock, just chagrin." By the same token, Schary concedes that the film sat on the shelves at RKO for years, noting, "the pathos in it previewed badly."

The first of director Nicholas Ray's three contributions, and the second of three by screenwriter Charles Schnee.

Reference   Selby, Silver and Ward

A NOVEL BY

THIEVES
LIKE
US

EDWARD ANDERSON

KEY LARGO

MAXWELL ANDERSON

Publisher   Washington, D.C.: Anderson House, 1939

Born in Atlantic, Pennsylvania Maxwell Anderson was educated at the University of North Dakota and Stanford. He became a playwright after careers as both a schoolteacher and a journalist. After several years of mixed success, he turned to historical drama for his recounting of the Elizabeth Essex story, *Elizabeth the Queen* (1930), and made the interesting choice of writing the play in blank verse. The play's success prompted him to write many of his subsequent dramas in the same style, making him the only major twentieth century American playwright to do so. One of the least successful of these was *Key Largo,* a drama set at the end of the Spanish Civil War, wherein an American loyalist, beset by guilt for having abandoned his comrades during the conflict, visits the families of the fallen men at a small hotel in Key Largo. He finds the opportunity to redeem himself by confronting a group of gangsters who have taken over the hotel. The play was one of the earliest productions staged by The Playwrights Company, which Anderson formed in 1938 along with S. N. Behrman, Elmer Rice, Robert E. Sherwood, Sidney Howard, and Kurt Weill.

The playwright's only contribution.

Gray cloth with titles in red at the front board and spine. Dark gray topstain and illustrated endpapers, repeating the design from the jacket. Title page shows a date 1939, with "First Printing, November 1939 / FIRST EDITION" stated on the copyright page. Front flap shows a price of $2.50 at the lower center; above the price is a plot summary, and below it is the publisher's name and address. Rear flap advertises "Plays by Maxwell Anderson," and shows listings for seventeen titles, beginning with *What Price Glory?* and ending with *Key Largo.* Rear panel is a continuation of the illustration from the front panel and the spine, with no text.

KEY LARGO

JOHN HUSTON

Screenwriter	John Huston, Richard Brooks
Cinematographer	Karl Freund
Composer	Max Steiner
Cast	Humphrey Bogart, Edward G. Robinson, Lauren Bacall, Lionel Barrymore, Claire Trevor
Studio	Warner Brothers, 1948
Runtime	100 minutes

John Huston recalls: "*Key Largo* was given to me by the studio. I liked to write away from the office, from the writers' building. [So] Richard Brooks and I went down to Florida, to Key Largo, and wrote the script there. It was quite a departure from the play, which was not one of Anderson's best. We went into a hotel on the Key, a remote, detached place. It had to be opened for us, and we brought our own cook. Presently there began to appear roulette wheels, a dice table and blackjack set up. We wrote the picture and gambled, alternately, and came back with the script, written I guess in six to eight weeks down there, and made the film. It was brought up-to-date, of course, to take place just after the Second World War. This man had returned and already disenchantment had set in—[after the] high hopes and aspirations of Roosevelt, the future was even then to be seen. And although we wrote it in Key Largo, it was filmed entirely in the studio." (Pratley)

Huston's eighth of nine contributions, and screenwriter Brooks' fourth of five.

Reference   Selby, Silver and Ward

THE UNSUSPECTED

CHARLOTTE ARMSTRONG

Publisher   New York: Coward-McCann, 1946

Charlotte Armstrong was born and raised in Vulcan, an iron-mining town on Michigan's Upper Peninsula. After receiving a degree from Barnard in 1925, she worked first as a secretary, then as a fashion reporter. She married in 1928, and while raising her three children, wrote stories and had poems published in *The New Yorker*. She also wrote two Broadway plays (in 1939 and 1941) but both had short runs. Following the failure of her second drama, she turned to the detective novel and soon sold *Lay On, MacDuff,* the first of three novels to feature Professor MacDougal Duff. It was with her fourth mystery, however, a suspense novel called *The Unsuspected,* that she achieved wider success. It was a controversial book, praised by many critics, including Howard Haycraft, but was criticized because of her disclosure of the murderer's identity almost at the outset—a technique that one day would be seen as groundbreaking. (Penzler)

Armstrong's only contribution, and a Haycraft Queen cornerstone.

Dark blue cloth with titles at the spine in gilt, no topstain. Endpapers illustrated with characters from the novel by Allen Pope (who also designed the dust jacket). No statement of edition or later printings on the copyright page. Front flap shows a price of $2.50 at the top right corner, followed by a plot summary that continues to the rear flap, ending with a blurb from *The Saturday Evening Post*. Rear panel begins with an illustration of the author, followed by a four-paragraph biography, credited to Douglas Gilbert of *The New York World-Telegram*.

THE UNSUSPECTED

MICHAEL CURTIZ

Screenwriter	Ranald MacDougall, Bess Meredyth
Cinematographer	Woody Bredell
Composer	Franz Waxman
Cast	Claude Rains, Joan Caulfield, Audrey Totter, Constance Bennett, Hurd Hatfield
Studio	Warner Brothers, 1947
Runtime	103 minutes

In the mid-1940s, the western world's cynicism about the inherent goodness of human nature manifested itself as a perverse fascination with evil and evildoing for its own sake. This mood influenced Michael Curtiz when his independent production company was on the verge of formation, and he selected Charlotte Armstrong's 1946 novel, *The Unsuspected* as the basis for his first film as a producer-director in Hollywood. Curtiz originally envisioned Orson Welles and Jennifer Jones as the leads, then Claude Rains and Joan Fontaine. When Fontaine was unavailable, Joan Caulfield took the female lead. The real stars of the film, however, are Woody Bredell's dazzling, shadow-drenched cinematography and Anton Grot's magnificent sets, transforming Claude Rains' wealthy and cultured radio mystery narrator into a killer with no conscience or qualms. (Robertson)

The second of three contributions by director Michael Curtiz, and screenwriter Ranald MacDougall's third of four.

Reference   Selby, Silver and Ward

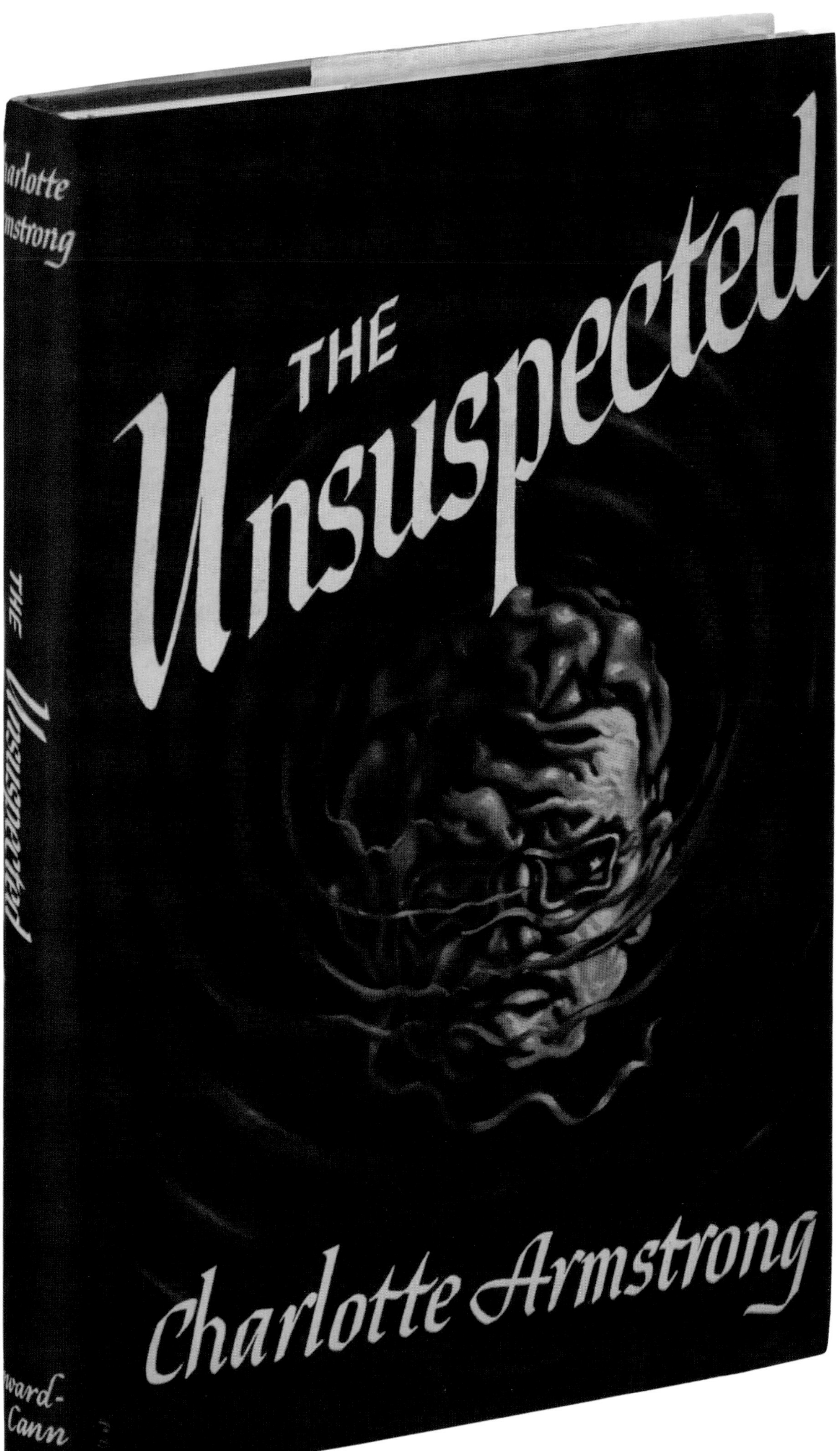
THE
Unsuspected
Charlotte Armstrong
THE
Unsuspected
Cann

MORTGAGE ON LIFE

VICKI BAUM

Publisher	Garden City: Doubleday, 1946

Born in Vienna, Vicki Baum began working as a professional harpist with the Vienna Konzertverein at the age of fifteen. As a young girl, she began writing and won prizes for her short stories. She worked as a magazine editor, and after several years of raising a family and writing late at night, suddenly broke through as a best-selling author with the publication of *Grand Hotel* in 1929. Her novel was made into a play, and in 1932, before she had even signed a contract with a film studio, she and her family set sail for America.

After a prolific decade of screenwriting, Baum began writing novels again, and *Mortgage on Life* was published during this period. Of her own literary talent she wrote: "When I've written potboilers I did so deliberately, to hone my tools, prove my skills, and, naturally, I needed money. I've also written a few good books. I know what I'm worth: I am a first-rate second-rate author. " (Feuchtwanger)

The author's second of two contributions, and her only contribution as a novelist.

Maroon cloth with gilt titles and illustration (similar to illustration at the lower portion of the front jacket panel) at the spine, maroon topstain. "FIRST EDITION" stated at the bottom of the copyright page. Front flap shows a price of $2.50 at the top right corner, followed by a photo of the author (with a photo credit for Elli Marcus), then a plot summary that continues to the rear flap, ending with a printer's code of 4344-46. Rear panel contains a biography of the author, ending with a printer's code of 22-46.

A WOMAN'S SECRET

NICHOLAS RAY

Screenwriter	Herman J. Mankiewicz
Cinematographer	George E. Diskant
Composer	Nacio Herb Brown, Frederick Hollander
Cast	Maureen O'Hara, Melvyn Douglas, Gloria Grahame, Bill Williams
Studio	RKO, 1949
Alternate Titles	The Long Denial (working title)
Runtime	84 minutes

First serialized in *Collier's* as "The Long Denial," Vicki Baum's novel, *Mortgage on Life,* was bought by RKO upon publication. Herman J. Mankiewicz was to produce and script this "modern and sophisticated drama with a music business background," and it would be his first screen credit since 1945. The studio originally slated Jacques Tourneur as director, but Tourneur, busy finishing another project (*Berlin Express*), was not able to make the film. On the same day, the young director Nicholas Ray, who had just completed work on his first film, *They Live by Night,* was assigned to take his place. The film was shot under the working title, *The Long Denial,* but upon his arrival at RKO as new studio boss, Howard Hughes himself chose "A Woman's Secret."

On June 1, 1948, actress Gloria Grahame (co-star of *A Woman's Secret* and screen femme fatale extraordinaire) obtained a divorce from her husband, actor Stanley Clements, in Las Vegas; at 6:30PM the same day, in her lawyer's Las Vegas office, she married Nicholas Ray. (Eisenschitz)

The second of Ray's three contributions, and the second of two by screenwriter Herman J. Mankiewicz.

Reference	Selby, Lyons

VICKI BAUM

A NEW NOVEL

MORTGAGE ON LIFE

CAMEL
Restaurant

club

DOUBLEDAY

THE HOUSE OF DR. EDWARDES

FRANCIS BEEDING

Publisher	London: Hodder and Stoughton, 1927

Francis Beeding was the pseudonym for the very prolific mystery writing team of Hilary St. George Saunders and John Palmer, both Oxford graduates, who began publishing crime fiction in 1925. Palmer was the drama critic for *The Saturday Review of Literature* and *The Evening Standard*. Saunders, who served with the Welsh Guards in World War I, was the anonymous author of the famous pamphlet, *The Battle of Britain* (1940), as well as *The Green Beret* (1949), an official history of the British commandos. Saunders once said, "Palmer can't be troubled with description and narrative, and I'm no good at creating characters or dialogue." (Penzler)

The writing duo's only contribution.

Blue cloth, no topstain. No statement of edition or later impressions on the copyright page. Front flap, rear flap, and rear panel are blank.

SPELLBOUND

ALFRED HITCHCOCK

Screenwriter	Ben Hecht, Angus McPhail, May E. Romm (uncredited)
Cinematographer	George Barnes
Composer	Miklós Rózsa ,
Cast	Ingrid Bergman, Gregory Peck, Leo G. Carroll, Michael Chekhov, Rhonda Fleming
Studio	United Artists, 1945
Alternate Titles	The House of Dr. Edwardes (working title)
Runtime	111 minutes

Producer David O. Selznick had concerns about the extreme nature of the source material proposed for the new Alfred Hitchcock film, noting in a production memo that the book was "filled with diabolical maniacs running loose; black magic; weird ceremonies, rites and incantations; violence; attempted murders, etc." Hitchcock remembers: "The original novel, *The House of Dr. Edwardes* [a title that the film retained until very near its release], was about a madman taking over an insane asylum. It was melodramatic and quite weird. In the book even the orderlies were lunatics and they did some very queer things. I wanted to make something more sensible, to turn out the first picture on psychoanalysis. So I worked with Ben Hecht, who was in constant contact with prominent psychoanalysts.

"I was determined to break with the traditional way of handling dream sequences through a blurred and hazy screen. I asked Selznick if he could get [Salvador] Dali to work with us and he agreed, though I think he didn't really understand my reasons for wanting Dali. He probably thought I wanted his collaboration for publicity purposes. The real reason was that I wanted to convey the dreams with great visual sharpness and clarity, sharper than the film itself. But Dali had some strange ideas. He wanted a statue to crack like a shell falling apart, with ants crawling all over it, and underneath there would be Ingrid Bergman, covered by ants! It just wasn't possible." (Truffaut)

Hitchcock's fourth of five contributions, and Ben Hecht's third of twelve.

Reference	Selby, Silver and Ward

14

THE HOUSE OF
DR. EDWARDES

FRANCIS
BEEDING

A tremendous thriller
by the author of
'The Seven Sleepers'
'The Hidden Kingdom'

H&S

7/6
NET

HODDER & STOUGHTON

THE LODGER

MARIE BELLOC LOWNDES

Publisher   London: Methuen, 1913

In the March 9, 1923, entry in her diary, Marie Belloc Lowndes wrote: "The story of *The Lodger* is curious and may be worth putting down if only because it may encourage some fellow author long after I am dead. *The Lodger* was first written as a short story after I heard a man telling a woman at a dinner party that his mother had had a butler and a cook who married and kept lodgers. They were convinced that Jack the Ripper had spent a night under their roof. When the literary editor of *The Daily Telegraph* commissioned a novel from me for serial publication, I remembered *The Lodger*. As soon as the serial began appearing, I began receiving letters from all parts of the world, from people who kept lodgings. When it was published as a book in the UK, I did not receive a single favorable review. When the American edition was published, I was not able to find even one sentence of tepid approval. Then, to my surprise, when *The Lodger* had been out two or three years, reviewers began to rebuke me for not writing another book like it."

Prior to being published as a novel, *The Lodger* was serialized in *The Daily Telegraph* in the UK, then appeared as a short story in the January 1911 issue of *McClure's* in the US.

The author's first of two contributions, and a Haycraft Queen cornerstone.

Blue cloth with titles in gilt at the front board and spine, no topstain. "First Published in 1913" stated in the middle of the copyright page, with no mention of later impressions. Thirty-one pages of advertisements at the rear. Jacket not seen. Later printings have been noted.

THE LODGER

JOHN BRAHM

Screenwriter   Barré Lyndon
Cinematographer   Lucien Ballard
Composer   Hugo W. Friedhofer
Cast   Laird Cregar, Merle Oberon, George Sanders, Cedric Hardwicke, Sara Allgood
Studio   Twentieth Century-Fox, 1944
Runtime   84 minutes

John Brahm was born in Germany, worked for many years in London and moved to Hollywood in 1937. Like Fritz Lang, Billy Wilder, Otto Preminger, and many others, Brahm brought to Hollywood a European and specifically German sensibility, refined by many years spent in theater and film. In his classic text, *The American Cinema,* American film historian and critic Andrew Sarris notes that Brahm hit his stride in the 1940s with "mood-drenched melodramas." And while his film work fell off after 1950, The director continued to contribute significant work to television in the 1950s and 1960s, most notably on *The Twilight Zone, The Alfred Hitchcock Hour,* and *The Man from U.N.C.L.E.*

The refined, English look of Brahm's adaptation of Lowndes' classic novel improves considerably on Hitchcock's worthy silent version from 1927 and was the first of two stunning collaborations with actor Laird Cregar.

The first of six contributions by Brahm, and the first of four by screenwriter Barré Lyndon.

Reference   Selby, Lyons

THE LODGER

BELLOC LOWNDES

METHUEN

THE STORY OF IVY

MARIE BELLOC LOWNDES

Publisher   London: William Heinemann, 1927

Born into a distinguished family in 1868, Marie Belloc Lowndes was the daughter of a French barrister, Louis Belloc, and an English mother. Her brother was the famous writer Hilaire Belloc; her great-great-grandfather was Joseph Priestley, the chemist who discovered oxygen; her grandmother wrote the first French translation of *Uncle Tom's Cabin* in 1852; and her husband, Frederic Sawrey Lowndes, was a respected journalist for the *London Times*.

Marie began writing at sixteen and wrote nearly every day. A perfectionist, she rewrote constantly and painstakingly, and yet she produced a large number of books. Although she is chiefly remembered for her crime and suspense thrillers, her major ability was character development—she was overwhelmingly concerned about the relationship between her male and female characters, with particular emphasis on discreetly handled sexual matters. (Penzler)

The second of two contributions by the author.

Dark blue cloth with titles and rule in gilt at the spine, no topstain. Title page shows a date of 1927, with "First Published, 1927" stated at the center of the copyright page. Jacket not seen.

IVY

SAM WOOD

Screenwriter	Charles Bennett
Cinematographer	Russell Metty
Composer	Daniele Amfitheatrof
Cast	Joan Fontaine, Patric Knowles, Herbert Marshall, Sir Cedric Hardwicke, Richard Ney, Lucille Watson, Sara Allgood
Studio	Universal, 1947
Runtime	99 minutes

Screenwriter Charles Bennett remembers: "I liked *Ivy*, but it wasn't very successful. Sam Wood was a strange director. There were a lot of great directors in those days who weren't really great—they were *dependent*. First on the writers, second on their art directors and people like that. Sam, in particular, was dependent on his art directors and *Ivy* is a good example of that." (McGilligan, *Backstory 1*).

Director Sam Wood's only contribution, and screenwriter Bennett's first of three.

Reference   Selby

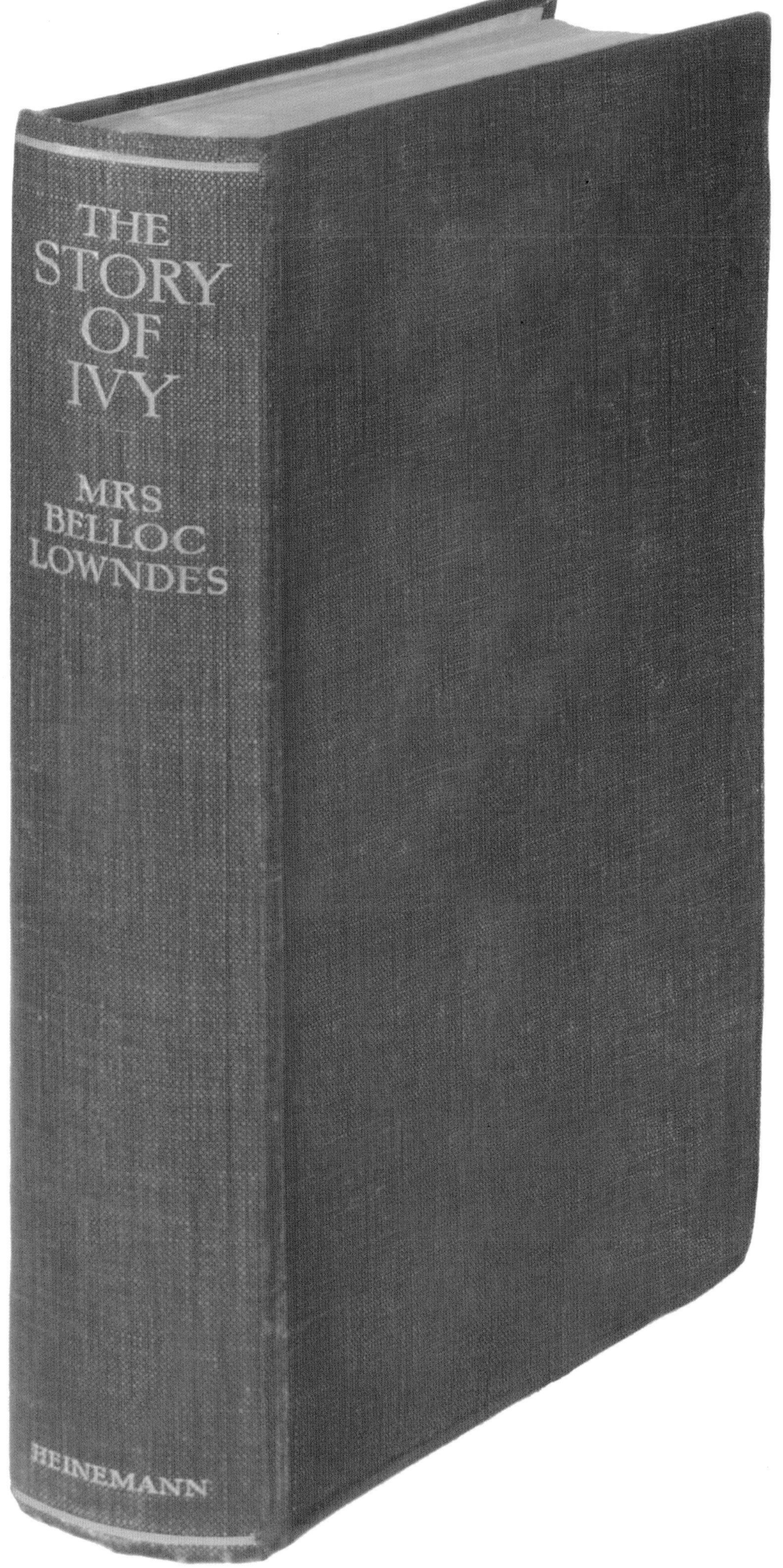
THE
STORY
OF
IVY
MRS
BELLOC
LOWNDES
HEINEMANN

BEFORE THE FACT

ANTHONY BERKELEY WRITING AS FRANCIS ILES

Publisher   London: Victor Gollancz, 1932

Before the Fact was the second of three novels written by Anthony Berkeley Cox under the pseudonym Francis Iles. Cox wrote far more prolifically under the shorter name, Anthony Berkeley, beginning in 1925 with *The Layton Court Mystery*. In 1931 Cox decided, as mystery authors often did in that era, to write a handful of books under a "mysterious" pen name.

The author's only contribution, and a Keating 100 selection.

Black cloth with green titles at the spine only. Title page shows a date of 1932, with no statement of edition or later impressions on the copyright page. Front flap, rear flap, and rear panel are devoted to "Opinions about *Malice Aforethought*," as follows: three blurbs on the front flap, with the fourth beginning on the front flap and ending on the rear flap, followed by the fifth and sixth, with the seventh beginning on the rear flap and ending on the rear panel, followed by six final blurbs.

SUSPICION

ALFRED HITCHCOCK

Screenwriter	Samson Raphaelson, Joan Harrison, Alma Reville
Cinematographer	Harry Stradling
Composer	Franz Waxman
Cast	Joan Fontaine, Cary Grant, Nigel Bruce, Sir Cedric Hardwicke
Studio	RKO, 1941
Alternate Titles	Before the Fact (working title)
Runtime	99 minutes

In *Hitchcock/Truffaut,* Alfred Hitchcock makes fond mention of writer Anthony Berkeley and sheds some light on how his preferred (but unused) notion of the film's ending was basically the same as that of the novel.

Hitchcock: "You might say *Suspicion* was the second English picture I made in Hollywood [the first being *Rebecca*]—the actors, the atmosphere, and the novel on which it's based were all British. I've often wanted to film Berkeley's first novel, *Malice Aforethought,* but could never find the right actor for the part.

"I've never been too pleased with the way *Suspicion* ends. I had something else in mind. The scene I wanted, but it was never shot, was for Cary Grant to bring Joan Fontaine a glass of milk that's been poisoned. Joan Fontaine has just finished a letter to her mother: 'Dear Mother, I'm desperately in love with him, but I don't want to live because he's a killer—I'd rather die." Then, Cary Grant comes in with the fatal glass and she says, 'Will you mail this letter to Mother for me, dear?' She drinks the milk and dies. Fade out and fade in on one short shot: Cary Grant, whistling cheerfully, walks over to the mailbox and pops the letter in."

The film retained the title *Before the Fact* until just prior to the film's release.

The only contribution to the American film noir cycle by noted playwright-screenwriter Samson Raphaelson, who wrote the screenplays for many of Ernst Lubitsch's classic films, including *Trouble in Paradise* (1932) and *The Shop Around the Corner* (1940).

Hitchcock's second of five contributions, Joan Harrison's second of five, and the first of two by longtime Hitchcock screenwriter Alma Reville (also known as Lady Hitchcock).

Reference   Selby, Silver and Ward

BEFORE THE FACT

by

"Francis Iles"

author of

MALICE AFORETHOUGHT

which The English Review called "possibly the best shocker ever written"

7/6 net

GOLLANCZ

LONG HAUL

A.I. BEZZERIDES

Publisher   New York: Carrick & Evans, 1938

Albert Isaac Bezzerides was born in Samsun, Turkey (then the Ottoman Empire), on August 9,1908, to an American mother and a Greek father. He was a year old when his parents emigrated to the United States, where he grew up in California's San Joaquin Valley, an area heavily populated with immigrants from Armenia and Europe and noted for its proliferation of fruit orchards.

As a young man, "Buzz" Bezzerides first worked as a truck driver, then studied electrical engineering at the University of California at Berkeley before dropping out to work as an engineer while fulfilling his ambition to write. His first novel, *Long Haul*, based on his own trucking experiences, was bought by Warners and became the basis for *They Drive By Night* (1940). This brought Bezzerides to Hollywood, where he would work as a screenwriter for the next three decades. He specialized in tough, unpretentious writing, providing pithy dialogue for several of Warners' "social conscience" films of the 1940s, many of which were films noir. His no-nonsense style was favored by such screen heroes as Humphrey Bogart, George Raft, and Robert Mitchum.

The author's first of three contributions.

Light orange cloth with brown and black design and rule at the front board and spine, light brown topstain. The second and third leaves (titled "A Letter from A.I. Bezzerides") are tipped in, and are slightly smaller than the rest of the text block. The letter "A" appears just below the copyright statement on the copyright page. Front flap shows a price of $2.00 at the top right corner, followed by a plot summary that continues to the end of the rear flap. Rear panel begins with a photo of the author, followed by a brief publisher's promotional blurb, ending with the publisher's name.

THEY DRIVE BY NIGHT

RAOUL WALSH

Screenwriter   Jerry Wald, Richard Macaulay
Cinematographer   Arthur Edeson
Composer   Adolph Deutsch
Cast   George Raft, Humphrey Bogart, Ann Sheridan, Ida Lupino, Alan Hale, Gale Page
Studio   Warner Brothers, 1940
Alternate Titles   The Road to Frisco (UK)
Runtime   93 minutes

Producer Mark Hellinger's wife Glad had little interest in her husband's business. She seldom knew how much money he was making, or what he planned to do. On the other hand, she was an omnivorous reader, and often sat long hours leafing through the scripts around the house. One night at dinner, in late 1939, she mentioned to her husband that she had read the Wald-Macaulay script for *They Drive by Night* and liked it. Hellinger said, "Who the hell is going to pay money to see a bunch of truck drivers? Answer me that. There's no glamour to driving a truck." But he eventually demurred, read the script more carefully, and saw the possibilities of a sleeper. The film was released in the summer of 1940, cost four hundred thousand dollars to make, and grossed over four million. The film also paired George Raft—then at the height of his career—with the up-and-coming Humphrey Bogart. It would be the last time Bogart played a secondary role. (Bishop)

The first of five contributions by director Raoul Walsh, screenwriter Jerry Wald's first of two, and Richard Macaulay's first of three.

Reference   Selby

LONG HAUL

A· I· BEZZERIDES

THIEVES' MARKET

A.I. BEZZERIDES

Publisher   New York: Charles Scribner's Sons, 1949

A.I. Bezzerides' style of "proletarian literature" was in keeping with the rising demand for hard-hitting, tough, and controversial movies with a social conscience in the 1940s. The author had no trouble finding work in Hollywood, first with Warner Brothers and then with other major studios. "I had been working as an engineer at the Department of Water and Power, writing on the side," Bezzerides recalls. "I'd written two novels, *Long Haul* [1938] and *Thieves' Market* [1949]. They were based on things I'd seen with my father or on my own. I worked with my father, trucking, going to the market to buy produce. There was corruption and they'd try to screw you. When he was selling grapes, the packing house would screw him on the price and then sell to New York for an expensive price. When I was trucking I wouldn't allow it. A guy once tried to rob me in such a blatant way [that] I picked up a two-by-four...I was going to kill him."

Bezzerides' last of three contributions, and second as a novelist.

Green cloth with titles in red at the front board and spine (spine title reads vertically, and upward), no topstain. Title page shows a date of 1949, with the Scribner "A" on the copyright page, and Scribner seal at the bottom. Front flap shows a price of $3.00, followed by a plot summary that continues to the rear flap, ending with the publisher's name and city. Rear panel begins with an author photo, followed by a one-paragraph biography.

THIEVES' HIGHWAY

JULES DASSIN

Screenwriter	A.I. Bezzerides
Cinematographer	Norbert Brodine
Composer	Alfred Newman
Cast	Richard Conte, Valentina Cortesa, Lee J. Cobb, Barbara Lawrence, Jack Oakie, Millard Mitchell, Joseph Pevney
Studio	Twentieth Century-Fox, 1949
Alternate Titles	Hard Bargain (working title), Collision (US re-release title), Thieves' Market (US re-release title)
Runtime	94 minutes

While highly regarded as one of the most realistic and finely-tuned films noir, compromises were still made for the adaptation of *Thieves' Market*. Bezzerides objected to some of the changes: "[Director Jules] Dassin said, 'For the prostitute, I want Valentina Cortesa, so rewrite it for her.' We were going to have Shelley Winters, who would have been perfect. This Italian, Cortesa, what would she be doing in this story? But I rewrote it."

Dassin shot *Thieves' Highway* in twenty-four days and had his share of troubles as well. After he turned in the finished film, which had a particularly cynical ending, producer Darryl F. Zanuck tacked on an upbeat and completely unnecessary moralistic scene in which a pair of cops lecture the hero and his pals about not taking the law into their own hands. Dassin had no knowledge of the new ending until he saw the finished film. (Vallance)

The last of Dassin's four contributions.

Reference   Selby, Silver and Ward, Lyons

THIEVES' MARKET

A Novel by
A. I. BEZZERIDES
Author of THEY DRIVE BY NIGHT

WILD CALENDAR
LIBBIE BLOCK

Publisher   New York: Alfred A. Knopf, 1946

Libbie Block was a very successful writer of women's fiction, with stories appearing frequently in periodicals and a string of highly successful novels. Hubin only credits the author with one crime novel, *Bedeviled* in 1947. Though *Wild Calendar* was essentially a soap opera (and not at all of the noir variety), Ms. Block's standing as a minor screenwriter, combined with the novel's extreme popularity in 1946, gained Hollywood's attention.

The author's only contribution.

Blue cloth with an illustration of a tree branch stamped in blind at the front board, and titles with a similar illustration stamped in copper at the spine. Burgundy topstain. Title page shows a date of 1946, with "FIRST EDITION" stated at the bottom of the copyright page. Front flap shows a price of $2.75 at the top right corner, and contains a plot summary. A brief essay about the book by Mary Chase (author of *Harvey*) takes up the rear flap. Rear panel shows a photo of the author and a separate photo of her Victorian residence, with a short biography and some lore about the house.

CAUGHT
MAX OPHÜLS DIRECTING AS MAX OPULS

Screenwriter	Arthur Laurents, Abraham Polonsky, Kathryn Scola, Paul Trivers (all except Laurents wrote uncredited early treatments)
Cinematographer	Lee Garmes
Composer	Frederick Hollander
Cast	James Mason, Barbara Bel Geddes, Robert Ryan, Frank Ferguson, Curt Bois, Ruth Brady
Studio	RKO, 1946
Alternate Titles	Wild Calendar (working title)
Runtime	88 minutes

The first treatment of *Caught*, then under the working title *Wild Calendar*, was written by screenwriter Kathryn Scola. The adaptation adhered very closely to the novel's story line about a woman whose early marriage to an eccentric, older millionaire named Smith Ohlrig who dramatically changes the "calendar" for her life. Abraham Polonsky was subsequently hired to work on a treatment, and at Ophüls' request changed the story's focus to Ohlrig. Ophüls was fascinated and repelled by RKO boss Howard Hughes (who had just fired him, along with Preston Sturges, on an early treatment of *Vendetta*), and asked Polonsky to have the Ohlrig character mirror some of Hughes' many eccentricities.

Polonsky wrote several drafts, but was eventually pulled away to direct another film that became a noir classic, *Force of Evil*. He was replaced by playwright Arthur Laurents, who was in good favor at the time from his work on *Rope* and *The Snake Pit*. Laurents finished the screenplay, and Howard Hughes (executive producer on the film) surprised everyone by quietly asking only that the most obvious references to himself be removed, and letting the majority of the Ohlrig character's dark, alcoholic behavior stand. Robert Ryan's portrayal of Ohlrig became a career highlight. (Bacher)

The first of two contributions by Ophüls. Polonsky's last of three, Laurents' second of two, and Scola's second of three.

Reference   Selby, Silver and Ward

WILD
Calendar

A NOVEL BY
LIBBIE BLOCK

HERE is a novel that tells the truth about the average, attractive, and agreeable American woman who — like Maud Eames, the heroine of this story — expects happiness as her natural right, without knowing of what happiness consists.

BORZOI BOOKS

Alfred · A ·
Knopf

MR. ANGEL COMES ABOARD
CHARLES GORDON BOOTH

Publisher   Garden City: Doubleday, 1944

Mr. Angel Comes Aboard was the eighth of ten crime novels by Charles Gordon Booth, a British-born author who settled in America when he was young and whose stories were nearly all set in the United States. Booth was also a successful screenwriter, contributing original stories and adaptations for *The General Died at Dawn* (1936), *Sundown* (1941), and *Fury at Furnace Creek* (1948). He went on to write three original stories that became films noir and he won both an Academy Award and an Edgar Award in 1946 for his screenplay for *The House on 92nd Street*.

The author's second of four contributions, and his only contribution as a novelist.

Green cloth with black titles and rule at the spine, no topstain. "First Edition" stated at the bottom of the copyright page. Front flap shows a price of "M.A.C.A. / $2.00" at the top right corner, followed by a "wartime conditions" notice, then a plot summary, ending with the Crime Club's "gun" symbol and a printer's code of 4575-44. Rear flap contains a "Buy War Bonds" advertisement. Rear panel is devoted to a Crime Club "Bullseyes" advertisement, with four book listings, beginning with Kathleen Moore Knight's *Design in Diamonds* and ending with Ruth Fenisong's *Jenny Kissed Me*. A printer's code of 746-44 appears at the bottom right corner. A book club edition was issued (an odd case for Crime Club titles during this period), with all points on the jacket being the same, except that there is no price on the front flap, and "BOOK CLUB EDITION" appears at the bottom of same.

JOHNNY ANGEL
EDWIN L. MARIN

Screenwriter   Steve Fisher, Frank Gruber
Cinematographer   Harry J. Wild
Composer   Leigh Harline
Cast   George Raft, Claire Trevor, Signe Hasso, Lowell Gilmore, Hoagy Caramichael, Marvin Miller
Studio   RKO, 1945
Runtime   79 minutes

Steve Fisher's long and highly successful screenwriting career began in earnest just after the adaptation of his hard-boiled novel, *I Wake Up Screaming,* in 1941. First came Fox's *Berlin Correspondent* in 1942, an anti-Nazi thriller, then the flag-waving, morale-boosting, action film, *To the Shores of Tripoli*, released the same year. The best of Fisher's work on war films was the adaptation of his own novel (written in collaboration with future blacklistee Albert Maltz), *Destination Tokyo* in 1943.

Fisher's second of six contributions, and his first as a screenwriter. Hard-boiled crime novelist Frank Gruber's first of three contributions, director Edwin L. Marin's first of three, and the only film in the noir cycle where singer-songwriter Hoagy Carmichael makes an appearance (as taxi driver "Celestial Jones").

Reference   Selby, Silver and Ward, Lyons

Mr. Angel Comes Aboard

CHARLES G. BOOTH

A deserted ship, a Havana night club, and an unlisted cargo were three signposts on the road to murder

THE CRIME CLUB

MURDER IN THE BUD

PHYLLIS BOTTOME

Publisher   Boston: Little, Brown, 1939

Phyllis Bottome was born on May 31, 1882, in Rochester, Kent, to a British mother of an aristocratic family and an American clergyman father. She was a prolific English novelist, memoirist, essayist, and short story writer. In addition to her fiction she was a political and social activist, and a staunch supporter of woman's suffrage. She traveled widely and lived in seven countries over the course of her life, and nearly all of her novels involve travel or are set in exotic locales. She made many literary friends during the period just before World War I, including Ezra Pound, Alice Meynell, Hilda Doolittle, Richard Aldington, and May Sinclair.

In 1935 Bottome's novel *Private Worlds* was made into a motion picture starring Charles Boyer and Claudette Colbert, and was also broadcast as a radio series by United Artists and adapted as a play. In the 1940s, her novels *The Mortal Storm* and *Murder in the Bud* were adapted to the screen as well.

The author's only contribution.

Taupe cloth with two red panels at the spine, against which author and book title are printed in reverse, then the publisher's name in the same color red. No topstain. "First published in Mcmxxxix / by Faber and Faber Limited" stated on the copyright page, with no mention of later impressions. Front flap shows a price of "7s. 6d. / net" at the bottom right corner, and contains a plot summary. Rear flap is an advertisement for *The Mortal Storm* by Phyllis Bottome, with six review blurbs, beginning with Phyllis Bentley in *The Yorkshire Post* and ending with *Punch*. Rear flap ends with a price notation of "Price 7s. 6d. net." Rear panel is an advertisement for "NEW FICTION" by the publisher, with notices for sixteen titles, beginning with *Hope of Heaven* by John O'Hara and ending with *My Best Mystery Story* by "Famous Authors," then the publisher's name and address.

DANGER SIGNAL

ROBERT FLOREY

Screenwriter	Adele Comandini, Graham Baker
Cinematographer	James Wong Howe
Composer	Adolph Deutsch
Cast	Faye Emerson, Zachary Scott, Dick Erdman, Rosemary DeCamp, Bruce Bennett
Studio	Warner Brothers, 1945
Runtime	94 minutes

Born on September 14, 1900, in Paris, Robert Florey was a French screenwriter, director of short films, and actor. After moving to Hollywood in 1921, he began his career as an assistant director to the likes of Josef von Sternberg, Frank Borzage, and Victor Fleming before making his feature directing debut in 1926. He directed over sixty films over the next twenty-three years, from the first Marx Brothers feature *The Cocoanuts* (1929) to skillful low-budget films noir like *The Crooked Way* (1949).

Florey made a significant but uncredited contribution to the script of the classic 1931 film adaptation of Mary Shelley's novel *Frankenstein*, which he was also originally slated to direct—but after script development was completed, he was assigned instead by Universal to direct *Murders in the Rue Morgue*.

The second of four contributions by Florey, the second of two by screenwriter Adele Comandini, and the first of two for screenwriter C. Graham Baker.

Reference   Selby, Silver and Ward, Lyons

MURDER
IN
THE BUD

Phyllis
Bottome

Faber and
Faber

MURDER
IN THE
BUD

Faber and Faber

a

novel

by

Phyllis

Bottome

TOMORROW IS FOREVER

GWEN BRISTOW

Publisher	New York: Thomas Y. Crowell, 1943

American author and journalist Gwen Bristow was born on September 16, 1903, in Marion, South Carolina. She became interested in writing while reporting on junior high school functions for her local newspaper, and after studying at Columbia University, wrote for a number of literary magazines and journals. Eventually she moved to New Orleans and worked there as a journalist for the *New Orleans Times-Picayune*. She became interested in the idea of writing novels and short stories by way of her husband, screenwriter Bruce Manning, and published her first book in 1929. Together she and Manning then published four novels for the subscription publisher *Mystery League* between 1930 and 1932. *Tomorrow is Forever* was her fifth novel, and she reached the pinnacle of her career with her sixth, the western romance *Jubilee Trail,* which became a bestseller in 1950 and was adapted into a moderately successful film in 1954. She continued to write novels and articles for magazines until her death in 1980.

Tan cloth with black titles at the spine, no topstain. Title page shows a date of 1943, with no statement of edition or later printings on the copyright page, only a wartime paper notice at the center. Jacket shows a price of $2.50, followed by a plot summary, which continues to the end of the rear flap, ending with the publisher's name. Rear panel is devoted to an author biography, with Ms. Bristow's photo at the top left corner and two blurbs at the bottom.

TOMORROW IS FOREVER

IRVING PICHEL

Screenwriter	Lenore J. Coffee
Cinematographer	Joseph Valentine
Composer	Max Steiner
Cast	Claudette Colbert, Orson Welles, George Brent, Lucile Watson, Richard Long, Natalie Wood
Studio	RKO, 1945
Runtime	105 minutes

Orson Welles biographer Simon Callow notes: "*Tomorrow is Forever* was one of many wartime films that dealt with the loss of loved ones. The plot has Welles being disfigured in action, having reconstructive surgery and returning to his wife under a pseudonym and with a foreign accent some twenty years later. It is a performance like none other in Welles' career as an actor, restrained and sensitive, with the impeccable German accent used to striking effect, as if Welles was moved by what was happening inside him."

Director Irving Pichel's first of four contributions, and screenwriter Lenore Coffee's first of two.

Reference	Silver and Ward

THE BRICK FOXHOLE

RICHARD BROOKS

Publisher   New York: Harper and Row, 1945

Richard Brooks was born Ruben Sax to Russian Jewish immigrants in Philadelphia in 1912. After graduating from Temple University, he was a sports reporter, a radio announcer, and a writer for NBC television. He eventually made the move to Hollywood as a staff writer, beginning with low-budget pictures and moving up quickly to critically acclaimed films noir including *The Killers, Key Largo,* and *Brute Force.* Brooks' first published novel was *Splinters* in 1940, but his 1945 novel, *The Brick Foxhole*, a story about a group of Marines who pick up and then murder a homosexual man, proved a larger success. He was contractually barred from working on the screenplay for the 1947 film version of the novel.

The third of five contributions by Brooks, and his only contribution as a novelist.

Brown cloth with the Harper & Brothers logo in black at the front board, with title, design and rule in black at the spine. No topstain. "FIRST EDITION / D-U" stated on the copyright page (with first edition statement removed for later printings). Front flap shows a price of $2.50 at the top right corner, followed by a plot summary, ending with a printer's code of 5868. Rear flap begins with a short biography of the author, followed by a "Buy War Bonds" statement from the author (with his facsimile signature), ending with a printer's code of 5869. Rear panel is devoted to quotes about Brooks from four authors, beginning with Richard Wright and ending with Niven Busch.

CROSSFIRE

EDWARD DMYTRYK

Screenwriter   John Paxton
Cinematographer   J. Roy Hunt
Composer   Roy Webb
Cast   Robert Young, Robert Mitchum, Robert Ryan, Gloria Grahame, Paul Kelly, Sam Levene
Studio   RKO, 1947
Alternate Titles   Cradle of Fear (working title)
Runtime   94 minutes

The film adaptation of *Crossfire* shifted the focus of the novel's anti-homosexual slant in the book to one of anti-Semitism. Director Edward Dmytryk and producer Dore Schary recall the sensitive politics of the film quite differently:

Dmytryk: "Dore Schary, one of the heads of the studio that held up our option for the picture, didn't want the picture made. He was a liberal, and that was his problem: he was sitting on the fence. He took all the credit for *Crossfire* after it was a success, and yet at the time when we were putting it together he wasn't even the head of the studio. Not only that, but he thought it was a very dangerous thing to make a picture about anti-Semitism."

Schary: "I felt that a number of things we changed made *Crossfire* a much more pertinent criticism of our society. Of course, homosexuality at that time was not as public as it is today; and if you mentioned it everything suddenly had a different coloration. I felt we might get negative reactions, even laughter; and I also felt that the audience really wouldn't care. I felt very strongly that changing the victim to a Jew was good, because then a point would be made about anti-Semitic feeling in the United States, something that no one could diminish the significance of." (Porfirio)

Dmytryk was one of the Hollywood Ten and was jailed in 1947 shortly after the release of *Crossfire*. He directed in the UK until 1951, when he was exonerated in the eyes of the HUAC after naming colleagues as communists.

The last of Dmytryk's three contributions, and screenwriter John Paxton's last of four.

Reference   Selby, Silver and Ward

Richard Brooks

the brick foxhole

HARPER & BROTHERS

ESTABLISHED 1817

Two O'Clock Courage

Gelett Burgess

Publisher   New York: Bobbs-Merrill, 1934

Born in 1866, Frank Gelett Burgess was an American author of juvenile fiction, mysteries, humorous novels and short stories. *Two O'Clock Courage* was the sixth of his eight crime novels. The first of these, and his best-known, is a Queen's Quorum selection called *The Master of Mysteries*. This novel features the Armenian-born Astrogon Kerby, known as Astro the Seer, one of the prototypes for a key figure in film noir, the fake spiritualist. *The Master of Mysteries* contains two now-famous ciphers, one, from the first letter of the first word of each of the twenty-four stories: "The author is Gelett Burgess"; the other, from the last letter of the last word of each story: "False to life and false to art." (Penzler)

The author's only contribution.

Orange-red cloth with titles in gilt at the front board, illustration of a church steeple in blind at the bottom right corner of same, titles in gilt at the spine. No topstain. "FIRST EDITION" stated near the top of the copyright page, removed on later printings. Front flap shows a price of $2.00 at the bottom right corner, and contains a plot summary, which continues to the middle of the rear flap. Rear panel is devoted to a biography of the author, beginning with a photo of him posed beside a miniature gallows, followed by two paragraphs of text.

Two O'Clock Courage

Anthony Mann

Screenwriter   Robert E. Kent, Gordon Kahn
Cinematographer   Jack MacKenzie
Composer   Roy Webb
Cast   Tom Conway, Ann Rutherford, Richard Lane, Lester Matthews, Roland Drew, Emory Parnell
Studio   RKO, 1945
Runtime   68 minutes

Director Anthony Mann's version of *Two O'Clock Courage* was a remake of Benjamin Stoloff's *Two in the Dark* (1936), and both were based on Burgess' novel. Stoloff had transitioned from director to producer by this time, and he served as producer of Mann's remake. The Mann version had a good amount of comedy relief not found in the original, but also had some stylistic touches that predicted the director's many full-blown noir efforts that were to come.

Mann's third of twelve contributions, and his only adaptation of a novel. Screenwriter Gordon Kahn's first of four contributions, and Robert E. Kent's first of three.

Reference   Lyons

A NOVEL OF MYSTERY

Two o'clock courage

by GELETT BURGESS

BOBBS
MERRILL

HIGH SIERRA

W.R. BURNETT

Publisher   New York: Alfred A. Knopf, 1940

William Riley Burnett was born on November 25, 1899, in Springfield, Ohio. He lived there until he was twenty-eight years old, when he impulsively decided to leave his civil service job in search of success as a writer in Chicago. He left Springfield with over a hundred short stories and five novels under his belt, all unpublished. In Chicago he found a job as a night clerk in a seedy hotel, where he met prize-fighters, hobos, and hoodlums. Two years later, in 1929, the author would transform these characters and their jargon into *Little Caesar*, a crime novel that was an overnight success and landed him a screenwriting job in Hollywood.

The author's first of five contributions.

Rust-brown cloth with the author's initials and design in blue at the front board, titles and design in blue at the spine, and the Borzoi logo in blue at the bottom right corner of the rear board. Red topstain. "FIRST EDITION" stated near the top of the copyright page. Front flap shows a price of "$2.00 / net" at the top right corner, followed by a plot summary. Rear flap reads "A Catalogue of recent & forthcoming Borzoi Books, with notes on their contents & authors, may be had upon request." Rear panel is devoted to a biography of W.R. Burnett, with the author's name at the top, with a photo below it at the left (credited to Alfred A. Knopf), followed by text, ending with the publisher's name, Borzoi logo, and city.

HIGH SIERRA

RAOUL WALSH

Screenwriter   John Huston, W.R. Burnett
Cinematographer   Tony Gaudio
Composer   Adolph Deutsch
Cast   Humphrey Bogart, Ida Lupino, Alan Curtis, Arthur Kennedy, Joan Leslie, Henry Hull,
                      Barton MacLane, Henry Travers, Jerome Cowan, Minna Gombell, Elizabeth Risdon,
                      Cornel Wilde
Studio   Warner Brothers, 1941
Runtime   100 minutes

Jack Warner bought the rights to *Little Caesar* on publication, and made a fortune for Warner Brothers with the film version starring Edward G. Robinson. During the 1930s, Warner continued to make pictures from Burnett stories, including *Iron Man,* his second novel. So it was not surprising when the studio bought the rights to *High Sierra* for $25,000 prior to its publication. The producer set Burnett to work on the screenplay with the emerging young talent John Huston (who had not yet made his directorial debut). The pair made a very successful writing team, and little about the novel was altered apart from an added opening.

The part for "Mad Dog Earle" in the film was turned down by a laundry list of the greatest stars of 1940, including George Raft (who would later also decline *The Maltese Falcon*), Paul Muni, James Cagney, and Edward G. Robinson. The part was finally offered to Humphrey Bogart, and the role made him a minor star. A year later, *The Maltese Falcon* would make him a major one.

Director Raoul Walsh's second of five contributions, and John Huston's first of nine.

Reference   Selby, Silver and Ward

NOBODY LIVES FOREVER

W.R. BURNETT

Publisher   New York: Alfred A. Knopf, 1943

With the 1929 publication of his first book, *Little Caesar*, W.R. Burnett established his lifelong interest. He did not write mysteries, and detective fiction did not concern him; rather, he was interested in crime, or more precisely, the criminal mentality. *Little Caesar* captured the archetypal 1920s Chicago gangster in protagonist Rico Cesare Bandello. It was, for its time, a powerful and insightful portrait that brought the author instant fame and a trip to Hollywood, where he labored at his typewriter for the rest of a long and productive career. Throughout the 1930s, Burnett demonstrated his versatility, writing historical fiction, Westerns, and several screenplay adaptations. But he never strayed far from his abiding interest in criminals. In *Nobody Lives Forever,* Burnett took aim at the "confidence man," with the story of a con man who falls in love with the wealthy young widow he and his gang intend to swindle out of a large sum of money. (Smiley, Penzler)

The author's fourth of five contributions, and his second as a novelist.

Gray cloth with author's initials and a small design in dark gray at the center of the front board, and titles in black at the spine, with design and the publisher's name in dark gray. Borzoi logo in the dark gray at the bottom right corner of the rear board. Gray topstain. Title page shows a date of 1943, with "FIRST EDITION" stated at the bottom of the copyright page. Jacket shows a price of $2.50 at the top right corner, followed by a plot summary, ending with a jacket designer credit for Gene Allen and a note that the story has recently appeared in *Collier's* magazine. Rear flap contains a war bonds advertisement. Rear panel is devoted to an author biography, beginning with a photo of the author at the top (with a photo credit for Alfred A. Knopf), ending with the publisher's name, logo and city.

NOBODY LIVES FOREVER

JEAN NEGULESCO

Screenwriter	W.R. Burnett
Cinematographer	Arthur Edeson
Composer	Adolph Deutsch
Cast	John Garfield, Geraldine Fitzgerald, Walter Brennan, Faye Emerson, George Coulouris
Studio	Warner Brothers, 1946
Runtime	94 minutes

With *High Sierra*, W.R. Burnett vaulted into the ranks of Hollywood's most proficient and highly paid screenwriters. He routinely turned out original stories (*Wake Island* in 1942, *Crash Dive* in 1943, and *San Antonio* in 1945), and his novels remained popular as the source material for successful films. In 1946 Warner Brothers paid him twelve weeks' salary to write a novel, *Nobody Lives Forever*, then kept him on salary to write the screenplay adaptation. (McGilligan, *Backstory 1*)

Director Jean Negulesco's third of six contributions.

Reference   Selby, Silver and Ward

Nobody Lives Forever

A NOVEL BY

W.R. BURNETT

BORZOI BOOKS

Knopf

KISS THE BLOOD OFF MY HANDS

GERALD BUTLER

Publisher   London: Nicholson and Watson, 1940

Born on July 31, 1907, British author Gerald Butler published seven crime novels between 1940 and 1951 (with a late last effort in 1972). *Kiss the Blood Off My Hands* was the first of these, and the first of three to be made into films. The next novel to be adapted was *Mad with Much Heart,* basis for the key 1952 film noir, *On Dangerous Ground* directed by Nicholas Ray, and the last was *They Cracked Her Glass Slipper,* basis for the 1948 British film noir, *Third Time Lucky.*

The author's only contribution.

Black cloth with red titles at the spine, no topstain."First published in 1940" stated on the copyright page, with no mention of later impressions. Front flap shows a price of "7s. 6d. / net" at the bottom right corner, set of with a diagonal dotted line, and contains a plot summary. Rear flap is an advertisement for *What Immortal Hand* by James Curtis, ending with the publisher's name and address. Rear panel is an advertisement for *Put Out That Light* by R.C. Woodthorpe, ending with the publisher's name.

KISS THE BLOOD OFF MY HANDS

NORMAN FOSTER

Screenwriter	Leonardo Bercovici, Hugh Gray, Ben Maddow, Walter Bernstein
Cinematographer	Russell Metty
Composer	Miklós Rózsa
Cast	Joan Fontaine, Burt Lancaster, Robert Newton, Lewis Russell, Aminta Dyne, Grizelda Harvey
Studio	Universal, 1948
Alternate Titles	Blood on My Hands (UK), The Unafraid (working title)
Runtime	79 minutes

Director and actor Norman Foster was born Norman Hoeffer on December 13, 1900, in Richmond, Indiana. He married twice, both times to leading ladies. His first wife, from 1928 to 1935, was Claudette Colbert. In 1937 he married actress Sally Blane (an elder sister of Loretta Young). Foster began his career as an actor, starring in over forty feature films between 1929 and 1936, including *Skyscraper Souls* (1932), *State Fair* (1933) and *Orient Express* (1934). In 1936, he made an abrupt switch to directing with *I Cover Chinatown* (in which he also starred), with only a handful of subsequent acting appearances. Some of Foster's notable directorial efforts outside film noir include *Rachel and the Stranger* (1948), *The Sign of Zorro* (1958), three *Charlie Chan* films, and no fewer than six films in the *Mr. Moto* series.

The second of two contributions by Foster, the second of two by screenwriter Leonardo Bercovici, and the second of two by Ben Maddow.

Reference   Selby, Silver and Ward, Lyons

KISS THE BLOOD OFF MY HANDS

by GERALD BUTLER

NICHOLSON AND WATSON

THREE OF A KIND

JAMES M. CAIN

Publisher   New York: Alfred A. Knopf, 1943

After the release of *The Postman Always Rings Twice,* James M. Cain was under some pressure from his agent to write a short, money-making piece for magazine submission. He began a novella that was basically a rewrite of *Postman,* except that this story was about a cynical insurance man instead of a drifter. When Knopf called to inquire how his next novel was coming, Cain mentioned the magazine piece offhand, saying that while his agent thought it was "a swell yarn," he thought it was "a piece of tripe, and will never go between the covers while I live." (Hoopes)

The author's first of four contributions.

Orange cloth with gilt titles, design and rule at the spine, maroon topstain. Cain's initials in blind at the front board, in a decorative design. Title page shows a date of 1943, and "FIRST EDITION" is stated at the bottom of the copyright page. Fuchsia topstain. Jacket has a price of "$2.50 / net" at the top right corner, followed by a brief plot summary, ending with a jacket drawing credit for E. McKnight Kauffer. Rear flap is an advertisement for "Mr. Cain's Other Novels," with listings for four books, ending with a printer's code of 1600-C-4-1944. Rear panel is a message "To the Purchaser of This Book" from Alfred A. Knopf about compliance with wartime paper restrictions. Second issue jacket has a printed price of "$2.75 / net," typically found clipped away, with a hand-stamped correction of $2.50 at the bottom right corner. The printer's code at the bottom of the rear flap is absent from the second issue jacket, and the rear panel is completely different, with a photo of Cain followed by a two-paragraph statement from the author about war bonds. The novella was first published in digest form as Avon Murder Mystery No. 16 in 1943, and was issued by Knopf in this hardcover edition later the same year.

DOUBLE INDEMNITY

BILLY WILDER

Screenwriter   Raymond Chandler, Billy Wilder
Cinematographer   John Seitz
Composer   Miklós Rózsa
Cast   Fred MacMurray, Barbara Stanwyck, Edward G. Robinson, Porter Hall, Jean Heather
Studio   Twentieth Century-Fox, 1944
Runtime   94 minutes

In adapting James M. Cain's novel, screenwriters Billy Wilder and Raymond Chandler explicitly established the fate of their narrator by "beginning at the end," thereby casting a specter of failure and death over the entire film. This made *Double Indemnity* one of three early 1940s films (the others being *Citizen Kane* and *The Killers*) to use of flashback structure as both a means of storytelling and creating a deterministic, noir atmosphere.

Double Indemnity not only marked Chandler's debut in the film noir cycle, it was also his first encounter of any kind with the film industry. After stumbling through a few attempts to write the screenplay on his own, he was assigned to director Billy Wilder, and although the two men were famously incompatible as human beings, each of them later claimed great mutual respect—and the status of the legendary film that resulted from their collaboration is beyond dispute.

Chandler's first of seven contributions, and director Wilder's first of two.

Reference   Selby, Silver and Ward

THREE OF A KIND

THREE OF A KIND

three short novels

JAMES M.
CAIN

JAMES M. CAIN
AUTHOR OF "SERENADE," ETC.

BORZOI
BOOKS

Knopf

MCK

MILDRED PIERCE

JAMES M. CAIN

Publisher   New York: Alfred A. Knopf, 1941

James M. Cain made several starts at *Mildred Pierce* over a period of years. First he made his lead character Mildred an airline stewardess, then a girl who had won a beauty contest and was on the make. But neither idea worked. He finally envisioned her as a commonplace suburban housewife with a nice figure and a way with men, but who had a weak husband and was faced with the problem of raising two girls at the beginning of the Depression. In the book, after throwing her philandering husband out of the house, Mildred begins selling her pies to restaurants, then buys a restaurant of her own, and ultimately becomes wealthy after opening a chain of restaurants. Cain then added a final dimension, the subtle turn of the story, where Mildred helps her oldest daughter, the very spoiled Veda, realize her ambition to become an opera singer. Mildred's dream of giving Veda all that she wants is revealed as her greatest weakness, and this is where the final betrayal, a thread common to nearly all of Cain's fiction, is established. (Hoopes)

The author's second of four contributions.

Teal cloth with the author's decorative initials in blind at the middle front board. Titles, decorative design and rule in gilt at the spine, with the Borzoi logo in blind at the bottom right corner of the rear board. Blue topstain. "FIRST EDITION" stated at the bottom of the copyright page, and a date of 1941 at the bottom of the copyright page. Front flap shows a price of "$2.50 / net" at the top right corner, followed by a plot summary, ending with a jacket design credit for Bob Smith and a reproduction notice. Rear flap is an advertisement for "Mr. Cain's Previous Novels," with listings for *The Postman Always Rings Twice* and *Serenade*, each with two blurbs. Rear panel is devoted to a biography of the author, with his name at the top in blue, followed by two paragraphs of text, ending with the Borzoi logo, publisher's name and city.

MILDRED PIERCE

MICHAEL CURTIZ

Screenwriter   Ranald MacDougall, William Faulkner (uncredited), Catherine Turney (uncredited)
Cinematographer   Ernest Haller
Composer   Max Steiner
Cast   Joan Crawford, Jack Carson, Zachary Scott, Eve Arden, Ann Blyth, Bruce Bennett
Studio   Warner Brothers, 1945
Runtime   111 minutes

Working to develop *Mildred Pierce* as a film, producer Jerry Wald worked with several writers in a row, including William Faulkner, before he finally read a script that satisfied him. But he never did satisfy the book's author, James M. Cain. In the new version, daughter Veda was not a singer, was much nastier than in the book, was having an affair with her mother's boyfriend, and ultimately committed murder out of jealousy. "I'm quite startled," Cain wrote Wald about the first script sent to him, "to discover the adaptation has deliberately scrapped the one element in the story that is its keystone. That is, having an opera singer in the family; without this, the story completely lacks a point." But Cain lost the fight, and the production went forward. New troubles soon arose: lead actress Joan Crawford was at a career low and considered director Michael Curtiz a maker of "men's pictures." Neither one liked the other, and in the midst of temperamental shoots, cinematographer Ernest Haller said that Crawford "could not be photographed." Slowly, however, matters improved, and in the end the film not only received rave reviews, it earned Joan Crawford her only Oscar and resuscitated her career. (Hoopes)

The first of three contributions by director Curtiz, the first of three by William Faulkner.

Reference   Selby, Silver and Ward

Mildred Pierce

A New Novel by

JAMES M. CAIN

BORZOI BOOKS

ALFRED·A·KNOPF

THE POSTMAN ALWAYS RINGS TWICE

JAMES M. CAIN

Publisher	New York: Alfred A. Knopf, 1934

After his tour in World War I, James M. Cain began working as a journalist for newspapers, with Mencken's *American Mercury*, then briefly as the managing editor of *The New Yorker*. After writing a nonfiction book, *Our Government,* Cain turned to fiction. Despite his dreams of becoming a writer of operas and stage dramas, he was forced by necessity to assume the mantle of hard-boiled American fiction writer. His first novel, *The Postman Always Rings Twice,* marked the debut of the plot formula that would dominate his work: A man falls for a woman, becomes involved in criminal activity with her, and is eventually betrayed by her.

Edmund Wilson saw James M. Cain as a leader of the tough, California-based, Hemingway-indebted writers he called "the boys in the back room," and observed, "All these writers are also preeminently the poets of the tabloid murder. Cain himself is particularly ingenious in tracing from their beginnings the tangles that gradually tighten around the necks of the people involved in those bizarre and brutal crimes that figure in the American papers." (Luhr)

The author's third of four contributions, and his last as a novelist. Haycraft Queen cornerstone, and a Keating 100 selection.

Orange cloth with dark blue titles, design and rule at the front board and spine, and Borzoi logo in the same dark blue at the bottom right corner of the rear board. Navy blue topstain. Title page shows a date of 1934, with "FIRST EDITION" stated on the copyright page. Front flap shows a price of "$2.00 net," followed by a plot summary, ending with a note regarding the release of the cheaper edition. Rear flap is devoted to a biography of Cain. Rear panel is an advertisement for eight "New Borzoi Novels," ending with *Belly Fulla Straw* by David Cornel DeJong, then the publisher's name, Borzoi logo, and city.

THE POSTMAN ALWAYS RINGS TWICE

TAY GARNETT

Screenwriter	Harry Ruskin, Niven Busch
Cinematographer	Sidney Wagner
Composer	George Bassman, Eric Zeisl (uncredited)
Cast	Lana Turner, John Garfield, Cecil Kellaway, Hume Cronyn, Leon Ames, Audrey Totter
Studio	MGM, 1946
Runtime	113 minutes

The final script for *The Postman Always Rings Twice* was written by Harry Ruskin and Niven Busch, the latter also a novelist and friend of Cain's, who had just published *Duel in the Sun*. Their script passed the Hays Office with little trouble. "The thing the Hays Office had objected to in the original," said the film's director, Tay Garnett, "was the sort of low-level quality of the people in it. So we raised the tone of the story. I guess you could say we've lifted it from the gutter up to, well, the sidewalk." (Hoopes)

Director Tay Garnett's only contribution, and the first of three for Niven Busch.

Reference	Selby, Silver and Ward

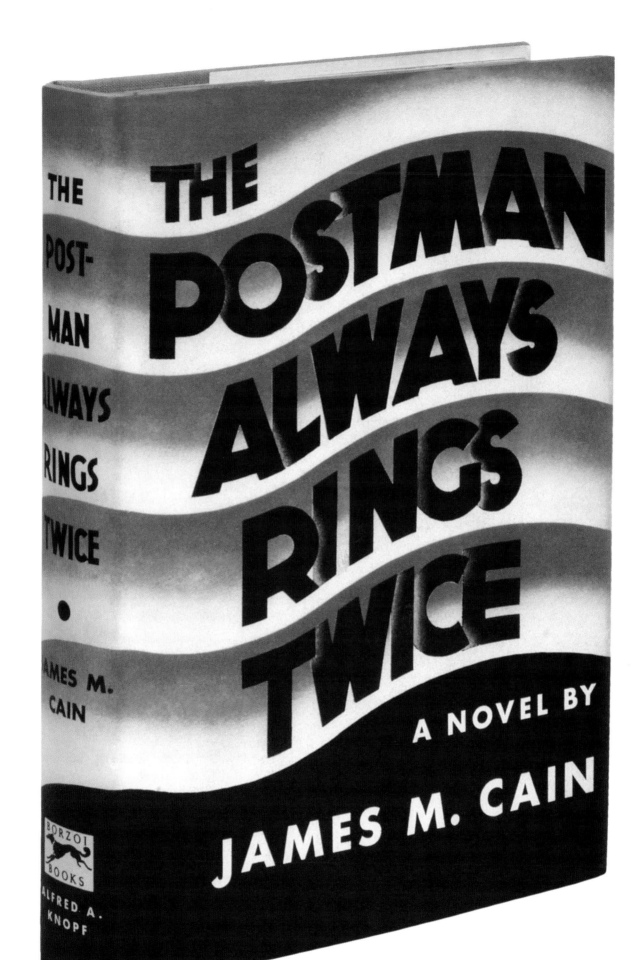

CRY WOLF

MARJORIE CARLTON

Publisher   New York: William Morrow, 1945

Born in 1897, Marjorie Carleton was an American author of crime fiction, short stories, and radio plays. *Cry Wolf* is the third of seven crime novels she wrote between 1924 and 1960, usually set in Massachusetts and New England, and often in rural settings.

The author's only contribution.

Yellow cloth with titles and Morrow logo in forest green at the spine, no topstain. Title page shows a date of 1945, with no statement of edition or later printings on the copyright page. Front flap shows a price of $2.50, followed by a plot summary that continues to the end of the rear flap, ending with the publisher's name and address. Rear panel is devoted to a biography of the author, with Ms. Carlton's photo at the top right (photo credit for Joseph Branzetti), her name at the top left, and the text below, ending again with the publisher's name and address.

CRY WOLF

PETER GODFREY

Screenwriter   Catherine Turney
Cinematographer   Carl Guthrie
Composer   Franz Waxman
Cast   Barbara Stanwyck, Errol Flyn, Geraldine Page, Richard Basehart, Jerome Cowan
Studio   Warner Brothers, 1947
Runtime   84 minutes

During a period when film noir was dominated by psychopathology, realistic backgrounds, and topical stories, director Peter Godfrey successfully harkened back to the old-style gothic melodrama with three films: *The Woman in White*, *Cry Wolf*, and *The Two Mrs. Carrolls*.

Godfrey was born on October 16, 1899, in London. As a young man he founded the Gate Theater on Villiers Street, and he served as its director for fifteen years. He directed over two hundred and fifty plays during this period, from Shakespeare to Eugene O'Neill, and worked with actors that included John Gielgud and Claude Rains. Godfrey came to America in 1937 to stage his first production and received good notices. By 1939 he had made his way to Hollywood, directing *The Lone Wolf Spy Hunt*, one of the better entries in the long running *Lone Wolf* series. After working for both Columbia and RKO, he spent the most successful years of his career at Warner Brothers before retiring to dramatic television in the 1950s. (Meyer)

The second of three contributions by Godfrey, and the last of three for screenwriter Catherine Turney.

Reference   Selby

CRY WOLF

CRY WOLF

BY
MARJORIE CARLETON

EXPERIMENT PERILOUS

MARGARET CARPENTER

Publisher   Boston: Little, Brown, 1943

Margaret Carpenter's first and only novel, a bestseller, and her only contribution.

Teal cloth with black titles on the front board and spine, in the style of those on the dust jacket. Mustard yellow topstain. Title page shows a date of 1943, with "FIRST EDITION" stated on the copyright page. Front flap shows a price of $2.50, followed by a plot summary, ending with a credit for jacket designer Charles Lofgren. Rear flap is devoted to an advertisement for Martha Albrand's *No Surrender,* and the rear panel advertises four books by John P. Marquand. Reprinted at least seven times as a trade edition in the US, then as book club edition. Beginning with its second printing, copies of the trade edition are printed in black cloth with teal titles. Later printings, oddly, are either so stated or have no statement of edition.

EXPERIMENT PERILOUS

JACQUES TOURNEUR

Screenwriter   Warren Duff
Cinematographer   Tony Gaudio
Composer   Roy Webb
Cast   Hedy Lamarr, George Brent, Paul Lukas, Albert Dekker, Carl Esmond, Olive Blakeney
Studio   RKO, 1945
Runtime   91 minutes

In adapting *Experiment Perilous,* screenwriter-producer Warren Duff changed the period from the then-present day of 1945 to 1903. Hedy Lamarr supposedly pushed for this change because she wanted to wear turn-of-the-century costumes, but executive producer Robert Fellows offered a more believable explanation: "It was felt that the slightly archaic quality of the heroine, who appears in the book as a cloistered and frustrated orchid, would lend itself to a clearer expression on the screen if presented against a less realistic background." The period change required the filmmakers to use some imagination in transposing the events of the novel. A key scene was moved from a restaurant to a department store because in researching the period, director Jacques Tourneur had learned that women never went unescorted to restaurants at the turn of the century. (Fujiwara)

Tourneur wished to make a film less ambiguous in its resolution than those he made under producer Val Lewton, but with the same dark, highly personal style. He also wanted to avoid inevitable comparisons to *Gaslight,* which had been released the year before in the United States and had strong plot similarities. Time has been kind to Tourneur's craft, and cinephiles now tend to agree that *Experiment Perilous,* while obviously not as well known, is a more personal film than *Gaslight* and benefits from a more atmospheric and complex approach.

The fourth of Tourneur's six contributions, and the second of four for screenwriter Warren Duff.

Reference   Selby

Margaret Carpenter
Experiment Perilous
xperiment
Perilous
argaret
arpenter
E, BROWN
COMPANY

LAURA

VERA CASPARY

Publisher   Boston: Houghton, Mifflin, 1943

In 1940, budding novelist Vera Caspary was struggling with an idea for a story about a detective who falls in love with a presumably dead, idealized woman, whose life he investigates. The author didn't know how to solve the problem of ending the story until she read an item in a newspaper about a young woman whose face was destroyed in an explosion. Caspary realized that her heroine wouldn't have to be dead after all.

Wilkie Collins' *The Moonstone*, a foundational mystery story from 1868 that is often cited as the first detective novel, was an inspiration to Caspary for her story's structure. In Collins' novel, the theft of the fictitious Moonstone diamond is recounted by several different people, bringing the various phases of the plot together. Caspary used this technique in her story by first having the story told by newspaper columnist Waldo, then by the detective Mark McPherson, and finally by the story's subject, Laura.

The author's only contribution, and a Haycraft Queen cornerstone.

Light blue cloth with titles and rule in red at the front board and spine, no topstain. Title page shows a date of 1943 (removed from later printings), with no statement of edition or later printings on the copyright page. Front flap shows a price of $2.50 at the top right corner, followed by a plot summary. Rear flap is an advertisement for a series of books by the publisher called "PSYCHOTHRILLERS." Rear panel is devoted to a piece about the author, beginning with a photo, followed by one paragraph of text, ending with the "Buy War Bonds" logo. An alternate binding has been noted, with a dark blue pebbled cloth, all other points the same. Later printings and a book club edition have been noted as well.

LAURA

OTTO PREMINGER, ROUBEN MAMOULIAN (UNCREDITED)

Screenwriter   Jay Dratler, Samuel Hoffenstein, Betty Reinhardt, Ring Lardner Jr. (uncredited)
Cinematographer   Joseph La Shelle, Lucien Ballard (uncredited)
Composer   David Raksin
Cast   Gene Tierney, Dana Andrews, Clifton Webb, Vincent Price, Judith Anderson
Studio   Twentieth Century-Fox, 1944
Runtime   88 minutes

Shortly after the publication of *Laura*, which enjoyed great success, Vera Caspary continued to develop her story as a stage drama. Otto Preminger, a young Hollywood director with an interest in directing for the stage, offered to help her, but the two eventually had a falling out over how to tell the story. After another year of unsuccessful attempts to stage her drama, Caspary decided "to offer *Laura* as a movie and be done with the bitch." When the manuscript was making the rounds in Hollywood, Preminger remembered it from the year before and convinced Fox to buy the rights for $30,000.

Screenwriter-novelist Jay Dratler was selected by the studio to do the adaptation, which was then reworked by several others, notably Ring Lardner, Jr. (who had just finished work on George Stevens' *Woman of the Year*). Directorial reins were initially given to Rouben Mamoulian, but after eighteen days of shooting, he was replaced by Preminger, who is said to have re-shot virtually all Mamoulian's initial footage. (Behlmer, *Behind the Scenes*)

Preminger's first of three contributions, screenwriter Samuel Hoffenstein's second of two, Jay Dratler's first of five, and the only contribution by Ring Lardner, Jr.

Reference   Selby, Silver and Ward

Laura

Laura

CASPARY

by Vera Caspary

A compelling novel of an impersonation under-
taken in malice and completed in panic

HOUGHTON MIFFLIN COMPANY

THE RED HOUSE

GEORGE AGNEW CHAMBERLAIN

Publisher   New York: Bobbs-Merrill, 1945

Born in 1879, George Agnew Chamberlain was an American author of novels and short stories that included juvenile fiction and romances. *The Red House* was the last of his five crime novels, all of which are set in New York, New Jersey, and Pennsylvania. One of seven short stories and novels by the author to be adapted to film, but the only crime film.

The author's only contribution.

Red cloth with titles in gilt at the front board and spine, red topstain. "First Edition" stated on the copyright page (and removed for later printings). Front flap shows a price of $2.50 at the bottom right corner, and contains a plot summary that continues to end of the rear flap. Rear panel is an advertisement for other titles by the publisher, with two columns of books, one "Fiction" (six titles beginning with *Lusty Wind for Carolina* by Inglis Fletcher and ending with *AWOL K-9 Commando* by Bertrand Shurtleff) and the other "General" (seven titles, beginning with *Lake Huron* by Fred Landon and ending with *Lost Waltz: A Story of Exile* by Bertita Harding). Rear panel ends with the publisher's name and city. Later printings have been noted.

THE RED HOUSE

DELMER DAVES

Screenwriter   Delmer Daves, Albert Maltz (uncredited)
Cinematographer   Bert Glennon
Composer   Miklós Rózsa
Cast   Edward G. Robinson, Judith Anderson, Lon McCallister, Allene Roberts, Rory Calhoun,
                      Julie London, Ona Munson, Harry Shannon, Arthur Space
Studio   United Artists, 1947
Alternate Titles   No Trespassing (US)
Runtime   100 minutes

The Red House was filmed in the Sonora region of California, about 350 miles from Hollywood, which was legendary for the variety of use it provided. Within ten miles in any direction, one could find a lush waterfall, rocky terrain suggestive of Wyoming or certain regions of Arizona or Nevada, and the Sonora Pass, which, while not as large as the Sahara desert, has enough sand to fool any viewer. The period from April until early November has many cloudless days, and the snowbound winters were perfect for films, including *For Whom the Bell Tolls*. *The Red House*, which takes place in a remote cabin in an unnamed wooded area, was an atypical project for location shooting in Sonora. and was probably one of only a few crime films made there. The filmmakers made use of a forested area, as the cabin's remoteness was key to the story line. A technician by background, director Delmer Daves employed infrared camerawork on location to shoot Edward G. Robinson's eerie repeated warning to a young boy. (Meyer, Hudgins)

Daves' first of two contributions, and the second of three for Albert Maltz.

Reference   Selby, Silver and Ward

The
RED
HOUSE

GEORGE AGNEW
CHAMBERLAIN

ONCE TOO OFTEN

WHITMAN CHAMBERS

Publisher   Garden City: Doubleday, 1938

Born in 1896, Whitman Chambers was an American screenwriter and novelist. He wrote seventeen crime novels between 1928 and 1960, with locales that included California, Florida, Mexico, and South America. He was the screenwriter for some thirteen films between 1933 and 1956, credited with adaptations of his own novels and stories as well as original screenplays and adaptations of works by other authors. His notable contibutions as a screenwriter include *To Have and Have Not* (1944), *Shadow of a Woman* (1946), and *Big Town After Dark* (1947).

The author's third of four contributions, and his only contribution as a novelist.

Red cloth with titles in black and reverse at the spine, red topstain. Title page shows a date of "MCMXXXVIII, " with "FIRST EDITION / CL" stated at the bottom of the copyright page. Front flap shows a price of "O.T.O. / PRICE, $2.00" at the top right corner, followed by a three-paragraph plot summary, ending with a printer's code of 2942-38 at the bottom right corner. Rear flap is an advertisement for *Hasty Wedding* by Mignon Eberhart, with two long paragraphs of text, ending with "PRICE, $2.00" and a printer's code of 2836-38 at the bottom right corner. Rear panel is an advertisement for the publisher's other books, with listings for six titles, beginning with *The Dead Don't Care* by Jonathan Latimer and ending with *Silent Witnesses* by John Stephen Strange. Rear panel ends with a printer's code of 598-38 at the bottom right corner.

BLONDE ICE

JACK BERNHARD

Screenwriter   Kenneth Gamet, Dick Irving Hyland (uncredited), Raymond L. Schrock (uncredited)
Cinematographer   George Robinson
Composer   Irving Gertz
Cast   Robert Paige , Leslie Brooks, Russ Vincent, Michael Whalen, James Griffith, Emory Parnell
Studio   Film Classics, 1948
Runtime   73 minutes

Blonde Ice was one of a fascinating series of Poverty Row genre pictures made by director Jack Bernhard and one of only a handful based on literature. While very much in the shadow of the more accomplished Edgar G. Ulmer, Bernhard took advantage of the relaxed moral standards afforded him while working for "B" studios such as Film Classics, Allied Artists, and Monogram, turning out films with some of the most ruthless (and most delightfully one-dimensional) femme fatales in the film noir canon. Photographed by master cinematographer George Robinson, who shot many of Universal's horror classics in the 1920s and 1930s, *Blonde Ice* serves up Leslie Brooks as Claire, a woman who murders her husband on the evening of their wedding day for his insurance money, then maintains a complicated alibi as she begins an affair with another man.

Edgar G. Ulmer in fact claims an off-handed right to *Blonde Ice*. In a 1971 interview with Peter Bogdanovich, the director said, "At the beginning of the season, [producer Leon] Fromkess would sit down with me and [Sigmund] Neufeld and we would invent forty-eight titles. We didn't have stories yet—they had to be written to fit the cockeyed titles. I am convinced, when I look back, that all this was a challenge. I knew that nothing was impossible. When *Double Indemnity* (1944) came out and was a huge success, I wrote a picture for Neufeld which we called *Single Indemnity*. We were able to write that junk in about two weeks. [*Single Indemnity*] was made, but not with that title—Paramount made us take that title off— I think it was called *Blonde Ice,* or something like that." (Bogdanovich)

Director Jack Bernhard's last of four contributions.

Reference   Lyons

ONCE TOO OFTEN

Whitman Chambers

DOUBLEDAY DORAN

By the Author of "13 STEPS"

A STARTLING AND REALISTIC NOVEL OF MURDER.

FAREWELL, MY LOVELY

RAYMOND CHANDLER

Publisher   New York: Alfred A. Knopf, 1940

Plot elements of Raymond Chandler's second novel, *Farewell, My Lovely*, were appropriated for two detective series vehicles in 1942: *Time to Kill* (featuring Brett Halliday's detective, Mike Shayne), and *The Falcon Takes Over*. This seems unusual now, but at the time, both The Falcon and Mike Shayne were much better known to audiences than Chandler's detective Philip Marlowe. *Murder, My Sweet* attempted not only to introduce Marlowe, but to make use of the story line, mood, and verbal textures of the novel. By placing most of the story in flashback, and by maintaining a constant sense of disorientation, the film is about Marlowe's perception of events as much as the events themselves. A great deal of description and dialogue was taken either directly or in slightly altered form from Chandler's text. (Luhr)

Chandler's second of seven contributions, and his first as a novelist. Haycraft Queen cornerstone.

Red-orange cloth with blue titles and rule at the front board and spine, and the Borzoi logo at the bottom right corner of the rear board. Dark blue topstain. Title page shows a date of 1940, with "FIRST EDITION" stated on the copyright page. Front flap shows a price of "$2.00 / net" at the top right corner, followed by a plot summary, which continues through the top two-thirds of the rear flap. The bottom third of the rear flap is an advertisement for *The Big Sleep* by Raymond Chandler, ending with the publisher's name and address. Rear panel shows an advertisement for four new "Borzoi" books, clockwise from the top left being *Farewell, My Lovely* by Chandler, *The Glass Triangle* by George Harmon Coxe, *Drink to Yesterday* by Manning Coles, and *Journey into Fear* by Eric Ambler. An advance copy in wrappers and a second printing have been noted.

MURDER, MY SWEET

EDWARD DMYTRYK

Screenwriter	John Paxton
Cinematographer	Harry J. Wild
Composer	Roy Webb
Cast	Dick Powell, Claire Trevor, Anne Shirley, Otto Kruger, Mike Mazurki, Miles Mander
Studio	RKO, 1944
Alternate Titles	Farewell, My Lovely (US pre-release title), Farewell, My Lovely (UK)
Runtime	95 minutes

Double Indemnity opened a few months before *Murder, My Sweet*, challenging Edward Dmytryk and his creative team to introduce Philip Marlowe to the screen with a much more ambitious, stylistic outing than they had made in the past. For Dmytryk, who was on the rise from "B" pictures, this meant a different approach than he had employed for films like *The Falcon Strikes Back* only a year earlier. In a 1974 interview with Robert Porfirio, the director recalls the origins of what became a seminal film noir: "The funny thing was that the original title was *Farewell, My Lovely*. They released it with [that title] in the New England states, in a few theaters, and everybody thought it was a musical because of Dick Powell. That's why we changed the title." Dmytryk saw Philip Marlowe in a more sensitive light than the archetype that would be so firmly established by Humphrey Bogart in *The Big Sleep* two years later. In the same interview, Dmytryk says, "[Vulnerability] is what makes Dick Powell the best of all the Philip Marlowes. [Sam] Spade was tough, and that's what was wrong with Bogey doing Marlowe. He made him Spade. Marlowe was actually kind of an Eagle Scout in the wrong business. I think all Eagle Scouts are weak, and this is exactly what I patterned him on."

The first of Dmytryk's three contributions, and screenwriter John Paxton's first of five.

Reference   Selby, Silver and Ward

FAREWELL, my Lovely

By Raymond Chandler

AUTHOR OF "THE BIG SLEEP"

THE BIG SLEEP

RAYMOND CHANDLER

Publisher   New York: Alfred A. Knopf, 1939

Raymond Chandler's first novel was a masterpiece right out of the gate and introduced a new kind of detective story, built on the hard-boiled foundation laid by Dashiell Hammett. Billy Wilder, who painstakingly coached Chandler through his first screenplay, said, "Chandler's novels have nothing to do with the Conan Doyle or Agatha Christie type of superb plotting. They aren't even as well plotted as Dashiell Hammett. But by God, a kind of lightning strikes on every page. The dialogue is sharp, and I must say that Chandler's great strength is a descriptive one." (Moffat)

Chandler's fifth of seven contributions, and his second as a novelist. Haycraft Queen cornerstone.

Brown-orange cloth with illustrative titles and design in dark blue at the front board and spine. Dark blue topstain. Title page shows a date of 1939, with "FIRST EDITION" stated at the bottom of the copyright page. Front flap shows a price of "$2.00 / net" at the top right corner, followed by a plot summary. Rear flap is a continuation of the plot summary, ending with the Knopf Borzoi logo. Rear panel shows reviews for six "BORZOI MYSTERIES," beginning with *The Dashiell Hammett Omnibus* and ending with *Three Star Omnibus,* then the publisher's name and city, separated by a variant of the Borzoi logo.

THE BIG SLEEP

HOWARD HAWKS

Screenwriter	William Faulkner, Leigh Brackett, Jules Furthman
Cinematographer	Sid Hickox
Composer	Max Steiner
Cast	Humphrey Bogart, Lauren Bacall, John Ridgley, Martha Vickers, Dorothy Malone, Peggy Knudsen, Regis Toomey
Studio	Warner Brothers, 1946
Runtime	114 minutes

William Luhr notes that, "Raymond Chandler expressed little interest in the notion of a film's 'fidelity' to his novels. He was aware of the many formal, cultural, and industry conditions that make such a notion untenable, and he did not complain about things being put in or left out. He looked rather for a film's own internal logic." Director Howard Hawks felt much the same way. He drew not upon the verbal texture of Chandler's descriptions but rather upon his perception of Los Angeles as a depraved place in which anything is possible and where confusion reigns. The well-known anecdote regarding the fact that neither the book nor the film provide an explanation for the death of the chauffeur has often been used to support the contention that the film makes no sense. One might reply that in actuality the film is tightly controlled but attempts to present an incoherent world. When asked how much the plot of Chandler's novel mattered to him, Hawks replied, "It didn't matter at all. Neither the author, the screenwriters, nor myself knew who killed whom. It was all what made a good scene."

Despite the fact that many aspects of the film version of *The Big Sleep* had little to do with Chandler's novel, it was the author's favorite of the four adaptations made in his lifetime, and Humphrey Bogart was his favorite Philip Marlowe. (Luhr)

Director Hawks' only contribution. William Faulkner's second of three, Jules Furthman's second of four, and author-screenwriter Leigh Brackett's only contribution.

Reference   Selby, Silver and Ward

THE LADY IN THE LAKE

RAYMOND CHANDLER

Publisher   New York: Alfred A. Knopf, 1943

After completing his original screenplay for *The Blue Dahlia,* Raymond Chandler contracted with MGM to write the screenplay adaptation for his novel, *The Lady in the Lake.* He originally took the job in a half hearted effort to protect his story from being ruined by a studio hack, but quickly lost interest in it. Once more he found himself writing in an office, this time on the fourth floor of the Thalberg Building on the Culver City lot. Defying studio policy, he left in frustration and continued to work on the screenplay at home. On August 18, 1945, he wrote to James Sandoe: "The last thing I'll ever do is a screenplay of a book I wrote myself. Just turning over dry bones." In the end, Chandler worked on the screenplay for thirteen weeks in the summer of 1945. Neither he nor the studio was satisfied with what he produced, and after another early treatment attempt by hard-boiled author David Goodis, Steve Fisher was called in to rewrite it. Chandler ultimately refused a screenwriting credit. (Chandler)

Chandler's sixth of seven contributions, and his third as a novelist.

Yellow-green cloth with titles in dark green at the front board, rear board and Borzoi logo at the spine. No topstain. Title page shows a date of 1943, with "FIRST EDITION" stated on the copyright page. Front flap shows a price of "$2.00 net," followed by a plot summary, ending with a reproduction notice. Rear flap is an advertisement for other books by Chandler, with listings for *The Big Sleep, Farewell, My Lovely* and *The High Window,* each with two blurbs. Rear panel contains "A Message to the Reader" from Chandler, ending with the publisher's name, the Borzoi logo, and city.

LADY IN THE LAKE

ROBERT MONTGOMERY

Screenwriter   Steve Fisher, David Goodis (early treatment), Raymond Chandler (early treatment)
Cinematographer   Paul C. Vogel
Composer   David Snell
Cast   Robert Montgomery, Lloyd Nolan, Audrey Totter, Tom Tully, Leon Ames, Jayne Meadows
Studio   MGM, 1947
Runtime   100 minutes

Robert Montgomery, who had been a major MGM star of the 1930s, starred in John Ford's *They Were Expendable* in 1945, after naval service in World War II. When Ford became ill toward the end of shooting, Montgomery took over some of the directing and liked it. He wanted to take the director's helm for his first postwar film, and made a proposal to the studio to experiment with point of view, making it entirely that of a single character—such that the character's face would only be seen only in reflections and mirrors. After complex negotiations, MGM allowed him to try the technique with Raymond Chandler's novel, as long as he also starred in the film.

As a result, *Lady in the Lake* was the first Hollywood film to be presented almost completely from a single point of view. Chandler, whose novels were all written in the first person, had little interest in first person point of view in his major film scripts and wrote most of them using a third person, "objective" viewpoint. When he learned that Montgomery was going to use a first person technique in *Lady in the Lake,* he mocked the idea. (Luhr)

Robert Montgomery's first of two contributions, Steve Fisher's fourth of six, and the first of three for David Goodis.

Reference   Selby, Silver and Ward, Lyons

64

The Lady
in the Lake

RAYMOND CHANDLER

BORZOI BOOKS

ALFRED A KNOPF

The Lady
IN THE LAKE

RAYMOND CHANDLER
A PHILIP MARLOWE MYSTERY

THE HIGH WINDOW

RAYMOND CHANDLER

Publisher   New York: Alfred A. Knopf, 1942

The High Window was Raymond Chandler's third Philip Marlowe novel, and his last effort as a novelist before going to Hollywood. The book took Chandler two years to complete, and his lack of enthusiasm showed. In his biography of Raymond Chandler, Tom Hiney notes: "Marlowe is bored and frustrated by what he is doing and by the people he meets." The novel did appeal to critics in England, and received a strong recommendation in the *Times Literary Supplement*. Sales were not good, however, and the film rights were ultimately sold for a mere $3500.

The author's last of seven contributions, and his fourth as a novelist. A Keating 100 selection.

Light gray-brown cloth with titles in dark maroon at the front board, spine and Borzoi logo at the rear board. No topstain. Title page shows a date of 1942, with "FIRST EDITION" stated on the copyright page. Front flap shows a price of "$2.00 net" at the top right corner, followed by a plot summary, ending with a reproduction notice. Rear flap advertises other books by Chandler, with listings for *The Big Sleep* and *Farewell, My Lovely*, each with two blurbs. Rear panel contains "a message to the reader" from Chandler, followed by three paragraphs of text, ending with the publisher's name and city, and the Borzoi logo in-between.

THE BRASHER DOUBLOON

JOHN BRAHM

Screenwriter	Dorothy Bennett (as Dorothy Hannah), Leonard Praskins
Cinematographer	Lloyd Ahern
Composer	David Buttolph
Cast	George Montgomery, Nancy Guild, Conrad Janis, Roy Roberts, Fritz Kortner
Studio	Twentieth Century-Fox, 1947
Alternate Titles	The High Window (UK)
Runtime	72 minutes

The Brasher Doubloon, in many ways, marked the end point for the wildly popular era of "the hard-boiled private eye," which had taken hold with *The Maltese Falcon* only seven years earlier. Released just four months after *Lady in the Lake*, the film version of *The High Window*, like *Murder, My Sweet*, was the "second run" at a Raymond Chandler novel, put to darker effect and using its real anti-hero (Philip Marlowe) instead of a substitute (Mike Shayne). It was the last Chandler adaptation to be made in the author's lifetime, and Marlowe would not be seen on the screen again for twenty years.

While not as ambitious in its narrative structure, and not as focused on the underlying existential malaise of its characters, director John Brahm's take on Chandler has a superb look, with exceptional use of *mise-en-scene*, an unconventional style that actually predicts the more experimental approaches that film noir would see in the decade to follow. *The Brasher Doubloon* tends to be overlooked as a Marlowe film, but it is one of German emigre Brahm's more distinctive efforts, with elements of German Expressionism put to more effective use than in any of the other Chandler adaptations.

Director John Brahm's fifth of six contributions.

Reference   Selby, Silver and Ward, Lyons

RAYMOND CHANDLER

the high window

RAYMOND CHANDLER
AUTHOR OF "THE BIG SLEEP"

HIGH WALL

ALAN R. CLARK

Publisher   New York: Harrison Smith and Robert Haas, 1936

High Wall was author Alan R. Clark's only novel, later adapted into an unpublished play co-authored by Bradbury Foote. Apart from a British edition also published in 1936 by Michael Joseph, it has never been reprinted.

The author's only contribution.

Pink cloth with black titles and rule at the front board and spine, no topstain. "FIRST PRINTING" stated on the copyright page. Front flap shows a price of $2.00 at the bottom right corner, and contains a plot summary. Rear flap is an advertisement for *More Studies in Murder* by Edmund Pearson. Rear panel advertises books available from the publisher, and lists nineteen authors (and thirty-six titles), beginning with Belomor and ending with Vivienne De Watteville, then the publisher's name and address at the bottom.

HIGH WALL

CURTIS BERNHARDT

Screenwriter	Sydney Boehm, Lester Cole
Cinematographer	Paul Vogel
Composer	Bronislau Kaper
Cast	Robert Taylor, Audrey Totter, Herbert Marshall, Dorothy Patrick, H.B. Warner, Warner Anderson
Studio	MGM, 1947
Alternate Titles	None
Runtime	100 minutes

High Wall was the first film noir contribution by three men who would go on to be important in the cycle: screenwriters Sydney Boehm and Lester Cole and cinematographer Paul Vogel. Vogel's camerawork and the film's classic noir techniques and themes (the wrong man as a fugitive, the wrong man in the insane asylum, blackouts, flashback structure) take what was a fairly straightforward and clearly minor stage play to a new level. *High Wall* was also one of the first films to make dramatic use of sodium pentathol, often referred to as "truth serum," a drug designed to make a person semi-conscious and restrict the ability to manipulate answers or use their imagination—a plot technique that would find no shortage of use in the decades to come.

The second of director Curtis Bernhardt's three contributions, and screenwriter Sydney Boehm's first of two.

Reference   Selby, Silver and Ward

MORE

HIGH
WALL

by ALAN R. CLARK

THE WOMAN IN WHITE

WILKIE COLLINS

Publisher   London: Sampson, Low, Son, 1860

Wilkie Collins was born in London in 1824, the son of William Collins, a noted landscape painter and member of the Royal Academy. After a spotty education, the sickly seventeen-year-old youth became an apprentice to a tea merchant, during which time he wrote his first novel. In 1851, after completing several years of legal studies, Collins met Charles Dickens while participating in an amateur theatrical production. The two became close friends, often collaborating on articles and stories. Collins also frequently contributed to Dickens' periodical, *Household Words*.

Collins never married but spent most of his adult years with Caroline Graves, whom he is said to have met in a setting that was later immortalized as the opening scene of his novel, *The Woman in White*. Collins, his younger brother, and the artist Millais were walking down a country lane one night when they heard a scream from a darkened garden and then saw a beautiful young woman dressed all in white. After he caught up with her, the woman told Collins an anguished story of her being held prisoner by a man. In later novels, he would explore similar themes, including prostitution and marital infidelity to emphasize the suffering of women in the context of Victorian society. (Penzler)

The author's only contribution, and a Haycraft Queen cornerstone.

Three volumes, each with a date of 1860 on the title page, and no statement of edition or later impressions on the copyright page. No topstain. Re-published in 1861 as a one-volume edition. Also rewritten as a drama by the author in 1871, and self-published in an edition bound in printed wrappers.

THE WOMAN IN WHITE

PETER GODFREY

Screenwriter	Stephen Morehouse Avery
Cinematographer	Carl Guthrie
Composer	Max Steiner
Cast	Alexis Smith, Eleanor Parker, Sydney Greenstreet, Gig Young, Agnes Moorehead, John Abbott
Studio	Warner Brothers, 1948
Runtime	109 minutes

Generally considered director Peter Godfrey's finest film, *The Woman in White* takes place in a territory not unfamiliar to the director: the doom-drenched mansion. Maintaining the nineteenth century setting of Wilkie Collins' classic novel (filmed no less than five times before this version, all in the silent era), this thriller concerns the scheme of Count Fosco (Sydney Greenstreet) to murder his two sisters and steal their fortune. Lurking at the edges of the frame are Fosco's tormented wife (Agnes Moorehead, in rare form) and the neurotic Frederick Fairlie (John Abbott). The third dimension, which makes the film a standout, is Godfrey's introduction of a strange, beautiful, and unknown woman in a white dress, who spirits through the trees in the moonlight.

The dinner scene at the center of the film story is the subtlest evocation of evil in the director's three 1940s films noir. Quick cuts from Fosco to the others at the table during the Count's verbal abuse of his wife are offset by Fosco's pet monkey Iago screeching in the background. Meanwhile, Fairlie remains cocooned in a world of silence, where the slightest noise is the equal of a murderous scream. (Meyer)

The last of Godfrey's three contributions.

Reference   Selby

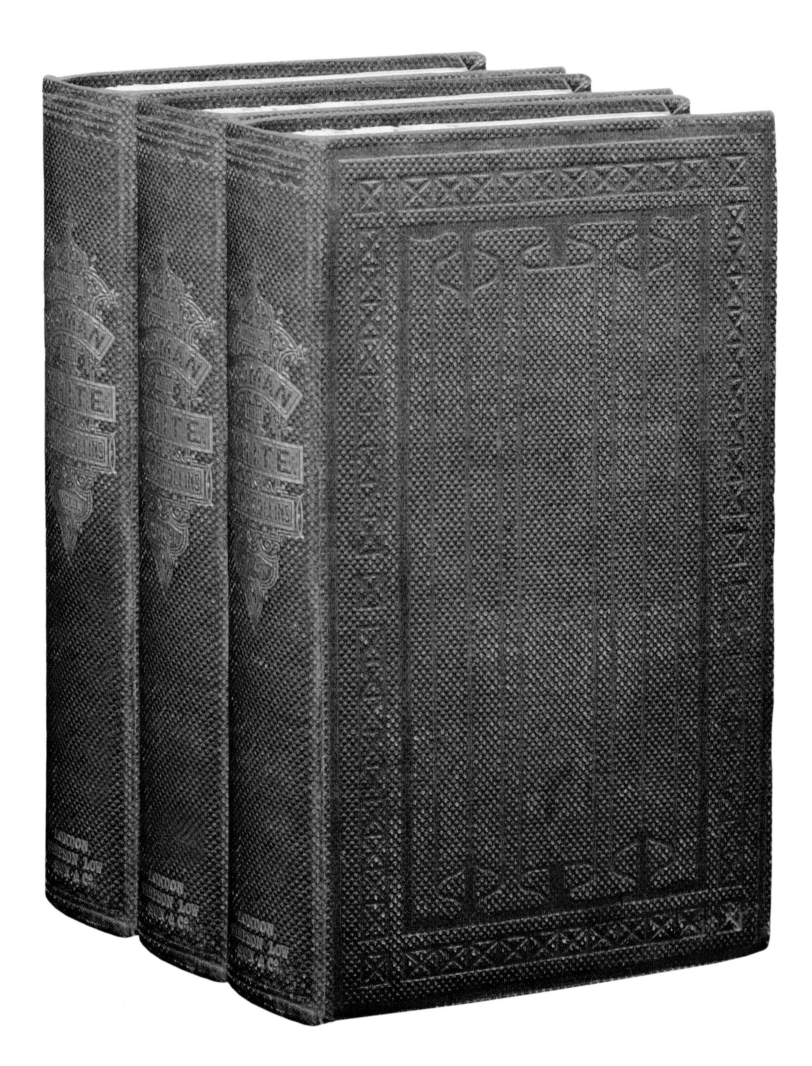

THE SHANGHAI GESTURE

JOHN COLTON

Publisher   New York: Boni and Liveright, 1926

Born is 1886, playwright John Colton was the son of an English diplomat who was serving in Yokohama, Japan at the time of his birth. He came to America as a young man and found work as the drama critic for the *Minneapolis Tribune*. His first play to be staged in New York was *Drifting* (1922), written with D. H. Andrews. Colton's biggest hits were *Rain* (1922), based on a Somerset Maugham story and written with Clemence Randolph, and *The Shanghai Gesture* (1926). His last plays, *Saint Wench* (1933) and *Nine Pine Street* (1933), were failures.

The playwright's only contribution.

Black cloth with a silver panel and outer rule with an illustrated dragon in reverse at the top right corner of the front board (no titles). Silver panels with author and title in reverse at the spine, with a small publisher's device stamped between the title and publisher's name, and the publisher's name stamped in silver at the bottom. No topstain. Title page shows a date of 1926, with no statement of edition or later printings on the copyright page. Front flap shows a price of $2.00 at the top right corner, followed by a plot summary. Rear flap contains an advertisement for W. Somerset Maugham's *Rain,* a dramatic version adapted by John Colton and Clemence Randolph, followed by five blurbs (beginning with John Corbin / *The Times* and ending with Burns Mantle / "*News*"), followed by "FIFTH EDITION," and ending with the publisher's name and address. Rear panel shows an advertisement for *The Shanghai Gesture,* followed by six blurbs (two columns of three each), beginning with Irwin Cobb and ending with *The New York Evening Journal.* At least five printings have been noted.

THE SHANGHAI GESTURE

JOSEF VON STERNBERG

Screenwriter	Geza Herczeg, Jules Furthman
Cinematographer	Paul Ivano
Composer	Richard Hageman
Cast	Gene Tierney, Walter Huston, Victor Mature, Ona Munson, Phyllis Brooks, Maria Ouspenskaya
Studio	United Artists, 1941
Runtime	106 minutes

In his 1966 book on Josef von Sternberg, Andrew Sarris writes: *The Shanghai Gesture* is a marvelous joke on the zeitgeist of the 1940s. At a time when screen censorship was so rigid that films of the early 1930s like *Arrowsmith* and *A Farewell to Arms* were re-released only after extensive editing, *The Shanghai Gesture* had no ostensible subject except the decadence and depravity of a horde of people who seem to have been left behind by history. Of course, all the depravity could not be spelled out exactly: "Mother" Goddam's joy house becomes "Mother" Gin Sling's gambling casino. Gene Tierney's name in the film is Poppy, but that is the only clue to her degradation the censors were willing to permit. It's strange to remember that all narcotics were legal in America until 1924, and that this noblest of noble experiments intersects film history at a point where an allegedly Victorian director like Griffith can be more explicit about the subject than an allegedly Baudelarian director like Sternberg."

Von Sternberg's only contribution, screenwriter Geza Herczeg's first of two, and screenwriter Jules Furthman's first of four.

Reference   Selby, Silver and Ward

THE SHANGHAI GESTURE

JOHN COLTON
Co-Author of "RAIN"

EAST SIDE, WEST SIDE

MARCIA DAVENPORT

Publisher	New York: Charles Scribner's Sons, 1947

Marcia Davenport was born in New York City on June 9, 1903, the daughter of opera singer Alma Gluck, and became the stepdaughter of violinist and noted book collector Efrem Zimbalist when her mother remarried. She traveled extensively with her parents and was educated at a variety of schools on the East Coast. After completing college and weathering a brief first marriage, she took an advertising copywriting job to support herself and her daughter. In 1928 she began her writing career on the editorial staff of *The New Yorker,* where she stayed until 1931. On May 13, 1929 she married Russell Davenport, who soon after became editor of *Fortune* magazine. Davenport wrote many popular novels, including *The Valley of Decision,* an epic saga that traces the Scott family, prototypical owners of an iron works in Pittsburgh, from 1873 to the events of Pearl Harbor. *East Side, West Side* is a novel that takes place over seven days, during which the personal lives of several troubled characters reach a dramatic peak.

The author's only contribution.

Black cloth with gilt titles and design, mustard yellow topstain. Title page shows a date of 1947, with an "A" at the top middle of the copyright page. Front flap shows a price of $3.00, followed by a plot summary that continues to the end of the rear flap, followed by a diagonal "proof of purchase" seal at the bottom left corner. Rear panel is devoted to an author biography, with Ms. Davenport's photo at the top right, her name at the top left, followed by text, ending with the publisher's name and city.

EAST SIDE, WEST SIDE

MERVYN LEROY

Screenwriter	Isobel Lennart
Cinematographer	Charles Rosher
Composer	Miklós Rózsa
Cast	Barbara Stanwyck, James Mason, Van Heflin, Ava Gardner, Cyd Charisse, Nancy Davis
Studio	MGM, 1949
Runtime	108 minutes

Born on October 15, 1900 in San Francisco, Mervyn LeRoy was an American film director, producer, and occasional actor. When his family was ruined financially by the 1906 earthquake, the young Mervyn sold newspapers and entered talent shows as a singer to make money. He eventually worked his way into vaudeville, forming a small-time act, and when the act broke up, he and his cousin, producer-to-be Jesse Lasky, went to Hollywood.

In Hollywood, LeRoy worked in costumes, processing labs, and as a camera assistant until he became a gag writer and actor in silent films. He became well-known for producing films that had the twin virtues of coming in under budget and making money at the box office. In 1930 he directed the groundbreaking gangster epic *Little Caesar,* and his career was made. By 1938, he was head of production at MGM, where he laid the groundwork for *The Wizard of Oz.* received an Oscar nomination for *Random Harvest* (1942), and discovered talent such as Clark Gable, Loretta Young, Robert Mitchum, and Lana Turner. After moving to Warner Brothers, he was responsible for such films as *Mister Roberts* (1955), *The Bad Seed* (1956), *No Time for Sergeants* (1958), and *The FBI Story* (1959).

LeRoy's second of two contributions.

Reference	Selby

EAST SIDE
WEST SIDE

a novel by
MARCIA DAVENPORT
author of "The Valley of Decision"

Roger Duvoisin

SCRIBNERS

Poor Sap
Georges de la Fouchardiere

Publisher   New York: Alfred A. Knopf, 1930

The original French edition of Georges de la Fouchardiere's novel was titled *La Chienne* and was published in 1930 as a wrappered edition by Albien Michel in Paris. The novel was a bestseller in France. It was published in translation by Knopf the same year with a very small print run.

The author's only contribution.

Light green cloth with titles in illustrative black title and design (two doves kissing) in red just below, and the author's name below, in regular black type. Spine titles in illustrative red, with the author and publisher's name in black. Borzoi logo in blind at the bottom right corner of the rear board. Gray topstain. Title page shows a date of MCMXXX, with the following stated on the copyright page "Copyright 1930 by Alfred A. Knopf / All rights reserved, no part of this book may be / reprinted in any form without permission / in writing from the publisher. / [break] / Originally published as / La Chienne / Copyright 1930 by Albin Michel." No price is present on the jacket. Front flap contains a plot summary. Rear flap begins with a photo of the author, followed by a short biography. Rear panel is an advertisement for "New Borzoi Fiction," listing eleven titles, beginning with *Parties* by Carl van Vechten and ending with *Smart Setback* by Wood Kahler, then the publisher's name, Borzoi logo, and address.

Scarlet Street
Fritz Lang

Screenwriter	Dudley Nichols
Cinematographer	Milton Krasner
Composer	H.J. Salter
Cast	Edward G. Robinson, Joan Bennett, Dan Duryea, Margaret Lindsay, Rosalind Ivan
Studio	Universal, 1945
Runtime	102 minutes

Fritz Lang remembers: "*Scarlet Street* was from an original film by Jean Renoir called *La Chienne* [released in 1931, based on de la Fouchardiere's novel], or "the bitch." Not even the war could make Joseph Breen [of the Hays Code] approve a title like that. Paramount bought the story for Lubitsch in the 30s but they could never work out the script. I had started my own company, Diana Productions, with Walter Wanger, who was married to Joan Bennett, and we were able to buy it very cheaply from Paramount. I didn't want to do another picture with Americans playing foreigners, in this case Frenchmen in Montmartre, so Dudley Nichols and I moved it to the US, to Greenwich Village. I did have a second fight with Joseph Breen over the "innocent" man being executed. But I pointed out that the ending was not just downbeat, but that Christopher Cross, the character played by Edward G. Robinson, received the greater punishment, [in that he] would either live on in complete despair or end his life. His work is gone, his life his torture, he can't forget he killed the woman he really loved, and if only someone knew this man on the street, broke, homeless, was this wonderful painter. But nobody knows it. Except the audience, of course." (Porfirio)

Lang's fifth of six contributions, and the only contribution by screenwriter Dudley Nichols.

Reference   Selby, Silver and Ward

THE PITFALL

JAY DRATLER

Publisher   New York: Crown, 1947

Jay Dratler was born in New York in 1911, and after attending college in North Carolina, extended his education by traveling to his mother's homeland of Austria, where during the 1930s he became a part of café society there. After receiving an international education, he returned to the United States with hopes of becoming a writer and a translator. His first novel, *Manhattan Side Street*, was published in 1936, and he would publish his first crime novel, *Ducks in Thunder*, in 1940. That same year would bring him to Hollywood, where he met with a success that far outstripped his efforts as a novelist. Dratler ultimately won an Oscar for his work as a screenwriter on *Laura* in 1944, and an Oscar nomination for *Call Northside 777* in 1948.

The Pitfall was Dratler's third novel, and found its way to the screen quickly due to his already-existing strong connections to the Hollywood establishment. While he would stay busy as a screenwriter, his remaining literary output drifted toward the romance genre, with titles like *Dream of a Woman* and *Doctor Paradise*.

The author's fourth of five contributions, and his only contribution as a novelist.

Tan cloth with red titles at the spine, red topstain. No statement of edition or later printings on the copyright page. Front flap shows a price of $2.00, followed by a plot summary. Rear flap is devoted to an author biography, and the rear panel is a photo of the author in a seated position, with his name just below.

PITFALL

ANDRÉ DE TOTH

Screenwriter	Karl Kamb, William Bowers (uncredited), André De Toth (uncredited)
Cinematographer	Harry J. Wild
Cast	Dick Powell, Lizabeth Scott, Jane Wyatt, Raymond Burr, John Litel, Byron Barr, Jimmy Hunt
Studio	United Artists, 1948
Runtime	86 minutes

In a February 2001 interview with Alain Silver, André De Toth notes: "I was hired to do a rewrite. They had purchased a book by Jay Dratler, but they could not get a script done. I said I needed about four weeks, and hired Bill Bowers, a great writer (and a beautiful drunk). Bill was under contract to Universal during the week, so we flew down to Palm Springs and delivered it in four weekends."

Dick Powell, the executive producer for the film, decided that he liked the script, and agreed to play the sympathetic leading role of Forbes if De Toth would direct. Only the "heavy," a character named MacDonald, remained to be cast. Despite pressure from his producer to cast a big star like Bogart in the role, De Toth resisted. The studio went back and forth with him for some time on this point. De Toth recalls, "Finally one afternoon, the casting agent we were using came to my office. He was a little fellow carrying a satchel full of photographs, so many I'm surprised he didn't get a hernia carrying it around. He opened up this satchel, and he couldn't hold it upright, so pictures started to fall out all over the desk and the floor. It was a waterfall of black-and-white glossies. And as he gathered them up, I noticed one of the floor right next to my foot. It was Raymond Burr, whom I had never seen before. And I said, 'That's him. That's the one.' And he got the part." (Silver, *Film Noir Reader 3*)

The last of De Toth's four contributions, and the second of four for screenwriter William Bowers.

Reference   Selby, Silver and Ward

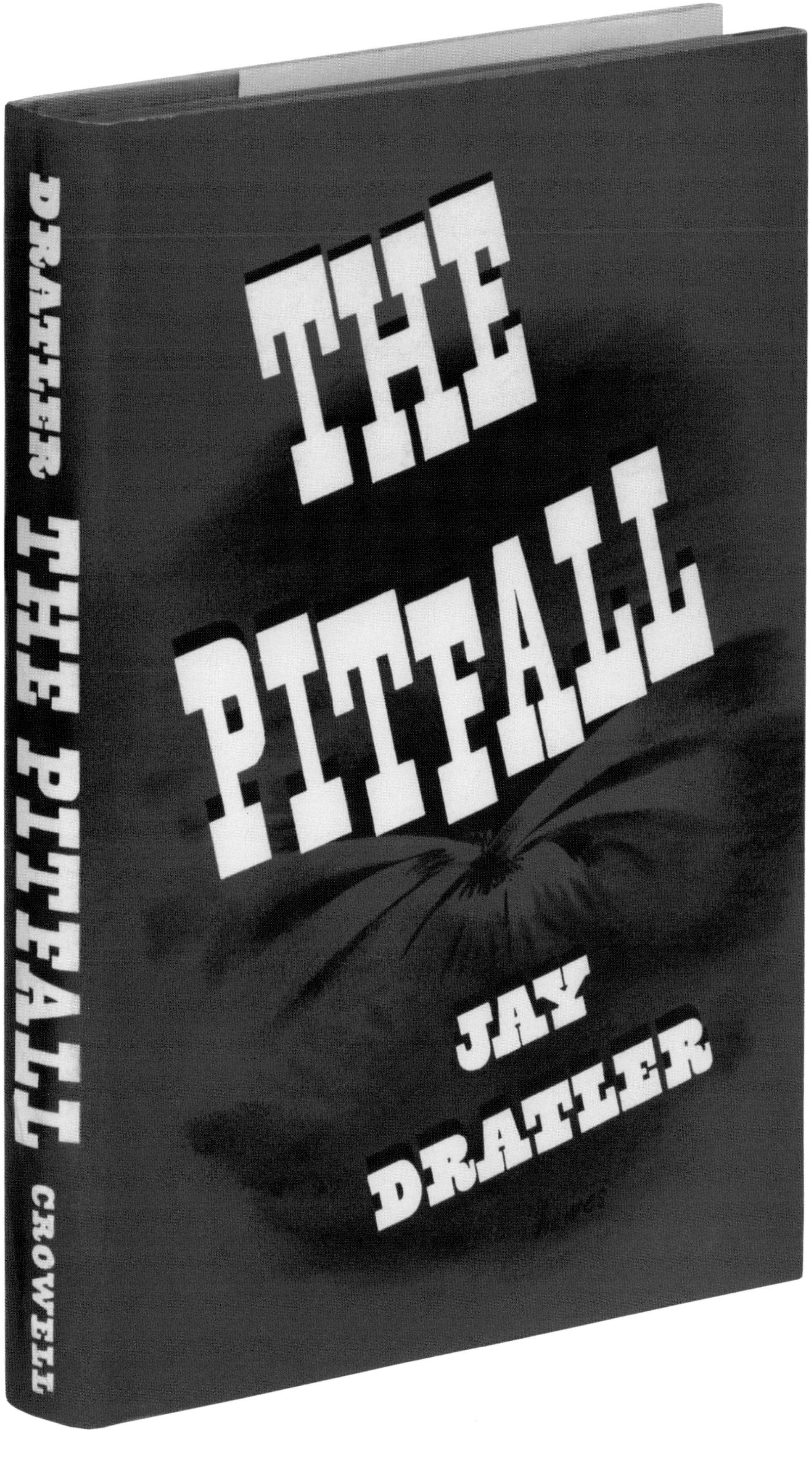
THE PITFALL
JAY DRATLER
DRATLER
THE PITFALL
CROWELL

REBECCA

DAPHNE DU MAURIER

Publisher	London: Victor Gollancz, 1938

Though she spent most of her life in her beloved Cornwall, Daphne Du Maurier was born in London in 1907. Her grandfather was the author and *Punch* cartoonist, George du Maurier, who created the character of Svengali in the novel *Trilby*. Du Maurier was also the cousin of the Llewelyn-Davies boys (George, Jack, Peter, Michael, and Nicholas), who were J.M. Barrie's inspiration for his play *Peter Pan*.

Rebecca has over time entered many aspects of popular culture. One edition of the book was used by the Germans in World War II as a code source. Sentences would be made using single words in the book, referenced by page number, line, and position in the line. One copy was kept at Rommel's headquarters, and the other was carried by German Abwehr agents infiltrated in Cairo. This code was never used, however, because the radio section of the HQ was captured in a skirmish and the Germans assumed that security had been compromised. This historical anecdote is incorporated into both Ken Follett's *The Key to Rebecca* and Michael Ondaatje's *The English Patient*.

The author's only contribution, and a Haycraft Queen cornerstone.

Black cloth with titles in gilt at the front board (title only, at the top left corner) and spine, no topstain. Title page shows a date of 1938, and copyright page reads "Printed in Great Britain by Purnell and Sons, Ltd. (p.u.) / Paulton (Somerset) and London," with no mention of edition or later impressions. Front and rear flaps are blank, with the rear panel blank as well but for "The Fanfare Press, London" printed at the bottom right corner. Preceded by a presentation edition (see *Appendix A: Secondary Books*).

REBECCA

ALFRED HITCHCOCK

Screenwriter	Robert E. Sherwood, Joan Harrison, Philip MacDonald, Michael Hogan
Cinematographer	George Barnes
Composer	Franz Waxman
Cast	Laurence Olivier, Joan Fontaine, George Sanders, Judith Anderson, Nigel Bruce
Studio	United Artists, 1940
Runtime	130 minutes

In *Hitchcock/Truffaut,* Hitchcock makes some interesting observations about the problem of adapting a British story to an American setting: "The American influence is obvious. First, because of David Selznick, and then because the screenplay was written by the American playwright Robert Sherwood, who gave it a broader viewpoint than it would have, had it been made in Britain. It's a completely British picture—the story, the actors, and director were all English. I've sometimes wondered what that picture would have been like had it been made in England with the same cast. I'm not sure I would have handled it the same way. *Rebecca* follows the novel very faithfully because Selznick had just made *Gone with the Wind*. He had a theory that people who had read the novel would have been very upset if it had been changed on the screen. Like the story of the two goats who are eating up cans containing the reels of a film taken from a bestseller. One goat says to the other, 'Personally, I prefer the book!'"

Hitchcock's first American film, and his first of five contributions. Playwright Robert E. Sherwood's only contribution, screenwriter Joan Harrison's first of five, and novelist-screenwriter Philip MacDonald's first of five.

Reference	Selby

DAPHNE
DU MAURIER

a new novel

REBECCA

a new novel

DAPHNE
DU MAURIER

GOLLANCZ

8/6
net

REBECCA | BY DAPHNE DU MAURIER

THE DEVIL THUMBS A RIDE

ROBERT C. DU SOE

Publisher	New York: Robert M. McBride, 1938

The Devil Thumbs a Ride, now a hard-boiled cult classic, was Robert Du Soe's first novel, and his only published work with criminous content. His career began as a writer for the pulps (as Bob Du Soe), for which he made a number of contributions between 1927 and 1934, including three short stories for *Black Mask,* as well as stories in *Strange Detective Stories, Underworld Detective, Mystery Stories,* and *Detective Dragnet.*

Publication of *The Devil Thumbs a Ride* in 1938 ostensibly had much to do with the author landing work in Hollywood, however brief. His sole film credit is as a co-writer for the 1940 Western, *20 Mule Team,* in which Wallace Beery braves Death Valley—where the film was actually shot on location—in search of a "motherlode" of Borax. Jack Kerouac cited the film as a "great old western" in *Big Sur,* quoting the film's final line, "Cuss a man for dyin' in Death Valley!"

The author's only contribution.

Blue-green cloth with red titles at the front board and the spine, no topstain. "FIRST EDITION" is stated on the copyright page. Front flap shows a price of $2.00 at the top right corner, followed by a plot summary, ending with the publisher address at the bottom. Rear flap contains an advertisement and plot summary for the simultaneously-published hard-boiled classic, *You Play the Black and the Red Comes Up* by Richard Hallis, with the publisher address again at the bottom. Rear jacket panel advertises five books by the publisher, beginning with *You Play the Black and the Red Comes Up* and ending with *The Second Mrs. Draper,* with the publisher's name and city at the bottom.

THE DEVIL THUMBS A RIDE

FELIX E. FEIST

Screenwriter	Felix E. Feist
Cinematographer	J. Roy Hunt
Composer	Paul Sawtell, Roy Webb (uncredited)
Cast	Lawrence Tierney, Ted North, Nan Leslie, Betty Lawford, Andrew Tombes, Harry Shannon
Studio	RKO Pictures, 1947
Runtime	62 minutes

Felix E. Feist adapted Robert Du Soe's novel to the screen faithfully, and in the best RKO tradition, quickly and cheaply. The director kept the novel's southern California setting intact, with extensive use of location shooting, specifically the "ride" from San Diego to Los Angeles and a fateful midnight stop at a beach house in between.

Contributing greatly to recent renewed interest in both the book and the film was author Barry Gifford's decision to make *The Devil Thumbs a Ride* the title subject of his 1988 book of essays on forgotten B-films.

Director-screenwriter Felix E. Feist's first of two contributions.

Reference	Selby, Silver and Ward, Lyons

THE DEVIL THUMBS A RIDE

ROBERT DU SOE

Blanchard

HASTY WEDDING

MIGNON EBERHART

Publisher   Garden City: Doubleday, Doran, 1938

Born in 1899 in Lincoln, Nebraska, Mignon Eberhart was an American crime author. She attended Wesleyan University for three years before marrying, after which she traveled extensively throughout the world. After a brief dalliance with journalism, she began writing crime fiction, authoring fifty-two books in all and earning a loyal readership.

Eberhart's first five books were about the detective team of Sarah Keate, a middle-aged spinster nurse, and Lance O'Leary, a promising young police detective in an unnamed Midwestern city. The unlikely duo functions effectively, despite Miss Keate's penchant for stumbling into situations from which she must be rescued. Keate is inquisitive and supplies O'Leary with considerable information, and crimes get solved, generally in a hospital setting. The duo enjoyed great popularity during the 1930s, with five film adaptations.

Hasty Wedding, a non-series novel, was the last of Eberhart's books to be adapted to the screen, and involves a woman who suspects that her husband has murdered her former flame. (Penzler)

The author's only contribution.

Red cloth with black titles, design and rule at the spine, red topstain. Title page shows a date of MCMXXXVIII, with "FIRST EDITION" stated at the bottom of the copyright page. Front flap shows a price of $2.00, followed by a plot summary, ending with a printer's code of 2836-38. Rear flap is an advertisement for Anthony Berkeley's *Trial and Error,* ending with a price of $2.50 and a printer's code of 2687-37. Rear panel is devoted to an advertisement for six titles by this publisher, beginning with *The Dead Don't Care* by Jonathan Latimer and ending with *Silent Witnesses* by John Stephen Strange.

THREE'S A CROWD

LESLEY SELANDER

Screenwriter   Dane Lussier
Cinematographer   William Bradford
Cast   Pamela Blake, Charles Gordon, Gertrude Michael, Pierre Watkin, Virginia Brissac, Ted Hecht
Studio   Republic, 1945
Runtime   58 minutes

Three's a Crowd is the misleadingly lighthearted title for this tense Republic murder mystery. When her fiance is mysteriously killed, heiress Diane Whipple (Pamela Blake) reluctantly agrees to marry Jeffrey Locke (Charles Gordon). Since both Diane and Jeffrey visited the dead man just before the murder, both are under suspicion, and neither completely trusts the other. Screenwriter Dane Lussier characteristically overloads the film with red herrings, misleading clues, and plot twists. A pleasurable crime film with nice noir touches throughout. (Hal Erickson)

The first of two contributions by director Lesley Selander, and the last of three by screenwriter Dane Lussier.

Reference   Lyons

HASTY
WEDDING

MIGNON G.
EBERHART

DOUBLEDAY
DORAN

HASTY
WEDDING

A MYSTERY
NOVEL

MIGNON G. EBERHART

THE VELVET FLEECE

LOIS EBY AND JOHN FLEMING

Publisher   New York: E.P. Dutton, 1947

Born in Indiana in 1908, Lois Eby was an American author who wrote crime fiction in the form of novels, radio teleplays, and screenplays, mostly between 1946 and 1952. She wrote her novels almost exclusively with her first cousin, John Fleming, the notable exception being a late effort, the 1966 paperback original *Nurse on Nightmare Island*. Her screen work was limited to *The Lone Ranger* (1938), which was a serial, and *Hi-Yo Silver* (1940), a feature film made by cobbling together episodes of the serial.

The writing duo's only contribution.

Green cloth with design in a darker green at the center of the front board, and a more elaborate design with titles added at the spine. No topstain. "FIRST EDITION" stated on the copyright page. Front flap shows a price of $2.50 at the bottom right corner, and begins with Dutton's "Guilt-Edged Mystery" logo, followed by a plot summary. Rear flap begins with the logo again, followed by a plot summary for the last Eby-Fleming mystery, *Hell Hath No Fury*. Three Eby-Fleming mysteries are advertised at the rear panel, with review blurbs for each, ending with the publisher's name and address.

LARCENY

GEORGE SHERMAN

Screenwriter   Herbert H. Margolis, Louis Morheim, William Bowers
Cinematographer   Irving Glassberg
Composer   Leith Stevens
Cast   John Payne, Joan Caulfield, Dan Duryea, Shelley Winters, Dorothy Hart, Richard Rober
Studio   Universal, 1948
Runtime   89 minutes

Born on July 14, 1908, George Sherman was a prolific director of action films, typically Westerns, beginning in the 1930s. He went on to direct two episodes of the noir-influenced television series *Naked City* in 1959 and 1962.

In *Larceny*, a gang of smooth con men prey on a war hero's widow. One of them romances her after pretending to be her late husband's war buddy, and convinces her to invest a hundred thousand dollars to set up a center for orphaned kids, supposedly at her late husband's request. The moll in the gang threatens to blow the whole scam when she arrives in town, seeking to continue her affair with the con man in question. A fast-moving noir with many plusses—a tight plot, witty dialogue, and convincing performances by Dan Duryea and John Payne as the con men at odds with each other over the tempestuous moll, played by Shelley Winters. (Keaney)

Director Sherman's second of two contributions, and screenwriter William Bowers' third of four.

Reference   Selby, Lyons

THE
Velvet
Fleece

LOIS EBY · JOHN C. FLEMING

DUTTON

GUILT
EDGED
MYSTERY

The Walls Came Tumbling Down

Jo Eisinger

Publisher   New York: Coward-McCann, 1943

Jo Eisinger began his writing career in radio, penning numerous segments for the *Adventures of Sam Spade* series. His film and television career spanned more than forty years, from the early 1940s to the 1980s. He is best remembered as the screenwriter of one of the most psychologically complex films noir, *Gilda* (1946), as well as his adaptation of Gerald Kersh's *Night and the City* (1950). After two decades in film, Eisinger returned to thriller and private eye series work in the 1960s, writing for ITV television program *Danger Man* and the mid-1980s HBO series *Philip Marlowe, Private Eye*. His script for an episode of the latter show, "The Pencil," earned him an Edgar Award in 1984. *The Walls Came Tumbling* down was Eisinger's only novel, and became the basis for an episode of the popular radio show *Suspense!* in 1944 before being filmed in 1946.

The author's last of three contributions.

Gray cloth with author and title in reverse against a green panel at the spine, followed by publisher logo and name. No topstain. No statement of edition or later printings on the copyright page. Front flap shows a price of $2.00, followed by a plot summary. Rear flap describes the "Requirements for Gargoyle Mysteries," with twelve enumerated points. Rear panel is an advertisement for "Gargoyle Mysteries," with listings for six titles, ending with *The Walls Came Tumbling Down* by Jo Eisinger, then a block of text describing the origins of the "Gargoyle" series motif.

The Walls Came Tumbling Down

Lothar Mendes

Screenwriter	Wilfred H. Petitt
Cinematographer	Charles Lawton Jr.
Composer	Marlin Skiles
Cast	Lee Bowman, Marguerite Chapman, Edgar Buchanan, George Macready, Lee Patrick
Studio	Columbia, 1946
Runtime	82 minutes

Like so many theatrically inclined Berliners of the teens and twenties, Lothar Mendes received his training under the watchful eye of Viennese impresario Max Reinhardt. In 1921, Mendes began his film career in Germany and Austria, and his last European film, *Die Drei Kuckucksuhren* (1925), is regarded as his best, if only because it is among the very few of his still extant silents. He moved to Hollywood in 1926, and spent the first half of the 1930s at Paramount, where he is best remembered for the 1932 Charles Laughton vehicle, *Payment Deferred*. After a brief time in England, he returned to Hollywood in 1939, where he directed mostly second features for a variety of studios until his retirement in 1946. *The Walls Came Tumbling Down* was his final directorial effort.

The only contribution by director Mendes, and the second of two for screenwriter Wilfred Petitt.

Reference   Selby

THE WALLS CAME TUMBLING DOWN

JO EISINGER

A GARGOYLE MYSTERY

(spine)

THE WALLS CAME TUMBLING DOWN

JO EISINGER

A GARGOYLE MYSTERY

COWARD McCANN

METHINKS THE LADY...

GUY ENDORE

Publisher   New York: Duell, Sloan, and Pierce, 1945

Guy Endore was born Samuel Guy Endore on July 4, 1900. Well-known for his work as a writer of horror fiction, screenwriter and left-leaning political activist, he received an Oscar nommination for *The Story of G.I. Joe* in 1945, and contributed screenplays to some of the classics of 1930s horror cinema, including *Mark of the Vampire* (1935), *The Raven* (1935), *Mad Love* (1935), and *Devil Doll* (1936). His novel, *The Werewolf of Paris* (Farrar and Rinehart, 1933), is considered a classic of horror literature.

The second of two contributions by Endore, and his only contribution as a novelist.

Brown cloth with light blue titles at the front board and spine, brown topstain. The copyright page has a roman numeral "I" set by itself at the top center. Front flap shows a price of $2.50 at the top right corner, followed by a teaser question, then a plot summary. Rear flap is an advertisement for *All Summer Long* by Wilder Hobson, beginning with a price of $2.50 at the top left corner, followed by one paragraph of text, ending with a four-line poem. Rear panel is devoted to a biography of the author, beginning with a photo, followed by his name and three paragraphs of text. The front flap, rear flap, and rear panel each end with the publisher's name and address.

WHIRLPOOL

OTTO PREMINGER

Screenwriter	Ben Hecht, Andrew Solt
Cinematographer	Arthur Miller
Composer	David Raksin
Cast	Gene Tierney, Richard Conte, Jose Ferrer, Charles Bickford, Barbara O'Neil, Eduard Franz
Studio	Twentieth Century-Fox, 1949
Runtime	98 minutes

From internal and external evidence, it's clear that the makers of *Whirlpool* (and its predecessor, *Fallen Angel*) made a conscious attempt to reproduce certain aspects of *Laura*. Signs of this effort are to be found in the records relating to the production histories of the films. On an early draft of the script of *Fallen Angel*, Twentieth Century-Fox production chief Darryl F. Zanuck penciled the notation: "Everything great up to last act—needs hypo like *Laura*." In script conferences for *Whirlpool*, Zanuck repeatedly urged Preminger and screenwriter Ben Hecht to draw on *Laura* for inspiration, noting that the villainous Korvo should be "just as interesting as Clifton Webb was in *Laura*," that *Whirlpool* "can have much of the quality and strangeness of *Laura*," and proposing changes to the ending (that were adopted in part) that would "put the heroine in jeopardy, after the manner of the last sequence of *Laura*." (Fujiwara, *4 x Otto Preminger*)

But *Fallen Angel* and *Whirlpool*, rather than seeming like bad copies of their more famous predecessor, were ultimately more sophisticated films, with complex dialogue, underlying themes of bitterness and frustration, and characters that have in common a quality of being lost in the world, despite trappings of wealth or devil-may-care poverty.

The last of Preminger's three contributions, and the last of twelve for Ben Hecht.

Reference   Selby, Silver and Ward

METHINKS THE LADY...

by Guy Endore

Duell Sloan
and Pearce

BEYOND THE FOREST

STUART ENGSTRAND

Publisher   New York: Creative Age Press, 1948

Born on March 13, 1905, in Chicago, Stuart Engstrand was an American crime author whose books tended to concentrate on abnormalities in marriage. *Beyond the Forest* was his third of four crime novels, and along with its predecessor, *The Sling and the Arrow*, was a bestseller.

The author's only contribution.

Green cloth with black quarter-binding; titles, design and rule in gilt at the spine, no topstain. Title page shows a date of 1948, with no statement of edition or later printings on the copyright page. Front flap shows a price of $3.00 at the top right corner, followed by a plot summary, ending with a jacket design credit for Christopher Williams. Rear flap is a continuation of the plot summary, ending with the publisher's name and address. Rear panel is devoted to a brief author biography, with a cut-out photo of the author's head at the top left corner, underneath which is a white panel which contains the text, set against a black background.

BEYOND THE FOREST

KING VIDOR

Screenwriter	Lenore J. Coffee
Cinematographer	Robert Burks
Composer	Max Steiner
Cast	Bette Davis, Joseph Cotten, David Brian, Ruth Roman, Minor Watson, Dona Drake, Regis Toomey, Sarah Selby
Studio	Warner Brothers, 1949
Alternate Titles	Rose Moline
Runtime	97 minutes

Originally titled *Rose Moline* (after the name of the main character), *Beyond the Forest* was the last film Bette Davis made for Warner Brothers. Being that it was at the low point of her mid-career, and being that the classic *All About Eve* would be her next film, *Beyond the Forest* marked an interesting turning point for the actress. In *Beyond the Forest,* she appears in a black wig and garish makeup throughout, a sideways reprisal of her horrific physical transformation in *Mr. Skeffington* a few years before. However, Davis seems thoroughly suited to her role here as the restless, promiscuous wife of a small-town doctor, who murders the old hunter who knows her cheating ways, and ultimately faces an agonizing death from peritonitis—all backed by variations of the musical standard, "Chicago." Noir melodrama at its trashy best. (Sennett)

Director King Vidor's only contribution, and screenwriter Lenore J. Coffee's second of two.

Reference   Selby, Silver and Ward

BEYOND the FOREST

STUART ENGSTRAND

Author of THE SLING AND THE ARROW

THE STORY OF A MAN AND A WOMAN DESTROYED BY "LOVE"

THE BIG CLOCK

KENNETH FEARING

Publisher   New York: Harcourt, Brace, 1946

Kenneth Fearing was born in Oak Park, Illinois, in 1902. After graduating from college, he moved to New York City, where he began working as a poet and was active in leftist politics. In the 1920s and 1930s, he published regularly in *The New Yorker* and *Poetry* and helped found *The Partisan Review*, while also working as an editor, journalist, and speechwriter.

Poetry remained Fearing's lifelong passion, but in the midst of his more serious literary pursuits, the author in his early days wrote and published pulp fiction and even pornography (sometimes published under the pseudonym Kurt Wolff) to earn spending money. Between 1941 and 1960, he would ultimately write eight novels, mostly crime fiction, that grew out of this sideline. The second of these, which turned out to be the biggest financial success of his career, was *The Big Clock*.

Released in the fall of 1946, *The Big Clock* made Fearing temporarily rich. Altogether he took in about $60,000. However, overestimating his own business acumen, he negotiated his own contract with Paramount, permanently and irrevocably signing away his film rights. (Ryley)

Fearing's only contribution.

Black cloth with titles in gilt at the spine, no topstain. First editiion stated on the copyright page. Front flap shows a price of $2.50, followed by a plot summary, ending with the publisher's name and address. Rear flap repeats the price of $2.50 at the top left corner, followed by a continuation of the plot summary, ending again with the publisher's name and address. Rear flap advertises recent fiction by the publisher, with seven listings, beginning with *All the King's Men* by Robert Penn Warren and ending with *Call the Next Witness* by Philip Woodruff.

THE BIG CLOCK

JOHN FARROW

Screenwriter   Jonathan Latimer
Cinematographer   Daniel L. Fapp, John Seitz
Composer   Victor Young
Cast   Ray Milland, Charles Laughton, Maureen O'Sullivan, George Macready, Rita Johnson, Elsa Lanchester, Harold Vermilyea, Dan Tobin, Harry Morgan (as Henry Morgan)
Studio   Paramount, 1948
Runtime   62 minutes

The Big Clock is one of the most visually arresting films of the 1940s noir cycle, but not due just to typical noir lighting. Director John Farrow and cinematographer John F. Seitz went to great pains to translate the Art Deco stylings of the 1930s onto the screen, with everything from the giant clock that is the story's centerpiece to the sophisticated sets used throughout.

Added to the sophisticated look of the film is a dazzling script by crime writer Jonathan Latimer, very faithful to Fearing's novel, that verges on the split-second wordplay of screwball comedy. Cinematographer John F. Seitz remembers: "Since we had so many people talking at once and so much camera movement I did practically the whole picture by reflected light, reflected from the ceiling and sometimes the floor. It was quite an innovation." (Ursini)

The second of director John Farrow's four contributions, and screenwriter Jonathan Latimer's fifth of seven.

Reference   Selby, Silver and Ward

2

3

4

THE
BIG CLOCK

8

1

7

5

A NOVEL BY

KENNETH FEARING

12

THE SIGN OF THE RAM

MARGARET FERGUSON

Publisher   London: Robert Hale, 1943

Born in 1904, Margaret Ferguson was a British novelist, and *The Sign of the Ram* was her only work of crime fiction. The American edition of the book was published by Blakiston, a publishing house normally associated with reprints, in 1945.

The author's only contribution.

Blue cloth with silver titles at the spine, no topstain. "First published 1943" stated on the copyright page. Front flap shows a price of "9/- net" at the bottom right corner, and contains a plot summary, beginning with the title and author. Rear flap is a an advertisement for "Britain Calls the World," a pro-Allies radio news slogan, beginning with a logo that shows a BBC microphone at the right, and compass points imposed on a picture of the earth at the left. Rear panel is devoted to an advertisement for "New and Forthcoming Novels from Robert Hale," and contains eight titles, beginning with John P. Marquand's *So Little Time* and ending with Hamilton Grieve's *Spring Manoeveurs*.

THE SIGN OF THE RAM

JOHN STURGES

Screenwriter   Charles Bennett
Cinematographer   Burnett Guffey
Composer   Hans J. Salter
Cast   Susan Peters, Alexander Knox, Phyllis Thaxter, Peggy Ann Garner, Ron Randell,
                      Dame May Whitty, Allene Roberts, Ross Ford, Diana Douglas, Margaret Tracy
Studio   Columbia, 1948
Runtime   84 minutes

The Sign of the Ram is an excellent example of a gothic melodrama with film noir stylings, the kind that first came to the screen with *Rebecca* in 1940. An intriguing aspect of the film is the conflict between its setting, Cornwall, England, and its cast, made up for the most part of American actors (with the notable exception of Dame May Whitty). Lines such as, "I was born in London" are spoken with a consummate American accent throughout, which along with the pervasive use of painted exteriors gives one the sense that the film is taking place in some mystical place that only vaguely resembles the world we know. This is of course an accident born of necessity, but it has a dreamlike and not unpleasant effect. Probably the father of this "dislocated character" approach is Ernst Lubitsch, who in the 1930s habitually set his comedies in places like Prague and Warsaw, yet with casts made up almost entirely of Americans, and with no particular need for the film to have taken place anywhere but the United States. The practice was typically taken up in films noir of the gothic variety, with *Love Letters* (1945) and *Ivy* (1947) being examples.

The first of two contributions by director John Sturges, and the second of three for screenwriter Charles Bennett.

Reference   Selby, Lyons

THE SIGN of THE RAM

Margaret
Ferguson

THE SIGN OF THE RAM

MARGARET FERGUSON

Robert
Hale

Abbey

I WAKE UP SCREAMING

STEVE FISHER

Publisher   New York: Dodd, Mead, 1941

Steve Fisher based the corrupt detective in *I Wake Up Screaming* on fellow crime novelist Cornell Woolrich, describing him thus: "He had red hair and thin white skin and red eyebrows and blue eyes. He looked sick. He looked like a corpse. His clothes didn't fit him...He was a misfit...He was frail, grey-faced and bitter...His voice was nasal. You'd think he was crying. He might have had T.B. He looked like he couldn't stand up in a wind."

I Wake Up Screaming was a bona fide hit for Fisher, and helped boost him out of the pulps and minor publishing houses and into favor as a published novelist. Even more significantly, it was the book that launched his career as a major Hollywood screenwriter. The story was powerful enough to merit a noir remake, *Vicki*, in 1953. This particular title is also an example of the "Hollywood novel," about a talent agent accused of murdering his own top-drawer star.

The author's first of six contributions, and his only contribution as a novelist.

Black cloth with the Dodd, Mead logo in blind at the middle of the front board, red titles and rule at the spine. Red topstain. No statement of edition or later printings on the copyright page. Front flap shows a price of $2.00 at the top right corner, followed by a plot summary, ending with the publisher's name. Rear flap advertises the semi-annual Red Badge $1000 Prize for the best mystery-detective story, ending with a listing of five previous winners and the publisher address. Rear panel is devoted to a biography of the author, with a large photo at the top. Later printings have been noted, and are stated on both the book and the jacket.

I WAKE UP SCREAMING

H. BRUCE HUMBERSTONE

Screenwriter	Dwight Taylor
Cinematographer	Edward Cronjager
Composer	Cyril J. Mockridge
Cast	Betty Grable, Victor Mature, Carole Landis, Laird Cregar, William Gargan, Elisha Cook, Jr.
Studio	Twentieth Century-Fox, 1941
Alternate Titles	Hot Spot (working title), Hot Spot (UK)
Runtime	82 minutes

Producer Darryl F. Zanuck at Twentieth Century-Fox, who paid Steve Fisher $7,500 for the film rights to *I Wake Up Screaming*, had specifically vetoed all film exposés of Hollywood. To avoid the hot end of Zanuck's cigar, the producers moved the film's setting from Hollywood to New York, which, in turn, necessitated changing certain elements of the story. California's sunny climes, palm trees, and restaurants like The Brown Derby and Ciro's were replaced in the film by bleak jazz clubs, police stations, apartments, and theaters. The script, which alternates between table-talk and cop-speak, was not Fisher's work, but that of writer Dwight Taylor who went on to pen Curtis Bernhardt's *Conflict* (1945) as well as Samuel Fuller's *Pickup on South Street*.

While films like *The Maltese Falcon* and *Rebecca* are credited as being among the first in the noir cycle, *I Wake Up Screaming* was a trendsetter in its own right, particularly with regard to cinematographer Edward Cronjager's shadow-drenched visuals and Laird Cregar's extraordinarily dark, complex performance. Another first was the use of Alfred Newman's "Street Scene Blues," a melody that was used again relentlessly in Fox noirs throughout the 1940s, including *The Dark Corner, Kiss of Death, Where the Sidewalk Ends,* and *Cry of the City.* (Haut)

Humberstone's only contribution, and the first of two for screenwriter Dwight Taylor.

Reference   Selby, Silver and Ward

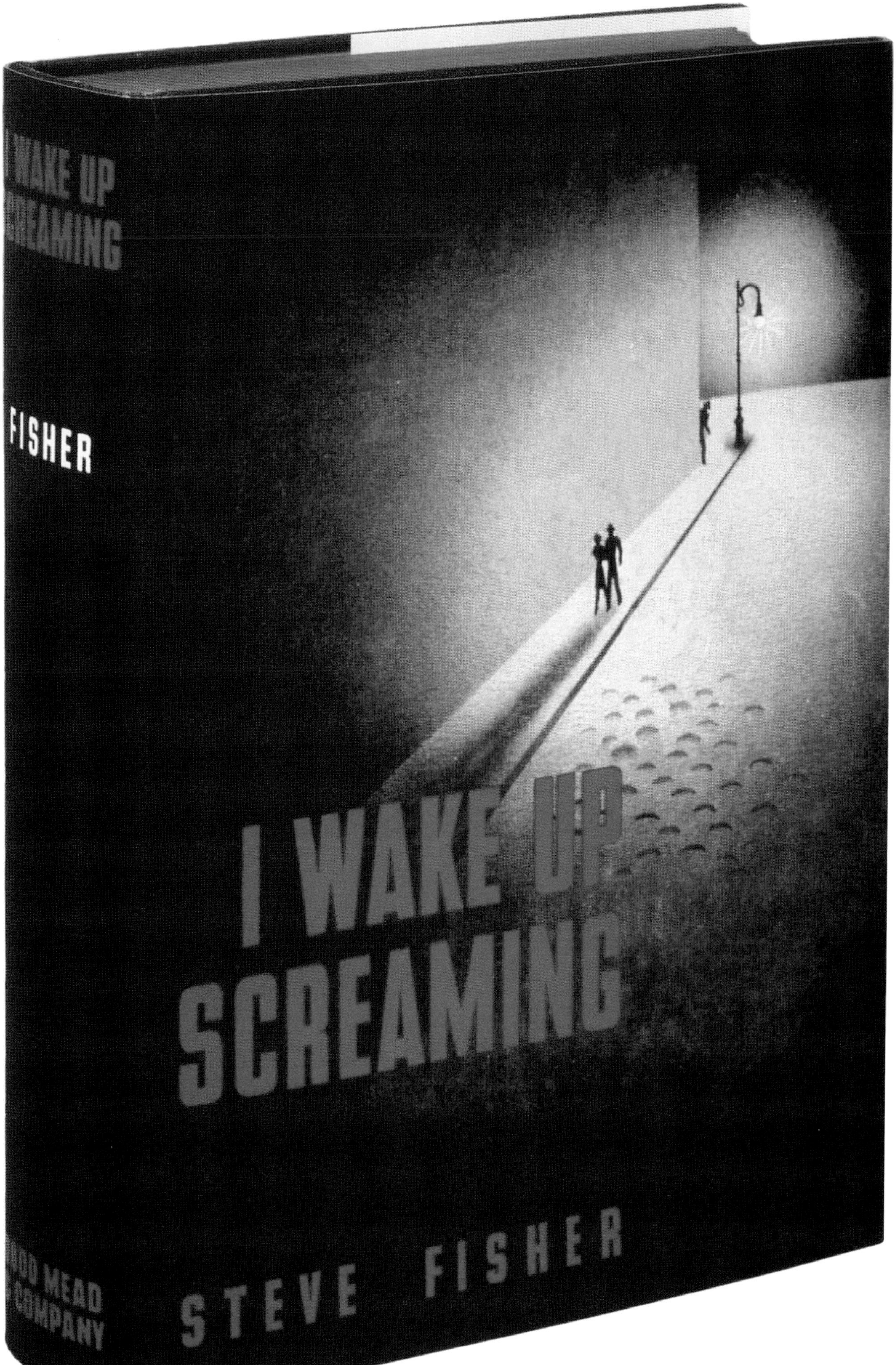
FISHER
I WAKE UP
SCREAMING
STEVE FISHER

THE GREAT GATSBY

F. SCOTT FITZGERALD

Publisher   New York: Charles Scribner's Sons, 1925

On August 24, 1924, F. Scott Fitzgerald wrote to his editor Maxwell Perkins: "I think my novel is about the best American novel ever written. It is rough stuff in places, runs only to about 50,000 words & I hope you won't shy at it." Perkins did not shy at it, but for several generations after its publication, many readers did. *The Great Gatsby* was not popular upon its initial printing in 1925, and sold fewer than 25,000 copies during the remaining fifteen years of Fitzgerald's life. Although it was adapted into both a Broadway play and a Hollywood film within a year of publication, it was largely forgotten during the Great Depression and World War II. After it was republished in 1945 and 1953, it found a wide readership, and is now regarded by many as the Great American Novel. (Kuehl)

The author's only contribution, and a Connolly 100 selection.

Dark blue cloth with titles in blind at the front board and in gilt at the spine, no topstain. Title page shows a date of 1925, with no statement of edition or later printings on the copyright page, and the Scribner seal at the bottom. The first issue of the book has six points, all of which must be present: (1) "chatter" for "echolalia," at page 60:16, (2) "northern" for "southern" Page 119:22, (3) "it's" for "its" on page 165:16, (4) "sick in tired" for "sickandtired" on page 205:9-10, and (5) "Union Street Station" for "Union Station" page 211:7-8. Front flap shows a price of "THE GREAT GATSBY $2.00" at the top edge, followed by advertisements for five Fitzgerald books, beginning with *This Side of Paradise* and ending with *The Vegetable,* then the publisher's name and address. Rear flap shows an advertisement for two books by Ring Lardner, each with an illustration. Rear panel contains a book and plot description, ending with the publisher's name. The "J" in "Jay Gatsby" has five issues as follows: (1) "j" mistakenly printed in lower case, uncorrected, (2) "j" in lower case, corrected by hand, (3) "j" in lower case, corrected by rubber stamp, (4) "j" in lower case, corrected by a press, and (5) Jay Gatsby (reprinted entirely). Jacket on all issues is slightly taller than the book.

THE GREAT GATSBY

ELLIOTT NUGENT

Screenwriter   Cyril Hume, Richard Maibaum
Cinematographer   John F. Seitz
Composer   Robert Emmett Dolan
Cast   Alan Ladd, Betty Field, Macdonald Carey, Ruth Hussey, Barry Sullivan, Howard Da Silva
Studio   Paramount, 1949
Runtime   91 minutes

Screenwriter Richard Maibaum recalls: "Fitzgerald represented everything that the Johnston office was against— unpunished murder, illicit sex, extramarital affairs, a low moral tone, and so on. I said to Joseph Breen, 'How can you object to this book? It's really just a version of the Faust story. A man makes some kind of pact with the devil and then discovers after achieving what he wants that it's all dust and ashes. *Gatsby* is really a morality play.' Breen said, 'Nonsense. If it's a morality play, where's the voice of morality? ' So I looked in the Bible for weeks, and finally one day I came across it. It's in Proverbs, and says, 'There is a way which seemeth right unto a man, but the end thereof are the ways of death.' So we had to put it right in the opening where Nick and Jordan, now married, stop at Gatsby's grave and quote the chapter and verse from Gatsby's tombstone." (McGilligan, *Backstory 1*)

The only contributions by director Elliott Nugent or producer-screenwriters Cyril Hume and Richard Maibaum.

Reference   Selby

The GREAT GATSBY
F·SCOTT·FITZGERALD
The GREAT GATSBY
FITZGERALD
SCRIBNERS

SORRY, WRONG NUMBER

LUCILLE FLETCHER AND ALLAN ULLMAN

Publisher   New York: Random House, 1948

Born in Brooklyn on March 28, 1912, Lucille Fletcher was a playwright as well as a film and television screenwriter. After graduating from Vassar in 1933, she took a clerical job at CBS, where she met her future husband, composer Bernard Herrmann.

Fletcher notes that *Sorry, Wrong Number* was inspired by personal experience. While Herrmann was sick at home one night, she went down to the corner drug store for medicine. Striking up a conversation with her pharmacist, a longtime friend, she raised the ire of an elderly woman who had apparently been waiting first. The woman interrupted and approached the druggist, complaining about poor service and demanding to know "who the interloper was," referring to Fletcher. Ms. Fletcher, finding the woman's shrill voice and demeanor particularly irritating, went home with the intention of writing a script based around a character with the same traits who becomes embroiled in a precarious, life-threatening situation.

One of Fletcher's best-known stories is the "The Hitchhiker," first turned into a radio drama by Orson Welles, then memorably filmed as an episode of *The Twilight Zone*. *Sorry, Wrong Number* first premiered in 1943 as a radio drama and was one of the most popular radio plays of that decade. Agnes Moorehead played the lead in the 1943 performance and again in several later radio productions, including *Suspense!* in 1959, which received an Edgar Award for Best Radio Drama.

The only contribution for Fletcher or Allan Ullman. Both Ullman and Fletcher contributed to the novelization, which drew from both the play and the screenplay, and was published just prior to the release of the film.

Black cloth with red titles at the front board and gilt titles at the spine. Red topstain. Title page shows a date of 1948, with "FIRST PRINTING" stated on the copyright page. Front flap shows a price of $2.00 at the top right corner, followed by a plot summary, then an explanation about the adaptation, ending with two credits ("Jacket photo by Aaron Sussman / Jacket design by Samuel Sugar"). Rear flap is an advertisement for *The Trial of Alvin Boaker* by John Reywall, ending with a "proof-of-purchase" tag, printed diagonally at the bottom left corner. Rear panel replicates the front panel exactly.

SORRY, WRONG NUMBER

ANATOLE LITVAK

Screenwriter   Lucille Fletcher
Cinematographer   Sol Polito
Composer   Franz Waxman
Cast   Barbara Stanwyck, Burt Lancaster, Ann Richards, Wendell Corey, Harold Vermilyea, Ed Begley
Studio   Paramount, 1948
Runtime   89 minutes

Hal Wallis: "[At Paramount], as at Warners, I regarded the writer as king. Scripts as excellent as Lucille Fletcher's *Sorry, Wrong Number*, based on her own play, made my work a pleasure. *Sorry, Wrong Number* had been a one-woman radio drama, so Lucille had to flesh out several new characters for the film. The rich woman's husband who plans her killing is seen as physically strong and handsome but morally and spiritually a weakling. We made no attempt to disguise the fact that the spoiled woman who married him had bought him. The only sympathetic character in the picture was played by the Australian actress Ann Richards, a friend whom the endangered Leona calls in the middle of the night, seeking help. This ordinary woman, living with her baby in a cramped apartment, was necessary as a counterpoint to the wealthy Leona in her mansion on Sutton Place." (Wallis)

The fourth of five contributions by director Litvak.

Reference   Selby, Siver, & Ward

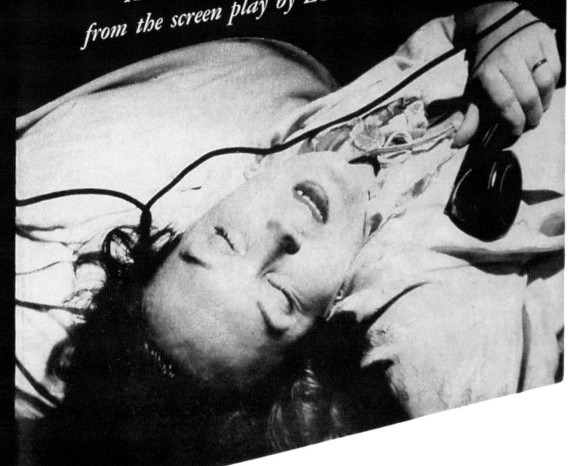

An adventure in *suspense*

SORRY, WRONG NUMBER

A novelization by ALLAN ULLMAN
from the screen play by LUCILLE FLETCHER

SONG OF THE DRAGON

John Taintor Foote

Publisher   New York: D. Appleton, 1923

Short story writer and playwright John Taintor Foote was born on March 29, 1881 in Leadville, Colorado. He began publishing short stories, principally about horses and dogs, in 1915, and worked sporadically as a screenwriter from 1919 to 1949. Apart from having penned the source for *Notorious*, he is best known for having written the original screenplay for *The Story of Seabiscuit,* a 1949 film starring Shirley Temple, based loosely on the true story of the famous racehorse.

Foote's short story, "The Song of the Dragon," was first published in two parts, in the November 12 and November 19, 1921 issues of *The Saturday Evening Post,* and was made the title story of a collection published by Appleton in 1923.

Red cloth with ornate gilt titles and design at the front board and spine, no topstain. Date of MCMXXIII on the title page, matching a date of 1923 on the copyright page, no other statement of edition or later printings. Two pages of advertisements at the rear. Front flap shows a price of $2.00 at the top left corner, followed by a plot summary. Rear flap advertises *Dumb-Bell of Brookfield* by Foote. Rear panel advertises four more books by Foote, ending with *Blister Jones*.

NOTORIOUS

Alfred Hitchcock

Screenwriter	Ben Hecht, Clifford Odets (uncredited)
Cinematographer	Ted Tetzlaff
Composer	Roy Webb
Cast	Cary Grant, Ingrid Bergman, Claude Rains, Lous Calhern, Madame Konstantin, Reinhold Schunzel
Studio	RKO, 1946
Runtime	101 minutes

Notorious began with an idea hatched by Hitchcock to build a film story around a confidence trick. Selznick story editor Margaret McDonell found a suitable property to base the idea on with Foote's story, "The Song of the Dragon," (referred to incorrectly by Hitchcock in *Hitchcock/Truffaut* as "The Song of the Flame"). In the story, a young woman falls in love with the son of a wealthy New York man, but is troubled about a secret in her past involving work as a government counterspy.

In late 1944, screenwriter Ben Hecht was brought on board to work with Hitchcock on the script, with the title *Notorious* chosen from the beginning. The two were superb collaborators, and worked on the screenplay steadily in Manhattan from December 1944 to early January 1945, then continuing in California until March. Several days a week, the pair would routinely work from nine in the morning until six at night. Hecht either paced or lay on the floor; Hitchcock "would sit primly on a straight-back chair, his hands clasped across his midriff, his round button eyes gleaming." Hecht handled narrative structure and development, and Hitchcock stuck with the visual pyrotechnics.

After a sale of the entire project to RKO in the summer of 1945, Clifford Odets was brought in to polish the dialogue, followed by a final tweaking by Hecht. Hitchcock, speaking of his work with Hecht, noted: "We were looking for a MacGuffin, and as always, proceeded by trial and error, going off in several different directions that all turned out to be too complex. Our original intention had been to show groups of German refugees training in secret camps in South America with the aim of setting up an enemy army. But we couldn't figure out what they were going to do with the army once it was organized. So we dropped the whole idea in favor of a sample of uranium contained in a wine bottle." (Truffaut, Leff)

Hitchcock's last of five contributions, Hecht's seventh of twelve, and Odets' second of three. The first of four contributions by Ted Tetzlaff, who was the cinematographer on this film and would go on to become a director for his remaining contributions.

Reference   Selby, Silver and Ward

The Song of the Dragon
Foote
Appleton
The Song of The Dragon
John Taintor Foote

HOLLOW TRIUMPH
MURRAY FORBES

Publisher   Chicago: Ziff-Davis, 1946

Born in Chicago, Murray Forbes began his radio career in 1931 on *The General Tire Show,* followed by regular work on radio soap operas like *The Guiding Light* and *Today's Children.* He went on to create the voice of Willie Fitz on the "Ma Perkins" radio show, which ran for thirty years. In the late 1940s, Forbes wrote his only novel, the thriller *Hollow Triumph,* about an ex-convict who kills a psychiatrist and becomes famous after assuming the dead man's identity.

The author's only contribution.

Dark olive-green cloth with titles and publisher's device in gilt at the spine, no topstain. No statement of edition or later printing on the copyright page. Front flap shows a price of $2.75 at the top right corner, followed by a plot summary that continues to the rear flap, ending with the publisher's name and city. The artwork from the front panel and spine wraps around to the rear panel, and the rear panel contains a biography of the author, with his photo at the top right. At least two later printings have been noted.

HOLLOW TRIUMPH
STEVE SEKELY

Screenwriter   Daniel Fuchs
Cinematographer   John Alton
Composer   Sol Kaplan
Cast   Paul Henreid, Joan Bennett, Eduard Franz, Leslie Brooks, John Qualen, Mabel Paige, Herbert Rudley, Charles Arnt, George Chandler, Sid Tomack, Alvin Hammer, Ann Staunton, Paul Burns, Charles Trowbridge, Morgan Farley
Studio   Eagle-Lion, 1948
Alternate Titles   The Scar (UK)
Runtime   82 minutes

The superb use of Los Angeles exteriors in *Hollow Triumph* (better known today by its original title in the UK, *The Scar*) demonstrates cinematographer John Alton's skill at photographing a location thriller. As in many of these "B" thrillers, the plot is contrived but executed with great confidence, and the grim conclusion makes the film as close to pure noir as *Criss Cross* or *Scarlet Street.* Joan Bennett, as the cynical Evelyn, has the film's best line: "You can't go back and start again. The older you get, the worse things get." (Silver, *Film Noir*)

The second of two contributions by director Steve Sekely, and novelist-screenwriter Daniel Fuchs' third of four.

Reference   Selby, Silver and Ward, Lyons

Hollow Triumph

Hollow Triumph

A Novel by
MURRAY FORBES

ZIFF-DAVIS PUBLISHING COMPANY

LOW COMPANY

DANIEL FUCHS

Publisher	New York: Vanguard, 1937

Born in Brooklyn on June 25, 1909, Daniel Fuchs was an American screenwriter, fiction writer, and essayist. He wrote three early novels depicting Jewish life in the Williamsburg neighborhood of New York: *Summer in Williamsburg* (1934), *Homage to Blenholt* (1936), and *Low Company* (1937). Fuchs' naturalistic, sincere style, combined with a point of view that was always skeptical and independent, led to his being called "the Brooklyn Chekhov." His limited reputation (as well as, perhaps, his lack of literary ambition) may plausibly be ascribed to the fact that after three fine novels, there wasn't much appeal in being even a Chekhov in Brooklyn. Fuchs also wrote short stories and personal essays, mainly for *The New Yorker*. When he was twenty-six, he moved to Hollywood, evidently without regret, to become a full-time screenwriter.

In a July 1977 essay, Fuchs remembers that he had hoped for a more "contrapuntal" style in the film adaptation of his novel *Low Company* (titled *The Gangster*), making reference to Robert Altman's ensemble films as an example. He said, "[In those days] you could do an ensemble [picture], but only if it were *Grand Hotel* or *Dinner at Eight,* some all-star affair taken from a stage smash." (Porfirio)

The author's second of four contributions.

Brown cloth with dark brown titles, design and rule at the front board and spine. Black topstain. No statement of edition or later printings on the copyright page. Front flap shows a price of $2.50 at the bottom right corner, and begins with a single blurb by Stanley Young of *The New York Times,* followed by a plot summary. Rear flap replicates the front flap, but with an order form for the publisher's catalog at the bottom. Rear panel is an advertisement for the author's book, *Homage to Blenholt,* with five blurbs, beginning with Fred T. Marsh of *The New York Herald Tribune* and ending with *The New Yorker*. At least two printings have been noted.

THE GANGSTER

GORDON WILES

Screenwriter	Daniel Fuchs, Dalton Trumbo
Cinematographer	Paul Ivano
Composer	Louis Gruenberg
Cast	Barry Sullivan, Belita, Joan Lorring, Akim Tamiroff, Harry Morgan (as Henry Morgan), John Ireland
Studio	Allied Artists, 1947
Alternate Titles	Low Company (US re-release title)
Runtime	84 minutes

After the 1946 success of their million-dollar musical noir *Suspense,* Monogram repeated the pairing of Barry Sullivan and British teenage skating wonder Belita when casting *The Gangster*. This star-power approach, combined with highly stylized sets and unusual cinematography, made for a truly strange adaptation that is not so much a gangster film as a moral tale of a corrupt, disintegrating criminal. For the film, Brooklyn's Brighton Beach was renamed Neptune Beach, with a plethora of cameos from actors who normally played the lead roles in films noir: Akim Tamiroff as the proprietor of a drugstore that fronts for a numbers racket; Harry Morgan as a soda jerk; Joan Lorring as cashier; Fifi D'Orsay, in a role that is difficult to describe; John Ireland and Virginia Christine as a compulsive gambler and his despairing wife; Sheldon Leonard as a predatory nemesis; Elisha Cook, Jr. and Charles McGraw as thugs; and finally, an uncredited Shelley Winters, in a ten-second spot as a waitress fixing her makeup. (Brennan)

Director Gordon Wiles' only Contribution, and the second of two for screenwriter Dalton Trumbo.

Reference	Selby, Silver and Ward, Lyons

DANIEL FUCHS
Author of "HOMAGE TO BLENHOLT"

Low Company

VANGUARD

"The date of Daniel Fuchs' next novel [LOW COMPANY is this novel] should appear in red on the calendar."

—STANLEY YOUNG in THE NEW YORK TIMES

Low Company

A Novel by DANIEL FUCHS
Author of "Homage to Blenholt"

THE WOMAN IN RED

ANTHONY GILBERT

Publisher   London: Collins, 1941

Anthony Gilbert was born Lucy Beatrice Malleson in 1899 and was an English author of novels and short stories. Although her mother wanted her to be a schoolteacher, Ms. Malleson succeeded in fulfilling her own ambition and became a novelist. After seeing John Willard's play, *The Cat and the Canary* in 1922, she became thriller-conscious, and in 1927 published her first mystery as Anthony Gilbert. For many years Gilbert's true identity was kept secret, and most readers assumed that the author was a man.

The detective in the early Gilbert novels including *The Body on the Beam* (1932) is generally Scott Egerton, a rising young British political leader. Egerton was dropped in 1936 with the introduction of a new character, Arthur Crook, who was an enormous success from the first time he appeared in *Murder by Experts* (1936). Though *The Woman in Red*, an Arthur Crook adventure, was the first of Gilbert's books to be filmed, the Crook character was dropped altogether from the film version. Instead, the film's eponymous heroine, Julia Ross, not only retained her name from the book, but became the center of the film story. (Penzler)

The author's only contribution.

Bright red cloth with black titles at the spine panel, no topstain. Title page shows a date of 1941, with no statement of edition or later printings on the copyright page. Front flap shows a price of "7s./6p." at the bottom right corner, and contains a plot summary of the book. Rear flap features four newspaper blurbs about Anthony Gilbert, beginning with the *Irish Independent* and ending with *The Sunday Times*. Rear panel is devoted to an advertisement for the Collins Crime Club, with the Club logo at the top right, followed by a block of text, then a small, hand-drawn "X," and ending with two columns showing fourteen authors who write for the series. The author list begins with Agatha Christie and ends with Nicholas Blake.

MY NAME IS JULIA ROSS

JOSEPH H. LEWIS

Screenwriter	Muriel Roy Bolton
Cinematographer	Burnett Guffey
Cast	Nina Foch, Dame May Whitty, George Macready, Roland Varno, Anita Bolster, Doris Lloyd
Studio	Columbia, 1945
Alternate Titles	The Woman in Red (working title)
Runtime	64 minutes

In a 1975 interview with Robert Porfirio, director Joseph H. Lewis noted: "I was given *My Name is Julia Ross* to do in twelve days, and after shooting for five days, I was three and a half days behind schedule. I was brought into the office of an executive who said, 'We'll give you an extra thousand-dollar bonus if you bring this picture in on time in just twelve days of shooting.' And I turned to this executive and I said, 'Not only am I not going to pick up the three days [I lost], but I expect to fall behind, oh, maybe six days. So if you're dissatisfied with me now or what I'm giving you, now's the time to fire me.' Now, it takes either a crazy man or one with great courage to make statements like this. It took me eighteen days. I did get the bonus, and I got a new contract, and I got many, many other blue ribbons from Harry Cohn and all the executives at Columbia. Those who didn't even say good morning to me on the day before my film was sneak-previewed were inviting me to their homes for dinner the following day."

The first of three contributions for director Lewis, and the first of three for screenwriter Bolton.

Reference   Selby, Silver and Ward, Lyons

THE WOMAN IN RED

ANTHONY GILBERT

ANTHONY GILBERT

THE CRIME CLUB

DETOUR

MARTIN M. GOLDSMITH

Publisher   New York: Macaulay, 1939

Very little is known about the filming of *Detour*, but so little is known about its book source that most references credit the film's source as an original screenplay. *Detour* was the second of only three books written by Martin M. Goldsmith, and was published by the small house of Macaulay in New York. It is reasonable to assume that Macaulay, after poor sales of the author's first book, *Double Jeopardy*, gave *Detour* an even smaller print run, enough to fulfill its contract with the author. *Detour* was not republished until 2006.

Though his actual birthdate is unknown, a quotation on the dust jacket for Goldsmith's third and final novel, *Shadows at Noon*, indicates that the author was thirty years old in 1943. This would place his birthdate at roughly 1913, making him about twenty-six years old when *Detour* was published in 1939.

Goldsmith's second of three contributions, and his only contribution as a novelist.

Olive cloth with red titles at the spine, no topstain. Copies also noted with black cloth and white titles, with no priority. No statement of edition or later printings on the copyright page. Front flap shows a price of $2.00 at the top right corner, followed by a plot summary, ending with the publisher's name and city. Rear flap is an advertisement for *My Family 'Tis of Thee* by Marguerite Brener, ending with the publisher's name and city. Rear panel is an advertisement for four new novels by the publisher beginning with *Detour* by Martin Goldsmith and ending with *My Family 'Tis of Thee* by Marguerite Brener.

DETOUR

EDGAR G. ULMER

Screenwriter	Martin M. Goldsmith, Martin Mooney (uncredited)
Cinematographer	Benjamin H. Kline
Composer	Leo Erdody (as Erdody)
Cast	Tom Neal, Ann Savage, Claudia Drake, Edmund MacDonald, Tim Ryan, Esther Howard
Studio	Producers Releasing Corporation, 1945
Runtime	67 minutes

Edgar G. Ulmer went from the heights to the basement, starting as a cameraman for F.W. Murnau in Germany, and winding up at what film historian Myron Meisel called "the lowest depths of Poverty Row, far beyond the pale of the B film and on into the seventh circle of the "Z" picture, employing absurd scripts and monotonal acting to reach the kind of controlled expression he felt compelled to create. *Detour*, a prime example, employs only three sets, plus a car driving interminably in front of an unceasing back-projection machine." Today it is considered a cornerstone of film noir.

In a 1970 interview, Peter Bogdanovich asked Ulmer how the idea evolved for *Detour*. The director replied: "Martin Goldsmith wrote a very bad book called *Detour*. I took it to Martin Mooney and rewrote the script. I was always in love with the idea, and with the main character—a boy who plays piano in Greenwich Village and really wants to be a decent pianist. He's so down on his luck that the girl who goes to the coast [with him] is the only person he can exist with sex-wise—*The Blue Angel* kind of thing. And then, the idea to get involved on that long road of Fate—where he's an absolute loser—fascinated me. We shot it in six days. The boy who played the leading character, Tom Neal, wound up in jail after he killed his own wife; he did practically the same thing he did in the picture." (Bogdanovich)

Ulmer's third of five contributions.

Reference   Selby, Silver and Ward, Lyons

DETOUR

BY
MARTIN M. GOLDSMITH
Author of "DOUBLE JEOPARDY"

DARK PASSAGE

DAVID GOODIS

Publisher   New York: Julian Messner, 1946

In January 1946, though his novel *Dark Passage* had not yet been published, Philadelphia crime novelist David Goodis sold the story rights to Warner Brothers for the respectable sum of $23,500. The story was first serialized in *The Saturday Evening Post,* then published by Messner in the fall. At about the same time, the author signed a six-year contract with Warner Brothers, with the unusual clause that he need spend only six months of the year in Hollywood, and the remaining months at home, writing fiction or film. This contract also allowed Goodis to bid farewell to the pulp magazines that had paid his bills for years, which included *Battle Birds, Daredevil Aces, Popular Sports,* and *Detective Fiction.* The author is said to have cranked out some half million words for such publications, sometimes contributing five or six stories in the same issue under various pseudonyms. He would publish his last magazine story of the 1940s, "Caravan to Tarim," in the more respectable *Colliers,* in 1946, along with an article in the *San Francisco Chronicle* about the murder in Los Angeles of Elizabeth Short, the "Black Dahlia," whose butchered body was found in a vacant lot. The Dahlia murder would become the stuff of legend, but for Goodis it was just another story.

Now making $750 a week at Warner Brothers, Goodis moved into the Oban, a rundown hotel on Yucca street, as opposed to more respectable Hollywood quarters like the Roosevelt or the Knickerbocker, which he could have easily afforded. (Haut)

The author's last of three contributions, and his only contribution as a novelist.

Black cloth with gilt titles at the spine, red topstain. No statement of edition or later printings on the copyright page. Front flap shows a price of $2.00 at the top right corner, followed by a plot summary. Rear flap is an advertisement for four mysteries by the same publisher, beginning with Dana Wilson's *Make with the Brains, Pierre* and ending with Audrey Gaines' *Omit Flowers, Please.* Rear panel is devoted to an advertisement for the publisher's "recommended mystery" label, which mentions a few authors but no titles, ending with the publisher's name and address.

DARK PASSAGE

DELMER DAVES

Screenwriter   Delmer Daves
Cinematographer   Sid Hickox
Composer   Franz Waxman, Max Steiner (uncredited)
Cast   Humphrey Bogart, Lauren Bacall, Bruce Bennett, Agnes Moorehead, Tom D'Andrea
Studio   Warner Brothers, 1947
Runtime   106 minutes

Upon graduation from Stanford law school in 1927, Delmer Daves began work in Hollywood as a prop man. By 1929 he was a freelance writer for several studios, and in 1943 he was given the opportunity to direct his own screenplay, an adaptation of Steve Fisher's *Destination Tokyo.* Never one to shy away from a technical challenge, Daves employed a subjective camera to record the first five reels of *Dark Passage* in 1947. Since Humphrey Bogart's character's face was not supposed to be seen until he has recovered from plastic surgery, the film's first half is told entirely from his point of view. In order to replace a person, the camera had to be especially small and light in order to simulate the pulse of human movement. To this purpose, Daves obtained a captured German camera from the Enemy Property Custody Office in Washington, DC. (Meyer)

Director-screenwriter Daves' second of two contributions.

Reference   Selby, Silver and Ward

GOODIS

DARK PASSAGE

DARK PASSAGE

DAVID GOODIS

A recommended mystery

GENE FOWLER:
"A lively mystery with atmosphere, pace, and suspense that will keep mystery fanciers awake without fail."

EMILY HAHN:
"A real thriller. It scared me but I couldn't stop until I found out what happened in the end."

CLIP BOUTELL:
"A fast-paced thriller by an up-and-coming writer who will give Raymond Chandler and James M. Cain a corpse for their money."

Recommended mystery

JULIAN MESSNER INC.

A GUN FOR SALE

GRAHAM GREENE

Publisher   London: William Heinemann, 1936

Graham Greene was notorious for juggling three or four writing projects at any given time, and he often wrote what he called his "entertainments" (*Brighton Rock, The Confidential Agent,* and *Orient Express* being examples) while working on weightier projects. *A Gun for Sale* was such a book—he called it a "shocker"—and he wrote it quickly in 1935 while also working on his first travel book, *Journey without Maps,* the final proofs of *England Made Me,* and the short stories that would constitute his collection, *The Basement Room.*

A Gun for Sale would be sold to Paramount upon publication in 1936, but the story did not see its way to the screen until 1942. When the film was announced, Greene's wife wrote while he was traveling to ask if Veronica Lake "was really to star in it." The film's setting was changed from England in the 1930s to California in the 1940s, where Fifth Columnists were selling secrets to Japan. Alan Ladd portrayed Greene's Raven, though without the harelip, and the film made him a star.

The author's first of three contributions.

Red cloth with titles in gilt at the spine, no topstain. Claret endpapers. "First published 1936" stated on the copyright page. Front flap shows a price of "7/6 / net" at the bottom right corner, and contains a plot summary that continues to the end of the rear flap. Rear panel advertises four other titles by Graham Greene, beginning with *The Man Within* and ending with *England Made Me,* with three general blurbs about the author from William Plomer, V.S. Pritchett, and Ezra Pound.

THIS GUN FOR HIRE

FRANK TUTTLE

Screenwriter	Albert Maltz, W.R. Burnett
Cinematographer	John F. Seitz
Composer	David Buttolph
Cast	Alan Ladd, Veronica Lake, Robert Preston, Laird Cregar, Tully Marshall, Marc Lawrence
Studio	Paramount, 1942
Alternate Titles	Guns for Sale, The Redemption of Raven [working titles]
Runtime	80 minutes

Paramount intended to make a film version of *This Gun for Hire* as early as May 1936, shortly after Graham Greene's novel was purchased by Paramount in London. Producer A. M. Botsford assigned Dore Schary to write the script and was considering Peter Lorre to play the role of Greene's character, Raven. Botsford soon began to have second thoughts about casting Lorre, however, with the concern that he might deliver a "one-key performance." After some other difficulties arose, the project was abandoned. In 1939, Paramount London considered making the film in the UK, but a version of the script developed by Anthony Quinn and writer Lester Koenig was rejected. Finally, in June 1941, Albert Maltz, who wrote the final screenplay with W. R. Burnett, began a story outline, and the film was rushed into production to capitalize on the growing popularity of Veronica Lake, who had been chosen as the female lead. Alan Ladd, who had played mostly bit parts up until this time, was chosen as the male lead, and had his blonde hair dyed black for the role. Ladd's portayal of Raven, "a contract killer with a heart of gold" became a template for many subsequent crime films.

Reference   Selby, Silver and Ward

A Gun
For Sale

GRAHAM
GREENE

author of
The Man Within,
Stamboul Train,
etc, etc,

THE MINISTRY OF FEAR

GRAHAM GREENE

Publisher   London: William Heinemann, 1943

Graham Greene was enthusiastic over the idea that Hollywood might have an interest in his new "entertainment," *The Ministry of Fear* (the title from a poem by Wordsworth), even before he had finished the manuscript. And indeed, after the success of *This Gun for Hire*, the rights were bought by Paramount on the strength of the title alone. But the resulting film, while entertaining and very successful at the box office, was a disappointment to both the director and the author. Greene: "Fritz Lang, whom I admire enormously, came up to me once in a bar in Los Angeles and apologized for what he had done with *The Ministry of Fear*. He said that he had signed the contract having read the book and [was then] presented with a ready-made script, which cut out the whole central part, where most of the point of the story lies. He had refused to do it, but he had signed the contract he couldn't get out of it." (Parkinson)

Greene's second of three contributions.

Mustard yellow or lemon yellow cloth (no priority) with titles in black at the spine, no topstain. "FIRST PUBLISHED 1943" stated at the top of the copyright page, followed by a statement about the book's compliance with the "authorised economy standards," with the War Economy Standard logo just above the compliance statement. Front flap shows the publisher's name and a price of 8s. 6d. at the bottom, with the title information at the top, as follows: "The / Ministry of Fear / An Entertainment / by Graham Greene." Rear flap is an advertisement for Greene's book, *The Power and the Glory*, with five blurbs, beginning with Sir Hugh Walpole and ending with V.S. Pritchett. Rear panel contains seven quotes about the author, which begin with Sir Hugh Walpole and end with *Spectator*. Some dust jackets were printed on the verso of other dust jackets (with no priority), part of an effort to conserve paper near the end of the war.

MINISTRY OF FEAR

FRITZ LANG

Screenwriter   Seton I. Miller
Cinematographer   Henry Sharp
Composer   Victor Young, Miklós Rózsa (uncredited)
Cast   Ray Milland, Marjorie Reynolds, Carl Esmond, Hillary Brooke, Dan Duryea, Alan Napier
Studio   Paramount, 1944
Runtime   86 minutes

A young producer named Seton I. Miller was brought in by Paramount to maintain strict supervision over Fritz Lang's activities, based on the studio's inability to control him in the past. Miller had finessed a breezy adaptation of Greene's novel, treating the story as Hitchcock might have—glossing over some puzzling clues that didn't quite add up, the alarming leaps in continuity, and superficial characterizations. Everything was sacrificed to create the style and momentum of a slick Hollywood thriller. Lang had no control over the film in the editing room, as Miller (referred to by Lang as "the supposed producer") presided over assembling a final cut that would meet studio approval.

But in the end, *Ministry of Fear* is an eminently watchable film, with a glossy studio patina, handsome production, atmospheric, and beautifully shot sequences throughout. Lang accommodates the suspense with a bitter, surreal, and truly dark point of view. (McGilligan, *Fritz Lang*)

Lang's third of six contributions, and screenwriter Seton I. Miller's first of three.

Reference   Selby, Silver and Ward

The
Ministry
of Fear
by
Graham
Greene

GRAHAM
GREENE

THE
MINISTRY
OF FEAR

A NOVEL

By the author of

The Power and the Glory

Heinemann

THE CONFIDENTIAL AGENT

GRAHAM GREENE

Publisher   London: William Heinemann, 1939

In May 1939, Graham Greene rented a studio in Mecklenburgh Square, Bloomsbury, to complete work on *The Power and the Glory* away from the distractions of family life. His plan was to work on a separate, lighter effort in the mornings, and continue writing *The Power and the Glory* in the afternoons. In his memoirs, Greene wrote: "Each day I sat down to work [on *The Confidential Agent*] with no idea of what turn the plot might take, and each morning I wrote, with the automatism of a planchette, two thousand words instead of my usual stint of five hundred words. In the afternoons *The Power and the Glory* proceeded towards its end at the same leaden pace, unaffected by the sprightly young thing who was quickly overtaking it." (Sherry, II)

The author's last of three contributions.

Blue cloth with red titles at the spine, no topstain. "First published 1939" printed at the top of the copyright page, with no mention of additional impressions. Front flap shows a price of "7s. 6d." at the bottom right corner, and contains a plot summary. Rear flap is an advertisement for Greene's previous novel, *Brighton Rock*, with six review blurbs. Rear panel contains four quotes about the author by various literary figures (William Plomer, V.S. Pritchett, Ezra Pound, and Richard Church), then six titles written by Greene, beginning with *The Man Within* and ending with *Brighton Rock*.

CONFIDENTIAL AGENT

HERMAN SHUMLIN

Screenwriter   Robert Buckner
Cinematographer   James Wong Howe
Composer   Franz Waxman
Cast   Charles Boyer, Lauren Bacall, Victor Francen, Wanda Hendrix, George Coulouris, Peter Lorre
Studio   Warner Brothers, 1945
Runtime   118 minutes

Graham Greene actually wrote a song for a nightclub sequence in *The Confidential Agent*, something generally known only to the author's most dedicated aficionados. In a interview with *The Guardian* at the National Film Theater on September 3, 1984, Greene noted: "[*Confidential Agent*] was one of the few, the only, American film which was faithful to one of my books. It was so faithful that I thought I was going to hear my song. But I didn't. They substituted another one."

Greene wrote a response to a poor review of the film in London's *Sunday Telegraph*: "This remains the only good film ever made from one of my books by an American director. For some reason the critics thought that a young American actress should not have played an English 'Honourable.' However the Honourable in my book was only removed by one generation from a coal miner." (Parkinson)

Director Herman Shumlin's only contribution.

Reference   Selby

The
Confidential
Agent

by

GRAHAM
GREENE

HEINEMANN

THE CONFIDENTIAL AGENT

landed at Dover on the 15th
he gave a false address to
resisted the detectives who
suspicion of murder. Later of
explosion at the colliery
reason to think the passport at S.
belongs to a man executed last year at
from his Government, but his confidential mission
all knowledge of it. Under these Embassy deny
stances, I consider the evidence circum-
insufficient to justify a charge of murder,
but a warrant should be issued at once on
the charges of fraud, theft and incitement
to violence.

I am etc.

by
GRAHAM
GREENE
author of BRIGHTON ROCK, etc.

NIGHTMARE ALLEY

WILLIAM LINDSAY GRESHAM

Publisher   New York: Rinehart, 1946

William Lindsay Gresham was born in Baltimore in 1909. As a child, he moved to New York with his family, where he became fascinated by the sideshow at Coney Island, an enchantment that would one day shape his writing. In 1937, after a brief stint as a folk singer in Greenwich Village, he served as a volunteer medic for the Loyalist forces during the Spanish Civil War. There he befriended a former sideshow employee, Joseph Daniel "Doc" Halliday, and their long conversations were an inspiration for the author's work, particularly his two books about the American carnival, the nonfiction *Monster Midway* and his best-known novel, *Nightmare Alley*.

Returning to the United States in 1939, after a bleak period that involved a stay in a tuberculosis ward and a failed suicide attempt, Gresham found work editing true crime pulp magazines. In 1942, he married Joy Davidman, who, although born Jewish, became a fan of the writings of C. S. Lewis and eventually converted to Christianity. Gresham was an abusive and alcoholic husband, and Davidman ultimately left him. Soon thereafter, she not only met C.S. Lewis, but also became his wife. On September 14, 1962, nearly blind, Gresham checked into the Dixie Hotel, the same hotel where he had stayed when he wrote *Nightmare Alley* sixteen years before, and took his own life with an overdose of sleeping pills.

The author's only contribution.

Black cloth with titles and brief decorative rule in gilt against a small green panel at the spine. Green topstain. Rinehart device present at the bottom of the copyright page (removed for later printings). Front flap shows a price of $2.50, followed by a plot summary, then a credit for jacket designer A.F. Arnold. Plot summary continues to the bottom of the rear flap. Rear panel is devoted to a biography of the author. Front flap, rear flap, and rear panel all end with the publisher's name and city.

NIGHTMARE ALLEY

EDMUND GOULDING

Screenwriter   Jules Furthman
Cinematographer   Lee Garmes
Composer   Cyril Mockridge
Cast   Tyrone Power, Joan Blondell, Coleen Gray, Helen Walker, Taylor Holmes, Mike Mazurki, Ian Keith
Studio   Twentieth Century-Fox, 1947
Runtime   110 minutes

Producer George T. Jessel's remarks to the *Herald Express* during the filming of *Nightmare Alley* help explain how a producer of musicals was put in charge of a film that probes a world of swindling and debasement: "I really gave birth to the picture. I read a review of the novel, rushed to Zanuck and told him to buy it. When Darryl got around to the book, he said, 'You so-and-so, you never even read this book, it's full of censorable stuff.' I admitted it, but the censorable stuff was not the picture I wanted to make. I was interested in the story of a carnival barker who hypnotizes a few hicks, decides to become a fake spiritualist, mocks the Deity and gets punished for his impudence." Jessel's vision was validated by Philip Scheuer of *The Los Angeles Times*, who found Tyrone Power "more convincing as a phony spirtualist than he was as the real thing the year before in *The Razor's Edge*." (Miller)

Director Edmund Goulding's only contribution.

Reference   Selby, Silver and Ward

NIGHTMARE ALLEY

WILLIAM
LINDSAY
GRESHAM

RINEHART

SIMON LASH, PRIVATE DETECTIVE

FRANK GRUBER

Publisher   New York: Farrar and Rinehart, 1941

Born on February 2, 1904, in Elmer, Minnesota, Frank Gruber was an American author and screenwriter, best known for his Westerns and detective stories. All told, Gruber wrote more than three hundred stories for over forty pulp magazines, as well as more than sixty novels and more than two hundred screenplays and television scripts—many of which appeared under a variety of pseudonyms.

Gruber worked on trade journals and taught writing in New York City as a young man before deciding to write for pulp magazines, which were peaking in the mid-1930s. For years, his stories were accepted only occasionally, and he was virtually penniless. But he wrote relentlessly, and eventually became one of the top-paid writers in the United States.

Simon Lash, Private Detective was the first of three novels to feature the Simon Lash character. Lash is a connoisseur of rare editions, as was Gruber. (Penzler)

The author's last of three contributions, and his only contribution as a novelist.

Silver cloth with decorative red titles at the front board and spine, maroon topstain. Farrar and Rinehart device present at the bottom of the copyright page (removed for later printings). Front flap shows a price of "Net, $2.00" at the top right corner, followed by a plot summary. Rear flap is an advertisement for Gruber's book, *The Talking Clock*, with three paragraphs of text. Rear panel is an advertisement for three more books by the author, *The Talking Clock* (two blurbs), *The Laughing Fox* (two blurbs), and *The French Key* (two blurbs). Front flap, rear flap, and rear panel all end with the publisher's name and city.

ACCOMPLICE

WALTER COLMES

Screenwriter	Irving Elman, Frank Gruber
Cinematographer	Jockey Arthur Feindel
Composer	Alexander Laszlo
Cast	Richard Arlen, Veda Ann Borg, Tom Dugan, Michael Brandon, Marjorie Manners, Earle Hodgins
Studio	Producers Releasing Corporation, 1946
Runtime	68 minutes

A trashy if intriguing "Z" budget thriller, *Accomplice* was shot on an achingly small budget, with many car chases and, within the car chases, many close-ups of spinning tires. Saving graces include Veda Ann Borg's monotone, the jaunty Richard Arlen, and occasionally snappy dialogue, courtesy of Irving Elman and hard-boiled novelist Frank Gruber. At one point Arlen, a rare book enthusiast, comments: "Most guys who get jilted at the altar go on a booze bender. Not me. I went on a book bender."

The first of two contributions by director Walter Colmes, and the first of three by screenwriter Irving Elman.

Reference   Selby, Lyons

SIMON LASH

PRIVATE DETECTIVE

a mystery by *Frank Gruber*

author of "THE TALKING CLOCK"

Farrar & Rinehart

DEADLIER THAN THE MALE

JAMES GUNN

Publisher   New York: Duell, Sloan, and Pearce, 1942

James Gunn was born on August 22, 1920, in San Francisco. *Deadlier Than the Male* was his only novel, and the following year would mark his debut as a Hollywood screenwriter. He contributed an original screenplay to the 1950s film noir, *Affair in Trinidad,* and probably his best-remembered film is the 1959 drama, *The Young Philadelphians.* After a prolific decade in Hollywood, Gunn began to write for television as well as film, with contributions to *Mike Hammer* and *77 Sunset Strip.*

Gunn's first of two contributions, and his only contribution as a novelist.

Orange-red cloth with titles in white at the spine, no topstain. "first edition" stated (in lower case) at the center of the copyright page. Front flap shows a price of $2.50 at the top right corner, followed by a biographical blurb about the author and a photo. Rear flap contains a plot summary. Rear panel is a variation on the plot summary, with quotes from the text. Front flap, rear flap, and rear panel each end with the publisher's name and address.

BORN TO KILL

ROBERT WISE

Screenwriter	Eve Greene, Richard Macaulay
Cinematographer	Robert de Grasse
Composer	Paul Sawtell
Cast	Claire Trevor, Lawrence Tierney, Walter Slezak, Phillip Terry, Audrey Long, Elisha Cook Jr.
Studio	RKO, 1947
Alternate Titles	Deadlier Than the Male (working title), Lady of Deceit (UK)
Runtime	92 minutes

Director Robert Wise notes: "I always preferred the original title, *Deadlier Than the Male,* the same as the novel (and the working title of the film until shortly before release). But because we had Lawrence Tierney in the lead male role, [RKO] wanted something stronger, with more kick, but also without any suggestion about male or female. Of course, *Deadlier Than the Male* was exactly what the movie was about, a very apt title." (Porfirio)

Born to Kill is notable for its use of location shooting at Ocean Beach, the wide strip of beach that separates San Francisco from the Pacific Ocean. While it has since become a popular nightlife spot, in 1947 it was a deserted piece of oceanfront property, perfect for the sequence in *Born to Kill* where the elderly Mrs. Kraft makes a narrow escape and Sam [Tierney] shows Marty [Elisha Cook, Jr.] the price of betrayal. Another prominently featured landmark is the San Francisco-Oakland Bay Bridge, a bridge that was used more often in film noir than the more famous Golden Gate Bridge—because of the ease with which it could be shot with the city in the background. (Rich)

The third of Wise's six contributions, and the last of three for screenwriter Richard Macaulay.

Reference   Selby, Silver and Ward, Lyons

deadlier than the male

JAMES GUNN

GAS LIGHT

PATRICK HAMILTON

Publisher   London: Constable, 1939

Born Anthony Walter Patrick Hamilton March 17, 1904, in Sussex, Patrick Hamilton was an English playwright and novelist. Well-regarded by Graham Greene and J. B. Priestley, Hamilton's work displays a strong sympathy for the dispossessed, as well as an acerbic black humor.

Due to his father's alcoholism and financial ineptitude, Hamilton spent much of his childhood living in boarding houses in Chiswick and Hove. His education was patchy and ended just after his fifteenth birthday when his mother withdrew him from Westminster School. After a short career as an actor, he became a novelist in his early twenties with the publication of *Monday Morning* (1925), written when he was nineteen.

Hamilton disliked many aspects of modern life. The end of his novel *Mr Stimpson and Mr Gorse* (1953), with its vision of England smothered in metal beetles, reflects his loathing of the motor car. He was in fact run over by an automobile in the late 1920s and badly disfigured.

The author's first of two contributions.

Green self-wrappers with white endpapers and pastedowns, no topstain. "First published 1939" stated on the copyright page, with no mention of later impressions. Front flap shows a price of "Price / 2/6 / net" at the bottom right corner, with a diagonal perforation; otherwise, both flaps are blank. Rear panel is an advertisement for other plays by the publisher in the "paper wrappers" format, listing Patrick Hamilton (two titles), James Bridie (thirteen titles), Hilda Vaughan & Laurier Lister (one title), John Brandane (three titles), Alfred Sangster (two titles), Hugh Ross Williamson (one title), Dan Burke (one title), ending with a mention that "Constable & Co also publish the plays of / BERNARD SHAW / For a full list apply to 10 Orange Street WC2."

GASLIGHT

GEORGE CUKOR

Screenwriter   John Van Druten, Walter Reisch, John L. Balderston
Cinematographer   Joseph Ruttenberg
Composer   Bronislau Kaper
Cast   Ingrid Bergman, Charles Boyer, Joseph Cotten, Dame May Whitty, Angela Lansbury
Studio   MGM, 1944
Alternate Titles   Murder in Thornton Square (UK)
Runtime   114 minutes

Screenwriter Walter Reisch notes: "MGM wanted to film [Hamilton's play], until they discovered that a minor company had already made it in England with Anton Walbrook and Diana Wynyard. They ran the picture and it turned out to be exactly like the stage play, not bad at all. [But] there was nothing that L.B. Mayer abhorred more than just taking a play and making it into a picture. So we were given the job of revamping it completely. Patrick Hamilton's original play was magnificent. You simply couldn't ruin it, whereas we had the chance of adapting it to the personalities who would [now] be playing it (Ingrid Bergman, Joseph Cotten, and Charles Boyer)—that was our real contribution. We wrote a [new] beginning and built the whole house from the idea of where the jewels were hidden. These were not in the play." (McGilligan, *Backstory 2*)

Director George Cukor's third of four contributions.

Reference   Selby

GAS LIGHT

*A Victorian thriller
in three acts
by*

PATRICK HAMILTON

Author of "ROPE"

HANGOVER SQUARE

PATRICK HAMILTON

Publisher   London: Constable, 1941

Hangover Square is regarded by many as Patrick Hamilton's most accomplished work, and contemporary authors including Iain Sinclair and Peter Ackroyd see it as an important contribution to the tradition of the London novel. It deals with both the alcohol culture of its day and the underlying political context, including the rise of Fascism and the responses to it.

The novel's main character is George Harvey Bone, a lonely borderline alcoholic who suffers from a split personality. He is obsessed with gaining the affections of Netta, a failed actress and one of the circle of "friends" with whom he drinks. George periodically suffers from what Hamilton calls "dead moods" in which he is convinced he must kill Netta; however, after recovering from these interludes, he cannot remember them.

The author's second of two contributions.

Beige cloth with red titles at the spine, no topstain. "First published 1941" at the center of the copyright page. Two pages of advertisements at the rear. Front flap shows a price of "8/6d. net" at the bottom right corner, with the top half showing three blurbs about Hamilton, beginning with *Spectator* and ending with J.B. Priestley. The bottom half advertises books by Hamilton, followed by listings for four novels and four plays. Rear flap is blank, and rear panel is a plot summary of the book, ending with the publisher's name and city. Two binding states have been noted, with no known priority. Both bindings and jackets are exactly the same in every respect, except that the board-to-board measurement of Binding "A" is 2 centimeters with off-white endpapers, and the board-to-board measurement of Binding "B" is 2.5 centimeters with white endpapers.

HANGOVER SQUARE

JOHN BRAHM

Screenwriter	Barré Lyndon
Cinematographer	Joseph La Shelle
Composer	Bernard Herrmann
Cast	Laird Cregar, Linda Darnell, George Sanders, Glenn Langan, Faye Marlowe, Alan Napier
Studio	Twentieth Century-Fox, 1945
Runtime	77 minutes

Fox purchased the screen rights to *Hangover Square* just after the book's publication in the US. Screenwriter Barré Lyndon made a number of changes, making the story a turn-of-the-century period piece and transforming George Harvey Bone into a classical composer-pianist. The period setting contributes to a dark, fantastical mood, especially in the unforgettable sequence where Bone (Laird Cregar), having strangled Netta (Linda Darnell) on Guy Fawkes Night, carries her wrapped body through cacaphonous streets filled with revelers and deposits it on top of a bonfire.

Seldom weighing less than three hundred pounds throughout his adult life, the great Laird Cregar came to a tragic end in 1945 because of his obsession to become slim, what he called a "beautiful man." His rapid loss of one hundred pounds, in conjunction with stomach-reducing surgery, contributed to a fatal heart attack at the age of thirty-one. He died two months before the release of *Hangover Square*, the only film in which he had ever received top billing. The unforgettable final scene shows Cregar as Bone, mesmerized, playing his masterpiece, "Concerto Macabre" (composed by Bernard Herrmann), blind to the conflagration and chaos around him.

The third of six contributions by director John Brahm, and screenwriter Barré Lyndon's second of four.

Reference   Selby, Lyons

HANGOVER SQUARE

by

PATRICK HAMILTON

CABLE

THE MALTESE FALCON

DASHIELL HAMMETT

Publisher   New York: Alfred A. Knopf, 1930

Dashiell Hammett made his debut in the October 1, 1923, issue of *Black Mask*, in which a short story titled "Arson Plus" introduced the world to his nameless Pinkerton agent, The Continental Op. The character proved popular with fans of the then-new hard-boiled style of mystery fiction, and nearly three dozen short stories featuring him were published over the next six years, followed by two novels published in quick succession in 1929 (*Red Harvest* and *The Dain Curse*).

In the same year as his debut as a novelist, Hammett would trump himself with the debut of world-weary private eye Sam Spade. Spade first appeared in the September 1929 issue of *Black Mask,* and in 1930 Knopf published Hammett's third novel, *The Maltese Falcon*, featuring his detective in a nearly unsolvable quest for a statue of the bird to which the title refers. For his new character, Hammett abandoned the familiar first-person narration of The Op, using instead a more detached, third-person narrative, and creating an even more unsentimental effect. It would become not only his best-loved work, but the foundation of the literature he had invented.

Hammett's first of two contributions. A Haycraft Queen cornerstone, and a Keating 100 selection.

Gray cloth with titles, rule and illustrations in black and dark green. Front board shows an illustration of a falcon in green; the spine is separated into five compartments, each with either titles or design within, with black-and-green rule separating each. Borzoi logo is stamped in black at the bottom right corner of the rear board. Front flap shows a price of "$ 2.00 / net" at the top right corner, followed by two paragraphs of text. Rear flap is devoted to a two-paragraph biography of the author. Rear panel advertises two books "BY DASHIELL HAMMETT," *Red Harvest* and *The Dain Curse*, each followed by two blurbs. Rear panel ends with the publisher's name and city, with the Borzoi logo in-between.

THE MALTESE FALCON

JOHN HUSTON

Screenwriter	John Huston
Cinematographer	Joseph La Shelle
Composer	Adolph Deutsch
Cast	Humphrey Bogart, Mary Astor, Gladys George, Peter Lorre, Sydney Greenstreet, Ward Bond
Alternate Titles	The Gent from Frisco (working title)
Runtime	100 minutes

Just after completing work on *High Sierra*, Warner Brothers offered screenwriter John Huston his first chance to direct, but warned that his budget would be small and his cast choices limited. After George Raft declined, Huston lobbied successfully for Humphrey Bogart (whom he had met while working on *High Sierra*), and added were Sydney Greenstreet, Mary Astor, and Peter Lorre. He noted many years later, "I've never had a better cast."

Huston kept his costs down by choosing a literary property already owned by Warner Brothers and by writing the screenplay himself. *The Maltese Falcon* had been filmed twice before, neither with great success. Huston recalls, "I decided to follow the book, which was considered at the time to be somewhat radical, and to transpose Hammett's style into camera terms. The book was told entirely from the standpoint of Sam Spade, and so too is the picture, with Spade in every scene except the murder of his partner. The audience knows no more and no less than he does. All the other characters are introduced only as they meet Spade, and upon their appearance I attempted to photograph them through his eyes. This too was something of an innovation at the that time." (Pratley)

Huston's second of nine contributions.

Reference   Selby, Silver and Ward

THE GLASS KEY

DASHIELL HAMMETT

Publisher   New York: Alfred A. Knopf, 1931

Dashiell Hammett was well known for his uncanny ability to put down on paper exactly what he wanted on his first draft, with only the most minimal revisions required afterward. In a letter to his publisher Alfred A. Knopf, dated December 20, 1930, Hammett wrote: "I am returning your invoice for excess corrections on *The Glass Key*. These corrections were made necessary by someone in your editorial department who, with unlimited amounts of time, energy, and red ink at his disposal, simply edited the Jesus out of my manuscript. If you'll take a look at the manuscript, which I think is still in your hands, you'll see you're very lucky I haven't billed you for the trouble I was put to unediting it."

The author's second of two contributions, and a Haycraft Queen cornerstone.

Green cloth with an illustration of a key in dark green and a maroon border, maroon and dark green design at the spine, with title and author name in reverse, and publisher's name in dark green. Borzoi logo in dark green at the bottom right corner of the rear board. Maroon topstain. Matching dates of 1931 on the title page and copyright page. Front flap has no price, and contains a plot summary, ending with a photo credit that reads, "(Jacket photograph reproduced through the / courtesy of Paramount)." Rear flap contains three reviews for *The Maltese Falcon,* two reviews for *The Dain Curse* and two reviews for *Red Harvest,* ending with a review blurb from *The New York Sun.* Rear panel repeats the front panel design exactly.

THE GLASS KEY

STUART HEISLER

Screenwriter   Jonathan Latimer
Cinematographer   Theodor Sparkuhl
Composer   Victor Young, Walter Scharf (uncredited)
Cast   Brian Donlevy, Veronica Lake, Alan Ladd, Bonita Granville, Joseph Calleia, Richard Denning, William Bendix, Frances Gifford, Donald MacBride, Margaret Hayes, Moroni Olsen, Eddie Marr
Studio   Paramount, 1942
Runtime   85 minutes

First filmed in 1935 with George Raft, the 1942 noir remake of *The Glass Key* today stands as the definitive interpretation of Dashiell Hammett's novel. Released just five months after *This Gun for Hire*, it was the second film to pair Alan Ladd with Veronica Lake, and the success of the two films catapulted them both to stardom. They appeared again as a couple in the 1946 film noir *The Blue Dahlia*, and finally in the 1948 war drama *Saigon*.

Reference   Selby, Silver and Ward

THE BEAST WITH FIVE FINGERS

WILLIAM FRYER HARVEY

Publisher   London and New York: J.P. Dent and Sons and E.P. Dutton, 1928

Born in 1885 to a wealthy Quaker family, William Fryer Harvey was an English writer of short stories, most notably in the mystery and horror genres. He took a degree in medicine from Leeds University, but during a long sabbatical due to ill health, he wrote what became his first book, a collection of short stories titled *Midnight House and Other Tales,* published in 1910. Harvey lapsed into obscurity after his death in 1937, but the 1946 release of the film version of his novel, *The Beast with Five Fingers,* caused a resurgence of interest in his work.

Black cloth with titles in white at the spine, no topstain. Title page shows a date of 1928, with publishers Dent and Dutton both present, and no statement of edition or later impressions on the copyright page. Front flap shows a price of "6s. / net" at the top right corner, followed by a blurb about the book. Rear flap advertises other books by the publisher, with listings for five titles, beginning with *The Bitter End* by John Brophy and ending with *Redemption Island* by C.M. Hale & Evan John, then the publisher's name and address. Rear panel repeats the artwork on the front panel exactly. *The Beast with Five Fingers* was published jointly by Dent in the UK and Dutton in the US, with the same pages used for both editions. Both the book and jacket for the Dutton edition have the same design, but note "Dutton" as the publisher at the lower spine, with the jacket showing a price in dollars and a different advertisement at the rear flap.

THE BEAST WITH FIVE FINGERS

ROBERT FLOREY

Screenwriter   Curt Siodmak
Cinematographer   Wesley Anderson
Composer   Max Steiner
Cast   Robert Alda, Andrea King, Peter Lorre, Victor Francen, J. Carrol Naish, Charles Dingle, John Alvin
Studio   Warner Brothers, 1946
Runtime   88 minutes

Time and speculation have embedded the production lore of *The Beast with Five Fingers* in Luis Buñuel scholarship. Some sources claim that Buñuel planned the entire severed hand sequence, and that producer William Jacobs had vetoed the result as too florid. Buñuel insisted in later interviews that his ideas were the entire basis for the script, and the film's Hispanic setting, morbid humor, and Victor Francen's Fernando Rey-like performance all argue for Buñuel's involvement. In any event, Buñuel had left Warners and the United States by the time the film was released. (Baxter)

Screenwriter Curt Siodmak recalls: "I wrote *The Beast with Five Fingers* not for Peter Lorre, but for Paul Henreid. Paul said, 'You want me to play against a goddamned hand? I'm not crazy.' I would love to have shot it with him, because I thought a man looking so debonair was a much more interesting murderer than that freakish Lorre." (McGilligan, *Backstory 2*)

The second of three contributions by novelist-screenwriter Siodmak, and the third of four by director Robert Florey.

Reference   Selby

THE
BEAST
WITH
FIVE
FINGERS

WILLIAM
FRYER
HARVEY

THE BEAST WITH FIVE FINGERS

AND OTHER STORIES BY
WILLIAM FRYER
HARVEY

DENT

THE COLLECTED STORIES OF BEN HECHT

BEN HECHT

Publisher   New York: Crown, 1945

After putting the finishing touches on the screenplay for *Gilda* in 1946, Ben Hecht adapted his short story, "Specter of the Rose" for the screen and convinced Herbert Yates, president of Republic Pictures, a small but smart studio in the San Fernando valley, to take it on. Hecht pitched a budget of $200,000, saying, "All I want is a pinch of the profits and no interference." He put together the creative team of Lee Garmes, George Antheil, and set designer Ernst Fegte to make the film, and offset their "A" picture salaries by shooting the entire picture in three weeks rather than three months. For his actors, he put veterans in the secondary roles, and for the two principal parts he chose unknowns, a former Olympic swimmer, Ivan Kirov, and a ballerina, Viola Essen. Said Hecht, "I wanted a girl who was a first rate dancer, who could act, and who didn't look actressy."

Blue cloth with Hecht's signature in gilt facsimile at the front board, titles and rule in gilt at the spine. Burnt orange topstain. No statement of edition or printing on the copyright page. Front flap shows a price of $3.00, followed by a summary of the book's stories. Rear flap contains a list of the story titles in this collection, and the rear panel shows an author biography, with a picture of Hecht in a noirish hat at the top.

SPECTER OF THE ROSE

BEN HECHT

Screenwriter   Ben Hecht
Cinematographer   Lee Garmes
Composer   George Antheil
Cast   Judith Anderson, Michael Chekhov, Ivan Kirov, Viola Essen, Lionel Stander, Charles (Red) Marshall
Studio   Republic, 1946
Alternate Titles   Spectre of the Rose (US alternate spelling)
Runtime   90 minutes

For his only outing as both sole screenwriter and director, Ben Hecht invoked as many cultural footnotes as one film noir has ever seen. The story was inspired by Carl Maria von Weber's *Invitation to the Dance,* adapted from Fokine's ballet *Le Spectre de la Rose* that Nijinsky made famous in 1911. Fokine's *Le Spectre de la Rose* is in turn based on a Theophile Gautier poem. The brilliant young dancer in the film is called Sanine, a name Hecht appropriated from Mikhail Artzybashev's 1907 novel of the same name. Finally, Hecht placed his own alter ego in the film by way of Lionel Stander, a poet who turns up at inopportune moments throughout, always with a shabby briefcase overflowing with poems. Stander's character was named Lionel Gans, a reference to Ganz, the real name of Hecht's fictitious autobiographical character in his novel *Count Bruga*. Ganz in turn was in actuality a thinly disguised Maxwell Bodenheim, a real-life wandering poet whom Hecht had first befriended in 1914 at Margery Curry's gatherings at the Fifty-Seventh Street colony. Hecht first parodied Bodenheim by way of a character named Rothenstein in his 1935 film, *The Scoundrel.* (MacAdams)

Slightly campy, dark, and far from plot-driven, *Specter of the Rose* wasn't for all tastes. Saul Bellow famously remarked that he "would rather eat ground glass" than sit through it a second time. (MacAdams, Fetherling)

The sixth of Hecht's twelve contributions, his second as a director, and his only contribution as an author.

Reference   Selby, Lyons

138

The Collected Stories of BEN HECHT

Crown

THE COLLECTED STORIES OF BEN HECHT

CONCERNING A WOMAN OF SIN · THE FIFTEEN MURDERERS · TH
CHAMPION FROM FAR AWAY · CAFE SINISTER · SPECTER OF THE ROS
THE ADVENTURES OF PROFESSOR EMMETT · CRIME WITHOUT PASSION
THE FABULOUS LAUNDRYMAN · DEATH OF ELEAZAR · REMEMBER TH
CREATOR · THE BULL THAT WON · ACTOR'S BLOOD · and many other

THE CHAIR FOR MARTIN ROME

HENRY EDWARD HELSETH

Publisher   New York: Dodd, Mead, 1955

The Chair for Martin Rome was Henry Edward Helseth's last novel, his remaining books all being novelizations. The author did find work as a screenwriter in the 1950s, penning original stories for two prison film dramas.

The author's third crime novel and only contribution.

Red cloth with titles in black at the spine only, no topstain. Title page shows a date of 1947, with no statement of edition or later printings on the copyright page. Front flap shows a price of $2.50 at the top right corner, followed by a plot summary, ending with the publisher's name. Rear flap contains an advertisement for *Cold Bed in the Clay* by Ruth Sawtell Wallis, with a price of $2.50 at the top left corner, ending again with the publisher's name. Rear panel is an advertisement for "Red Badge Detective Mysteries of Spring 1947," and lists eight titles, beginning with *Uneasy Terms* by Peter Cheyney and ending with *Murder Stalks the Circle* by Lee Thayer, then the publisher's name and city.

CRY OF THE CITY

ROBERT SIODMAK

Screenwriter   Richard Murphy, John Monks, Jr., Ben Hecht (early draft), Charles Lederer (early draft
Cinematographer   Lloyd Ahern
Composer   Alfred Newman
Cast   Victor Mature, Richard Conte, Fred Clark, Shelley Winters, Betty Garde, Berry Kroeger
Studio   Twentieth Century-Fox, 1948
Alternate Titles   The Chair for Martin Rome (working title), The Law and Martin Rome (working title)
Runtime   95 minutes

Producer Darryl F. Zanuck chose Ben Hecht and Charles Lederer, who had just completed the screenplay for the very successful film noir, *Kiss of Death,* to adapt *The Chair for Martin Rome* to the screen. Hecht and Lederer completed a first draft, incorporating suggestions by Zanuck to use a flashback structure, and to move the setting from San Francisco to Brooklyn. The next two drafts were written by John Monks, Jr., and the final draft was completed by Richard Murphy, who had written screenplays for *Panic in the Streets* and *Boomerang!* winning an Oscar nomination for the latter. The final draft dropped Zanuck's suggestion of a flashback structure, but kept the action in New York City, as well as a strong sociological theme of local cop vs. local hood, more along the lines of *Panic in the Streets* than the police procedural approach used in *Boomerang!*

Working against his preferences (and on Zanuck's orders), director Robert Siodmak shot *Cry of the City* mostly on location, with the rain-soaked nighttime scenes shot in Los Angeles, and almost all of the daylight sequences in New York City, with all interiors completed in the studio. Siodmak's contempt for the "documentary style" that was becoming popular in crime films of the mid-1940s (and would greatly influence many films noir of the 1950s) was well known. Fifteen years later, the director devalued the widely used approach as "cinema's gift to television." Had he a choice, he would have created the city entirely within the studio. (Greco)

The ninth of Siodmak's ten contributions, and the eleventh of twelve for Ben Hecht.

Reference   Selby, Silver and Ward

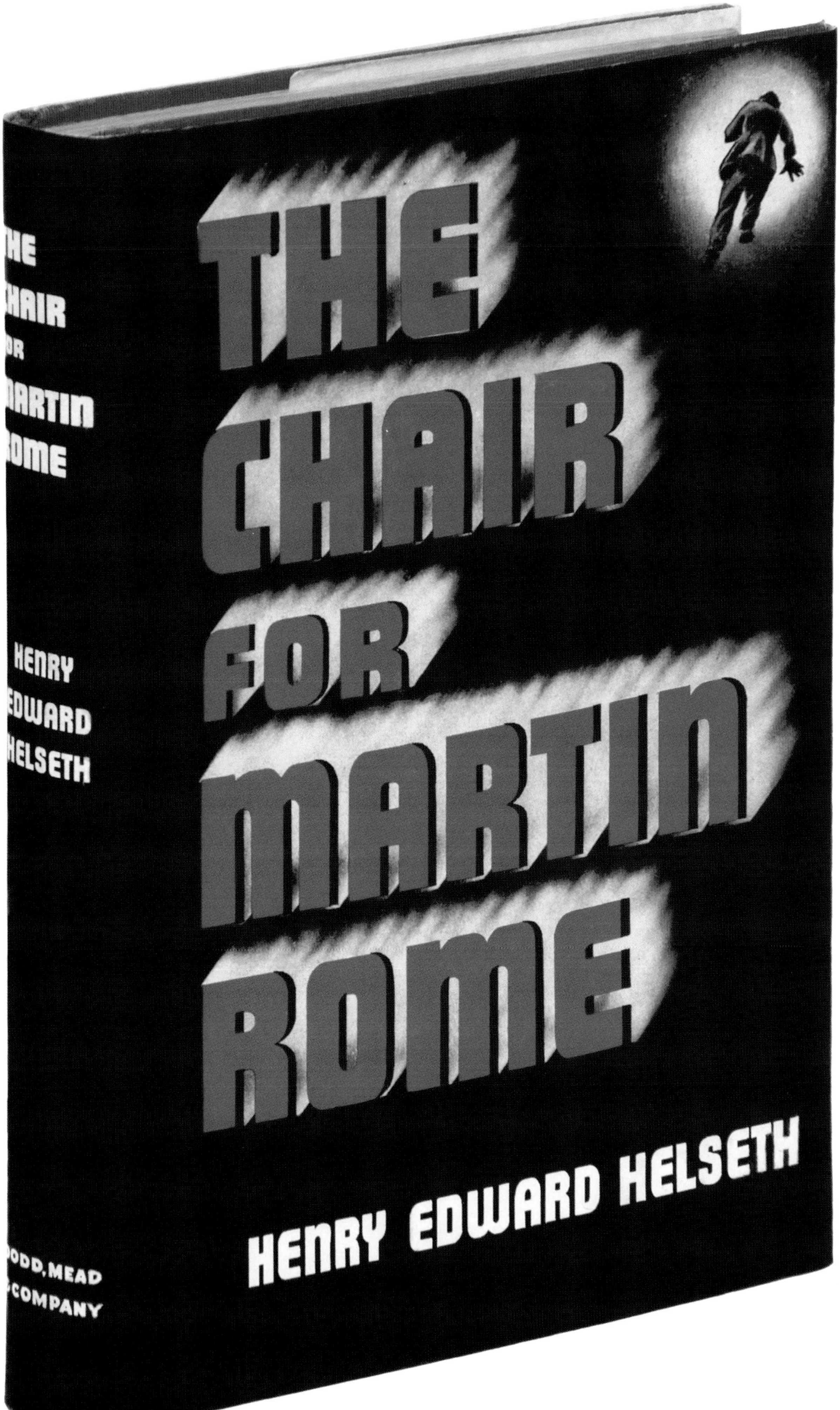
THE
CHAIR
FOR
MARTIN
ROME
HENRY EDWARD HELSETH
DODD, MEAD
& COMPANY

MEN WITHOUT WOMEN

ERNEST HEMINGWAY

Publisher   New York: Charles Scribner's Sons, 1927

Perhaps the most famous of all Ernest Hemingway's short stories, "The Killers" first appeared in the 1927 hardcover collection, *Men Without Women*. Ernest Hemingway's biographer Carlos Baker says that the film noir adaptation of the story "was the first film from any of his work that Ernest could geniunely admire." As far as director Robert Siodmak was concerned, Hemingway loved it. "We gave him a print," Siodmak wrote in 1959, "and I know that he has run it over 200 times." A remarkable fact, given that 90% of the film is an addendum to Hemingway's original ten-page short story.

The new material was mostly the work of John Huston, whose contract wth Warner Brothers prevented him from receiving a screen credit. Huston and Richard Brooks, along with Anthony Veiller, left much of Hemingway's laconic dialogue intact, a practice studiously avoided in most other early Hemingway adaptations.

The first of Hemingway's two contributions.

Black cloth with gold labels (titles and rule in black) at the front board and spine, orange topstain. Endpapers are orange with a design that replicates the front panel design, but with no titles. Title page shows a date of 1927, and the copyright page shows no statement of edition or later printings, with six copyright dates and the Scribner seal present at the bottom. The first issue of the book has a weight of at least 15.8 ounces, whereas later issue copies weight about 15 ounces. Front flap shows a price of $2.00, followed by a plot summary. Rear flap shows six blurbs about the author. Rear panel is an advertisement for Hemingway's *The Sun Also Rises*, with ten blurbs, ending with the publisher's name and city.

THE KILLERS

ROBERT SIODMAK

Screenwriter	Anthony Veiller, Richard Brooks (uncredited), John Huston (uncredited)
Cinematographer	Woody Bredell
Composer	Miklós Rózsa
Cast	Burt Lancaster, Edmond O'Brien, Ava Gardner, Albert Dekker, Jeff Corey, Virginia Christine
Studio	Universal, 1946
Alternate Titles	Ernest Hemingway's The Killers (US complete title)
Runtime	105 minutes

While most of the film's narration is original, its narrative format is not. Huston, Brooks, and Veiller chose to use the style of "posthumous inquiry" made famous by Herman J. Mankiewicz in his screenplay for *Citizen Kane*. Using multiple flashbacks—eleven in all, over an eleven-year period—the nature of an ex-fighter's life and death is explored from different points of view, recollection by recollection, until a conclusion is reached. This approach, however, wasn't even new for *Citizen Kane*. Preston Sturges arguably invented it years before in *The Power and the Glory* (1933), and Mankiewicz experimented with Sturges' technique prior to Kane in *John Meade's Woman* (1937). In the end, the remarkable thing about the narrative structure of *The Killers*, when its antecedents are considered, is that its "prismatic" story concerns a rather lowbrow subject, a prize-fighter, who is accorded a relentless, almost obsessive inquiry throughout the film. Swede is ennobled by the inquiry, and is made to seem more important than he really is, more like the mystery man of the Hemingway story, someone for whom no story is needed because all that matters in the end is that he was remarkable simply for having endured. (Greco)

The seventh of Siodmak's ten contributions, screenwriter Huston's sixth of nine, Richard Brooks' first of five, and Veiller's second of two.

Reference   Selby, Silver and Ward

MEN
WITHOUT
WOMEN

HEMINGWAY

MEN WITHOUT WOMEN

BY
ERNEST HEMINGWAY
AUTHOR OF
THE SUN ALSO RISES

CHARLES SCRIBNER'S SONS

SCRIBNERS

THE FIFTH COLUMN AND THE FIRST FORTY-NINE STORIES

ERNEST HEMINGWAY

Publisher	New York: Charles Scribner's Sons, 1938

"The Short Happy Life of Francis Macomber" first appeared in the September 1936 issue of *Cosmopolitan* magazine, and is the lesser-known noir cousin to Hemingway's more famous noir story, "The Killers." The author wrote "Macomber" after his return from the African safari described in his nonfiction book, *The Green Hills of Africa* (1935). Its companion story, "The Snows of Kilmanjaro," owes its inception to this same 1934 safari, and the creative spark that fired Hemingway's imagination for both was kindled by Philip Percival, the sagacious guide who accompanied him on the trip.

In the evenings by the campfire Percival would often regale Hemingway over whiskey with bits of African lore and stories of his previous safaris. Several of the safari tales were about the growth in courage of inexperienced hunters. Hemingway appropriated one such story, and called his protagonist Francis Macomber. Of Macomber's wife, Margaret, Hemingway later said: "I invented her complete with handles from the worst bitch I knew, and when I first knew her she'd been lovely."

The author's second of two contributions.

Red cloth with Hemingway's signature in facsimile in black on the front board, black design and gilt titles at the spine, no topstain. Title page shows a date of 1938, and the Scribner "A" appears at the center of the copyright page. Front flap shows a price of $2.75 at the top right corner, followed by a plot summary. Rear flap contains four reviews for *To Have and Have Not,* beginning with *Time* magazine and ending with Clifton Fadiman of *The New Yorker*. Rear panel begins with a photo of Hemingway in the upper half (with a photo credit for Joris Ivens), followed by additional text about the book.

THE MACOMBER AFFAIR

ZOLTAN KORDA

Screenwriter	Casey Robinson, Seymour Bennett, Frank Arnold
Cinematographer	Karl Struss
Composer	Miklós Rózsa
Cast	Gregory Peck, Joan Bennett, Robert Preston, Reginald Denny, Carl Harbord, Jean Gillie
Studio	United Artists, 1947
Alternate Titles	The Short Happy Life of Francis Macomber (working title), The Great White Hunter (US re-release title)
Runtime	89 minutes

The most significant departure from Hemingway's story is a romance introduced between Wilson (Gregory Peck) and Macomber's widow Margaret (Joan Bennett), who has killed her husband for mysterious reasons. In Hemingway's text, Wilson and Margaret have an attraction that is purely sexual and short-lived. In the film, the attraction is romantic, and Margaret's motives are shifted to invite the viewer's sympathy. (Phillips, *Hemingway*)

The first of two contributions by director Zoltan Korda.

Reference	Selby

ERNEST
HEMINGWAY

THE FIFTH COLUMN
AND THE FIRST
FORTY-NINE
STORIES

NEELY

SCRIBNERS

THE BURNING BUSH

HEINZ HERALD AND GEZA HERCZEG

Publisher   Beverly Hills, CA: Shirley Collier, 1947

Born Georg Pinner on October 24, 1890, Heinz Herald was a playwright, screenwriter, and film director. Geza Herczeg was born on March 1, 1888, in Budapest and was a playwright and screenwriter. Together they won an Oscar for their first joint effort at screen adaptation, *The Life of Emile Zola* in 1937, based on Matthew Josephson's biography, *Zola and His Time*. The only other credit for the writing team was the screen adaptation of their only play, *The Burning Bush*, retitled *Vicious Circle* for the screen.

The second of two contributions by Herczeg, the second of two by Herald, and the only contribution by either as a playwright.

Blue-gray cloth with gilt borders and type against a rectangular panel of deep blue on both the front board and spine. Blue topstain. Title page and copyright page show matching dates of 1947, with no statement of edition or later printing on the copyright page. No price on the dust jacket. Front flap contains short biographical blurbs for Heinz Herald and Geza Herczeg, with Herczeg's blurb continuing to the rear panel, ending with a biographical blurb for Noel Langley, who provides the adaptation for this edition. Rear panel is blank.

VICIOUS CIRCLE

W. LEE WILDER

Screenwriter   Guy Endore, Heinz Herald, Noel Langley
Cinematographer   Paul Dessau
Composer   George Robinson
Cast   Conrad Nagel, Fritz Kortner, Reinhold Schünzel, Philip Van Zandt, Lyle Talbot, Edwin Maxwell
Studio   United Artists, 1948
Alternate Titles   The Circle, Shadows of Fire, The Woman in Brown (US re-release titles)
Runtime   77 minutes

Wilhelm Lee Wilder spent most of his Hollywood career estranged from his younger, more famous brother Billy, who in a 1998 interview with Cameron Crowe, remembered him this way: "He was a fool. He lived in America many years before I even came here. I came here, really kind of pushed by Hitler. [Wilhelm] was in the leather-goods business—he manufactured handbags. And then one day he said, "Well, if my brother can do it, I can do it too." He sold his business, he bought a house [in Hollywood], and started making pictures, one worse than the other, and then he died."

Arthur Lyons notes: "This film, dubbed noir by some critics and a period piece and courtroom drama by others, and [its inclusion as film noir] is for those buffs of the genre whose primary criterion is cinematographic. This has to be one of the darkest films ever made, as every scene [appears to be] lighted with ten-watt bulbs. The movie packs every frame of its seventy-seven minutes with boredom. Truly one of the oddball films of all time, as it is hard to envision for what commercial audience it was aimed."

Director W. Lee Wilder's last of three contributions.

Reference   Lyons

THE
BURNING
BUSH

·

A PLAY IN THREE ACTS
BY
HEINZ HERALD
AND
GEZA HERCZEG

ADAPTED BY
NOEL LANGLEY

·

SHIRLEY COLLIER AGENCY
BEVERLY HILLS

BELLA DONNA
ROBERT S. HICHENS

Publisher   London: William Heinemann, 1909

Born in Spedhurst, Kent, on November 14, 1864, Robert Smythe Hichens was an English journalist and novelist. He was educated at Clifton College, the Royal College of Music, and the London School of Journalism. He is today perhaps best remembered in the literary world for his 1894 satire on Oscar Wilde, *The Green Carnation*. However, many of his novels were made into films, including *The Paradine Case* (published in 1933, and filmed by Hitchcock in 1947) and *The Garden of Allah* (published in 1904, and filmed three times, twice as a silent film and most famously in 1936 with Marlene Dietrich and Charles Boyer).

The author's only contribution.

Two volumes, green topstain. Front and rear pastedowns of both volumes show a printed advertisement for "HEINEMANN'S / [Heinemann logo] / LIBRARY OF / MODERN / FICTION / [decorative device]," both volumes have a "Heinemann's Library of Modern Fiction" title page preceding the actual title page, and both volumes show matching dates of 1909 on the title page and the copyright page. No advertisements at the rear of either volume. Jacket(s) not seen.

TEMPTATION
IRVING PICHEL

Screenwriter   Robert Thoeren
Cinematographer   Lucien Ballard
Composer   Daniele Amfitheatrof
Cast   Merle Oberon, Paul Lukas, George Brent, Charles Korvin, Lenore Ulric, Arnold Moss
Studio   Universal, 1946
Runtime   98 minutes

Irving Pichel had wanted to be in the theater from childhood, influenced by one of his oldest friends, playwright George S. Kaufman. Pichel attended Harvard University and tried other lines of work, but acting finally won out. He proved a valuable character player and villain in such Paramount films as *Murder by the Clock* (1931), *An American Tragedy* (1931), and *The Cheat* (1932). His deep, kindly voice tended to be a poor match for his villainous roles, so he had to become as proficient at vocal manipulations as he was at character makeup. Pichel was slated to star in the 1931 version of *Dr. Jekyll and Mr. Hyde* (1931), but director Rouben Mamoulian, complaining that he would have been "Mr. Hyde and Mr. Hyde," chose Fredric March instead. Reviews were mixed on Pichel's subsequent portrayal of Fagin in the 1933 filmization of *Oliver Twist*, one critic bestowing upon him the "worst actor of the year" award. Pichel began his directing career in collaboration with Ernest B. Schoedsack on the 1932 classic, *The Most Dangerous Game*. His subsequent directorial efforts of the 1930s were largely potboilers, but the quality improved when he joined the Fox directing staff in the 1940s. His better non-noir efforts include *Hudson's Bay* (1940), *The Pied Piper* (1942), *The Moon Is Down* (1942), and, for Paramount, *A Medal for Benny* (1945). By the mid-1940s, Pichel had all but abandoned film acting, though he played small parts in several of the films that he directed, performed on radio, and was the narrator of John Ford's *She Wore a Yellow Ribbon* (1949).

Pichel's second of four contributions.

Reference   Selby

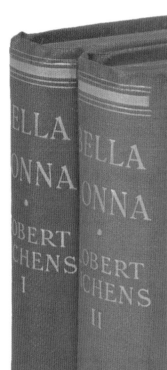

THE DAWN OF RECKONING

JAMES HILTON

| Publisher | London: Thornton and Butterworth, 1925 |

Born in Lancashire, England, on September 9, 1900, James Hilton found literary success at the age of twenty with the publication of his first novel, *Catherine Herself*. Several of his subsequent books were international bestsellers and inspired successful film adaptations, notably *Lost Horizon* (1933), *Goodbye, Mr. Chips* (1934), and *Random Harvest* (1941). *Lost Horizon,* which sold briskly in the 1930s as one of the first Pocket Books, is sometimes referred to as the book that began the paperback revolution.

Hilton's novels are sometimes dismissed as sentimental celebrations of English virtues. This is true of *Mr. Chips,* but some of his writing had a darker side. Flaws in English society of his time, particularly prejudice and class-consciousness, were frequently his targets. His novel *We Are Not Alone,* despite its inspirational-sounding title, is a grim story of legally approved lynching brought on by wartime hysteria in Britain.

The author's only contribution.

Burgundy cloth with thick horizontal rule running the along the top edge, with titles in blind at the top left corner of the front board, and the Thornton Butterworth Limited circular logo in blind at the bottom right corner of same. Copper-colored titles at the spine, with the publisher's circular logo is repeated at the bottom left corner of the rear board. No topstain. "First published - - - - - 1925" stated at the middle of the copyright page. Front flap contains a plot summary. Rear flap advertises other titles by the publisher, with listings for forty-five enumerated titles, beginning with *Where the Pavement Ends* by John Russell and ending with *Michael Forth* by Mary Johnston. Rear panel advertises more fiction by the publisher, with two sets of books: "New Volumes" and "Previous Volumes," then the publisher's name and address.

RAGE IN HEAVEN

W.S. VAN DYKE, ROBERT B. SINCLAIR (UNCREDITED), RICHARD THORPE (DIRECTOR OF RETAKES, UNCREDITED)

Screenwriter	Christopher Isherwood, Robert Thoeren
Cinematographer	Oliver T. Marsh, George J. Folsey (uncredited)
Composer	Bronislau Kaper, Mario Castelnuovo-Tedesco (uncredited), Eugene Zador (uncredited)
Cast	Robert Montgomery, Ingrid Bergman, George Sanders, Lucile Watson, Oscar Homolka
Studio	MGM, 1941
Runtime	85 minutes

The adaptation of *Rage in Heaven* by Christopher Isherwood and Robert Thoeren went for psychological depth, but the direction was straight suspense, with a noir touch. This was an early role for Ingrid Bergman (her third film in Hollywood), and Robert Montgomery reprised the maniac he played so well in *Night Must Fall* (1937). Here Montgomery does his stalking in a tuxedo and with a faux British accent, in order to be husband to Bergman and best friend to George Sanders. (Eames)

The only contribution by novelist-screenwriter Christopher Isherwood and directors W.S. Van Dyke and Richard Thorpe; Robert B. Sinclair's first of two, Edward Chodorov's first of three, and Robert Thoeren's first of four.

| Reference | Selby |

THE
DAWN
OF
RECKONING

JAMES
HILTON

A new version of
the eternal triangle.

3/6
NET

THORNTON
BUTTERWORTH

The
Dawn of Reckoning

James
Hilton

3/6
NET

What the Story
is about

THE BLANK WALL

ELISABETH SANXAY HOLDING

Publisher   New York: Simon and Schuster, 1947

In a July 10, 1951, letter to Frederic Dannay, Raymond Chandler wrote: "...does the [detective] category include writers of suspense stories in which there is little mystery, or none at all? If it does not, you eliminate some of the best performers, including Elisabeth Sanxay Holding, certainly one of my favorites." (Chandler)

Born in 1889, Elisabeth Sanxay Holding was brought up in New York and educated at Miss Whitcombe's and other schools for young ladies. In 1913 she married a British diplomat, with whom she had two daughters and lived in various South American countries, as well as Bermuda. Holding wrote six romantic novels in the 1920s, but after the stock market crash turned to the more profitable genre of detective fiction. From 1929 to 1954 she wrote eighteen novels, as well as numerous short stories for magazines. *The Blank Wall* was the first to feature a brief series character named Lieutenant Levy, but the story itself was so strong that Levy was written out of both the 1949 film noir adaptation and the 2001 neo-noir remake.

The author's only contribution.

Mauve cloth with gilt titles, rule and publisher's "Inner Sanctum" logo at the spine in gilt, yellow topstain. or no topstain, no priority. Title page shows a date of 1947, with no statement of edition or later printings on the copyright page. Front flap shows a price of $2.50 at the bottom right corner, and contains a plot summary, which continues to the rear flap, ending with a jacket design credit for H. Lawrence Hoffman and a diagonal proof-of-purchase tag with at the bottom left corner. Rear panel is an advertisement for *The Innocent Mrs. Duff* by Elisabeth Sanxay Holding, with a two-paragraph review excerpt from Joseph Henry Jackson of *The San Francisco Chronicle*.

THE RECKLESS MOMENT

MAX OPHÜLS

Screenwriter   Henry Garson, Robert W. Soderberg, Mel Dinelli, Robert E. Kent
Cinematographer   Burnett Guffey
Composer   Hans Salter
Cast   James Mason, Joan Bennett, Geraldine Brooks, Henry O'Neill, Shepperd Strudwick, Roy Roberts
Studio   Columbia, 1949
Alternate Titles   The Blank Wall (working title)
Runtime   82 minutes

A film noir from Max Ophüls's postwar Hollywood period, *The Reckless Moment* is usually overlooked in favor of the masterpieces he would direct upon his return to Europe (*Lola Montès, The Earrings of Madame de . . .*). But it is one of his most perverse stories of doomed love, with Joan Bennett as a bored middle-class housewife whose teenage daughter accidentally kills her sleazy suitor, and James Mason as an engagingly exotic Irishman, whose attempts to blackmail the mother are in conflict with his attraction to her. Ophüls spins a network of fine irony out of the lurid material, and Joan Bennett is surprisingly effective as a typical Ophüls heroine, who discovers in herself a long-suppressed streak of masochism. (Lee)

The 2001 neo-noir remake of Holding's novel, titled *The Deep End*, reinvents the problem child as the son rather than the daughter, and the son's suitor as an older man, introducing a homosexual element to the story that deepens its already significant noir content.

The second of two contributions by Ophüls, and the last of three films he directed during his brief tenure in Hollywood; the last of three contributions by Mel Dinelli.

Reference   Selby, Silver and Ward, Lyons

152

THE
Blank Wall

A NOVEL OF SUSPENSE BY
Elisabeth Sanxay Holding

FALLEN ANGEL

MARTY HOLLAND

Publisher	New York: E.P. Dutton, 1945

Fallen Angel was the first of two crime novels written by Marty Holland, a pseudonym for Mary Holland. The author had a brief career in Hollywood as a screenwriter, and is noted for the original screenplay for the 1950 film noir, *The File on Thelma Jordon*.

The author's only contribution.

Mauve cloth with decorative titles in dark blue at the front board and spine, no topstain. Title page shows a date of 1945, with "FIRST EDITION" stated at the top of the copyright page. Front flap shows a price of $2.00 at the bottom right corner, and begins with a notice reading "WATCH FOR THE MOVIE:" containing an advertisement for the forthcoming film to be directed by Otto Preminger as a "major picture for 1945," followed by a plot summary. Rear flap is an advertisement for *Death Visits the Apple Hole* by A.B. Cunningham, ending with a price of $2.00 at the bottom left corner. Rear panel is a photo of the author, with her autograph in facsimile below the photo.

FALLEN ANGEL

OTTO PREMINGER

Screenwriter	Harry Kleiner
Cinematographer	Joseph LaShelle
Composer	David Raksin
Cast	Alice Faye, Dana Andrews, Linda Darnell, Charles Bickford, Anne Revere, Bruce Cabot, John Carradine, Percy Kilbride, Olin Howlin, Hal Taliaferro, Mira McKinney, Broderick O'Farrell
Studio	Twentieth Century-Fox, 1945
Runtime	98 minutes

With *Fallen Angel,* Otto Preminger's follow-up to *Laura,* the director's work began to form what would become something of a film noir canon, consisting of six films in all, ending with *Angel Face* in 1952. Part of what gives these six films their unity is Preminger's extremely consistent directorial style. Another crucial aspect is the recurring presence of certain actors. Finally, the films have a remarkable sensitivity to their female characters, something one would find surprising after reading just about any interview with Preminger.

Following up on his career-making performance in *Laura,* actor Dana Andrews returned to film noir and Preminger in 1945 with *Fallen Angel,* starring alongside Linda Darnell and Alice Faye. Andrews portrays an impecunious loner who arrives in a small town in Northern California by bus (getting off because he has run out of bus fare), and immediately entangles himself with two women and murder.

The film was Alice Faye's first starring role in a non-musical, and the second film noir for Linda Darnell. Both Darnell and Andrews would return to work with Preminger in films noir of the 1950s.

The second of three contributions by Preminger, and screenwriter Harry Kleiner's first of two.

Reference	Selby, Silver and Ward

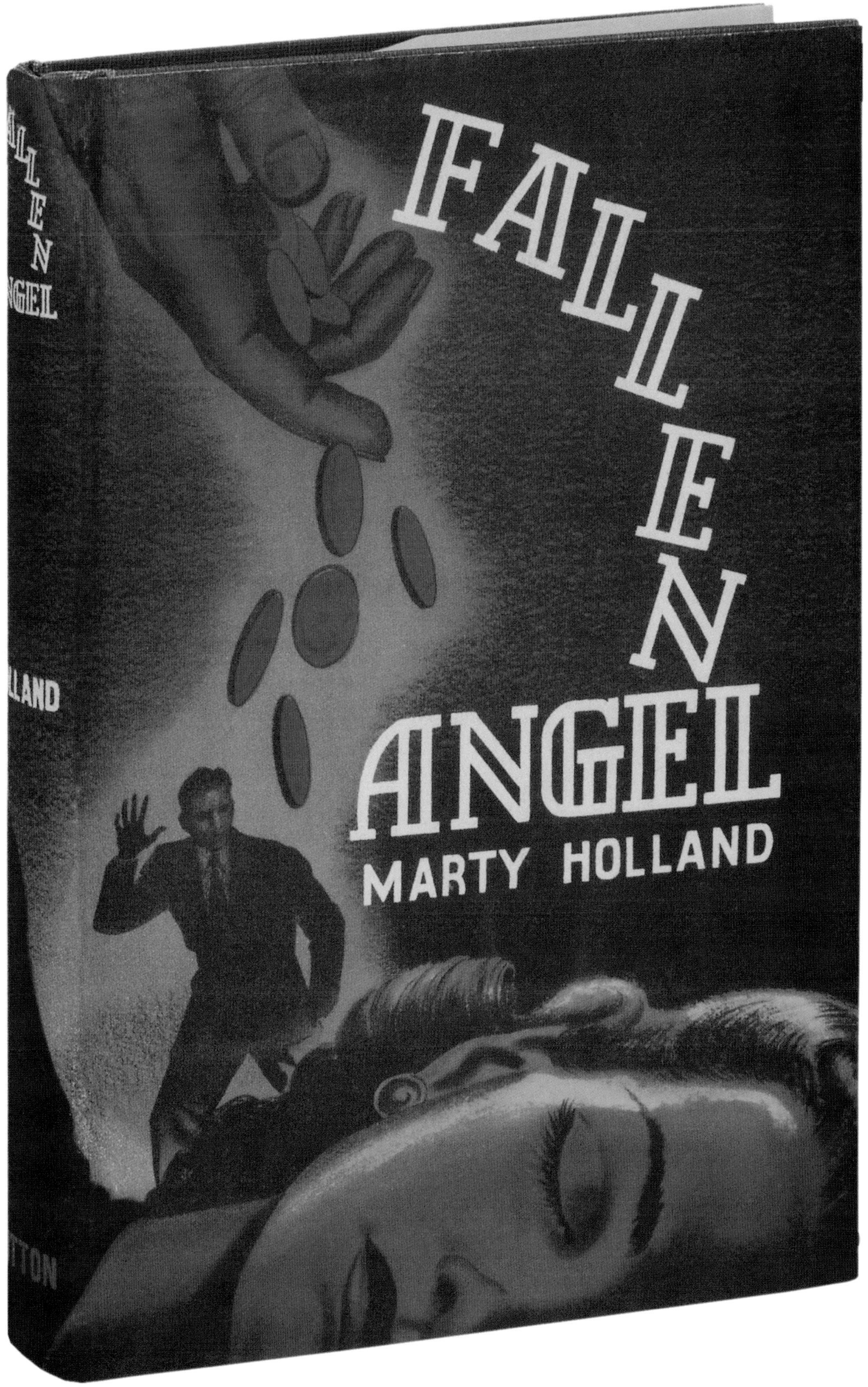
FALLEN
ANGEL
MARTY HOLLAND

THE DOUBLE TAKE

ROY HUGGINS

Publisher   New York: William Morrow, 1946

Born on July 18, 1914, Roy Huggins was a novelist, a screenwriter, and an influential originator of humorous, character-driven US television programs, with creations that typically featured misfits and rascals rather than conventional heroes. He is best known as the creator of long-running shows including *Maverick*, *77 Sunset Strip*, *The Fugitive*, and *The Rockford Files*. He also produced *Alias Smith and Jones* and *Baretta* and, after being lured out of retirement by protege Stephen J. Cannell, served for three years as the executive producer of *Hunter*.

A member of the Communist Party in the US until the Nazi-Soviet Non-Aggression Pact of 1939, Huggins appeared before the HUAC in 1952, where he named nineteen former comrades who had already been named before the Committee.

The third of four contributions by Huggins, and his first as a novelist.

Black cloth with red titles at the spine, ending with the Morrow "X" device, red topstain. Title page shows a date of 1946, with no statement of edition or later printings on the copyright page. Front flap shows a price of $2.00 at the top right corner, followed by a summary of the "great mystery characters" that the publisher has introduced in the past two decades, beginning with Mr. Tolefree and ending with Roy Huggins' Stuart Bailey, followed by a plot summary of *The Double Take* that continues to the rear flap. Rear flap ends with a list of six characters found in the book. Both flaps have "A MORROW MYSTERY" printed at the bottom. Rear panel is devoted to a five-paragraph biography of the author, which begins with "This is ROY HUGGINS" and ends with the publisher's name and address.

I LOVE TROUBLE

S. SYLVAN SIMON

Screenwriter   Roy Huggins
Cinematographer   Charles Lawton Jr.
Composer   George Duning
Cast   Franchot Tone, Janet Blair, Janis Carter, Adele Jergens, Glenda Farrell, Steven Geray
Studio   Columbia, 1947
Runtime   93 minutes

I Love Trouble is more hard-boiled than its title would suggest, a noir gem that follows directly in the footsteps of Hammett and Chandler, with terse, cynical dialogue at every turn and Los Angeles as its stomping ground. Huggins, who wrote the screenplay based on his novel, ultimately resurrected its private eye Stuart Bailey for his popular television series, *77 Sunset Strip*, which debuted in 1958 and ran for six years.

The first of two contributions by director S. Sylvan Simon.

Reference   Selby, Lyons

Too Late for Tears

Roy Huggins

Publisher	New York: William Morrow, 1947

As a civilian employee of the US government during the war, Roy Huggins spent his spare time writing hard-boiled crime fiction and was inspired by the work of Raymond Chandler. In 1946 his first novel, *The Double Take*, was published. Thereafter, he sold several serialized mysteries to *The Saturday Evening Post*, and soon published two more novels, *Too Late for Tears* and *Lovely Lady, Pity Me*. When Columbia Pictures purchased the rights to *The Double Take* in 1947, Huggins recognized an opportunity for more steady employment and signed on to adapt the script. From there he entered the movie industry, working as a contract writer at United Artists, Columbia, and RKO. In 1949, he again adapted the screenplay for one of his own novels, *Too Late for Tears*. In 1952 he wrote and directed the feature film *Hangman's Knot*, a Randolph Scott Western produced by Harry Joe Brown for Columbia. Later in 1952, he signed a contract with Columbia, where he worked as a staff writer until 1955.

The last of four contributions by Roy Huggins, and his second as a novelist.

Dark gray cloth with maroon titles at the spine, ending with the Morrow "X" device, no topstain. Title page shows a date of 1947, with no statement of edition or later printings on the copyright page. Front flap shows a price of $2.50 at the top right corner, followed by a plot summary that continues to the rear flap. Both flaps have "AND PUBLISHED BY MORROW" at the bottom. Rear panel is devoted to a five-paragraph biography of the author, which begins with "Author with an Aptitude—ROY HUGGINS" and ends with the publisher's name and address.

Too Late for Tears

Byron Haskin

Screenwriter	Roy Huggins
Cinematographer	William Mellor
Composer	Dale Butts
Cast	Lizabeth Scott, Don DeFore, Dan Duryea, Arthur Kennedy, Kristine Miller, Barry Kelley
Studio	United Artists, 1949
Alternate Titles	Killer Bait (US re-release title)
Runtime	98 minutes

In *Too Late for Tears*, Jane (Lizabeth Scott) says, "We were the worst kind of poor. White collar poor." When Jane and her husband become the unexpected custodians of a bag full of mob money, husband Don wants to go to the police. But when Don asks Jane to say goodbye to the cash, Jane says, "When I think of it, I get sick inside."

It's enough to drive two people apart, and indeed it does. *Too Late for Tears* is launched by a ridiculous coincidence, but still succeeds under its own logic. Jane is trouble from the first, and like Mrs. Dietrichson in *Double Indemnity* she's always two double-crosses ahead of the men in her life. Many films noir put the blame on Mame, and this is one of the more extreme cases: Lizabeth Scott has her poor husband convinced she's redeemable, while simultaneously twisting a hard-boiled bad man around her finger like he was made of taffy—the bad man being Dan Duryea, who goes from tough-guy abuser to hapless fool in four easy steps. (Glenn Erickson)

Director Byron Haskin's second of two contributions.

Reference	Selby, Silver and Ward, Lyons

ROY HUGGINS

AUTHOR OF "THE DOUBLE TAKE"

TOO
LATE FOR
TEARS

THE FALLEN SPARROW

DOROTHY B. HUGHES

Publisher   New York: Duell, Sloan, and Pearce, 1942

Dorothy Huges was born Dorothy Belle Flanagan in Kansas City, Missouri in 1904. Early in her writing career, she worked for newspapers and wrote poetry. Her first book of poems, *Dark Certainty,* was published in 1931 and won an award in the Yale Series of Younger Poets competition. Soon afterward she settled in Santa Fe, New Mexico, and after marrying and starting a family, launched her career as a mystery novelist and reviewer. Her most prolific decade as a fiction writer would be the 1940s, during which she would write her most famous novels: *The So Blue Marble* (1940), *The Fallen Sparrow* (1942), *Ride the Pink Horse* (1946) and *In a Lonely Place* (1947).

Most of Hughes' detective fiction involves outsiders, haunted loners, or upper-class characters involved in evil intrigues. Hughes herself has acknowledged her debt to such writers as Eric Ambler, Graham Greene, and William Faulkner in this regard. In *The Fallen Sparrow,* her protagonist is a veteran of the Spanish Civil War, who returns home to find himself facing unexpectedly the vestiges of that experience. (Penzler)

The author's first of two contributions.

Blue cloth with titles in white at the front board and spine, and publisher's "Bloodhound" logo at the bottom of the spine. Pink-red topstain. "first edition" stated on the copyright page. Front flap shows a price of $2.50 followed by a plot summary, ending with the publisher's name and address. Rear flap is devoted to a three-paragraph biography of the author, ending again with the publisher's name and address. Rear panel has an illustration of the author in black-and-white, with her name and the titles of her first four books below it, and a backdrop showing a "spread" of various newspaper reviews for her work.

THE FALLEN SPARROW

RICHARD WALLACE

Screenwriter	Warren Duff
Cinematographer	Nicholas Musuraca
Composer	Roy Webb
Cast	John Garfield, Maureen O'Hara, Walter Slezak, Patricia Morison, Hugh Beaumont
Studio	RKO, 1943
Runtime	94 minutes

The Fallen Sparrow is a film noir that, in the tradition established by *The Maltese Falcon,* defies rational plot analysis as it becomes lost in the convolutions of its own story line. Overflowing with murder, mania, and vague implications of Nazi cruelty, it ultimately becomes a film that is principally about paranoia and lost identity. The hero, played by John Garfield, attempts to uncover the person responsible for killing his childhood friend, while also trying to understand who was responsible for torturing him during his long internment at a Franco prison camp during the Spanish Civil War. The two quests, of course, turn out to be linked.

Maureen O'Hara recreated her role as Garfield's lover the following year, on February 14, 1944, in a new version of the story adapted for the *Lux Radio Theater*. (Parish)

The first of two contributions by director Richard Wallace, and the first of four by screenwriter Warren Duff.

Reference   Selby, Silver and Ward

Dorothy B. Hughes
THE FALLEN SPARROW
author of THE SO BLUE MARBLE,
THE CROSS-EYED BEAR and THE BAMBOO BLONDE
Dorothy B. Hughes
THE FALLEN SPARROW
SLOAN
PEARCE

RIDE THE PINK HORSE

DOROTHY HUGHES

Publisher   New York: Duell, Sloan, and Pearce, 1946

With the end of World War II, Dorothy Hughes turned her attentions as a novelist to postwar social problems. *Ride the Pink Horse* was an attempt to build into a suspense story the three cultures that had by that time fused in New Mexico, which was the author's place of residence for most of her adult life. Against the setting of Santa Fe's annual fiesta, Hughes tells of the collision of Indian, Spanish and "Anglo" societies and also explores in depth the mind of a murderer. (Penzler)

The author's second of two contributions.

Issued in two binding colors, taupe with red titles and brown with purple titles, no priority. No topstain. "First Printing" stated on the copyright page. Jacket shows a price of $2.50 at the top right corner, followed by a plot summary, ending with "A Bloodhound Novel" and the publisher's name and address. Rear flap is an advertisement for *Dread Journey* by Dorothy Hughes, with a short descriptive paragraph followed by a single blurb by Anthony Boucher of the *San Francisco Chronicle,* ending with the publisher's name and address at the bottom. Rear panel shows a photo of the author, with eight of her titles below it, beginning with *Dread Journey* and ending with *Johnnie*. The photo and text are set against a gathering of review blurbs praising the author's work, all colored in purple against a white background.

RIDE THE PINK HORSE

ROBERT MONTGOMERY

Screenwriter	Ben Hecht, Charles Lederer, Joan Harrison (uncredited)
Cinematographer	Russell Metty
Composer	Frank Skinner
Cast	Robert Montgomery, Thomas Gomez, Wanda Hendrix, Rita Conde, Iris Flores, Andrea King, Art Smith, Fred Clark, Richard Gaines, Tito Renaldo, Grandon Rhodes, Martin Garralaga
Studio	Universal, 1947
Runtime	101 minutes

Robert Montgomery went to great pains in *Ride the Pink Horse* to bring a hard-boiled element into the carnival atmosphere of a border town during fiesta. The antique Vivo Carousel in Taos, New Mexico, author Dorothy Hughes' model for the carousel in her novel, was purchased by Universal and shipped from Taos to Universal City, where it was reconstructed for use in the film. (Silver, *Film Noir*)

Ride the Pink Horse was remade as a television movie directed by Don Siegel in 1964, titled *The Hanged Man*.

Director Robert Montgomery's second of two contributions, screenwriter Ben Hecht's tenth of twelve, screenwriter Joan Harrison's last of five, and screenwriter Charles Lederer's third of five.

Reference   Selby, Silver and Ward

RIDE THE pink HORSE

DOROTHY B. HUGHES

Duell, Sloan
and Pearce

HUMORESQUE

FANNIE HURST

Publisher   New York: Simon and Schuster, 1919

Born on October 19, 1889, in Hamilton, Ohio, Fannie Hurst was an American novelist and screenwriter. She was the only child of a well-to-do family and spent the first twenty years of her life in St. Louis, Missouri, where she graduated from Washington University in 1909. In 1921, Hurst was among the first to join the Lucy Stone League, an organization that fought for the right to allow women to preserve their maiden names. She was active in the Urban League and was appointed to the National Advisory Committee to the Works Progress Administration in 1940. She was also a delegate to the World Health Organization in 1952.

Hurst was an extremely successful screenwriter, with credits for nearly three dozen films made between 1912 and 1945. The best of these include *Imitation of Life* (based on her novel, and filmed in 1934 and 1959), and *Humoresque*, based on the title story from the 1919 collection published by Simon and Schuster.

The author's only contribution.

Maroon cloth with titles and rule in gilt at the front board and spine, no topstain. "Published March, 1919 / B-T" stated at the bottom of the copyright page. Front flap contains an advertisement for "Popular Fiction," with listings for four titles, beginning with *Land's End* by Wilbur Daniel Steele and ending with *Panama Plot* by Arthur B. Reeve, then "Established 1817." Rear flap is an advertisement for *Harper's Magazine*. Rear panel is an advertisement for the publisher's "Fiction in Many Fields," with listings for five titles, beginning with *The Highflyers* by Clarence Budington Kelland and ending with *Humoresque* by Fannie Hurst, then the publisher's name and city.

HUMORESQUE

JEAN NEGULESCO

Screenwriter	Clifford Odets, Zachary Gold
Cinematographer	Ernest Haller
Cast	Joan Crawford, John Garfield, Oscar Levant, J. Carrol Naish, Tom D'Andrea, Craig Stevens
Studio	Warner Brothers, 1946
Runtime	125 minutes

In 1942 playwright Clifford Odets was hired by Warner Brothers to write a script based loosely on the life of George Gershwin. After much revision work by Sonya Levien and Elliot Paul, the resulting film was the 1945 drama, *Rhapsody in Blue*. But since very little of Odets' original script was used in the final version, producer Jerry Wald took a large portion of it, changed the names of the characters, and merged it with an ongoing adaptation of a Fannie Hurst short story titled "Humoresque." Hurst's story is about a violin player who goes from rags to riches, only to be brought to his knees by one of his more attractive high society patrons. All references to Gershwin's life were removed from Odets' script, and the film noir *Humoresque* was born. (Behlmer)

John Garfield's violin "performances" in *Humoresque* were actually played by two professional violinists standing on either side of him, one to bow and one to finger. The actual music was performed by Isaac Stern.

Clifford Odets' last of three contributions, and Negulesco's fourth of six.

Reference   Selby

Humoresque

by

Fannie Hurst

HARPER & BROTHERS
Publishers
ESTABLISHED 1817

Spine:

Humoresque

By

FANNIE HURST

augh on life h a tear be-d it.

$1.50 net

RPERS

MORTAL COILS

ALDOUS HUXLEY

Publisher   London: Chatto and Windus, 1922

Born on July 26, 1894, Aldous Leonard Huxley was an English writer. Best known for his novels and essays on a wide range of topics, he also published short stories, poetry, travel writing, film stories, and scripts. Through his novels and essays Huxley functioned as an examiner and sometimes critic of social mores, norms, and ideals.

Mortal Coils is a collection of five pieces of short fiction, each about a different character. One of the stories, "The Gioconda Smile," is a crime story, and is among Huxley's most famous fictional works. The other stories involve a nun, a little girl, an old artist, and the patrons of a bar. The term "mortal coils" originated in Shakespeare's *Hamlet*, meaning "the activities and troubles of life." The stories each concern themselves with some sort of trouble, normally of an amorous nature, and often end in disappointment.

The author's only contribution, for which he also wrote the screenplay.

Blue cloth with title, author name and rule in reverse against a panel of white at the top of the spine. Blue topstain. Title page shows a date of 1922, with no statement of edition or later impressions on the copyright page. Front flap advertises three titles by Huxley, each with a mention of the impression currently in print, the format, and the price. Rear flap is blank, and the rear panel is an advertisement for recent fiction by the publisher, with listings for eight titles, beginning with *The Veneerings* by Sir Harry Johnson and ending with *The Mercy of Allah* by Hillaire Belloc, then a mention of the publisher's catalogue and address.

A WOMAN'S VENGEANCE

ZOLTÁN KORDA

Screenwriter   Aldous Huxley
Cinematographer   Russell Metty
Composer   Miklós Rózsa
Cast   Charles Boyer, Ann Blyth, Jessica Tandy, Cedric Hardwicke, Mildred Natwick, Cecil Humphreys
Studio   Universal, 1948
Alternate Titles   The Gioconda Smile
Runtime   96 minutes

Born on June 3, 1895 in Austria-Hungary (now Hungary), Zoltán Korda (birth name Zoltán Kellner) was a screenwriter, director, and producer. A former cavalry officer, Korda made a number of military adventure films, many of which were filmed in Africa or India. Of his directorial efforts, *The Four Feathers* (1939) starring Sir Ralph Richardson is considered his greatest cinematic accomplishment, and was nominated for the Palme d'Or at the 1939 Cannes Film Festival.

The Macomber Affair and *A Woman's Vengenance*, filmed back-to-back in 1947 and 1948, respectively, form an interesting pair of noir adaptations of literature by the director. *A Woman's Vengeance*, by virtue of having been written for the screen by Aldous Huxley, author of the source material, is less compromised.

The second of two contributions by Korda.

Reference   Selby

MORTAL COILS

BY ALDOUS HUXLEY

CONTAINING:
The Gioconda Smile
Permutations among the
Nightingales
The Tillotson Banquet
Green Tunnels
Nuns at Luncheon

6/-
NET

CHATTO &
WINDUS

THE LOST WEEKEND

CHARLES JACKSON

Publisher   New York: Farrar and Rinehart, 1944

Author Charles Jackson's first and by far best-known novel was *The Lost Weekend,* a semi-autobiographical account of his own struggles with alcohol, and he used his celebrity to become an advocate against substance abuse. Jackson is noted for being one of the first speakers in Alcoholics Anonymous to acknowledge drug dependence as part of his recovery story. He wrote a handful of novels in the years that followed, but never quite repeated his initial success. He committed suicide in 1968.

The author's only contribution, and only book to be adapted to the screen.

Red cloth with black panels that have titles in reverse on the front board and spine, publisher's name in black at the heel. Farrar and Rinehart colophon symbol present at the bottom of the copyright page (and removed for later printings). Front flap shows a price of $2.50 at the top right corner, followed by a plot summary, which continues to the rear flap. Both flaps have the publisher's name and address at the bottom. Rear panel is devoted to a biography of the author, with a photo of him sitting in his yard at the top left corner.

THE LOST WEEKEND

BILLY WILDER

Screenwriter	Charles Brackett, Billy Wilder
Cinematographer	John F. Seitz
Composer	Miklós Rózsa
Cast	Ray Milland, Jane Wyman, Phillip Terry, Howard Da Silva, Doris Dowling, Frank Faylen, Mary Young, Anita Bolster, Lilian Fontaine, Frank Orth, Lewis L. Russell
Studio	Paramount, 1945
Runtime	101 minutes

In a 1997 interview with Cameron Crowe, Billy Wilder recalls that he picked up a copy of *The Lost Weekend* in Chicago during the summer of 1944 while changing trains, and immediately selected it as the source material for his next film. Much of the shooting was done on location in New York City, including the Ray Milland character's favorite daytime roost, P.J. Clarke's on New York's Upper East Side. The liquor industry reportedly offered the studio five million dollars to "bury" the film, which went on to win Academy Awards for Best Picture and Best Actor.

The Lost Weekend foreshadowed the emergence of the kind of social issues that would dominate films during the next three decades. While its popular appeal was largely due to a then-new kind of sensational content and intensity, it remains striking and unusually fresh today. This has much to do with Wilder's grim and rather unapologetic depiction of his protagonist's five-day drinking binge. While the same kinds of topics would be exploited to the point of exhaustion in cinema for years to come, including many noirs of the 1950s and 1960s, they would almost always be accompanied by long, theatrical speeches, overacting, and redemptive endings. In his series of 1998 interviews with Cameron Crowe, Wilder said that Paramount was not enthusiastic about making the film the way he wanted to make it, saying, "How can you make a [successful] picture about a drunk man who does not suddenly awake one day and say, 'I will not drink anymore'?"

The second of Billy Wilder's two contributions.

Reference   Selby

The
Lost
Weekend

CHARLES
JACKSON

The Lost
Weekend

A story by

CHARLES JACKSON

*Five Days Out of a Man's Life—One
of the Strangest, Most Remarkable
Narratives Ever Written*

Farrar &
Rinehart

THE ASPERN PAPERS

HENRY JAMES

Publisher   London and New York: Macmillan, 1888

In the 1880s, as Henry James moved on from explorations of European-American clashes and the young American woman in his novels, his shorter works also explored new subjects. "The Aspern Papers" (1888) is one of James' best longer tales, and bears a gothic connection to his more famous novella, "The Turn of the Screw." The story line is based on an anecdote that James heard about a Mary Shelley devotee who tried to obtain some valuable letters written by the poet. Set in a brilliantly described Venice, the story demonstrates James's ability to generate almost unbearable suspense while never neglecting the development of his characters.

The author's only contribution.

Two volumes. The first volume contains "The Aspern Papers" (the story on which the film is based), and the second volume contains two other thematically-related stories, "Louisa Palant" and "The Modern Warning." Title page and copyright page both read 1888, in both volumes. No advertisements at the rear of volume one. Six pages of advertisements in volume two, the first page beginning with *The Reverberator* by Henry James (followed by other titles), and the last page beginning with *New Novels* by F. Marion Crawford.

THE LOST MOMENT

MARTIN GABEL

Screenwriter	Leonardo Bercovici
Cinematographer	Hal Mohr
Composer	Daniele Amfitheatrof
Cast	Robert Cummings, Susan Hayward, Agnes Moorehead, Joan Lorring, John Archer, Eduardo Ciannelli, Frank Puglia, Minerva Urecal, William Edmunds, Eugene Borden, Chris Drake, Martin Garralaga, Micholas Khadarik, Saverio LoMedico, Donna De Mario, Lillian Molieri, Julian Rivero, Wallace Stark, Robert Verdaine
Studio	Universal, 1947
Runtime	89 minutes

The Lost Moment, as with the following year's *A Portrait of Jennie*, is a strange trip into a gothic netherworld, where romantic obsessions take the upper hand and the rules of reality are of little or no significance. Screenwriter Leonardo Bercovici adapted the screenplays for both films, taking *The Lost Moment* from Henry James' "The Aspern Papers." As in *A Portrait of Jennie,* the story takes a haunting plunge into nineteenth-century romanticism, a meditation on obsession and loss.

The only contribution and sole directorial effort by Martin Gabel, a character actor who also produced the 1947 film noir *Smash-Up: The Story of a Woman*, which, like *The Lost Moment,* uses Susan Hayward as its muse. The first of two contributions by screenwriter Leonardo Bercovici.

Reference   Selby

THE ASPERN PAPERS
HENRY JAMES
VOL. I
MACMILLAN & Co.
THE ASPERN PAPERS
HENRY JAMES
VOL. II
MACMILLAN & Co.

Uncle Harry

Thomas Job

Publisher   New York: Samuel French, 1942

Uncle Harry, British playwright Thomas Job's second of four plays, opened on Broadway in 1942 and ran for nearly a year. Joseph Schildkraut played the title character Harry, who lives with his two sisters in a classic co-dependent relationship (they care for him, and he works to pay the bills). Harry meets a woman, falls in love, and becomes engaged to marry. Lettie, the more dependent of the two sisters, feigns illness in order to postpone the marriage, causing Harry's fiancée to break their engagement. Consumed with rage upon discovering Lettie's trickery, Harry attempts to poison her, but the poison is consumed instead by his innocent sister Hester. Lettie is blamed for the murder, and despite Harry's attempts to claim responsibility, she is convicted and hanged.

The first of Job's two contributions, and his only contribution as a playwright.

Dark blue cloth with titles in gilt at the front board and spine, no topstain. No statement of edition or later printings on the copyright page. Front flap shows a price of $1.50 at the bottom center, and contains a plot summary. Rear flap is blank, and rear panel shows six reviews for the stage play, ending with *New York Daily News,* then the publisher's name and address.

The Strange Affair of Uncle Harry

Robert Siodmak

Screenwriter   Stephen Longstreet, Keith Winter
Cinematographer   Paul Ivano
Composer   Mario Castelnuovo-Tedesco (uncredited), Paul Dessau (uncredited), Hans J. Salter (uncredited)
Cast   George Sanders, Geraldine Fitzgerald, Ella Raines, Sara Allgood, Moyna MacGill
Studio   Universal, 1945
Alternate Titles   Uncle Harry (UK), Guilty of Murder? (US re-release title)
Runtime   80 minutes

British producer Harry Wilcox first submitted *Uncle Harry* to Hays Code chief Joseph Breen three years before its Broadway debut in 1939, as a proposed vehicle for his wife, actress Anna Neagle. Breen was not so much concerned with the incestuous implications of the relationship between Harry and his dependent sister as he was with the dispensation of justice in response to an act of murder. Breen objected to the vague moral implications of the play's ending, writing, "Wrong must always be characterized as wrong, and not as something else." Wilcox agreed and concluded that, in the film's ending, Harry should be "locked up for life as a lunatic."

The project was shelved until 1944, when writer-producer Joan Harrison brought it to director Robert Siodmak, with whom she had just completed work on *Phantom Lady.* The ending originally suggested by Wilcox was incorporated, but ultimately, Siodmak cut no fewer than five different endings for the film for preview audiences, one of which was buoyed by an optional prologue. The ending used in the final version was tepid indeed, with Harry waking in his telescope room having realized the whole mess was a dream. (Greco)

The fifth of Siodmak's ten contributions.

Reference   Selby, Silver and Ward, Lyons

Uncle Harry

A PLAY IN THREE ACTS

by Thomas Job

SAMUEL FRENCH

MUSEUM PIECE No. 13

RUFUS KING

Publisher   Garden City: Doubleday, 1946

Born in 1893 in New York City, Rufus King was an American crime writer. After serving in World War I, he went to sea as a wireless operator, and claims he learned how to live on six cents a day while beachcombing along the Buenos Aires waterfront. On his return to the US, he began to write mysteries, creating the dandyish Reginald De Puyster, "the wealthiest detective of all time. " (Penzler)

Museum Piece No. 13 was a non-series effort by King, and was first serialized in *Redbook*.

The author's only contribution.

Dark gray pebbled cloth with titles, design and rule in blue at the front board and spine. No topstain. Title page shows a date of 1946, with "FIRST EDITION" stated at the bottom of the copyright page (at the end of the copyright statement as opposed to the usual position of just below it). Front flap shows a price of "M.P.N. 13 / Price, $2.00" at the top right corner, followed by a plot summary, ending with a printer's code of 2438-46 at the bottom left corner. Rear panel is an advertisement for the Crime Club series, with fifteen author names in two columns, ending with a printer's code of 4743-45 at the bottom right corner. Rear panel is a advertisement for Crime Club "Bullseyes," and ends with a printer's code of 880-46.

SECRET BEYOND THE DOOR

FRITZ LANG

Screenwriter   Sylvia Richards
Cinematographer   Stanley Cortez
Composer   Miklós Rózsa
Cast   Joan Bennett, Michael Redgrave, Anne Revere, Natalie Schaefer, Paul Cavanagh
Studio   Universal, 1948
Runtime   98 minutes

The time required for script preparation of *Secret Beyond the Door* was the longest of any Fritz Lang film, including *Metropolis*. Nearly all of 1946 was taken up with the adaptation, in which Lang altered Rufus King's novel to the point where it was practically no longer recognizable as a source. The book's millionaire newspaper magnate had become an architect; the female protagonist's name had been changed from Lily to Celia; a prologue in Mexico had been added, where the architect Mark and Celia were married; flashback structure *within* the prologue was added; a secondary but major character in the novel was dropped entirely; and Lang wanted to use voiceover narration, but with a different woman's voice (the voice of "her mind"). Most of the time Lang dictated the dialogue and scenes, with new screenwriter Sylvia Richards trying to organize his flow of words. She remembers, "I was working against the grain, and had no feeling for the story. I wrote good English sentences, so the language looked fine on paper—at least to Fritz. It was labor every inch of the way. I couldn't talk to him about it. I swear I was too much in awe of him." (McGilligan, Fritz Lang)

Fritz Lang's last of six contributions, and the second of two for Sylvia Richards.

Reference   Selby, Silver and Ward

A Crime Club Selection
MUSEUM PIECE
NO. 13
Rufus King
RUFUS
KING
THE

IF I DIE BEFORE I WAKE

SHERWOOD KING

Publisher	New York: Simon and Schuster, 1938

Born in Yonkers, New York in 1904, Sherwood King was a graduate of Marquette University and worked in advertising and sales, in addition to being a freelance journalist in Chicago. *If I Die Before I Wake* is the second of two crime novels he wrote for Simon and Schuster's "Inner Sanctum" series.

The author's only contribution.

Black cloth with gilt titles and publisher's device at the spine, red topstain. Title page shows a date of 1938, with no statement of edition or later printings on the copyright page. Front flap shows a price of $2.00 at the bottom right corner, and contains a short essay on the writing of the book. Rear flap contains an author biography, and the rear panel is an advertisement for two books by the publisher, the first a board game called *Reward*, the second a book by Rudd Fleming titled, *Cradled in Murder*.

THE LADY FROM SHANGHAI

ORSON WELLES

Screenwriter	Orson Welles, William Castle (uncredited), Charles Lederer (uncredited), Fletcher Markle (uncredited)
Cinematographer	Charles Lawton, Rudolph Maté (uncredited), Joseph Walker (uncredited)
Composer	Heinz Roemheld
Cast	Rita Hayworth, Orson Welles, Everett Sloane, Glenn Anders, Ted de Corsia, Erskine Sanford
Studio	Columbia, 1947
Alternate Titles	Black Irish, The Girl from Shanghai, Take This Woman (all US working titles)
Runtime	86 minutes

The truth about Orson Welles' first contact with Sherwood King's novel remains somewhat mysterious. Accounts from Peter Bogdanovich, Welles biographer Simon Callow, and the lore spun by Welles himself all differ greatly. The composite story seems to be that after some critical bashing over his performance in *The Stranger*, Welles returned to the stage and was desperately trying to climb out of debt incurred in an expensive production of Jules Verne's *Around the World in Eighty Days*. Welles struck a deal with Columbia chief Harry Cohn to shoot a picture with his then-wife Rita Hayworth as the star. After pitching *Carmen* as the vehicle to Cohn without success, Welles, a great lover of thrillers, sold him on King's book.

Welles' screenplay, while quite faithful to King's basic plot and characters, made significant shifts in locale and dialogue. The book is set entirely on Long Island, whereas the film launches in New York City and resolves in San Francisco, with a long yachting expedition to Acapulco in between (all shot on location). Added are two visually stunning set-piece climaxes, first in a Chinese Opera, then in a House of Mirrors.

Welles' third of four contributions, screenwriter Charles Lederer's fourth of five, William Castle's seventh of nine, and Fletcher Markle's first of two.

Reference	Selby, Silver and Ward

IF I DIE
BEFORE
I WAKE

SHERWOOD
KING

IF I DIE
BEFORE
I WAKE

A MYSTERY STORY BY

SHERWOOD KING

SIMON AND
SCHUSTER

Sing a Song of Homicide

James R. Langham

Publisher   New York: Simon and Schuster, 1940

Sing a Song of Homicide was the first of two crime novels written by James R. Langham, both published by Simon and Schuster. Both books were set in Los Angeles, and both featured a detective named Samuel G. Abbott.

The author's only contribution.

Red cloth with black titles and design at the front board and spine. No topstain. Title page shows a date of 1940, with no statement of edition or later printings on the copyright page. Front flap shows a price of $2.00, followed by a plot summary, which continues to the middle of the rear flap, followed by a photo of the author, then a two-paragraph biography. Rear panel is a publisher's advertisement for their "Inner Sanctum" series, with listings for *The Wrong Murder* by Craig Rice and *The Goose is Cooked* by Emmett Hogarth.

Night in New Orleans

William Clemens

Screenwriter   Jonathan Latimer
Cinomatographor   Merritt B. Gerstad, Leo Tover
Cast   Preston Foster, Patricia Morison, Albert Dekker, Charles Butterworth, Dooley Wilson, Paul Hurst, Jean Phillips, Cecil Kellaway, William Wright, Noble Johnson, Joe Pope
Studio   Paramount, 1942
Runtime   75 minutes

Born on September 10, 1905 in Saginaw, Michigan, William Clemens was an American film director known primarily for low-budget crime dramas. He began his Hollywood career as a film editor in 1931, and his first directing project was the 1936 film *Man Hunt*. His subsequent major credits include two Perry Mason films (*The Case of the Velvet Claws* and *The Case of the Stuttering Bishop*), three films in the "Falcon" series featuring detective Tom Lawrence, four films based on the Nancy Drew series, *and Calling Philo Vance.*

The first of two contributions by Clemens (his second, *The Thirteenth Hour,* would be his last directorial effort), and the first of seven for screenwriter Jonathan Latimer.

Reference   Selby

JAMES R. LANGHAM

SING A SONG
OF HOMICIDE

Sammy Abbott, the hardboiled
sleuth, and Ethel, his adoring wife,
find a corpse, invent a murderer,
and make their dreams come true!

AN INNER SANCTUM MYSTERY

AN INNER SANCTUM MYSTERY

SIMON AND SCHUSTER

SING A SONG OF HOMICIDE

JAMES R. LANGHAM

ROUND UP: THE STORIES OF RING W. LARDNER

RING W. LARDNER

Publisher   New York: Charles Scribner's Sons, 1929

Born Ringgold Wilmer Lardner on March 26, 1885 in Niles, Michigan, Ring Lardner's ambition from adolescence was to become a sports reporter, one he fulfilled in 1907 by landing a job as a writer for the *Chicago Inter-Ocean*. He contributed variously to *The Sporting News* in St. Louis, the *Boston American*, the *Chicago American* and others until 1919 when he joined a newspaper syndicate.

"Ring Lardner thought of himself as primarily a sports columnist whose stuff wasn't destined to last, and he held to that absurd belief even after his first masterpiece, *You Know Me Al*, was published in 1916 and earned the awed appreciation of Virginia Woolf, among other very serious, unfunny people", wrote Andrew Ferguson, who in a *Wall Street Journal* article named it one of the top five pieces of American humor writing. Many years later, In J.D. Salinger's *Catcher in the Rye*, Lardner assumed permanent immortality when he was revealed as Holden Caulfield's second favorite writer.

One of the best stories in *Round Up* is "Champion" a rags-to-glory tale about a boxer who comes to believe in his own mythology, and pays dearly on the way down.

Green cloth with Lardner's facsimile signature stamped in gilt to the center of the front board, no topstain. Title page shows a date of MCMXXIX under the publisher's name, and the Scribner seal id present at the bottom of the copyright page. Front flap shows a price of $2.50 at the top right corner, followed by a long appreciation by Carl Van Doren (expanded from the one on the front panel), which continues to the rear flap. Rear panel contains four reviews, by Sir James Barrie, Edmund Wilson, Harry Hansen, and H.L. Mencken. A "cheap" edition of the book was issued by Scribner in the same year as the first, bound in red cloth (lacking the signature stamped in gilt), a black, gold and white jacket design, and a price of $1.00 on the front flap.

CHAMPION

MARK ROBSON

Screenwriter	Carl Foreman
Cinematographer	Frank Planer
Cast	Kirk Douglas, Marilyn Maxwell, Arthur Kennedy, Paul Stewart, Ruth Roman, Lola Albright
Studio	United Artists, 1949
Runtime	99 minutes

Mark Robson's *Champion* was one of three films noir made about boxing in the late 1940s. Nastier in tone than *Body and Soul* (1947) or *The Set-Up* (1949), *Champion* is perhaps the harshest example of the genre, a descent into a moral abyss in which its hero—Kirk Douglas at his brashest and most intense—leads the charge and never looks back at what he's given up. Douglas was so compelling in a vile and irredeemable role that he almost singlehandedly changed the rules governing acceptable roles that could be played by Hollywood's leading men. (Eder)

Director Mark Robson's second of two contributions, and screenwriter Carl Foreman's first of two.

Reference   Selby

ROUND UP
The Stories of
RING W. LARDNER

" 'Round Up,' the collected short stories of Ring W. Lardner, is a characteristically, completely, unmistakably American book, truly a native product of a native art. Up to the present Mr. Lardner has had two rather distinct audiences: a large popular audience which has read him chiefly for his comedy, and a small, sophisticated one which has read him for his insight. It is time for these two audiences to meet on common ground."

—CARL VAN DOREN
Editor-in-chief, *The Literary Guild.*

SCRIBNERS

THE KISS OF DEATH

ELEAZAR LIPSKY

Publisher   New York: Penguin, 1947

Born in 1911 in Bronx, New York, Eleazar Lipsky was a prosecutor, lawyer, novelist, and playwright. He was an assistant district attorney for Manhattan in the 1940s, and later had a law practice in the city. He also served for many years as legal counsel to the Mystery Writers of America.

Eleazar Lipsky wrote the first draft of *Kiss of Death,* then titled *Stoolpigeon,* under the pseudonym Lawrence L. Blain. He sold the hundred-page manuscript to Fox, but retained the rights to publication just prior to the film. According to the Twentieth Century-Fox legal department records, producer Darryl F. Zanuck changed the title from *Stoolpigeon* to *Blind Date,* then retitled it *Kiss of Death* after stumbling upon a newspaper article by famed columnist, Hedda Hopper, referring to an event in a politician's life as "the kiss of death." Lipsky then appropriated the title for his book.

The author's only contribution.

"First Penguin Books Edition, August, 1947" stated at the top of the copyright page. Page edges stained reddish-brown. One page of advertisements at the rear, with two categories. The first category is "RECENT PENGUIN MYSTERIES," beginning with *The Cask* by Freeman Wills Crofts and ending with *Murder! Great True Crime Cases* by Alan Hynd. The second category is "RECENT PENGUIN NOVELS," beginning with *Manhattan Transfer* by John Dos Passos and ending with *Portrait of Jennie* by Robert Nathan. Rear panel begins with a photo of the author at top center with his name to the right, followed by a two-paragraph biography.

KISS OF DEATH

HENRY HATHAWAY

Screenwriter	Ben Hecht, Charles Lederer
Cinematographer	Norbert Brodine
Composer	David Buttolph
Cast	Victor Mature, Brian Donlevy, Coleen Gray, Richard Widmark, Taylor Holmes, Howard Smith, Karl Malden, Anthony Ross, Mildred Dunnock, Millard Mitchell, Temple Texas, Jay Jostyn
Studio	Twentieth Century-Fox, 1947
Alternate Titles	Stoolpigeon (working title), Blind Date (working title)
Runtime	98 minutes

While *Kiss of Death* has some remarkably brutal moments, there were still parts of the script that didn't make the final cut. Patricia Morison, who originally appeared in an early version of the film as Victor Mature's wife, is attacked and raped by the gangster hired to watch out for her while Mature is in prison. After the attack, she commits suicide by sticking her head in the kitchen oven and turning on the gas. Both of these scenes were cut from the original print at the insistence of the censors, who wanted no depiction of either a rape or a suicide. Thus, although Morison's name appears in the credits, she actually does not appear in the film at all (though her suicide is a major plot point).

Kiss of Death was the film debut of noir icon Richard Widmark, and the first of three noir important collaborations by the writing team of Ben Hecht and Charles Lederer. On January 12, 1948, Widmark, Victor Mature, and Coleen Gray reprised their screen roles for a *Lux Radio Theater* broadcast. Mature and Widmark also reprised their screen roles for a three-part television broadcast on *The Screen Guild Theater,* which first aired on October 28, 1948.

Director Henry Hathaway's third of four contributions, Hecht's ninth of twelve, and Lederer's second of five.

Reference   Selby, Silver and Ward

642

A CRIME 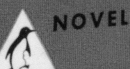 NOVEL

THE KISS OF DEATH

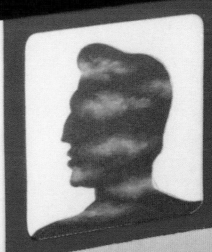

ELEAZAR LIPSKY

complete **PENGUIN BOOKS** unabridged

642

THE KISS OF DEATH — ELEAZAR LIPSKY

BUILD MY GALLOWS HIGH

DANIEL MAINWARING WRITING AS GEOFFREY HOMES

Publisher   New York: William Morrow, 1946

Build My Gallows High was Daniel Mainwaring's last of thirteen crime novels written under the Geoffrey Homes pseudonym in a long relationship with Morrow. He would concentrate the next twenty years exclusively on screenwriting for films and then television. In an interview with Patrick McGilligan, the author said, "*Build My Gallows High* was a different kind of book, entirely different. [At] first I had a detective named Robin Bishop. [He] got married and then got awfully soft, and I got fed up with him. I changed to Humphrey Campbell, who was a tougher one. With *Build My Gallows High* I wanted to get away from straight mystery novels. Those detective stories are a bore to write. I'd get to the end and have to say whodunit and be so mixed up I couldn't decide myself." (McGilligan, *Backstory 2*)

The author's first of two contributions, and his only contribution as a novelist.

Black cloth with titles in white at the spine and decorative rule above and below the title. No topstain. Title page shows a date of 1946, with no statement of edition or later printings on the copyright page. Front flap shows a price of $2.50 at the top right corner, followed by a plot summary, which continues to the end of the rear flap, with "AND PUBLISHED BY MORROW" printed at the bottom of both flaps. Rear panel is devoted to a biography of the author, ending with the publisher's name and address.

OUT OF THE PAST

JACQUES TOURNEUR

Screenwriter   Daniel Mainwaring (as Geoffrey Homes), James M. Cain, Frank Fenton (both uncredited)
Cinematographer   Nicholas Musuraca
Composer   Roy Webb
Cast   Robert Mitchum, Jane Greer, Kirk Douglas, Rhonda Fleming, Richard Webb, Steve Brodie
Studio   RKO, 1947
Alternate Titles   Build My Gallows High (UK)
Runtime   97 minutes

Jeff Schwager notes in a 1991 *Film Comment* essay that screenwriter Frank Fenton, working from Mainwaring's novel, decisively influenced the characterizations in the film adaptation of *Out of the Past,* and "was responsible for the bulk of the film's best dialogue," as well as for several key plot points. Fenton was the third writer to work on the project. James M. Cain wrote two drafts, contributing little that was used in the final film. Daniel Mainwaring, an experienced screenwriter and the author of the source novel, was called in to finish the script, and was credited in the film with the same pseudonym he used to write the novel, Geoffrey Homes.

Daniel Mainwaring's reflections on his participation as a screenwriter in films noir have always combined modesty with a bit of malice. In a 1975 interview with Robert Porfirio, he said, "The book and the film are entirely different. The film is better, a lot less confused." In an earlier interview, he minimized Tourneur's reportedly large contribution, saying, "He did what was in the script—very much so," and says nothing regarding Fenton's contribution other than, "Frank Fenton had worked on it for a while."

The fifth of director Tourneur's six contributions, Cain's last of four, and Fenton's second of two.

Reference   Selby, Silver and Ward

Geoffrey
Homes
Build My Gallows High
morrow
Build
My
Gallows
High
a novel by
Geoffrey Homes

THE SET-UP

JOSEPH MONCURE MARCH

Publisher	New York: Covici-Friede, 1928

Joseph Moncure March was born on July 27, 1899, in New York. After serving in World War I and graduating from Amherst College (where he was a protégé of Robert Frost), he worked as managing editor for *The New Yorker* in 1925—the magazine's inaugural year—and helped create the magazine's long-standing "Talk of the Town" front section. After leaving the magazine, March wrote the first of his two important long Jazz Age narrative poems, *The Wild Party*. Due to its risqué content, the book could not find a publisher until 1928. Once published, it was a great success, despite being banned in Boston. March's follow-up to *The Wild Party* was *The Set-Up*, another epic poem about a washed-up African-American boxer.

In 1929, March moved to Hollywood and was hired to turn the silent version of Howard Hughes' classic *Hell's Angels* into a talkie, a rewrite that brought the phrase "Excuse me while I put on something more comfortable" into the American cultural lexicon. He continued to work as a screenwriter in Hollywood until 1940, and his most fascinating late work is probably the left-leaning John Wayne curio, *Three Faces West*, a knockoff of *The Grapes of Wrath* that ends with a faceoff between Okies and Nazis.

The screenwriter and poet's only contribution.

Gray cloth with an illustration of a silhouetted boxer in blind and colored dark brown at the front board. Dark brown topstain. Title page shows a date of MCMXXVIII, with no statement of edition or later printing on the copyright page. Front flap shows a price $2.00 is at the top right corner, followed by a brief author biography, then a mailing list request form and the publisher's name and address. Rear flap is an advertisement for five other titles by the publisher. Rear panel contains a plot summary, and ends with a jacket design credit for Alexander King. As many as four printings have been noted, each with the printing stated on the front panel at the bottom left corner. Covici-Friede also issued a signed and numbered edition in 1928, with a limitation of 275 copies, in a slipcase with a paper spine label and no dust jacket.

THE SET-UP

ROBERT WISE

Screenwriter	Art Cohn
Cinematographer	Milton Krasner
Composer	Constantin Bakaleinikoff
Cast	Robert Ryan, Audrey Totter, George Tobias, Alan Baxter, Wallace Ford, James Edwards
Studio	RKO, 1949
Runtime	72 minutes

In a 2001 interview with Alain Silver, Robert Wise noted: "RKO bought the rights to *The Set-Up,* and in the original the fighter was black. Robert Ryan was under contract to RKO, and he had been an intercollegiate heavyweight champion when he was at Dartmouth. Since he knew his way around the ring and fit the other aspects of the character, he was a natural choice for the part."

The Set-Up has become a landmark for cinephiles because of its use of compressed time, meaning that the story takes place in real time, with clocks used throughout the film to mark the passing of its sixty-minute running time.

The last of six contributions by Wise, and screenwriter Art Cohn's first of two.

Reference	Selby, Silver and Ward, Lyons

THE SET-UP

JOSEPH MONCURE MARCH

AUTHOR OF
THE WILD PARTY

SHED NO TEARS

DON MARTIN

Publisher   New York: Murray and Gee, 1948

Don Martin was better known as a screenwriter than a novelist, which can likely be explained by the fact that he wrote over two dozen screenplays and only one novel. Many of his original screenplays were for films noir, particularly in the late 1940s and 1950s, when he worked on *The Pretender* (1947), *Destination Murder* (1950), *Shakedown* (1950), *Double Jeopardy* (1955), *No Man's Woman* (1955), and *The Man is Armed* (1956).

The text on the front flap of the jacket for *Shed No Tears* reflects the level of popularity the femme fatale was enjoying by 1948: "Using a scalpel for a pen, the author has etched a novel-sized portrait of Edna, a woman met once and remembered always—as one remembers a venereal disease. With James Cain microscopy, he dissects the warped thinking behind her triumphs and her tragedies."

Martin's second of two contributions, and his only contribution as a novelist.

Red cloth with black titles on the front board and spine, no topstain. Title page shows a date of 1948, with no statement of edition or later printings on the copyright page. Front flap shows a price of $2.75 at the top right corner, followed by a plot summary, ending with the publisher's name (Murray and Gee, Inc.) at the bottom. Rear flap has a list of eighteen other titles available from the same publisher, and the rear panel shows an "About the Author" biography with no photo.

A variant jacket, using the same book, was issued to promote the film adaptation, which was released the same year. See *Appendix A: Secondary Book Sources*.

SHED NO TEARS

JEAN YARBROUGH

Screenwriter   Brown Holmes, Virginia Cook
Cinematographer   Frank Redman
Cast   Wallace Ford, June Vincent, Robert Scott, Johnstone White, Dick Hogan, Frank Albertson
Studio   Eagle-Lion, 1948
Runtime   70 minutes

After attending the University of the South, Jean Yarbrough entered the film business in 1922, first as a propman, then steadily rising in the ranks to assistant director. By 1936, he was directing comedy and musical shorts for RKO, and in 1938 he directed his first feature, *Rebellious Daughters*. Yarbrough hit his stride as a horror film director in the 1940s, with such memorable classics as *The Devil Bat*, *King of the Zombies*, and *She-Wolf of London*. He also made a number of Abbott and Costello and Bowery Boys comedies during this period. In the 1950s, when the traditional "B" movie was on the decline, he moved to television and is best remembered as producer-director of *The Abbott and Costello Show*.

Shed No Tears is yet another argument for the dominance of the single-minded femme fatale—and the downer ending—in the world of inexpensive 1940s "B" pictures. Arthur Lyons notes, "At the urging of his wife, Wallace Ford fakes his own death to collect the insurance money. The wife collects the dough but has been having an affair on the side for some time and double-crosses her husband. When Ford finds out about his wife's infidelity, he commits suicide."

Yarbrough's second of two contributions.

Reference   Selby, Lyons

Shed no tears
By
DON MARTIN
A Novel of Surprise
SHED NO TEARS • Martin • M & G

PITY MY SIMPLICITY

CHRIS MASSIE

Publisher   London: Faber, 1944

Born in 1880, Chris Massie was a prolific British crime author. He published sixteen novels between 1925 and 1959, *Pity My Simplicity* being the tenth.

The author's only contribution.

Blue cloth with gilt titles at the spine, tan topstain. "First published in Mcmxliv" stated on the copyright page, with no mention of later impressions. Front flap shows a price of "8s. 6d. / net" at the bottom right corner, and contains a plot summary. Rear flap is an advertisement for *The Green Orb* by Chris Massie. Rear panel is an advertisement for new fiction by the publisher, with listings for nineteen titles, ending with the publisher's name and address.

LOVE LETTERS

WILLIAM DIETERLE

Screenwriter   Ayn Rand
Cinematographer   Lee Garmes
Composer   Victor Young
Cast   Jennifer Jones, Joseph Cotten, Ann Richards, Cecil Kellaway, Gladys Cooper, Anita Louise
Studio   Paramount, 1945
Runtime   101 minutes

Ayn Rand's tenure in Hollywood was brief, but unlike many other literary figures who spent time there, she relished the opportunity. She had long been a movie fan, and had a strong desire to become involved in the filmmaking process. In 1945, she wrote two screenplays that were made into films, *You Came Along* and *Love Letters*.

About the adaptation of *Love Letters,* Rand had the following to say: "The truth about *Love Letters*, as I see it, is this: it is essentially a very silly and meaningless story by the mere fact that it revolves around so unnatural a thing as somebody's amnesia. No, it has no moral lesson to teach, nor any kind of lesson whatever. So, if you look at it from the standpoint of content, it has none. But it has one valuable point as a story: a dramatic situation involving a conflict. This permits the creation of suspense. If the basic premise, amnesia, doesn't interest you, then of course the rest of the story won't interest you. A basic premise in a story is always like an axiom, [in that] you take it or you don't. If you accept the premise, the rest will hold your interest. As for me, I accept the premise out of sheer curiosity, nothing more deep or important than that. That is, granting such a setup, let's see what can be made of it. My only interest in that picture was purely technical—how to create a good construction that would be dramatic and suspenseful, out of practically nothing. The novel on which the picture was based was a holy mess. Whatever story interest and unity it has, I had to invent. But we picked this particular novel because it had elements of a possible situation. That is very rare in picture stories." (Rand)

Ayn Rand's only contribution, and director William Dieterle's first of three.

Reference   Selby

Pity My Simplicity

CHRIS MASSIE

THE CASUARINA TREE

W. SOMERSET MAUGHAM

Publisher   London: William Heinemann, 1926

W. Somerset Maugham's short story "The Letter" first appeared in hardcover in 1926, as part of a collection titled *The Casuarina Tree*. Maugham dramatized the story the same year. The theatrical version opened in London in February of 1927, and later the same year in New York. The story is based on an actual incident that took place in Singapore in 1911, and comes straight from trial testimony. Mrs. Ethel Proudlock, wife of a headmaster in Kuala Lumpur, shot the manager of a tin mine, William Steward, on the veranda of her home, in what she claimed was self-defense against an attempted rape. As in the story, Mrs. Proudlock fired not once, but six times. Public sympathy was with Proudlock, but it was soon revealed that Steward had been her lover, and that Proudlock had shot him in a jealous rage after discovering he was carrying on another affair. She was eventually pardoned at the behest of her husband, only to return to England and die in an asylum. The only element that Maugham added to the story was a letter, which served as the damning evidence. (Morgan)

Maugham's first of two contributions, and a Connolly 100 selection.

Navy blue cloth with titles in gilt at the front board and spine, with the publisher's "Maugham" device in black at the bottom right corner of the front board. No topstain. "First published 1926" stated on the copyright page, with no mention of later impressions. Front flap shows only a brief publisher blurb in a deep green at the top.Rear flap is an advertisement for seven other novels by Maugham, beginning with *The Explorer* ("6s. net") and ending with *The Painted Veil* ("3/6 net"). Rear panel contains a plot summary, ending with the italicized phrase, "*Extract from the preface.*"

THE LETTER

WILLIAM WYLER

Screenwriter   Howard Koch
Cinematographer   Tony Gaudio
Composer   Max Steiner
Cast   Bette Davis, Herbert Marshall, James Stephenson, Frieda Inescort, Gale Sondergaard,
                      Bruce Lester, Elizabeth Earl, Cecil Kellaway, Sen Yung, Doris Lloyd, Willie Fung, Tetsu Komai
Studio   Warner Brothers, 1940
Runtime   95 minutes

Director William Wyler was intent on making the opening of *The Letter* sensational. He recalls: "The script said something like, 'You hear a gunshot and you see a woman coming out shooting at a man.' I thought the shot should shock you. To get the full impact of it I thought everything should be very quiet. At the same time I wanted to show [exactly] where we were—and [all] in a single camera move. This two-minute sequence was all we did on the first day. And since all of this was not in the script [i.e., no dialogue], we ended the day with only a quarter of a page filmed. Normally, you're supposed to do three or four pages a day. Jesus, the whole studio was in an uproar. But when they saw the footage they didn't mind." (Herman)

Director Wyler's only contribution, and screenwriter Howard Koch's first of two.

Reference   Selby, Silver and Ward

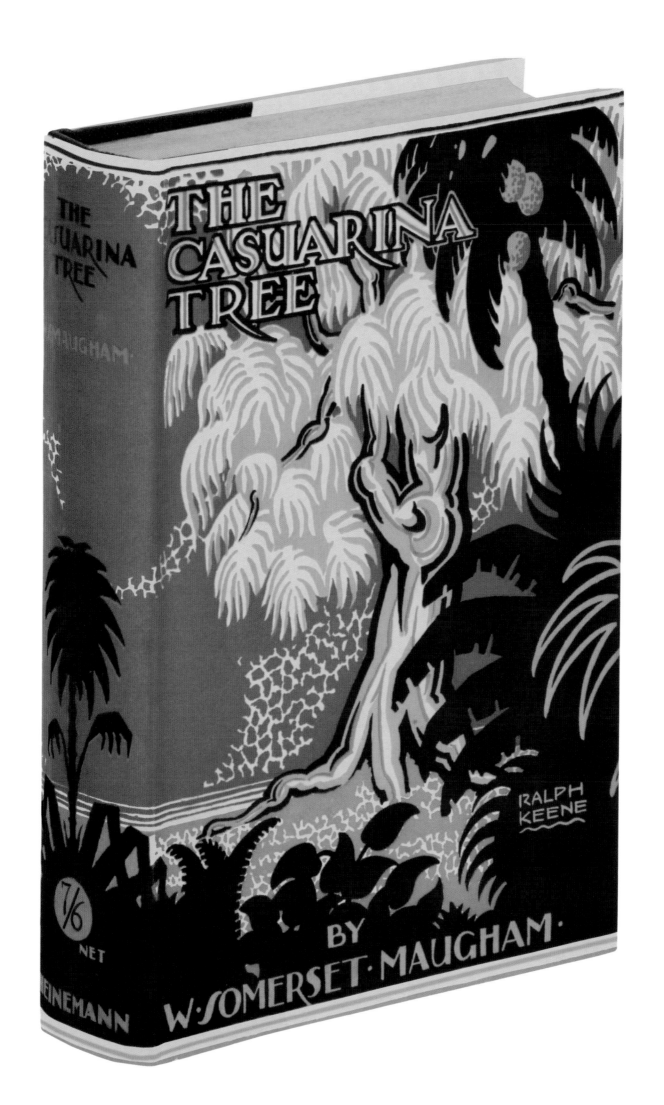

CHRISTMAS HOLIDAY

W. SOMERSET MAUGHAM

Publisher   London: William Heinemann, 1939

In December of 1932, W. Somerset Maugham went to Paris to attend the trial of Guy Albert Davin, who had been sentenced to life for murdering his rich American friend Richard Wall. The crime had homosexual overtones, but Maugham was more interested in the character of the murderer and the French penal system. From the trial and a subsequent visit to French Guiana he fashioned his 1939 novel, *Christmas Holiday*. The story was not for the prudish, and has never been one of the author's best-known works. But it epitomizes his love—and concern—for the morbid details found in ordinary lives and remote locales. (Morgan)

Maugham's second of two contributions.

Dark blue cloth with titles at the front board in gilt and the publisher's "Maugham" device in black at the bottom right corner. Book title and author in gilt at the spine, with the publisher's name in black at the bottom. Heinemann device is in black at the bottom right corner of the rear board. No topstain, dark blue endpapers. No statement of edition or later impressions on the copyright page, and no date on the title page. Front flap shows a price of "7/6 / NET" at the bottom right corner, and contains a simple publisher's blurb about the book, ending with a note reading, "Details of the various editions of Mr. / Somerset Maugham's books will be / found on the back and the back flap / of this wrapper." Rear flap advertises other books by Maugham, with listings for six titles, beginning with *The Summing Up* (three blurbs) and ending with a "Half-bound leather edition" of *Cakes and Ale* and *Of Human Bondage*. Rear panel advertises two Maugham omnibus titles, ending with a statement referring the reader to the rear flap to see the non-collected editions.

CHRISTMAS HOLIDAY

ROBERT SIODMAK

Screenwriter	Herman J. Mankiewicz
Cinematographer	Woody Bredell
Composer	H.J. Salter
Cast	Deanna Durbin, Gene Kelly, Richard Whorf, Dean Harens, Gladys George, Gale Sondergaard
Studio	Universal, 1944
Runtime	93 minutes

Christmas Holiday took some time to receive Production Code approval, but in the end it was in the hands of one of the most magnificent filmmaking teams of the 1940s. It began in 1939, when independent producer Walter Wanger sent Maugham's novel to Joseph Breen to see whether Breen would deem it worthy by Hays Code standards. Seeing that the novel's principal themes were homosexuality, prostitution, and incest, Breen's rejection was not unexpected. Four years later, in 1943, producer Felix Jackson, facing the same objections from the code, managed to get the film passed by characterizing it as a vehicle for his then-wife Deanna Durbin, who was at the time a bankable actress, along with the up-and-coming Gene Kelly, who would soon become a major star at MGM. For the delicate job of writing a screenplay, Jackson hired Robert Siodmak, who had gained notice for *Phantom Lady* the year before; then Herman J. Mankiewicz, who at the time was riding high from his success as the screenwriter for *Citizen Kane*. In Jackson's words, "Mank was very erudite *and* knew what to do with material. And believe me, that is a rare distinction." Mankiewicz later counted *Christmas Holiday* among his greatest successes, and Siodmak considered it his most personal film. (Greco)

The second of Siodmak's ten contributions, and Herman J. Mankiewicz's first of two.

Reference   Selby, Silver and Ward

CHRISTMAS HOLIDAY

W. Somerset Maugham

HEINEMANN

THEY WON'T BELIEVE ME

GORDON MCDONELL

Publisher   London: George G. Harrap, 1947

In *Hitchcock/Truffaut*, discussing his classic film noir *Shadow of a Doubt,* Alfred Hitchcock recalls: "A woman called Margaret McDonell, who was head of Selznick's story department, had a husband who was a novelist. One day she told me her husband had an idea for a story but he hadn't written it down yet. So we went to lunch at the Brown Derby and they told me the story, which we elaborated together as we were eating. Then I told him to go home and type it up. In this way we got the skeleton of the story into a nine-page draft that was sent to Thornton Wilder." *Shadow of a Doubt* was completed based on Wilder's screenplay in 1943, and is today considered by many to be Hitchcock's finest film.

They Won't Believe me is the third of McDonell's nine crime novels. Though he was born and raised in England, the writer spent much of his life in the United States working as a screenwriter, while continuing to publish novels in England. Many of his nine books were published in England with no American equivalent, this title being an example.

The second of McDonell's two contributions, and his only contribution as a novelist.

Fuchsia cloth with titles at the spine in gilt, no topstain. "First published 1947" stated on the copyright page. Front flap shows a price at the bottom right corner, and contains a plot summary. Rear flap is blank but for a printer's code of APT/K125 at the bottom. Rear flap is a generic design built around the publisher's "horse-and-letter" device.

THEY WON'T BELIEVE ME

IRVING PICHEL

Screenwriter	Jonathan Latimer
Cinematographer	Harry J. Wild
Composer	Roy Webb
Cast	Robert Young, Susan Hayward, Jane Greer, Rita Johnson, Tom Powers, Don Beddoe, George Tyne, Frank Ferguson, Harry Harvey
Studio	RKO, 1947
Runtime	95 minutes

Produced by Alfred Hitchcock's longtime assistant and collaborator, Joan Harrison, *They Won't Believe Me* was a sideways take on *Double Indemnity,* the principal difference being that the male protagonist's guilt is held in doubt until the film's final moments. An effective noir atmosphere is maintained by both Robert Young's alternating personalities and use of flashback structure. Micheal Keaney: "This is an intriguing tale of a reprehensible cad, the three women in his life, and how fate deals them all a dirty hand. [Robert] Young is wonderfully cast against type as a loathsome husband who get his noirish come-uppance when he tries to capitalize on an unfortunate accident."

Director Irving Pichel's third of four contributions, and screenwriter Jonathan Latimer's fourth of seven.

Reference   Selby, Silver and Ward

They Won't Believe Me

GORDON McDONELL

ALL MY SONS

ARTHUR MILLER

Publisher   New York: Reynal and Hitchcock, 1947

Arthur Miller debuted on Broadway in 1944 with *The Man Who Had All the Luck,* but it closed after only four performances. Miller decided to give himself one more chance. If he did not have success with his next play, he would quit the business and find "another line of work." He returned three years later with *All My Sons,* openly modeling the drama on the "problem play" style established by Ibsen, and the more commercial approach to dramatic scripting that had proven successful for Tennessee Williams. Miller solicited the assistance of Elia Kazan, who had just directed the debut of Williams' *The Glass Menagerie* on Broadway, and ultimately dedicated the play to him. Kazan's influence got the play funded, and Ed Begley and Arthur Kennedy starred in the two principal roles of father and son. Though now completely overshadowed by Miller's *Death of a Salesman,* the play was a bona fide hit in its day, running for nearly all of 1947 and earning Miller and Kazan a Tony Award each.

Both publication and motion picture rights were optioned during the first run of *All My Sons,* and in 1947 it became the first Miller play to be published in book form. The film was released the following year, with Edward G. Robinson and Burt Lancaster assuming the two lead roles. The success of *All My Sons* gave Miller the financial stability, status, and confidence necessary to pen *Death of a Salesman,* now considered by many to be the greatest stage drama of the twentieth century, as well as a 1950s film noir. (Gottfried, Griffin)

The playwright's only contribution.

Gray cloth with titles in blue at the spine. No statement of printing on the copyright page. Front flap shows a price of $2.00 at the top right corner, and the flap begins with two blurbs at the top (*The Boston Herald* and The *Christian Science Monitor*), followed by a plot summary. Rear flap is devoted to reviews of Miller's first two books, listing seven blurbs, ending with the publisher's name and address.

At least three later printings of the book have been noted, all in a light celery cloth rather than gray, and with the later printing clearly stated on the copyright page. Beginning with the second printing, the two review blurbs on the front flap are replaced by a single, longer blurb from Brooks Atkinson of *The New York Times.*

ALL MY SONS

IRVING REIS

Screenwriter   Chester Erskine (also Producer)
Cinematographer   Russell Metty
Composer   Leith Stevens, Dave Torbett (uncredited)
Cast   Edward G. Robinson, Burt Lancaster, Mady Christians, Louisa Horton, Howard Duff,
                             Frank Conroy, Lloyd Gough, Arlene Francis, Harry Morgan (as Henry Morgan)
Studio   Universal, 1948
Runtime   95 minutes

In his *New York Times* review of *All My Sons* in 1948, Bosley Crowther notes that Chester Erskine, probably on the direction of a higher authority, took pains to narrow the play's indictment of the entire capitalist system down to the greed and narrowmindedness of one man. This was likely part of a larger design to make the film a powerhouse vehicle for its star, Edward G. Robinson, and draws the film out of the realm of social criticism and into the noir frame.

Irving Reis' second of two contributions, and the first of two for screenwriter Chester Erskine.

Reference   Selby

ALL MY SONS

A PLAY

By Arthur Miller

KNOCK ON ANY DOOR

WILLARD MOTLEY

Publisher	New York: Appleton-Century, 1947

Born into a middle-class, Roman Catholic, African-American family in 1909, Willard Motley enjoyed some early advantages. His family lived comfortably in Englewood, a white neighborhood on the south side of Chicago. At the age of thirteen, after winning a short story contest sponsored by the African-American newspaper *The Chicago Defender*, Motley began writing a weekly column, "Bud Says," in the children's section of the paper. Motley wrote under the byline Bud Billiken, a name invented by the paper's founder that was later used to inaugurate the annual "Bud Billiken Parade" in 1929 (which is held to this day). His dreams of attending the University of Wisconsin and becoming a writer were sidelined by the Great Depression, and after the death of his parents, he took a slum apartment in the Maxwell Street neighborhood. It was ethnically diverse and downtrodden, full of the kinds of characters that would inhabit his future novels.

During this time, Motley began writing his first novel, *Knock On Any Door*. The story dealt with Nick Romano, an Italian altar boy turned murderer, whose life is shaped by poverty and who is ultimately executed for his crimes. With its release in 1947, Motley's novel enjoyed immediate popular success, selling 47,000 copies during its first three weeks in print. It soon became popularized as a King Features comic-strip, and was adapted to the screen in 1949.

Critics hailed Motley's first book as a superior "naturalist" novel and compared it favorably to the work of Richard Wright and Theodore Dreiser. Due to the HUAC witch hunts of the early 1950s, Motely emigrated to Mexico, where he would spend the rest of his life.

The author's only contribution.

Gray cloth with titles in dark blue at the front board and spine, no topstain. No statement of edition or later printings on the copyright page. Front flap shows a price of $3.00 at the top right corner, followed by a plot summary that continues to the rear flap, ending with the publisher's name and city. Rear panel contains a biography of the author, ending again with the publisher's name and city.

KNOCK ON ANY DOOR

NICHOLAS RAY

Screenwriter	Daniel Taradash, John Monks, Jr.
Cinematographer	Burnett Guffey
Composer	George Antheil
Cast	Humphrey Bogart, John Derek, George Macready, Allene Roberts, Susan Perry, Mickey Knox
Studio	Columbia, 1949
Runtime	100 minutes

Upon its publication in 1947, *Knock on any Door* was purchased by producer Mark Hellinger in association with David O. Selznick and Humphrey Bogart. When Hellinger died unexpectedly later that year, Bogart bought out the remaining shares and formed his own production company, Santana, offering the film to Nicholas Ray to direct. The experience would prove to be a major period of growth for the young Ray, who learned a lot by working with a wise and patient Bogart (who was not only the film's more experienced lead, but its producer and financer).

The last of Ray's three contributions, and the last of three for screenwriter John Monks, Jr.

Reference	Selby, Silver and Ward

KNOCK ON ANY DOOR

A Novel by
WILLARD MOTLEY

APPLETON CENTURY

REPEAT PERFORMANCE

WILLIAM O'FARRELL

Publisher   Boston: Houghton, Mifflin, 1942

Born in 1904, William O'Farrell was an American author of crime fiction, and *Repeat Performance* was the first of fifteen novels he wrote between 1942 and 1963. He also wrote numerous short stories for magazines, including *Ellery Queen's Mystery Magazine, Manhunt, Alfred Hitchcock's Mystery Magazine,* and *The Saint* between 1955 and 1966, and won an Edgar Award in 1959 for his short story, "Over There, Darkness." O'Farrell was also a television screenwriter for vintage crime programs of the 1950s and 1960s, including *Alfred Hitchcock Presents, Perry Mason, Thriller,* and *Suspense!*

The author's only contribution.

Yellow cloth with purple titles at the front board and spine, no topstain. Title page shows a date of 1942 (removed for later printings), with no statement of edition or later printings on the copyright page. Front flap shows a price of $2.50 at the top right corner, followed by a plot summary. Rear flap is a separate advertisement for the book (noting what "type" of book it is, with comparisons to others of the same type), with the title "PSYCHOTHRILLERS." Rear panel is devoted to a biography of the author, beginning with his photo at the top left, followed by his name and the start of the text at the right, and four paragraphs of text, ending with a "Buy War Bonds" logo at the bottom right.

REPEAT PERFORMANCE

ALFRED WERKER

Screenwriter	Walter Bullock
Cinematographer	L.W. O'Connell
Composer	George Antheil
Cast	Louis Hayward, Joan Leslie, Virginia Field, Tom Conway, Richard Basehart, Natalie Schafer, Benay Venuta, Ilka Grüning
Studio	Eagle-Lion, 1947
Runtime	91 minutes

Director Alfred Werker was born in Deadwood, South Dakota on December 2, 1896, and was a prolific Hollywood director, working almost exclusively on "B" pictures between 1917 and 1957. He directed over fifty films in all, and was known for having an efficient, uncomplicated style. Apart from his efforts in film noir, he is known for *The Adventures of Sherlock Holmes* (1934), which paired Basil Rathbone with future noir actress and director Ida Lupino.

Michael Keaney: "New Year's Eve, 1947. Broadway actress [Joan] Leslie shoots and kills her adulterous, alcoholic husband, has-been playwright [Louis] Hayward. After confiding in her poet friend Basehart (in his film debut), Leslie wishes that she had the year to live over so she could do things differently. Surprisingly, her wish is granted. The actress thinks she's tricked destiny, but the same events seem to be reoccuring."

Werker's second of three contributions.

Reference   Selby

A novel of one man's struggle
with an overpowering presentiment

O'Farrell

REPEAT PERFORMANCE

Repeat Performance

by William O'Farrell

Houghton Mifflin Company

LADIES IN RETIREMENT

EDWARD PERCY AND REGINALD DENHAM

Publisher   New York: Random House, 1940

Reginald Denham was an American playwright, theater director, film director, and sometimes screenwriter who contributed to twenty-six films between 1920 and 1948. Denham had a very successful career on the New York stage as well, between 1929 and 1966, with twenty-eight Broadway plays to his credit, mostly of the thriller variety. *Ladies in Retirement*, which debuted on March 26, 1940, at Henry Miller's Theater in New York, was one of his earliest productions. He went on to direct and/or stage the Broadway debuts of many plays that became noted crime films, including *Guest in the House, The Two Mrs. Carrolls, Dial "M" for Murder,* and *The Bad Seed*.

Edward Percy was a playwright with four Broadway plays to his credit between 1926 and 1949, of which *Ladies in Retirement* was the second.

The only contribution by Percy or Denham.

Red cloth with titles in gilt at the spine. The book title and author name run vertically, and the publisher's name is set horizontally at the bottom. Black topstain. "First Printing" stated at the top of the copyright page. Front flap shows a price of $2.00 at the top right corner, followed by a publisher's blurb for the play, an introductory paragraph, then five review blurbs, beginning with Burns Mantle of *New York Daily News* and ending with Sidney Whipple of *New York World Telegram*, then the publisher's name. Rear flap is an advertisement for Random House plays, followed by eleven listings, beginning with *The Man Who Came to Dinner* by Kaufman and Hart and ending with *The Complete Plays of J.M. Synge*. The bottom portion of the flap is an advertisement for a new edition of the plays of Eugene O'Neill in three volumes, followed by a per-copy price and a boxed set price, ending with the publisher's name and city. Rear panel is an advertisement for Random House plays in book form, followed by four listings, beginning with *The New 1940 Edition of The Pulitzer Prize Plays* and ending with *The Complete Greek Drama*, followed by a list of Random House playwrights and the publisher's name and address.

LADIES IN RETIREMENT

CHARLES VIDOR

Screenwriter   Garrett Fort, Reginald Denham
Cinematographer   George Barnes
Composer   Ernst Toch
Cast   Ida Lupino, Louis Hayward, Evelyn Keyes, Elsa Lanchester, Edith Barrett, Isobel Elsom, Emma Dunn, Clyde Cook, Queenie Leonard
Studio   Columbia, 1941
Runtime   92 minutes

Director Charles Vidor was born Vidor Károly on July 27, 1900, in Budapest, Hungary. Arriving in Hollywood at the dawn of the sound era, he directed over thirty-five films between 1929 and 1960. His penultimate effort was the 1957 film version of Hemingway's *A Farewell to Arms*.

The first of two contributions by Vidor (who would go on to direct the film noir classic, *Gilda,* in 1946), and the first of four for screenwriter Garrett Fort.

Reference   Selby, Lyons

HE FELL DOWN DEAD

VIRGINIA PERDUE

Publisher   Garden City: Doubleday, 1943

Born in 1899, Virginia Perdue wrote five crime novels between 1941 and 1944, of which *He Fell Down Dead* was the fourth. The novel is a story of a young wife who is fearful of the man she has just married. What follows is a complex tangle of daughters, sisters, children, and mistresses, which despite some murders is more a suspense yarn than a detective story. (Barzun)

The author's only contribution.

Blue-gray cloth with the "Crime Club selection" ribbon device running along the top of the front board and spine in red, with titles and Crime Club logo also in red at the spine. Title page shows a date of MCMXLIII, with "FIRST EDITION" stated at the bottom of the copyright page (removed for later printings). Front flap shows a price of "H.F.D.D. / Price, $2.00," followed by a Wartime Conditions and Standards notice, then a plot summary. Front flap ends with a reproduction notice and a printer's code of 4307-43 at the bottom right corner. Rear flap is devoted to a "Buy War Bonds" advertisement, with a cut-out donation coupon at the bottom. Rear panel is an advertisement for other Crime Club titles, with four listings, beginning with *Trademark of a Traitor* by Kathleen Moore Knight and ending with *A Variety of Weapons* by Rufus King, then a printer's code of 496-43 at the bottom right corner.

SHADOW OF A WOMAN

JOSEPH SANTLEY

Screenwriter	Whitman Chambers, C. Graham Baker
Cinematographer	Bert Glennon
Composer	Adolph Deutsch
Cast	Helmut Dantine, Andrea King, William Prince, John Alvin, Becky Brown, Dick Erdman, Peggy Knudsen, Don McGuire, Lisa Golm, Larry Geiger, Monte Blue, Jack Smart
Studio	Warner Brothers, 1946
Runtime	78 minutes

Shadow of a Woman is an interesting dip into Hitchcock territory, but with "B" movie trimmings. While on vacation, a lonely and depressed young woman meets an "alternative medicine practitioner" and marries him after a whirlwind romance. Like Joan Bennett in *The Secret Beyond the Door*, the new bride receives a few surprises when she moves into her husband's stately old house, which is occupied by his widowed sister and her crippled son, along with her husband's five-year-old son from a previous marriage. The plot becomes a bit hard to swallow, but King is enjoyable as the bride with second thoughts. (Keaney)

Director Joseph Santley's second of two contributions, the first of three for screenwriter Whitman Chambers, and the second of two for C. Graham Baker.

Reference   Selby, Lyons

He fell down dead

VIRGINIA PERDUE

A HASTY MARRIAGE BRINGS LEISURE TO EXPECT AND DREAD MURDER

THE CRIME CLUB

ARCH OF TRIUMPH

ERICH MARIA REMARQUE

Publisher   New York: Appleton-Century, 1945

Erich Paul Remark was born on June 22, 1898, in Osnabrück, Germany, into a working-class Roman Catholic family. Conscripted into the German army at age eighteen, he was transferred to the Western Front. He was wounded in battle by shrapnel in the left leg, right arm, and neck, and repatriated to an army hospital in Germany, where he spent the rest of the war. After the end of World War I he changed his last name to Remarque, which had been the family name until his grandfather changed it due to nineteenth-century German xenophobia. He worked at a number of different jobs, including librarian, businessman, teacher, journalist, and editor.

In 1929, Remarque published his most famous work, *All Quiet on the Western Front* (*Im Westen Nichts Neues*) under the name Erich Maria Remarque (changing his middle name in honor of his mother). The novel described the cruelty of the war from the perspective of a twenty-year-old soldier, based mostly on his own experience. A number of similar works followed, and in simple, emotive language they realistically described wartime and the postwar years.

The author's only contribution.

Blue cloth with decorative titles in gilt at the front board and spine, no topstain. No statement of edition or later printings on the copyright page, and "(1)" should appear at the end of the text. Front flap shows a price of $3.00 at the top right corner, followed by a plot summary that continues to the rear flap, ending with a jacket design credit for George Salter, then the publisher's name and city. Rear panel shows a photo of the author, followed by his name and a one-paragraph blurb that ends with the statement, "He expects his final naturalization papers in 1946,"

ARCH OF TRIUMPH

LEWIS MILESTONE

Screenwriter   Lewis Milestone, Harry Brown, Irwin Shaw (uncredited)
Cinematographer   Russell Metty
Composer   Louis Gruenberg
Cast   Ingrid Bergman, Charles Boyer, Charles Laughton, Louis Calhern, Ruth Warrick, Roman Bohnen
Studio   United Artists, 1948
Runtime   120 minutes

Arch of Triumph is set in Paris in the winter of 1938, a time when the city was crowded with Nazi refugees. At the story's center is Dr. Ravic, who practices medicine illegally and stalks an old Nazi enemy named Haake with murder in mind.

Irwin Shaw spent five months writing a screenplay for *Arch of Triumph,* but quit when director Lewis Milestone wanted him to add a love story to the plot. Milestone then rewrote the script to include a romance, which met with the approval of both the studio and Ingrid Bergman. Joseph Breen then forced the studio to tone down the excessive violence in the script. The offending footage included Ravic stuffing Haake into a trunk, stripping him naked, burying him and burning his clothes—all eventually cut from the film. Breen also objected to the murder going unpunished, but later rationalized it as an act of war, since it was committed on the eve of the outbreak of World War II.

Cut after its initial release to 120 minutes, *Arch of Triumph* was restored to its original length of 133 minutes in 1990.

Director Lewis Milestone's last of three contributions, and Irwin Shaw's second of three.

Reference   Selby

Arch of Triumph

ERICH MARIA REMARQUE

APPLETON-CENTURY

THE LUCKY STIFF

CRAIG RICE

Publisher   New York: Simon and Schuster, 1945

Craig Rice (pseudonym of Georgiana Ann Randolph) was an American crime novelist and screenwriter. Born in 1908 in Chicago, the author spent most of her life in that city, where she did radio and public relations work. Although she wrote under several names, her most famous series, about sleuthing Chicago lawyer John J. Malone, was written under the Rice pseudonym. Owing something to Jonathan Latimer's Bill Crane character, Malone was billed as "Chicago's noisiest and most noted criminal lawyer," a hard-drinking hard-boiled ne'er-do-well with a reputatation for courtroom pyrotechnics, far more likely to be found at Joe the Angel's City Hall Bar than in the courtroom. Along with his boozing buddies, the affable Jake and Helene Justus, he drank his way through a whole slew of novels and short stories, not to mention later film, radio, and television appearances.

The Lucky Stiff was the seventh Malone novel. Rice also penned a couple of original screenplays for the "Falcon" series in the early 1940s, *The Falcon's Brother* (1942) and *The Falcon in Danger* (1943), as well as the original screen story for a key 1950s film noir, *The Underworld Story* (1950).

The author's only contribution.

Black cloth with gilt titles at the spine, yellow topstain. Title page shows a date of 1945, with no statement of edition or later printings on the copyright page. Front flap shows a price of $2.00 at the bottom right corner, and contains a plot summary that continues to the end of the rear flap. Rear panel is an advertisement for recent Inner Sactum publications, followed by three listings, *Net of Cobwebs* by Elisabeth Sanxay Holding, *A Time to Die* by Hilda Lawrence, and *The Outsiders* by A.E. Martin, ending with the statement, "THERE'S A NEW INNER SANCTUM MYSTERY EVERY MONTH."

THE LUCKY STIFF

LEWIS R. FOSTER

Screenwriter   Lewis R. Foster
Cinematographer   Ernest Laszlo
Composer   Heinz Roemheld
Cast   Dorothy Lamour, Brian Donlevy, Claire Trevor, Irene Hervey, Marjorie Rambeau, Robert Armstrong, Warner Anderson, Virginia Patton, Richard Gaines, Joe Sawyer, Larry J. Blake
Studio   United Artists, 1949
Runtime   99 minutes

The Lucky Stiff was a rare attempt at what might be called "noir screwball comedy," the second, more hard-boiled shot at Craig Rice's lawyer-turned-private-eye on the silver screen. Malone was first introduced to viewers in *Having Wonderful Crime* (1945) where the role was played more for laughs by Pat O'Brien, with Carole Landis as a walking advertisement for 1940s fashion as Helene Justus. In the second outing, the talented team of Brian Donlevy and Dorothy Lamour made for quite an upgrade, adding welcome nuance to Rice's creation.

The first of two contributions by director Lewis R. Foster.

Reference   Selby

AN INNER SANCTUM MYSTERY

the LUCKY stiff

JAKE, HELENE and
MALONE find a beau-
tiful ghost and help
her haunt a murderer

CRAIG RICE

MOON TIDE

WILLARD ROBERTSON

Publisher   New York: Carrick and Evans, 1940

Born in 1886, Willard Robertson has the unusual career distinction of being a one-time novelist, a two-time playwright, and a full-time Hollywood character actor. His career spanned 1921 to 1948, with nearly 150 films to his credit, typically in roles playing official figures. He was the sheriff in both *The Ox-Bow Incident* (1943) and *Deep Valley* (1947), a prison warden in *My Favorite Brunette* (1947), a colonel in *Men with Wings* (1938), *Wake Island* (1942), and *Air Force* (1943), and played judges, inspectors, ministers, and policemen in too many films to mention. *Moon Tide* was his first of three novels, all written between 1940 and 1944.

Robertson's only contribution.

Light blue cloth with titles and slightly jagged rule at the spine, yellow topstain. Copright page has a letter "A" just below the copyright notice (in the manner of Scribner, and like Scribner, removed for later printings). Front flap shows a price of $2.50, followed by a plot summary that continues to the rear flap, ending with the publisher's name and address. Rear flap is devoted to an author biography, beginning with an author photo at the left, author and title at the right, with three paragraphs of text below, ending with the publisher's name and address.

MOONTIDE

ARCHIE MAYO AND FRITZ LANG (UNCREDITED)

Screenwriter   John O'Hara, Nunnally Johnson (uncredited)
Cinematographer   Charles Clarke, Lucien Ballard (uncredited)
Composer   David Buttolph, Cyril J. Mockridge
Cast   Jean Gabin, Ida Lupino, Thomas Mitchell, Claude Rains, Jerome Cowan, Helene Reynolds, Ralph Byrd, Sen Yung, William Halligan, Chester Gan, Robin Raymond, Arthur Aylesworth
Studio   Twentieth Century-Fox, 1942
Runtime   94 minutes

Jean Gabin, the archetypal French leading man, had finally reached the US, among the many actors and filmmakers fleeing Western Europe in 1942. Gabin had signed with Twentieth Century-Fox, and the studio swiftly arranged for him to make his Hollywood debut in *Moontide*, from Robertson's novel about a seaman who befriends suicidal waif Ida Lupino. The script would be penned by John O'Hara, and Mark Hellinger would produce. Marlene Dietrich encouraged Gabin to request Fritz Lang, her former lover, as his director. Upon receipt of the script, both Lang and Gabin began to complain of its verbosity, and in an unrelated incident, Lang took Gabin aside and had a "man-to-man talk" with him, boasting of his own previous affair with Dietrich. Gabin stormed away, incensed, and the production began to deteriorate.

Lang was soon replaced by the stout and savvy Archie Mayo, and the film took shape. In addition to his technical prowess, Mayo knew something about fishing boats, something about the French, and something about how to make a moody picture. Most of the film was shot in a big tank on a back lot at Fox. Each afternoon, Gabin wanted to buy wine for the working crew, and each day Hellinger had to explain that this was not permitted at an American studio. The film was finished on time, and in the end made money for the studio.. (McGilligan, *Fritz Lang*; Bishop)

Lang's first of six contributions, author-screenwriter John O'Hara's only contribution, and screenwriter Nunnally Johnson's first of three.

Reference   Selby, Lyons

WILLARD ROBERTSON

MOON
TIDE

MOON
TIDE

CARRICK
& EVANS

THIS WAY OUT

JAMES RONALD

Publisher   London: Rich and Cowan, 1940

This Way Out was British crime author James Ronald's nineteenth novel in a prolific eight years after his debut in 1932 with *Counsel for the Defense*. He wrote primarily non-series books, many based on actual events. *This Way Out* was a fictional adaptation of the Crippen murder case that captivated London for six months in the summer and fall of 1910. Hawley Harvey Crippen was a 50-year-old American doctor living in London's North End who poisoned his wife Cora, an American music-hall singer known as Belle Elmore, and buried her dismembered body under his own house. Crippen and his new female companion fled London, but were arrested for the murder onboard a steamship as it docked in Quebec. Though he claimed his innocence to the end, he was hanged on November 24, 1910.

The author's only contribution.

Light blue cloth with titles at the spine in a paler shade of blue, no topstain. No statement of edition or later impressions on the copyright page. Front flap shows a price of "7/6 net" at the bottom right corner, and contains a plot summary. Rear flap is devoted to a brief invitation from the publisher to be on a mailing list, ending with the publisher's address. Rear panel is an advertisement for six other James Ronald titles by the publisher (beginning with *Murder for Cash* and ending with *They Can't Hang Me*), ending with the publisher's name and address. The US edition precedes the UK edition by one year, published by Lippincott in 1939.

THE SUSPECT

ROBERT SIODMAK

Screenwriter	Bertram Millhauser, Arthur T. Horman
Cinematographer	Paul Ivano
Composer	Frank Skinner
Cast	Charles Laughton, Ella Raines, Henry Daniell, Rosalind Ivan, Dean Harens, Stanley Ridges, Molly Lamont, Raymond Severn, Eve Amber, Maude Eburne, Clifford Brooke, John Berkes, Katherine Yorke, Rebel Randall, Barbara Gray, Sheila Roberts, Edgar Norton
Studio	Universal, 1944
Runtime	85 minutes

Released in the same prolific year as *Christmas Holiday* and *Phantom Lady*, *The Suspect* was a straightforward and very enjoyable effort for director Robert Siodmak. Shot without flashback structure, the adaptation was more of a traditional drama than a crime film, a scene-by-scene adaptation of Ronald's novel, much in the style that the director would use two years later in *The Spiral Staircase*. The few changes that were made involved accommodating the formidable presence of actor Charles Laughton, who had mastered the sort of character the film required—a sedate, henpecked husband—on both the stage and screen with C.S. Forester's *Payment Deferred*.

The third of Siodmak's ten contributions.

Reference   Selby, Lyons

HIS
WAY
OUT
JAMES
ONALD
CH & COWAN
This Way Out
OISON
JAMES RONALD
AUTHOR OF MURDER IN THE FAMILY

DRAGONWYCK

ANYA SETON

Publisher	Boston: Houghton, Mifflin, 1944

Anya Seton was an American novelist, born on January 23, 1906, in New York City. She was the daughter of the English-born naturalist and pioneer of the Boy Scouts of America, Ernest Thompson Seton. An only child, Ann (later Anya), was unusual for both her haunting beauty and her intelligence. Yet she never attended college, married at nineteen, and remained an accomplished if restless housewife until her late thirties. Her first novel became a bestseller, and all ten of her historical novels followed suit, beginning with *My Theodosia* in 1941 and ending with *Green Darkness* in 1973. One of the most popular of these was *Dragonwyck*, a nineteenth-century drama that takes place in a mansion in New York's Hudson Valley. (MacKethon)

The author's only contribution.

Two variant bindings and dust jackets, each conjoined, with no priority. The following applies to Binding "A": Rose-orange cloth with titles and design at the front board and spine in burgundy. Binding from board to board measures three centimeters. Title page shows a date of 1944 (removed for later printings). "Riverside Press" is noted on both the title page and copyright page as the printer, with no statement of edition or later printings on the copyright page. Front flap shows a price of $2.50, followed by a plot summary. Rear flap is an advertisement for *My Theodosia* by Anya Seton, ending with a notice regarding wartime paper. Rear panel is devoted to a biography of the author, beginning with her name at the left and photo at the right, followed by two paragraphs of text. For points on Binding "B", see *Appendix A: Secondary Book Sources*.

DRAGONWYCK

JOSEPH L. MANKIEWICZ

Screenwriter	Joseph L. Mankiewicz
Cinematographer	Arthur Miller
Composer	Alfred Newman
Cast	Gene Tierney, Walter Huston, Vincent Price, Glenn Langan, Anne Revere, Spring Byington
Studio	Twentieth Century-Fox, 1946
Runtime	103 minutes

After nearly fifteen years as a successful screenwriter, Joseph Mankiewicz made his directorial debut with *Dragonwyck*, and wrote the screenplay adaptation as well. He decided to lean heavily on set design, adding spectacle and detail in the Ernst Lubitsch manner. This was perhaps a direct consequence of the film's production circumstances, as Lubitsch was the original producer, and picked Mankiewicz to be the director for the project, no doubt recognizing the young screenwriter's promise. But the two often disagreed during the initial phases of shooting, and Mankiewicz found Lubitsch, then quite ill with the heart condition that would soon kill him, difficult to work with. Lubitsch withdrew early on from the project, and Mankiewicz was ultimately given credit as both producer and director. (Lower & Palmer)

The first of three contributions by Mankiewicz.

Reference	Selby

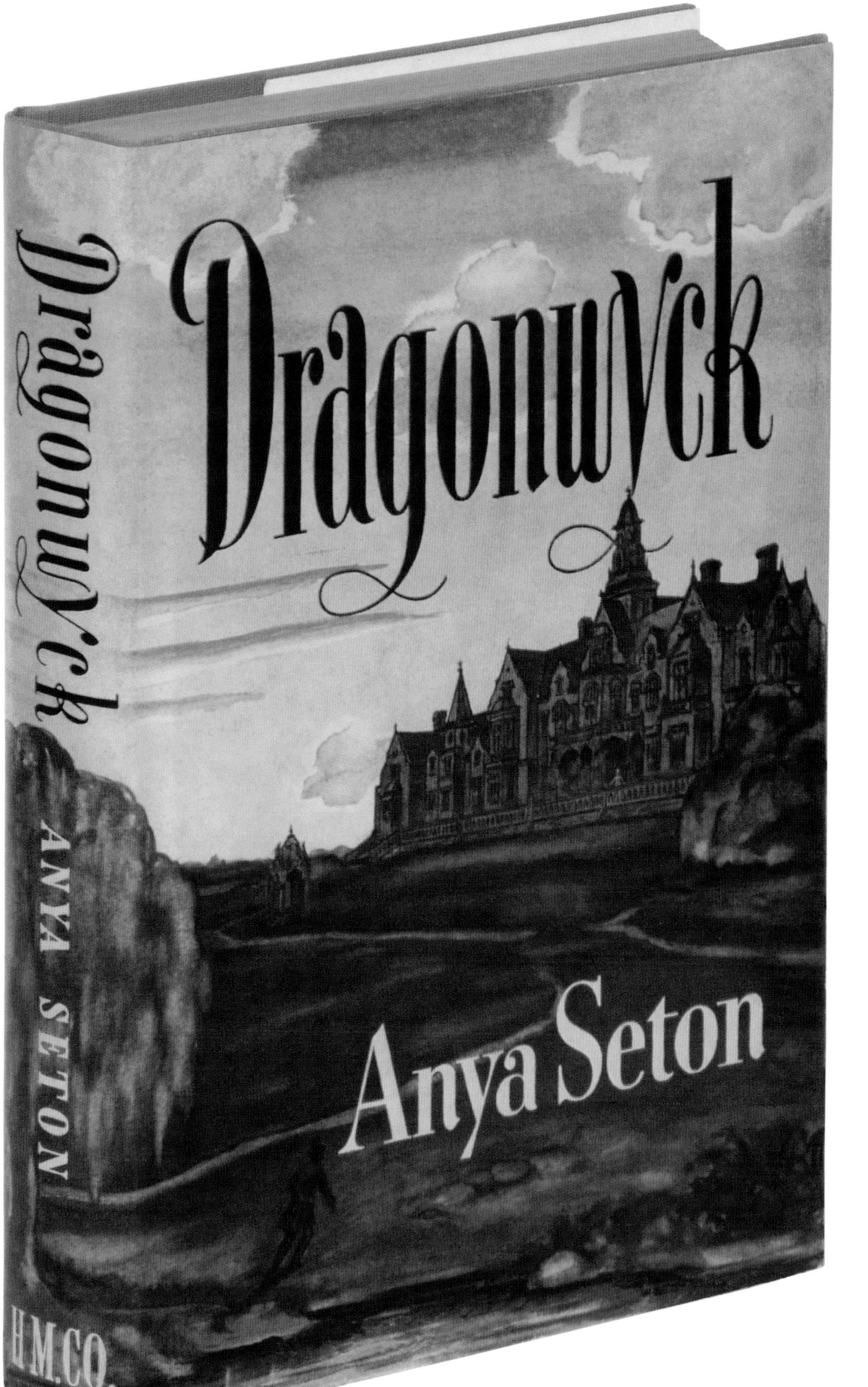
Dragonwyck
Anya Seton
Dragonwyck
ANYA SETON
H.M.CO.

THE GENTLE PEOPLE

IRWIN SHAW

Publisher   New York: Random House, 1939

The Gentle People was one of a number of plays published in hardcover by Random House in the 1930s and 1940s wherein the entire cast of the premiere production is printed at the beginning of the book, along with a frontispiece still from that production. This particular premiere featured two minor actors who would eventually become powerful Hollywood directors, Martin Ritt and Elia Kazan. Kazan debuted in 1945 with *A Tree Grows in Brooklyn,* Ritt in 1957 with *Edge of the City.*

Irwin Shaw's first of three contributions, and his only contribution as a playwright.

Burnt orange cloth with a panel of brown at the center of the front board, upon which the title and the Random House name and logo are stamped in gilt. The spine titles and rule are stamped in gilt against a brown panel in the same style. Brown topstain. Frontispiece with a photo of the cast from the original production of the play opposite the title page, with "FIRST EDITION" stated on the copyright page. Front flap shows a price of $2.00 at the top right corner, and contains nine reviews of the play. Rear flap is devoted to an advertisement for the Modern Library series. Rear panel is an advertisement for eight other Random House plays.

OUT OF THE FOG

ANATOLE LITVAK

Screenwriter   Robert Rossen, Jerry Wald, Richard Macaulay
Cinematographer   James Wong Howe
Composer   Heinz Roemheld, Max Steiner (both uncredited)
Cast   Ida Lupino, John Garfield, Thomas Mitchell, Eddie Albert, John Qualen, George Tobias,
                     Jerome Cowan
Studio   Warner Brothers, 1941
Alternate Titles   The Gentle People (working title)
Runtime   86 minutes

This strange and compelling early film noir centers on two simple fishermen who are being victimized by a racketeer on Brooklyn's waterfront. The screenwriters cleverly sidestepped a Production Code requirement that murder must always result in punishment by changing a key scene: in the play, the two fishermen rid themselves of their enemy by murdering him during a boat ride across the bay. In the film the hood still takes the ride and still dies, but by falling into the water during a scuffle and drowning because he cannot swim.

The first of five contributions by director Anatole Litvak, the first of seven by screenwriter Robert Rossen (who would later direct), the first of three by Richard Macaulay, and the second of two by Jerry Wald (who would later become a very successful Hollywood producer).

Reference   Selby, Lyons

THE GENTLE
PEOPLE
A PLAY BY IRWIN SHAW

PUBLISHED BY RANDOM HOUSE

MOSS ROSE

JOSEPH SHEARING

Publisher   London: William Heinemann, 1934

Born on Hayling Island, Hampshire in 1912, Joseph Shearing was a pseudonym for Gabrielle Margaret Vere Campbell, an extremely prolific British author who wrote principally as Marjorie Bowen, but also as George Preedy, Robert Paye, and John Winch.

Moss Rose is based on an actual 1872 murder, but at its core is about the seduction of the innocent, which like the use of historical crimes, is a recurrent motif in Shearing's novels, along with madness and religious fanaticism. The attraction to a psychopath, against her better judgment, is what motivates the novel's otherwise cool and self-posessed heroine Belle. (Reilly)

The author's first of two contributions.

Fuchsia cloth with gilt titles and two small rose devices at the spine, with the first device separating the author and title, and the second device just above the publisher's name. No topstain. "FIRST PUBLISHED 1934" stated at the top center of the copyright page. Front flap shows a price of "3'6 / net" at the bottom center, and contains a plot summary. Rear flap is an advertisement for *Album Leaf* by Joseph Shearing. Rear panel is an advertisement for *Forget-Me-Not* by Joseph Shearing, with three blurbs, the first being Norman Collins in the *News Chronicle* and the last being Rebecca West in the *Daily Telegraph*.

MOSS ROSE

GREGORY RATOFF

Screenwriter	Jules Furthman, Tom Reed, Niven Busch
Cinematographer	Joe MacDonald
Composer	David Buttolph
Cast	Peggy Cummins, Victor Mature, Ethel Barrymore, Vincent Price, Margo Woode
Studio	Twentieth Century-Fox, 1947
Runtime	82 minutes

Born on April 20, 1897 in Samara, Russia, Gregory Ratoff was a Russian-born American film director, actor and producer who first came to the United States in 1922. His most famous role as an actor was that of Max Fabian, the producer who feuds with star Margo Channing (Bette Davis) in *All About Eve* (1950). Outside of acting, he is known for having directed the pro-Soviet propaganda film *Song of Russia* (1944), and for being one of the two producers to have purchased and developed the original rights to the James Bond franchise from Ian Fleming in 1955.

Director Ratoff's first of two contributions, the last of three for screenwriter Niven Busch, and Jules Furthman's third of four.

Reference   Selby, Lyons

MOSS ROSE

MOSS ROSE

JOSEPH SHEARING

JOSEPH SHEARING
AUTHOR OF
"FORGET-ME-NOT" "ALBUM LEAF"

HEINEMANN

FOR HER TO SEE

JOSEPH SHEARING

Publisher   London: William Hutchinson, 1947

In *For Her to See*, Marjorie Bowen used not only the outline of the unsolved 1876 Charles Bravo case, where a husband was supposedly poisoned by his wife, but its secondary characters as well, including Florence Bravo's dead first husband, her lover, her doctor (the famous Dr. Gully, called Sir John Curle in the novel), and her antagonistic mother-in-law. The fiction even reproduces portions of the two inquests. (Reilly)

The author's second of two contributions. Published in the US as *So Evil My Love*.

Black cloth with the publisher's name in decorative gilt at the bottom right corner of the front board, with gilt titles at the spine. No topstain. No statement of edition or later printings on the copyright page. Front flap shows a price of "9s. 6d. / net" at the bottom right corner, and contains a plot summary. Rear flap is an advertisement for new books by the publisher, with listings for fourteen titles, beginning with *Where the Road Ends* by Dorothy Buck and ending with *Path to the Stars* by Dorothy Upson. "Printed in Great Britain" appears at the bottom of the flap. Rear panel is a continuing advertisement for new books by the publisher, in the categories of General Fiction (sixteen titles), Historical Fiction (seven titles), and Thrillers (eight titles).

SO EVIL MY LOVE

LEWIS ALLEN

Screenwriter   Leonard Spigelgass, Ronald Millar
Cinematographer   Max Greene
Composer   William Alwyn, Victor Young
Cast   Ann Todd, Ray Milland, Geraldine Fitzgerald, Moira Lister, Raymond Huntley, Leo G. Carroll
Studio   Paramount, 1948
Runtime   112 minutes

In his autobiography, producer Hal Wallis delineates Hollywood's shift toward what would later become known as film noir: "[Beginning in the 1940s], I very consciously made a series of melodramatic films with strong characters and situations, films that proved to be extremely popular. Movie-going audiences had matured during the war and no longer required false and sentimental portraits of human nature. I dealt again and again with the psychology of murderers. I showed, and encouraged my writers to show, how frustration, poverty and a desperate need for money could drive people to psychotic extremes. Miss Marjorie Bowen [Joseph Shearing], specialized in stories based on actual Victorian crimes, and her novel *So Evil, My Love* had echoes of two or three such cases. Lewis Allen and I agreed that Welshman Ray Milland would be perfect for the lead role of the story's wastrel painter. He had recently made a big hit in *The Lost Weekend* as Charles Jackson's pathetic drunk, and audiences would easily accept him as a beaten human being. The picture presented a problem insofar as I wanted to shoot on location as much as possible. London had changed enormously since the Victorian era, and we had to very carefully select areas that still looked of that period, arranging our shots so that electric lights, store windows, and even the pavements were not clear. We were one of the first American [film studios] to shoot in London after the war, and crowds gathered to watch our actors stepping into carriages or hurrying in period costume through dimly-lit streets."

Director Lewis Allen's third of four contributions.

Reference   Selby

For her to See
Joseph Shearing
Author of Abode of Love (6th Thousand)
HUTCHINSON
HINSON

GUNMAN'S CHANCE
LUKE SHORT

Publisher   Garden City: Doubleday, Doran, 1941

Born in Kewanee, Illinois on November 19, 1908, Luke Short was a popular writer of Western fiction. His birth name was Frederick Dilley Glidden, and he attended the University of Illinois at Champaign-Urbana for two and a half years before transferring to the University of Missouri at Columbia to study journalism. Following graduation in 1930, he worked for a number of newspapers before becoming a trapper in Canada, then later moved to new Mexico to be an archaeologist's assistant.

Short was an avid reader of Western pulp magazines, and trying to escape poverty he started writing Western fiction. He sold his first short story and novel in 1935 under the pen name of Luke Short (which was also the name of a famous gunslinger in the Old West, though it's unclear if he was aware of that when he assumed the pen name).

After publishing over a dozen novels in the 1930s, Short began writing for films in the 1940s. In 1948 alone, four of his novels were adapted to the screen. Some of the more memorable film credits include *Ramrod* (1947) and *Blood on the Moon* (1948). He continued to write novels, despite increasing trouble with his eyes, until his death in 1975. He is buried in Aspen, Colorado, his home at the time of his death.

Blood on the Moon is the only Western in the 1940s American noir cycle based on a literary source. It was adapted for the screen by the author, and is his only contribution.

Tan cloth with brown titles and design at the spine, no topstain. Title page shows a date of 1941, and "FIRST EDITION" is stated at the bottom of the copyright page. Front flap shows a price of "G.C. / Price, $2.00" at the top right corner, followed by a plot summary and a printer's code of 3888-41. Rear flap is an advertisement for *Red Clark Takes a Hand* by Gordon Young, ending with a price of $2.00 and a printer's code of 3810-41. Rear panel is an advertisement for Double D Westerns, with an illustration at the top half and a blurb at the bottom, ending with the publisher's name and a printer's code of 663-41.

BLOOD ON THE MOON
ROBERT WISE

Screenwriter	Luke Short, Harold Shumate, Lillie Hayward
Cinematographer	Nicholas Musuraca
Composer	Roy Webb
Cast	Robert Mitchum, Barbara Bel Geddes, Robert Preston, Walter Brennan, Phyllis Thaxter
Studio	RKO, 1948
Runtime	88 minutes

Robert Wise notes: "*Blood on the Moon* was my first Western. I told Nick Musuraca, the cameraman, the kind of feeling I wanted. We never used the term 'film noir,' of course, but we knew what a dark mood meant. We knew it couldn't be lit like a normal Western, but that it had to have a heaviness to it that matched the nature of the story. It had nothing to do with [Robert] Mitchum or the casting. It was the tone of the script—how the script felt dictated how it should look."

The fourth of six contributions by director Robert Wise, and Lillie Hayward's first of three.

Reference   Selby

GUNMAN'S
CHANCE

Luke Short

GUNMAN'S CHANCE

Luke Short

A girl and a
gunman meet
in a western
range war.

THE AMBOY DUKES

IRVING SHULMAN

Publisher   Garden City: Doubleday, 1947

Irving Shulman's career was defined by his first book, *The Amboy Dukes,* a tough novel about hard-boiled juvenile delinquents in Brooklyn that was in its day one of the most scandalous titles in print, as well as being the first novel to address the topic. It was a huge bestseller, and two years after its release, Shulman adapted it for a film version, which in turn launched his screenwriting career. His Hollywood work reached its creative zenith with *Rebel Without a Cause,* where he adapted an original treatment by Nicholas Ray into a screen story that actually owed much to *The Amboy Dukes.* The estimable influence of Shulman's seminal novel led to a whole subgenre of films that had juvenile delinquency as a theme, many of which, particularly in the 1950s, were films noir.

The Amboy Dukes is considered the first book of a juvenile crime trilogy, followed by *Cry Tough* (made into the 1959 film noir of the same name) and *Children of the Dark* (Shulman's adaptation of his own screen story for *Rebel Without a Cause,* released the year after the film).

The author's only contribution.

Taupe cloth with an illustration similar to that of the one on the front jacket panel in maroon at the front board, and maroon titles at the spine. No topstain. Title page shows a date of 1947, with "FIRST EDITION" stated at the bottom of the copyright page. Front flap shows a price of "T.A.D. / Price, $2.50," followed by a plot summary, ending with a printer's code of 338-46 at the bottom left corner. Rear flap is an advertisement for *Angry Dust* by Dorothy Stockbridge, ending with proof-of-purchase tag at the bottom left corner, and a printer's code of 353-46 at the bottom right corner. Rear panel is an advertisement for four books by the publisher, beginning with *For One Sweet Grape* by Kate O'Brien and ending with *Idols of the Cave* by Frederic Prokosch, then a printer's code of 25-46 at the bottom right corner.

CITY ACROSS THE RIVER

MAXWELL SHANE

Screenwriter	Maxwell Shane, Dennis J. Cooper, Irving Shulman
Cinematographer	Maury Gertsman
Composer	Walter Scharf
Cast	Stephen McNally, Thelma Ritter, Luis Van Rooten, Jeff Corey, Sharon McManus, Sue England
Studio	Universal, 1949
Runtime	91 minutes

Born on August 26, 1905, Maxwell Shane was a film and television director, screenwriter and producer. After studying law at the University of Southern California and UCLA, he made his start in Hollywood as a publicist, then began working in 1937 as a screenwriter on low-budget films. The 1947 film noir *Fear in the Night* marked his directorial debut, and in 1949 he wrote, adapted, and directed Irving Shulman's *The Amboy Dukes,* retitled *City Across the River.* In 1960, Shane became a writer-producer for the Boris Karloff television anthology series *Thriller.*

The last of Shane's three contributions.

Reference   Selby, Lyons

IRVING SHULMAN

the Amboy Dukes

the Amboy Dukes

IRVING SHULMAN

A NOVEL OF YOUTH AND CRIME IN BROOKLYN

DOUBLEDAY

E.B

THE BODY SNATCHER
ROBERT LOUIS STEVENSON

New York: The Merriam Company, 1895

Robert Louis Stevenson based his grim short novel, *The Body Snatcher*, on an equally grim historical practice. In the early nineteenth century, graverobbers, known as "resurrection men," would sell dug-up corpses to medical practitioners who needed cadavers, particularly research doctors with students to train. Things got out of hand in 1827, when two Scottish canal workers named William Burke and William Hare took the established method to a horrific extreme, committing cold-blooded murder and selling the corpses of their seventeen victims to the Edinburgh Medical College for dissection. Their principal customer was doctor Robert Knox, and the case became known as the "West Port murders."

The author's only contribution. First published in the *Pall Mall* Christmas supplement in 1883.

Title page shows the Merriam Company logo and the publisher's name below the logo, with a date of 1895 on the copyright page. Three pages of advertisements at the rear, beginning with *Merriam's Violet Series* and ending with *Episodes* by G.S. Street. Rear board design matches that of the front board exactly.

THE BODY SNATCHER
ROBERT WISE (PRODUCED BY VAL LEWTON)

Screenwriter	Philip MacDonald, Val Lewton (as Carlos Keith)
Cinematographer	Robert De Grasse
Composer	Roy Webb
Cast	Boris Karloff, Bela Lugosi, Henry Daniell, Edith Atwater, Russell Wade, Rita Corday
Studio	RKO, 1945
Alternate Titles	Robert Louis Stevenson's The Body Snatcher (US complete title)
Runtime	77 minutes

The Body Snatcher was one of Robert Louis Stevenson's shorter and lesser-known works (though no less original and terrifying than the better-known *Dr. Jekyll and Mr. Hyde*), and provided producer Val Lewton with a rough template from which he could draw a sophisticated tale of jealousy, corruption, and madness. A number of interesting ironies were added to Lewton's adaptation, and the climax is grislier than anything Stevenson managed to achieve.

Lewton took his first screenplay credit for this film along with novelist-screenwriter Philip MacDonald, but in fact wrote all of the final screenplay himself. Lewton wrote, "In the case of *The Body Snatcher*, I had rewritten the script so completely that Phil MacDonald, who did not trust my work, wanted someone to share the blame if it were a flop. After considerable discussion, recognizing the justice of my viewpoint, the Screen Writers Guild allowed me to use the pseudonym of Carlos Keith."

The Edinburgh setting of the shoot allowed Lewton full range to indulge his love of authentic period detail. Although the film was shot on a budget only a few thousand dollars more than his usual pittance, the producer managed to make every dollar count by using fragments and details to suggest the larger panorama of the city as it would have appeared in 1831. This part-for-whole method grants the film a sense of historical intimacy which many Hollywood films, for all their massive reconstructions, never begin to approach. (Siegel)

The last of producer Val Lewton's five contributions, the first of six for Wise, and the third of five for novelist-screenwriter MacDonald.

Reference	Selby

THE
BODY SNATCHER

ROBERT L. STEVENSON

MERRIAM'S
VIOLET
SERIES

DESERT TOWN

RAMONA STEWART

Publisher   New York: William Morrow, 1946

Author Ramona Stewart wrote five crime fiction novels in her career, but her first book, *Desert Town* (1946), preceded the other four by nearly twenty-five years. Her second novel, *The Possession of Joel Delaney,* was published by Little, Brown in 1970, and was made into a thriller starring Shirley MacLaine in 1972.

The author's only contribution.

Tan cloth with purple titles at the spine, no topstain. Title page shows a date of 1946, with no statement of edition or later printings on the copyright page. Front flap shows a price of $2.50 at the top right corner, followed by a plot summary that continues to the end of the rear flap. A photo of the author appears at the top of the rear panel, followed by a short biography and publisher address. A reprint was published by World/Forum shortly after the first edition, and confusingly states "First Printing" on the copyright page.

DESERT FURY

LEWIS ALLEN

Screenwriter	A.I. Bezzerides, Robert Rossen
Cinematographer	Edward Cronjager
Composer	Miklós Rózsa
Cast	John Hodiak, Lizabeth Scott, Burt Lancaster, Wendell Corey, Mary Astor, Kristine Miller
Studio	Paramount, 1947
Alternate Titles	Desert Town (working title)
Runtime	96 minutes

One of the few noirs shot in color during the 1940s, *Desert Fury* got the full Technicolor treatment and an "A" picture budget, with the best talent of the hard-boiled variety that Hollywood had to offer (Burt Lancaster, Lizabeth Scott, William Bendix, A.I. Bezzerides, and Robert Rossen). But strangely, the result is a hot-blooded "B" movie melodrama, albeit the best kind—a companion of sorts to the 1950s Technicolor 3-D film noir, *Inferno,* also shot in the desert.

Desert Fury was filmed on location in the town of Piru, Ventura County, California, with the northwest corner of Center Street and Main used as the exterior of Fritzi's saloon and casino (center for much of the film's action). The Piru Mansion was used as the Haller family home, and the historic Piru bridge was used as the locale of the car crash that brings the film to its climax.

Director Lewis Allen's second of four contributions, screenwriter Robert Rossen's fifth of seven, and A.I. Bezzerides' second of three.

Reference   Selby

DESERT TOWN

DESERT TOWN

RAMONA STEWART

a novel by
RAMONA STEWART

MORROW

PRELUDE TO NIGHT

DAYTON STODDART

Publisher   New York: Coward-McCann, 1945

Prelude to Night was author Dayton Stoddart's only novel. He did, however, write a 1941 biography of Sime Silverman, the man who started out broke, made millions, and created *Variety*, "the spicy, terse, ribald, slang-spawning Bible of the show business."

The author's only contribution, and his only Hollywood credit.

Black cloth with titles in pink at the spine, no topstain. No statement of edition or later printings on the copyright page. Front flap shows a price of $3.00 at the top right corner, followed by a plot summary, ending with a wartime restrictions notice. Plot summary continues on the rear flap, ending with a single blurb by Shepard Butler of *Redbook*. Rear panel is devoted to a biography of the author, with a large photo of Stoddart at his typewriter, and one paragraph of text.

RUTHLESS

EDGAR G. ULMER

Screenwriter   S.K. Lauren, Gordon Kahn (both names a front for Alvah Bessie)
Cinematographer   Bert Glennon
Composer   Werner Janssen
Cast   Zachary Scott, Louis Hayward, Sydney Greenstreet, Diana Lynn, Lucille Bremer, Martha
                                   Vickers, Raymond Burr, Edith Barrett, Dennis Hoey, Joyce Arling, Charles Evans, Bob Anderson,
                                   Arthur Stone, Ann Carter, Edna Holland, Fred Worlock, John Good, Claire Carleton
Studio   Eagle-Lion, 1948
Alternate Titles   Prelude to Night (working title)
Runtime   104 minutes

Ruthless has been called Edgar G. Ulmer's *Citizen Kane*, because it attacks wealth and because its protagonist Horace, like Charles Foster Kane, strives in vain to earn the love of an abusive parent. Using the plot of Dayton Stoddart's novel for its structure, the moral emphasis of *Ruthless* actually resembles Dreiser's *An American Tragedy* more than *Kane*. While Welles deals with the frivolity of inherited money, Ulmer's story is more about an ethnic community of "rising capitalists." (Gallagher)

Like many Eagle-Lion films of its period, *Ruthless* was top-heavy with contract players loaned out from Warner Brothers, and was one of only a few big-budget films made by Ulmer. The director notes that three large sequences were cut from the film, all due to the HUAC hearings (what Ulmer called "the panic time") which in 1948 were just beginning to cause Hollywood writers, directors, and actors to be blacklisted. The director recalls, "[I wanted to make a film about] the complete evilness and ruthlessness of money. They cut [that] out, though there is still something still left in the picture about it. I wanted to do a morality play—a Jesuitic morality film—on three levels, earth, hell and heaven. But they fought me every step, because it was a very bad indictment against 100 percent Americanism." (Bogdanovich)

Edgar G. Ulmer's fourth of five contributions.

Reference   Selby, Lyons

232

PRELUDE
to NIGHT

DAYTON
STODDART

THUNDER GODS GOLD

BARRY STORM

Publisher   Tortilla Flat, AZ: Southwest Publishing Company, 1945

Barry Storm was a modern-day American prospector, writer, and promoter of sorts, and *Thunder Gods Gold* is a nonfiction history of the famed "Lost Dutchman" gold mine. This mine is a fabled spot just east of Phoenix, Arizona near Superstition Mountain (actually an area of rough terrain) that has taken on a Bermuda Triangle-esque mystique since its discovery, due to the violence, death, and mystery surrounding it. The Apache Indians were probably the first to lay eyes on the mountain, followed by the Spanish, led by Francisco Vasquez de Coronado, who rode up out of Mexico on an expedition in 1540. When the Spaniards tried to explore the mountain on their own, their men began to vanish mysteriously, and it was said that if one of them strayed more than a few feet from his companions, he was never seen alive again. The bodies of the men were later found mutilated and with their heads cut off. The terrified survivors refused to return to the mountain and so Coronado dubbed the peaks "Monte Superstition."

Storm's only contribution, and one of only two nonfiction books used as film sources.

Brown cloth with titles in purple at the front board and spine, no topstain. Title page begins with a quote from Napoleon, followed by the author, title, subtitle, then the publisher's name, city and date of 1945. Copyright page begins with a dedication "To The Prospector," followed by "TREASURE TRAIL EDITION / 1st printing: June, 1945," ending with the copyright date and printer's information. Front flap shows a price of $2.75 at the top right corner. Beyond these points, at least three variants with no known priority have been noted. The variants differ principally in the placement of the yellow boxes outlined in blue with either plot summary or review blurbs, and different blue-tinted terrain photos used on the rear flap. A second printing of the book has been noted as well, with "Second edition" stated on the copyright page, along with the date and the print run (5500 copies).

LUST FOR GOLD

S. SYLVAN SIMON

Screenwriter   Ted Sherdeman, Richard English
Cinematographer   Archie Stout
Composer   George Duning
Cast   Ida Lupino, Glenn Ford, Gig Young, William Prince, Edgar Buchanan, Will Geer, Paul Ford
Studio   Columbia, 1949
Alternate Titles   For Those Who Dare (US re-release title)
Runtime   90 minutes

The film version of *Thunder Gods Gold* integrates an impressive number of details from Barry Storm's book into its story line. Brought to life on the screen, for example, is German prospector Jacob Walz, who, despite his country of origin, came to be known in the West as "The Dutchman." Walz spent a reported twenty years in the Arizona territory known as "Superstition Mountain" on a relentless search for gold. According to lore, Walz would disappear into the fabled region for months at a time, only to reappear suddenly with pockets full of gold, buying drinks and spending freely, after which he would disappear again. Walz died on October 25, 1891, reportedly with a sack of rich gold ore beneath his deathbed. Immediately after word of his passing reached town, a group of prospectors who had heard him speak of the mine over the years rode out to the mountain in search of the mysterious mother lode. They never found it, although two of them, Sims Ely and Jim Bark, spent the next twenty-five years searching in vain for what came to be known as "The Lost Dutchman Mine."

The second of two contributions by director S. Sylvan Simon.

Reference   Selby

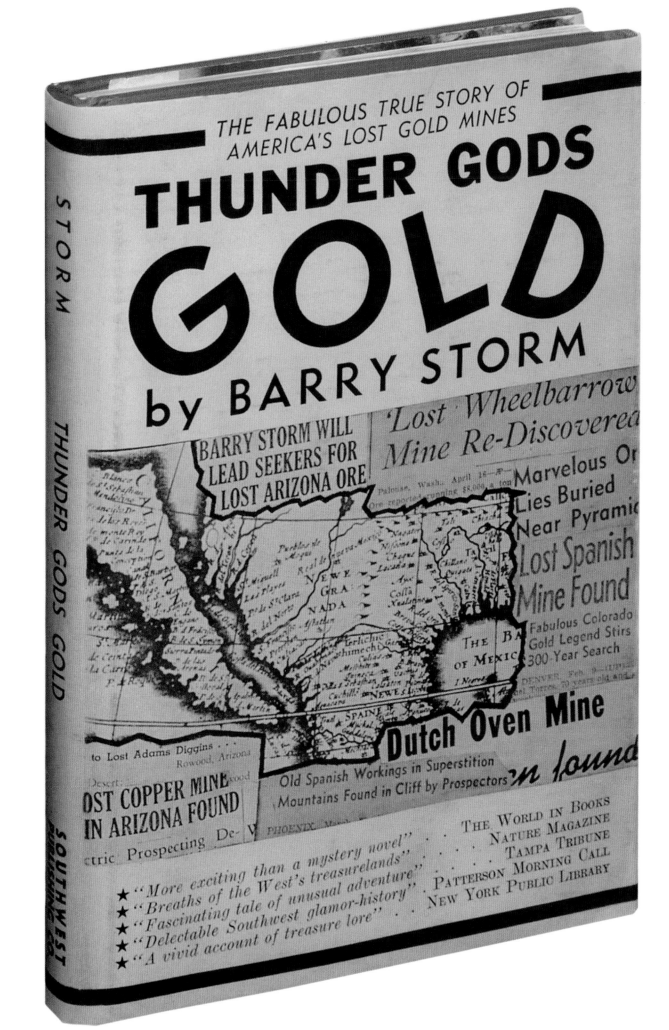

MOONRISE

THEODORE STRAUSS

Publisher   New York: Viking, 1946

Born in New York City on February 17,1912, Theodore Strauss was a drama critic for *The New York Times*. He was also a minor American author and screenwriter who wrote two novels, of which *Moonrise* is the second. His first, *Night at Hogwallow,* was published by Little, Brown in 1937. In Hollywood, Strauss contributed original stories to five films between 1946 and 1949, along with a late producing effort, *The Bridge at Remagen,* a war film released in 1969.

The author's only contribution.

Both book and jacket have two variants, each conjoined, with no known priority. The description that follows is for Variant "A": red cloth with yellow titles at the front board and spine, yellow topstain, and illustrated endpapers. Title page shows a date of 1946, and the statement, "Published by the Viking Press in October 1946" at the top of the copyright page. Jacket is very slightly short, does not have a man's face present in the front panel illustration, and is on close inspection an entirely different painting than the one found on Variant "B". Front flap shows a price of "Moonrise $2.50" at the top right corner, followed by a photo of the author, then a biography, ending with a jacket design credit for H. Lawrence Hoffman (and no mention of The Viking Press). Rear flap is an advertisement for recent and forthcoming Viking fiction, followed by four listings, beginning with *End Over End* by Nelson Gidding, ending with *An Afternoon* by Elizabeth Parsons. Rear flap ends with a statement reading, "Descriptive list of other current books / sent on request," followed by the publisher's name and address (with no "PRINTED IN THE U.S.A. statement at the bottom right corner). Rear panel is devoted to a plot summary, beginning with the book title, the author's name, then three paragraphs of text, then a "Printed in the U.S.A." statement, ending with the publisher's name and city. A description of Variant "B" can be found in *Appendix A: Secondary Book Sources*.

MOONRISE

FRANK BORZAGE

Screenwriter   Charles Haas
Cinematographer   John L. Russell
Composer   Walter Kent, William Lava
Cast   Dane Clark, Gail Russell, Ethel Barrymore, Rex Ingram, Harry Morgan (as Henry Morgan)
Studio   Republic, 1948
Runtime   90 minutes

Moonrise was first serialized in *Collier's* in 1945 and, after subseqent publication as a novel by Viking in 1946, was much in demand as a film property. Several companies competed to bring the book to the screen, beginning with Paramount, then Garson Kanin for actor John Garfield, and finally John Farrow for his protégé Alan Ladd. The option finally went to young independent producer Marshall Grant, who paid the author $50,000 for the rights. The lead was then offered to James Stewart and Burt Lancaster, both of whom declined. Eventually United Artists agreed to make the film, with William Wellman directing, Vladmir Pozner writing the script, and John Garfield in the lead role. Eight weeks into pre-production, however, Grant ran into financial difficulty with his lenders and had to quickly jump ship to a smaller studio. Charles K. Feldman, creator of the "one-picture deal" in the shadow of the collapsing Hollywood studio system, took the project, and the reins were finally handed to Republic, with *Moonrise* becoming the second most expensive film ever produced there. Frank Borzage directed, and the resulting film was a career highlight for the director, who applied his well-established dreamlike approach in what would be his only dalliance with a crime story.

The only contribution by Borzage.

Reference   Selby, Silver and Ward

ROUGH SKETCH

ROBERT SYLVESTER

Publisher   New York: Dial Press, 1948

Born in 1907, Robert Sylvester was a newspaper columnist, drama editor at the *New York Mirror,* and a minor American author of crime fiction. His two published novels were both made into films noir, *Rough Sketch* being the first, and *The Big Boodle* (filmed in 1957) the second. He wrote the original screenplay for The *Joe Louis Story* in 1953, but has no other recorded work in Hollywood.

The author's only contribution.

Light gray cloth with black titles and rule on the spine, no topstain. Title page shows a date of 1948, with no statement of later printings on the copyright page. Front flap shows a price of $3.00 at the top right corner, followed by a plot summary that continues to the end of the rear flap. Rear panel contains an author biography, with a photo of Sylvester at the top. At least three printings have been noted.

WE WERE STRANGERS

JOHN HUSTON

Screenwriter   John Huston, Peter Viertel
Cinematographer   Russell Metty
Composer   George Antheil
Cast   Jennifer Jones, John Garfield, Pedro Armendáriz, Gilbert Roland, Ramon Novarro, Wally Cassell, David Bond, José Pérez, Morris Ankrum, Tito Renaldo, Paul Monte, Leonard Strong
Studio   Columbia, 1949
Runtime   106 minutes

In his autobiography, *An Open Book,* John Huston recalls, "After the completion of *Key Largo,* Sam Spiegel and I formed our first independent company, Horizon Pictures. [We] were eager to get the company going, so...we decided upon *We Were Strangers* as our first picture. This was from a book called *Rough Sketch* by Robert Sylvester. A New York columnist suggested in print that I make the story into a picture. Sam and I both saw the item, read the story and thought, "Why not?" We acquired the property, and Peter Viertel and I wrote the script. This was the first time I worked with Peter, whom I'd known since he was a boy."

Huston went on to shoot second unit footage for the film in Cuba, and there met Ernest Hemingway by way of Viertel. Four years later, Viertel wrote a novel based on Huston's hunting escapades in Africa, titled *White Hunter, Black Heart.* (Huston)

Author-screenwriter Peter Viertel's only contribution, and John Huston's last of nine.

Reference   Selby

Current

rough sketch

A NOVEL BY
ROBERT SYLVESTER
AUTHOR OF DREAM STREET

DIAL

ONE WOMAN

TIFFANY THAYER

Publisher   New York: William Morrow, 1933

Born in Freeport, Illinois on March 1, 1902, Tiffany Thayer was a novelist, screenwriter, editor, and one-time actor. He wrote five crime novels under his own name, and two pseudonymous novels in 1932 under the names John Doe and O. B. King, respectively. Five films were made from his novels and stories between 1932 and 1949. *One Woman* was his last novel, and the last story to be filmed.

Thayer quit school at age of fifteen and worked variously as an actor, reporter, and used-book clerk in and around Detroit. In 1924 he made contact with his philosophical hero, author Charles Fort, a critic associated with anomalous phenomena and the debunking of "scientists' claim to ultimate knowledge," and in 1931 founded The Fortean Society in Britain. Toward the end of his life, Thayer championed increasingly idiosyncratic ideas, including that of a Flat Earth, and opposed others, such as the fluoridation of water supplies. The *Fortean Society Magazine* (also called *Doubt*) was published regularly until Thayer's death in Nantucket, Massachusetts in 1959, when both the Society and the magazine came to an end.

The author's only contribution.

Purple-brown cloth with title and author name in blind at the center of the front board and at the spine. Black topstain, illustrated endpapers. Title page shows a date of 1933, with no statement of edition or later printings on the copyright page. Front flap shows a price of $2.50 at the top right corner, followed by a plot summary that continues to the end of the rear flap (with no other reviews). Rear panel begins with a publisher's blurb for *One Woman*, followed by five reviews of the author's previous novel, *Thirteen Men*, beginning with Burton Rascoe and ending with *The New York Sun*, then, "AND PUBLISHED BY MORROW."

CHICAGO DEADLINE

LEWIS ALLEN

Screenwriter   Warren Duff
Cinematographer   John F. Seitz
Composer   Victor Young
Cast   Alan Ladd, Donna Reed, June Havoc, Irene Hervey, Arthur Kennedy, Berry Kroeger,
                      Harold Vermilyea, Shepperd Strudwick, John Beal, Tom Powers, Gavin Muir
Runtime   86 minutes

In *Chicago Deadline*, Alan Ladd stars as journalist Ed Adams, who discovers the body of a young woman, dead of tuberculosis in a cheap southside hotel. He is intrigued by the exquisite corpse and steals the woman's address book before the police arrive. He begins to investigate the girl's past, discovering that her real name is Rosita Jean D'Ur. Her seedy backstory is recounted in flashback (in the form of Donna Reed), through the memories of people who knew her. Adams uncovers a world of murder and blackmail, where Rosita is just one link in a twisted, deadly chain of crime and violence.

By way of flashback and the necrophilic fascination of the main character, *Chicago Deadline* is a darker, more unseemly re-imagining of *Laura*, with a fatalistic romanticism that makes it something of a darker cousin to the better-known film.

Director Lewis Allen's last of four contributions, and the third of four by screenwriter Warren Duff.

Reference   Selby, Silver and Ward

DEEP VALLEY

DAN TOTHEROH

Publisher   New York: L.B. Fischer, 1942

Born July 22, 1894, in San Francisco, Dan Totheroh was a successful Hollywood screenwriter, with a number of screenplay credits between 1929 and 1954. Notable films include both the 1930 and 1941 versions of *The Dawn Patrol*, *The Count of Monte Cristo* (1934), and *The Devil and Daniel Webster* (1941).

Deep Valley is his only known published work as a novelist, and his only contribution.

Green cloth with black titles at the center of the front board and the publisher's device in white at the bottom right corner of the same. From the crown, the spine shows the author's name in white caps, followed by four compartments set off by white-and-black double rule. The second compartment is a black panel with the book title in reverse, and the other compartments are blank, with the publisher's name in white caps just below the fourth compartment. Black topstain. No statement of edition or later printings on the copyright page. Front flap shows a price of $2.50, followed by a plot summary that continues to the end of the rear flap, ending with the publisher's device, then the publisher's name. Rear panel is an advertisement for *Mud on the Stars* by Hendrik Wilhelm Van Loon, with the title in pink, followed by a blurb by Eugene Lyons, then a four-paragraph summary in two columns. The bottom quarter of the panel is devoted to a War Bonds advertisement.

DEEP VALLEY

JEAN NEGULESCO

Screenwriter	Salka Viertel, Stephen Morehouse Avery, William Faulkner (uncredited)
Cinematographer	Ted McCord
Composer	Max Steiner
Cast	Ida Lupino, Dane Clark, Wayne Morris, Fay Bainter, Henry Hull, Willard Robertson
Studio	Warner Brothers, 1947
Runtime	104 minutes

Darryl F. Zanuck could get swept up in a director's enthusiasm for a project, and director Jean Negulesco liked that quality in him. In 1947, Negulesco directed *Deep Valley* for Warner Brothers, another one of his "tough romances," dealing with an escaped convict who brings meaning to the life of a farm girl. There was a general strike at Fox, so Negulesco shot the film on location at Big Sur and Big Bear. The production became an archetype for a new kind of film made away from the process screen—but not in the city. The film is more striking than ever today, with the naturalistic scenes of prison inmates mining the entire side of a mountain striking and fresh. Even more remarkable is the film's morally complex, downbeat, and philosophically dense ending, which somehow sailed past the Production Code. (Meyer)

Director Jean Negulesco's fifth of six contributions, and William Faulkner's last of three.

Reference   Selby

Deep
Valley

DAN
TOTHEROH

Deep
Valley

A NOVEL BY
DAN TOTHEROH

Salter

CRISS-CROSS

DON TRACY

Publisher	New York: Vanguard, 1934

Don Tracy was a regular contributor to the pulps of the 1930s and 1940s, and while his first four novels were hard-boiled crime stories, he also wrote adventure and historical fiction. He was also one of the earliest writers to credit Alcoholics Anonymous (which he joined in the early 1950s after many years of alcohol abuse) with having saved his life and career.

Criss-Cross is, in the words of Otto Penzler, "pretty bad." With clunky dialogue, racist overtones, and a dated style, it is the perfect example of a book where plot lines and basic ideas were appropriated by a superior screenwriter as a framework to make a classic film.

Tracy worked both as a guard on an armored car and as a night-club manager, both professions that figure heavily in the story.

The author's first novel, and only contribution.

Blue cloth with black titles and diagonal line design at the front board and spine. No statement of edition or later printings on the copyright page. Front flap shows a price of $2.00 at the bottom right corner, and contains a plot summary. Rear flap contains an author biography, with a clip-out catalogue request form for other Vanguard titles at the bottom. Rear panel has advertisements for two other Vanguard titles, *I'm the Happiest Girl in the World* by John Held, Jr., and *Nina* by Alfred Bourne.

CRISS CROSS

ROBERT SIODMAK

Screenwriter	Daniel Fuchs, Robert Siodmak (uncredited), Mark Hellinger (original treatment)
Cinematographer	Frank Planer
Composer	Miklós Rózsa
Cast	Burt Lancaster, Yvonne De Carlo, Dan Duryea, Stephen McNally, Esy Morales, Tom Pedi, Percy Helton, Alan Napier, Griff Barnett, Meg Randall, Richard Long, Joan Miller, Edna M. Holland, John Doucette, Marc Krah, James O'Rear, John 'Skins' Miller, Tony Curtis (uncredited)
Studio	Universal, 1949
Runtime	87 minutes

After working successfully with Robert Siodmak on *The Killers,* producer Mark Hellinger reconceived Tracy's novel as involving a detailed heist at a race track. However, Hellinger died before the film became a reality, with the screenplay only half finished. Siodmak and screenwriter Daniel Fuchs ultimately returned to Tracy's original idea of an armored car robbery, transplanted Don Tracy's Baltimore setting to Los Angeles, and filmed on location there.

Burt Lancaster was displeased with the changes from Hellinger's draft, as it shifted the film's focus from him as a strong leading man to a participant in a romantic triangle involving Yvonne De Carlo and Dan Duryea. The resulting film, however, has become a noir cornerstone where a single poor choice made by the protagonist at the beginning " governs his destiny with an irresistible force," leading him down a relentlessly bleak path of lust, greed, and betrayal, ending in a shotgun shack on a county road, where everyone dies and only the money remains. (Greco, Silver and Ward)

Reference	Selby, Silver and Ward

CRISS-CROSS

CRISS-CROSS

by
DON TRACY
Author of
"ROUND
TRIP"

by
DON TRACY
Author of
"ROUND
TRIP"

VANGUARD

THE TREASURE OF THE SIERRA MADRE

B. TRAVEN

Publisher   London: Chatto and Windus, 1934

B. Traven's classic story was first published in German as *Der Schatz Der Sierra Madre* (Buchergilde Gutenberg, 1927), and is the author's only contribution.

While the first UK edition of *The Treasure of the Sierra Madre* precedes the American edition by a year, the UK edition is a translation from the German by Basil Creighton, a version reportedly much admired by Traven. The American edition was re-written by Traven himself in conjunction with his American publisher, and is an expanded version. Thus, both the American and British editions given equal weight. Following are the points for the UK edition: Burnt orange cloth with titles in gilt at the spine, orange-brown topstain. Title page shows a date of 1934, with no statement of edition or later printings. Front flap shows a price of "7s. 6d. / NET" at the bottom right corner, and contains a short blurb about the book. Rear flap and rear panel are blank. For points on the American edition, see *Appendix A: Secondary Book Sources*).

THE TREASURE OF THE SIERRA MADRE

JOHN HUSTON

Screenwriter	John Huston
Cinematographer	Ted McCord
Composer	Max Steiner, Buddy Kaye (title song)
Cast	Humphrey Bogart, Walter Huston, Tim Holt, Bruce Bennett, Barton MacLane, Alfonso Bedoya
Studio	Warner Brothers, 1948
Runtime	126 minutes

Not long after John Huston wrote to author B. Traven regarding his desire to make a film of *The Treasure of the Sierra Madre*, Huston awoke one morning in Mexico City to find "a shadowy figure of a man" at the foot of his bed. Huston recalls: "He took out a card and gave it to me...it said, 'Hal Croves, Interpreter, Acapulco and San Antonio.'" Croves announced to Huston that he would represent Traven in every way, as he "knew as much about his work as [Traven] himself did and knew as much about the circumstances and the country." Croves ultimately did just that, working as an on-site consultant for script revision, pre-production, and all of the principal shooting. Although Croves' manner did not resemble that of the Traven Huston had known from correspondence in any way, he suspected throughout that Traven and the quiet, mysterious man were in fact one and the same. Finally Huston notes, "After I'd made *Treasure* and time passed, I heard that Croves was living in Mexico City and he was generally accepted as Traven, although he was still calling himself Croves." In the wake of the film's success, Croves-Traven became quite a celebrity in Mexico City, and by some accounts, eventually permitted himself to be called Traven. Huston ultimately concedes, "I'm still quite mystified by the whole thing." (Pratley)

The Treasure of the Sierra Madre was the first American studio feature film to be made entirely on location outside the borders of the United States. Huston's seventh of nine contributions.

Reference   Selby

THE
TREASURE
OF THE
SIERRA MADRE

B. TRAVEN

CHATTO
AND WINDUS

BE STILL, MY LOVE

JUNE TRUESDELL

Publisher   New York: Dodd, Mead, 1947

June Truesdell was a minor American crime writer. She wrote three novels between 1945 and 1951, and *Be Still My Love* was the second of two published by Dodd, Mead. Her last book, *Burden of Proof,* was published only in the UK, by Boardman.

The author's only contribution.

Yellow cloth with the Dodd, Mead logo in red at the top center of the front board, and titles in red at the spine. Yellow topstain. Title page shows a date of 1947, with no statement of edition or later printings on the copyright page. Front flap shows a price of 2.50 (with no "$" sign), followed by a plot summary. Rear flap contains a plot summary for another book by the publisher, *Fortune's Gift* by Susan Kerby. Rear panel is devoted to an author biography, with a photo of Ms. Truesdell at the top (with a photo credit for Whitey Schafer at the bottom edge), the author's name to the left of the photo, and the biography below. The front flap, rear flap, and rear panel all end with the publisher's name.

THE ACCUSED

WILLIAM DIETERLE

Screenwriter   Ketti Frings
Cinematographer   Milton Krasner
Composer   Victor Young
Cast   Loretta Young, Robert Cummings, Wendell Corey, Sam Jaffe, Douglas Dick, Suzanne Dalbert,
                             Sara Allgood, Mickey Knox, George Spaulding, Francis Pierlot, Ann Doran, Carole Mathews
Studio   Paramount, 1949
Alternate Titles   Strange Deception (working title)
Runtime   101 minutes

The Accused was one of the earliest films about what is today known as "date rape." Loretta Young portrays a teacher who, when molested by one of her own students, accidentally kills him and must face prosecution. The fact that the murder in the story was self-defense—but murder nonetheless—made for an interesting challenge to the Hays Code. *The New York Times* review of the film noted that the film's ambiguous ending must have "been quite a concession for the Production Code people, who are usually quite fussy about exacting retribution. The departure should not be construed as a body blow to morality, however, for it is made quite evident that the heroine acted instinctively to protect her honor. And, even the policeman who doggedly pieces together the fragments of evidence which expose her has nothing but sympathy and admiration in his heart for the lady."

The second of three contributions by director William Dieterle, and the second of two for screenwriter Ketti Frings.

Reference   Selby, Silver and Ward

BE STILL, my Love

JUNE TRUESDELL

BE STILL, MY LOVE

Truesdell

DODD MEAD COMPANY

THE TWO
MRS. CARROLLS

MARTIN VALE

Publisher	London: George Allen and Unwin, 1936

Born in 1881, Martin Vale was the pseudonym of Marguerite Veiller. *The Two Mrs. Carrolls* was her only published work, and debuted in New York at the Booth Theater on August 3, 1943. It was a bona fide hit, running for just over two years and 585 performances.

The playwright's only contribution.

Orange cloth with titles in black at the front board and spine, no topstain. "First published in 1936" stated at the top of the copyright page, with no mention of later impressions. Front flap shows a price of "3s. 6d. *net*" at the bottom center, with no other text present. Rear flap is blank, and the rear panel is an advertisement for *One-Act Play Parade*, an omnibus of "twelve new one-act plays," followed by three blurbs, ending with the publisher's name. At least five printings have been noted between 1936 and 1949, and the later bindings and jackets vary considerably, some in card covers and self-wrappers, others in hardcover with dust jackets.

THE TWO
MRS. CARROLLS

PETER GODFREY

Screenwriter	Thomas Job
Cinematographer	Peverell Marley
Composer	Franz Waxman
Cast	Humphrey Bogart, Barbara Stanwyck, Alexis Smith, Nigel Bruce, Isobel Elsom, Pat O'Moore, Ann Carter, Anita Bolster, Barry Bernard
Studio	Warner Brothers, 1947
Runtime	99 minutes

The film version of *The Two Mrs. Carrolls* is neither a brilliant chiller nor a contrived mystery, but rather a curious blend of those elements, with the relationship between Humphrey Bogart and Barbara Stanwyck being not about chemistry but rather complete alienation. The story's conceit is that the psychopathic Bogart finds a lover, paints her, and then murders her. Director Peter Godfrey fills the intended void with the standard gothic conventions of creaking boards, long silences, slamming doors, haunting paintings, and pulsating music, but also brings a new kind of blackness to the proceedings by focusing on the utter lack of warmth in the large drafty house where the action comes to a close. Only occasional visits from Bogart's screen daughter in the film maintain a slender thread of humanity, just enough to keep things interesting. (Meyer)

Peter Godfrey's first of three contributions.

Reference	Selby

The Two Mrs. Carrolls

a play in three acts

by

Martin Vale

The text of the brilliant poisoning drama, which was staged at the St. James's Theatre with such success. The setting of the play is the South of France and the theme that of Geoffrey Carroll's deliberate and cold-blooded plan to murder his unsuspecting wife by poison. Sally Carroll is warned only just in time, and her husband, realising that she knows, tries to strangle her. When he is discovered in this attempt he commits suicide.

GEORGE ALLEN & UNWIN LTD

George Allen
Unwin Ltd

The Two Mrs. Carrolls—Martin Vale

LOVE FROM A STRANGER

FRANK VOSPER

Publisher   London: Collins, 1936

Born in London in 1899, Frank Vosper was an actor who performed both on the stage and in films. He made his dramatic debut in 1919 at the age of twenty, and his typical role on the stage was that of a smooth villain.

Vosper was also an occasional playwright. The last of his three dramas, *Love from a Stranger* is a three-act play based on a short story by Agatha Christie titled "Philomel Cottage" (Christie's story originally appeared in *The Grand Magazine* in 1924). Vosper drowned after falling from a transatlantic liner in 1937, the year after *Love from a Stranger* was published.

The actor-playwright's only contribution.

Black cloth with gilt lettering at the spine only, no topstain. No statement of edition or later impressions on the copyright page. Front flap shows a price of "3/6 paper 5/- cloth," and contains four quotes about the book, beginning with Charles Morgan of *The Times* and ending with *The Daily Express*. Rear flap leads with Agatha Christie's name, followed by five quotes, beginning with *The Bystander* and ending with *the Observer* (with the lower case "t" in "the" being a typo). Rear panel is an advertisement for "Famous Poirot Detective Stories by Agatha Christie," followed by ten titles, beginning with *Murder in Mesopotamia* and ending with *The Big Four*.

LOVE FROM A STRANGER

RICHARD WHORF

Screenwriter	Philip MacDonald
Cinematographer	Tony Gaudio
Composer	Hans J. Salter
Cast	Sylvia Sydney, John Hodiak, Isobel Elsom, Ernest Cossart, Ann Richards, John Howard, Philip Tonge, Anita Sharp-Bolster, Frederick Worlock
Studio	Eagle-Lion, 1947
Alternate Titles	A Stranger Walked In (UK)
Runtime	81 minutes

Born in Winthrop, Massachusetts on June 4, 1906, Richard Whorf was an American film actor who later became a director. He began his acting career on the Boston stage as a teenager, and made his Broadway debut at age twenty-one. He moved to Hollywood and became a contract player in movies of the 1930s and 1940s before his directorial debut in1944.

Whorf appeared as an actor in films noir including *Christmas Holiday* (1944), *Blues in the Night* (1941), and *Keeper of the Flame* (1942). He directed a number of notable television programs in the 1950s and 1960s, the best known being the long-running CBS comedy *The Beverly Hillbillies,* for which he directed twenty episodes between 1962 and 1964.

Love from a Stranger was first filmed with Basil Rathbone and Ann Harding in 1937, and was set in contemporary England. The 1947 remake, based on Frank Vosper's play more than Christie's short story, capitalized somewhat on the popularity of films noir like *Gaslight*, *Hangover Square*, and *The Woman in White* by moving its setting to late Victorian England, where the husband of a newly-married couple plots to murder his wife for her money.

Whorf's only contribution, and screenwriter Philip MacDonald's fourth of five.

Reference   Selby, Lyons

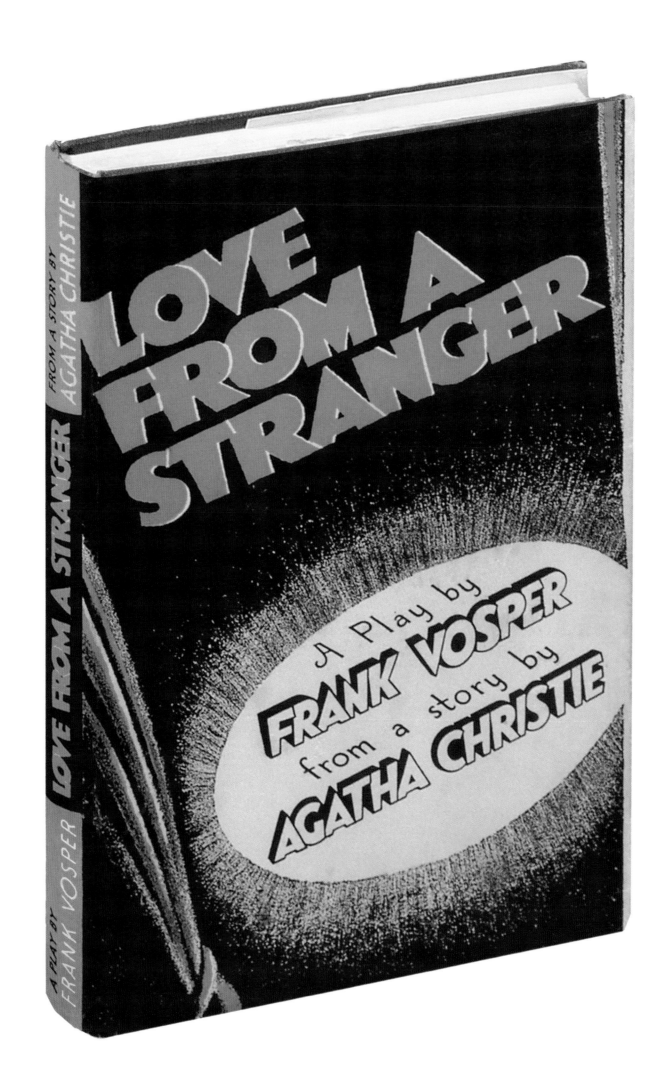

ONCE OFF GUARD

J.H. WALLIS

Publisher   New York: E.P. Dutton, 1942

J.H. Wallis was born in Iowa in 1885, was educated at Yale, and began his career as a newspaperman in Iowa. He moved to New York in 1931 to become a full-time writer, publishing his first novel, *Murder by Formula* with Dutton, who would remain his publisher until the end of his writing career in 1943. His mysteries were set mostly in New York City (with detours to Connecticut, and once to Illinois), and he was known for his series character, Inspector Wilton Jacks. *Once Off Guard* was his ninth crime novel, a non-series effort.

Wallis' first of two contributions, and his only contribution as a novelist.

Black cloth with titles and rule in gilt at the front board and spine, yellow topstain. Small ornamental device at the spine in reverse, all other spine titles and rule in gilt. Yellow topstain. Title page shows a date of 1942, with "FIRST EDITION" stated on the copyright page. Front flap shows a price of $2.50 at the bottom right corner, and contains a plot summary that continues to the rear flap, then to the rear panel, followed by the book title and author, with an illustration of a woman and the heading, "What would you have done?"

THE WOMAN IN THE WINDOW

FRITZ LANG

Screenwriter   Nunnally Johnson
Cinematographer   Milton Krasner
Composer   Arthur Lange
Cast   Edward G. Robinson, Joan Bennett, Raymond Massey, Dan Duryea, Edmond Breon
Studio   RKO, 1945
Runtime   99 minutes

The Woman in the Window has always had a little black cloud over its head in the mind of film noir purists, in that it has a "dream" ending, where Edward G. Robinson wakes up at his Gentleman's Club and realizes that he really didn't commit adultery (and ultimately, suicide) after all. In the eyes of the Hays Code, suicide would have certainly been an agreeable counterbalance for infidelity, and it turns out the "dream" ending was actually a creative addition by director Fritz Lang, not one required by the Production Code as is sometimes assumed.

In a 1972 interview with Alain Silver, Lang said: "*The Woman in the Window* was too dark at first. So I used a cheap trick to change the ending, to make it upbeat. But in the film's introduction, looking at the picture of the woman in the shop window then having her appear as a reflection in the glass, that was always there and it set a symbolic groundwork for the dream. At the end it's all tied in, the people in the dream are people in real life and then, of course, it threatens to start again and the professor runs home. Some critics ridiculed the dream ending, but they were wrong. This movie was not about evil, it was certainly not *Scarlet Street*, it was about psychology, the subconscious desires, and what better expression of those than in a dream, where the libido is released and emotions are exaggerated?"

Lang's fifth of six contributions, and screenwriter Nunnally Johnson's second of three.

Reference   Selby, Silver and Ward

THE SNAKE PIT

MARY JANE WARD

Publisher   New York: Random House, 1946

The Snake Pit is an autobiographical novel by Mary Jane Ward that tells of her experiences of in a crowded mental hospital, where therapy for schizophrenia included being wrapped in wet, cold sheets, "boiled" in a bathtub and given electric shock treatment. Her few moments of gentle care come when she talks to the psychiatrist named Dr. Chrzanowski (whom she calls "Dr. Kik"). The book was hailed as one of the first honest looks at life in a mental institution. The film, starring Olivia de Havilland as the patient and Leo Genn as the doctor, earned six Academy Award nominations.

The book's title refers to the medieval practice of lowering the mentally ill into snake pits in the belief that a fright intense enough to unhinge a sane person would similarly cure an insane one.

Mary Ward suggests in her book that Dr. Kik believed she was in danger of a recurrence of her problems after her release from the mental hospital. She suffered a second breakdown in 1957, and a third in 1969. She died in 1981. (McCoubrey)

Blue-green cloth with title in gilt at the front board, author name and publisher's device in gilt at the spine. Gray topstain. "FIRST PRINTING" stated on the copyright page, with no mention of later printings. Front flap shows a price of $2.50 at the top right corner, followed by a plot summary of the book. Rear flap contains an author biography, with a photo of Mary Jane Ward at the top, and the rear panel contains a statement by the author regarding the factuality of the book.

THE SNAKE PIT

ANATOLE LITVAK

Screenwriter	Millen Brand, Frank Partos, Arthur Laurents (uncredited)
Cinematographer	Leo Tover
Composer	Alfred Newman
Cast	Olivia de Havilland, Mark Stevens, Leo Genn, Celeste Holm, Glenn Langan, Helen Craig, Leif Erickson, Beulah Bondi, Lee Patrick, Howard Freeman, Natalie Schafer, Ruth Donnelly
Studio	Twentieth Century-Fox, 1948
Runtime	108 minutes

Arthur Laurents: "What brought me to Hollywood was needing money. Anatole Litvak wanted me to do *The Snake Pit* after having seen [the stage version of] *Home of the Brave*, because they were both 'psychiatric.' I didn't want to go to Hollywood. I wanted to stay in the theater, but by that time I was in debt. So I ended up going to Hollywood for MGM. [Then] MGM loaned me to Fox to do *The Snake Pit*, because Fox paid MGM more than I was getting in salary. Anatole was on deadline, because they were ready to go into shooting and the script was no good. I sat all day and all night with him, rewriting at the Fox studio. After the picture was shot, the screenwriting credit went to the Screen Writers Guild [for arbitration], and they ruled that Millen Brand and Frank Partos [authors of the first draft] had written it. The hearing was during the shooting of another picture, and Anatole was too busy to attend and testify. So I didn't get the screen credit. I was a little annoyed, but not really, because I thought, and I still think, what's the difference? I mean, I know I wrote it." (McGilligan, *Backstory 2*; Laurents)

The last of five contributions by director Litvak, and the first of two for Laurents.

Reference   Selby

the snake pit

a novel by MARY JANE WARD

ALL THE KING'S MEN

ROBERT PENN WARREN

Publisher   New York: Reynal and Hitchcock, 1947

Robert Penn Warren was born in Guthrie, Kentucky, on April 24, 1905. He graduated from Clarksville High School in Tennessee, Vanderbilt University in 1925 and the University of California at Berkeley in 1926. He later attended Yale University and obtained a degree from New College in Oxford as a Rhodes Scholar in 1930. While still an undergraduate at Vanderbilt, Warren became associated with the group of poets there known as the Fugitives, and later, during the early 1930s, along with some of the same writers formed a group known as the Southern Agrarians.

Warren served as the Poet Laureate of the United States from 1944 to1945, and went on to win the Pulitzer Prize in 1947 for his best known work, *All the King's Men*. The story's main character, Willie Stark, was based largely on the radical populist governor of Louisiana, Huey Pierce Long (1893-1935), whom Warren was able to observe closely while teaching in Baton Rouge at Louisiana State University from 1933-1942. He won Pulitzer Prizes in poetry in 1958 for *Promises: Poems 1954-1956*, and in 1979 for *Now and Then*.

The author's only contribution, winner of the Pulitzer Prize for Literature.

Maroon cloth with gilt lettering at the spine, no topstain. Copyright page states "first edition" (in lower case) stated near the top of the copyright page. Front flap shows a price of $3.00 in the top right corner, followed by a plot summary, which continues to the rear flap, ending with the publisher's name and address (and an early New York zip code of "17"). Rear panel contains a single blurb by Sinclair Lewis, replaced by multiple reviews on later issue jackets.

ALL THE KING'S MEN

ROBERT ROSSEN

Screenwriter	Robert Rossen
Cinematographer	Burnett Guffey
Composer	George Duning, Louis Gruenberg, Marlin Skiles (all uncredited)
Cast	Broderick Crawford, John Ireland, Joanne Dru, John Derek, Mercedes McCambridge, Shepperd Strudwick , Ralph Dumke, Anne Seymour, Raymond Greenleaf, Walter Burke, Will Wright, Grandon Rhodes
Studio	Columbia, 1949
Runtime	109 minutes

Just after working on an aborted adaptation of B. Traven's *Treasure of the Sierra Madre* (relinquished to John Huston), Robert Rossen turned to Robert Penn Warren's novel, *All the King's Men*, which would be his first effort working both as sole screenwriter and director. He later said, "I tried as I do always when I adapt a book that I like, to render the spirit of it rather than the letter." Warren, with whom Rossen consulted frequently through some ten drafts of the screenplay, had much the same view, saying, "I think that it is an extraordinarily good movie, with his very special touch. I can praise it, because it seems to me that when a movie is made from a novel, the novel is merely raw material, the movie is a new creation, and the novelist can properly attract neither praise nor blame for it. The movie, as a matter of fact, does not 'mean' what I think my book meant. It is Bob's movie." (Casty)

The last of seven contributions by Rossen.

Reference   Selby

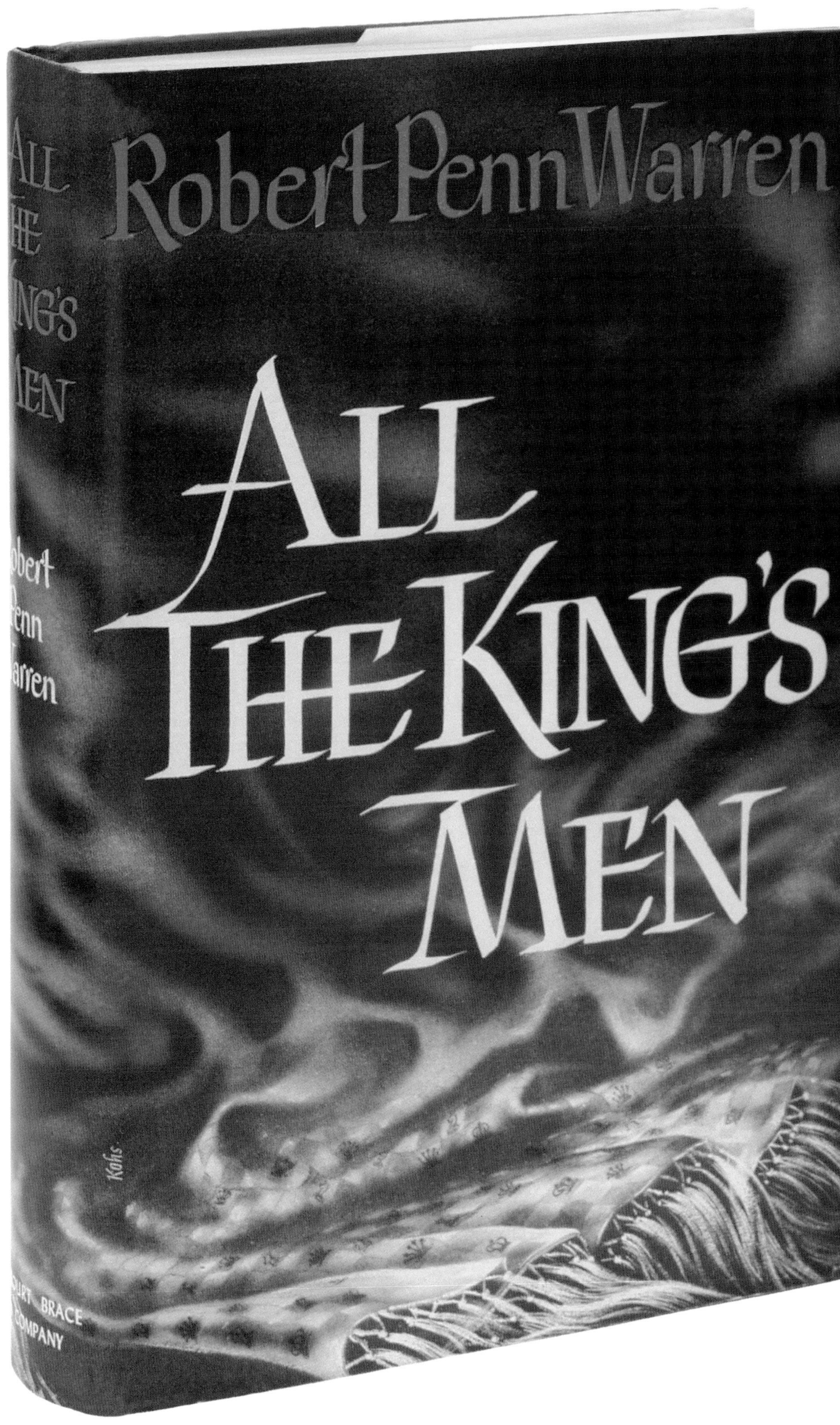
Robert Penn Warren
ALL THE KING'S MEN

I'll Never Go There Anymore

Jerome Weidman

Publisher   New York: Simon and Schuster, 1941

The fictional character of Max Maggio in Jerome Weidman's *I'll Never Go There Again* was drawn from incidents relating to the life of A.P. Giannini. Giannini was an Italian immigrant who founded his bank on the notion of lending money to hard-working immigrants with no collateral during the depression. His bank flourished, and in spite of much scandal over the years, eventually became what is today the Bank of America.

Jerome Weidman's six-year tenure in Hollywood began with this adaptation. His only other contribution to the film noir cycle is as a screenwriter on *The Damned Don't Cry* (1950). He is perhaps best known for his novel, *I Can Get It For You Wholesale*, basis for the 1951 film.

Black cloth with Weidman's signature in gilt at the center of the front board, titles and rule in gilt at the spine. Mauve topstain. The title page and copyright page show matching dates of 1941. Front flap shows a price of $2.50, followed by a plot summary that continues to the end of the rear flap. Rear panel has a photo of the author at the top, followed by six reviews (one by Rebecca West) for four of the author's other books, printed in two columns.

House of Strangers

Joseph L. Mankiewicz

Screenwriter	Philip Yordan, Joseph L. Mankiewicz (uncredited)
Cinematographer	Milton Krasner
Composer	Daniele Amfitheatrof
Cast	Edward G. Robinson, Susan Hayward, Richard Conte, Luther Adler, Debra Paget
Studio	Twentieth Century-Fox, 1949
Alternate Titles	East Side Story (working title)
Runtime	101 minutes

Producer Sol C. Siegel originally asked screenwriter Philip Yordan to prepare an adaptation of Weidman's book, focusing on a chapter devoted to Max Maggio (the chapter titled "Max"), a lawyer who ultimately goes to jail for his father's crimes, in the shadow of three brothers who were too cowardly to become involved. Yordan was unable to complete a screenplay on the studio's schedule, and the job was given to Joseph L. Mankiewicz, who had already been slated to direct. Mankiewicz wrote the entire script, faithful to Weidman's story, but added his own hard-boiled dialogue. Upon completion of the script, the Screen Writer's Guild demanded that Mankiewicz share screenwriter's credit with Yordan. Having completed a script that Yordan had barely started, Mankiewicz refused, and Yordan was ultimately given the entire screenwriting credit.

Mankiewicz, following Weidman's lead, used the source material to retell what was in part a true story: the founding of the Bank of America by the Giannini family, and the foreclosure early in its history due to the illegal and careless practices of its directors. He even asked the Fox art department to construct a faithful copy of the actual Giannini bank (in San Francisco) that would be relocated for the film in a fictionalized Manhattan. (Lower & Palmer)

The last of four contributions by Joseph L. Mankiewicz, and the sixth of seven for Yordan.

Reference   Selby, Silver and Ward

I'll never go there any more

THE NEW NOVEL BY
Jerome Weidman

LIEBERMAN

MIDNIGHT HOUSE
ETHEL LINA WHITE

Publisher   London: Collins, 1932

Ethel Lina White was born in 1884, in Abergavenny, a small English town on the Welsh border. She was raised as one of a family of twelve, and worked for most of her adult life at the Ministry of Pensions. She gave up her job just prior to retirement, at age 53, to write fiction, and had a brief but very successful career as a writer. Her first three books were mainstream novels, but she then moved to writing thrillers, which along with her superb storytelling style, would become her trademark. Altogether she authored twenty books over a period of fourteen years, passing away in Chiswick in 1944, the same year that her last novel, *They See in Darkness,* was published. She specialized in brisk, economical mysteries, all of which took place in England, and never wrote using a series character.

The author's first of two contributions.

Red-orange cloth with titles in black at the spine, no topstain. No statement of edition or later impressions on the copyright page, but a date of 1942 appears at the very bottom, just below the printing notice, and two pages of advertisements at the rear. Front flap shows a price of "8/- / net" at the bottom right corner, and contains a plot summary. Rear flap is an advertisement for other books by the author, beginning with *She Faded Into Air* and ending with *The First Time He Died.* Rear panel is an advertisement for other Collins Crime Club titles, with seven listings, beginning with *Slocombe Dies* by L.A.G. Strong and ending with *The Fourth Bomb* by John Rhode.

THE UNSEEN
LEWIS ALLEN

Screenwriter   Raymond Chandler, Hagar Wilde, Ken Englund
Cinematographer   John F. Seitz
Composer   Ernst Toch
Cast   Joel McCrea, Gail Russell, Herbert Marshall, Phyllis Brooks, Isobel Elsom, Norman Lloyd
Studio   Paramount, 1945
Alternate Titles   Fear (working title), Her Heart in Her Throat (working title)
Runtime   80 minutes

After the writing team of Billy Wilder and Charles Brackett broke up, Brackett produced *The Uninvited* in1944, an English ghost tale that was an unexpected success. Hoping to capitalize upon its good fortune, the studio took a story that it already owned, based on the novel *Midnight House* by Ethel Lina White, renamed it *The Unseen,* and assigned both the director (Lewis Allen) and the female lead (Gail Russell) of *The Uninvited* to the project. John Houseman, who had just come to Paramount as a producer, took it as his first assignment.

The earliest screenplay of the film uses the title of the American first edition of White's novel, *Her Heart in Her Throat,* lists Ken Englund as the screenwriter, and is dated July 6, 1943. The next four, all entitled *Fear,* are credited to Hagar Wilde, and are dated November 1943 through April 1944. Chandler's name appears only on a censorship dialogue script titled *The Unseen,* dated five months later. Hagar Wilde fell ill before a suitable ending to the screen story could be devised, and Houseman hired Chandler to polish the script, but recalls that it "was not a good idea, and except for a friendship that lasted for fifteen years, little came of Ray's three weeks' work." (Luhr)

Director Lewis Allen's first of four contributions, Raymond Chandler's third of seven, and the second of two for screenwriter Hagar Wilde.

Reference   Selby, Lyons

Some Must Watch

Ethel Lina White

Publisher — London: Ward, Lock, 1933

The author's second of two contributions.

Blue cloth, no topstain. "First published in 1933" stated at the top of the copyright page, with no mention of later impressions. No number should be present on the jacket spine, as this indicates a later impression. Front flap shows a price of "7/6 net" at the bottom right corner, and contains a plot summary. Rear flap is an advertisement for *The Windsor Magazine*. Rear panel is an advertisement for five novels by Ethel Lina White, beginning with *Put Out the Light* and ending with *Fear Stalks the Village,* then the publisher's imprint and city.

The Spiral Staircase

Robert Siodmak

Screenwriter	Mel Dinelli
Cinematographer	Nicholas Musuraca
Composer	Roy Webb
Cast	Dorothy McGuire, George Brent, Ethel Barrymore, Kent Smith, Rhonda Fleming, Gordon Oliver
Studio	RKO, 1945
Alternate Titles	Silence of Helen McCord (working title), Some Must Watch (working title)
Runtime	83 minutes

Seven years after the highly successful Alfred Hitchcock adaptation of Ethel Lina White's *The Wheel Spins* (filmed as *The Lady Vanishes*), producer Dore Schary purchased the story rights to an even earlier thriller by the author, *Some Must Watch*. Schary made the decision on the strength of his wife's recommendation (she had just read the novel), and had Mel Dinelli write a screenplay before a director was attached.

In the script development process Dinelli and Schary made a change to the story that would make all the difference. Schary: "I was sorry I had bought it because I saw something very funny about it. Mel kept saying, 'What is it that bothers you?' I said, 'I don't know why the hell she doesn't yell for help. I think that's ridiculous.' Then suddenly it hit me. 'That's the answer, Mel, she can't talk. She can hear; but she's mute. A person can go into shock and become kind of autistic where they can hear but they can't speak.'" Schary checked his hypothesis with a doctor, who confirmed that it was a real medical condition, and Dinelli had the turn he needed to write a great script.

It was Siodmak's idea to place beneath the title sequence an overhead shot of a spiral staircase that would be central to the film's claustrophobic, housebound atmosphere. The design in turn prompted Dinelli to change the title from *Some Must Watch* to something a bit more Hitchcockian. Thus, *The Spiral Staircase* was born. (Porfirio, Greco)

The sixth of Siodmak's ten contributions, and screenwriter Dinelli's first of three.

Reference — Selby

SOME MUST WATCH

ETHEL·LINA WHITE

SOME MUST WATCH

ETHEL LINA WHITE

AUTHOR·OF
FEAR·STALKS
THE·VILLAGE·Etc.

WARD·LOCK
&CO

THE HARD-BOILED OMNIBUS

Raoul Whitfield (story), Joseph T. Shaw (editor)

Publisher   New York: Simon and Schuster, 1946

In his *Encyclopedia of Mystery and Detection*, Otto Penzler states flatly that *Black Mask* was "the most important pulp magazine ever published in the United States," a contention that would provoke little debate among crime fiction enthusiasts. Founded in 1920 by H.L. Mencken and George Jean Nathan, *Black Mask* was initially devoted to general fiction and thrillers. However, it is remembered today chiefly for the hard-boiled school of detective fiction inaugurated by Carroll John Daly, then developed further by Dashiell Hammett, Raymond Chandler, Frank Gruber, and others. The magazine achieved preeminence under the editorship of Joseph T. Shaw between 1926 and 1936.

Born in 1898, Raoul Whitfield was an American author of hard-boiled detective fiction. Although less remembered than other *Black Mask* writers, Whitfield was one of the most popular and highly paid writers of his time. He sold his first story at the age of twenty-five, in 1923, and wrote prolifically for the next decade, after which poor health curtailed his activities.

The film noir *High Tide* is based on a short story by Whitfield titled "Inside Job," which originally appeared in the February 1932 issue of *Black Mask*. *The Hard-Boiled Omnibus,* a collection of some of the best stories from *Black Mask*, edited by Joseph T. Shaw, was the first hardcover appearance of the story and was published the year before the film was released. (Penzler)

The author's only contribution.

Green cloth with titles in gilt at the spine, black topstain. No statement of edition or later printings on the copyright page. Front flap shows a price of $3.00 at the bottom right corner, and contains a plot summary. Rear flap contains a biography of *Black Mask* editor Joseph T. Shaw, and begins with "ABOUT THE EDITOR," followed by three paragraphs of text, ending with a jacket design credit for Jackson Lowell. Rear panel is a table of appendix a for the book, with a listing of it's fifteen authors and story titles.

HIGH TIDE

John Reinhardt

Screenwriter   Peter Milne, Robert Presnell Sr.
Cinematographer   Henry Sharp
Composer   Rudy Schrager
Cast   Lee Tracy, Don Castle, Julie Bishop, Anabel Shaw, Douglas Walton, Regis Toomey, Francis Ford
Studio   Monogram, 1947
Runtime   72 minutes

Born on February 24, 1901, in Vienna, John Reinhardt was an enterprising young Austrian actor-writer who arrived in Hollywood shortly before the advent of sound. A highlight of his acting career was his performance as Jean Hersholt's lovesick son in Universal's first version of Edward Locke's 1910 melodrama *The Climax* (1930). As a director, Reinhardt worked on both sides of the Atlantic, but is perhaps best remembered for *Mr. Moto in Danger Island* (1938) and the Cold War melodrama *Sofia* (1948).

Reinhardt's second of four contributions, screenwriter Peter Milne's second of two, and the second of three for Robert Presnell, Sr.

Reference   Selby, Lyons

J. J. des ORMEAUX
REUBEN JENNINGS SHAY
DASHIELL HAMMETT
RAMON DECOLTA
RAYMOND CHANDLER
NORBERT DAVIS
GEORGE HARMON COXE
PAUL CAIN

THE HARD-BOILED OMNIBUS

THEODORE TINSLEY
LESTER DENT
CHARLES G. BOOTH
TOM WALSH
ED LYBECK
ROGER TORREY
RAOUL WHITFIELD

EARLY STORIES FROM *BLACK MASK*

SIMON AND SCHUSTER

LOWELL

GUEST IN THE HOUSE

HAGAR WILDE AND DALE EUNSON

Publisher   New York: Samuel French, 1942

Guest in the House was a stage drama based on an unpublished story by popular novelist Dale Eunson's wife, Katherine Albert (also a minor novelist). It debuted at the Plymouth Theater on Broadway in February of 1942 and ran for six months, introducing a psychologically damaged villainess that *Time* magazine called, "a kind of grown-up version of the brat in Lillian Hellman's *The Children's Hour*." The screen rights were optioned immediately by United Artists, but the resulting film retained none of the cast from the original stage production.

Dale Eunson was best known to readers as an author of down-to-earth novels about rural life, based on his own boyhood experiences. Eunson and Albert would go on to collaborate on two very successful films, *The Star* (1952, featuring Bette Davis) and their biggest hit, *How to Marry a Millionaire* (1953, starring Marilyn Monroe and Betty Grable, based on the Eunson/Albert play, *Loco*).

Hagar Wilde was a minor novelist and successful playwright, but was best known for her contributions to film and television. Her career highlight was the original screenplay for the screwball comedy, *Bringing Up Baby* in 1938.

The only contribution to the noir cycle by Eunson or Albert, and Wilde's first of two.

Beige cloth with lilies and rule in black at the front board and the spine panel, no topstain. Frontispiece of the play's set opposite the title page, with no statement of edition or printing on the copyright page. Front flap shows a price of $1.50 at the lower middle, contains a plot summary, and notes that the book is also published in a "paper covered edition." Rear flap shows five reviews of the play, beginning with *The Newark News* and ending with *The Newark Star-Ledger*. Rear panel shows five more reviews, beginning with *The New York Times* and ending with *Women's Wear*.

GUEST IN THE HOUSE

JOHN BRAHM, LEWIS MILESTONE (UNCREDITED), AND ANDRÉ DE TOTH (UNCREDITED)

Screenwriter	Ketti Frings, André De Toth (uncredited)
Cinematographer	Lee Garmes
Composer	Werner Janssen
Cast	Anne Baxter, Ralph Bellamy, Aline MacMahon, Ruth Warrick, Jerome Cowan, Scott McKay, Marie McDonald, Margaret Hamilton, Percy Kilbride, Connie Laird
Studio	United Artists, 1944
Alternate Titles	Satan in Skirts (working title)
Runtime	121 minutes

John Brahm set the standard for what would become known as his "touch for the bizarre" by taking *Guest in the House* outside its stagey confines, though he waits until the last fifteen minutes to provide a surreal cinematic twist on what would have otherwise been a standard thriller. The director would continue to show a talent for highly effective visual disorientation as a storytelling technique, notably in *The Lodger* (1944) and *Hangover Square* (1945).

The second of Brahm's six contributions, and the first of two for screenwriter Ketti Frings. Also notable for early, uncredited screenwriting and partial directorial contributions by André De Toth and Lewis Milestone.

Reference   Selby, Silver and Ward

GUEST IN THE HOUSE

By

HAGAR WILDE

and

DALE EUNSON

From a Story by Katherine Albert

SAMUEL FRENCH

Founded 1830

Incorporated 1899

25 WEST 45th STREET
NEW YORK

811 WEST 7th STREET
LOS ANGELES

THE PICTURE OF DORIAN GRAY

OSCAR WILDE

Publisher	London: Ward, Lock, 1891

Born Oscar Fingal O'Flahertie Wills Wilde on October 16, 1854, Oscar Wilde was an Irish playwright, novelist, poet, and short story writer. Known for his barbed wit, he was one of the most successful writers in late Victorian London and one of the greatest celebrities of his day. *The Picture of Dorian Gray* was his only published novel, and originally appeared as the lead story in *Lippincott's Monthly Magazine* on June 20, 1890. Wilde later revised the story, making several alterations and adding new chapters, and the amended version was published by Ward, Lock in April 1891. In addition to being one of the best works of nineteenth-century gothic horror fiction, *The Picture of Dorian Gray also* deals with both the artistic movement of the Decadents and homosexuality. The book caused some uproar upon publication, and was even used by the prosecution when the author was later put on trial. Today it is considered one of the great works of nineteenth-century literature.

Wilde's only contribution.

No date shown on either the title page or the copyright page, with four pages of advertisements at the rear. First issue with the letter "a" missing from the word "and" on page 208. Jacket not seen. Also issued by Ward, Lock in an edition limited to 250 large paper copies, bound in parchment and signed by Oscar Wilde.

THE PICTURE OF DORIAN GRAY

ALBERT LEWIN

Screenwriter	Albert Lewin
Cinematographer	Harry Stradling
Composer	Herbert Stothart, William Hargreaves, and C.W. Murphy ("Good-Bye, Little Yellow Bird")
Cast	George Sanders, Hurd Hatfield, Donna Reed, Angela Lansbury, Peter Lawford, Lowell Gilmore
Studio	MGM, 1945
Runtime	110 minutes

The Pandro Berman production of *The Picture of Dorian Gray* was directed in high style by Albert Lewin. As Dorian Gray, actor Hurd Hatfield's deadpan expression and flat mid-Atlantic accent somehow manages to suggest perfectly Oscar Wilde's English aristocrat of great beauty and limitless depravity. Suggestion was everything, in fact. The undescribed vices and unshown orgies that Lewin could only imply under the Production Code made for a model that Stanley Kubrick would follow two decades later with *Lolita*. Cinematographer Harry Stradling won an Academy Award for his elegant black-and-white interiors, and broke into Technicolor for the portrait bearing Dorian's sins. George Sanders was given a rare opportunity to show no restraint while rattling off epigrams as Lord Henry Wotton, and Angela Lansbury received the second of her two Academy Award nominations in what was only her third film. All of these elements make the film a keystone of melodramatic noir, one of several in the cycle that are American realizations of utterly British stories. (Eames)

Director-screenwriter Albert Lewin's only contribution.

Reference	Selby

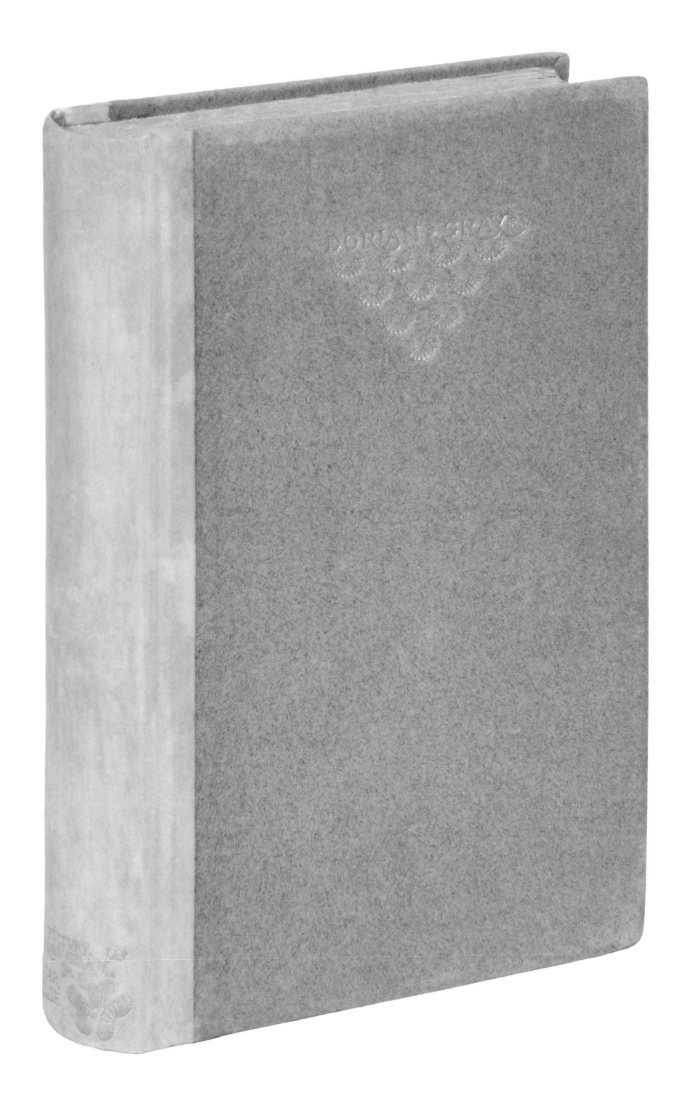

FLAMINGO ROAD

ROBERT WILDER

Publisher   New York: Putnam, 1942

Born in Richmond, Virginia in 1901, Robert Wilder was the son of a minister-turned-lawyer-turned-doctor-turned-dentist, whose own moves through different professional lives seemed to set the pattern that Robert would follow in his own life. He spent much of his youth in Daytona Beach, Florida, and served in the United States Army during World War I. He then completed his education at Columbia University, and his career as a writer started when he was employed as an assistant to theatrical press agent Dixie Hines. Wilder subsequently formed his own agency, representing the publicity interests of Claudette Colbert, among others. He also tried his hand at writing for the theater, authoring a pair of plays, *Sweet Chariot* and *Stardust*. *Stardust* premiered in 1930, and was an especially surprising and daring work for its time, with an almost all-black cast (including Frank Wilson and Fredi Washington) and a plot based on the life and career of renowned black activist Marcus Garvey. Wilder later joined the National Broadcasting Company, working on publicity for the radio network before becoming chief of publicity for WOR radio. In 1935, he turned to journalism, joining the *New York Sun* as a rewrite man and eventually getting his own column. He also wrote articles for *Smart Set, The New Yorker,* and other magazines. At the end of the 1930s, he turned to fiction writing and saw his first novel, *God Has a Long Face*, published in 1940. Two years later came the publication of his first major success, *Flamingo Road,* and he would reach his peak as a writer in 1946, with *Written on the Wind.*

Wilder's only contribution.

Mauve cloth with black decorative titles and rule at the front board and spine, mauve topstain. Front flap shows a price of $2.50 at the top right corner, followed by a plot summary, and the rear flap is an advertisement for Wilder's novel, *Written on the Wind,* with five paragraphs of text, ending with a tiny "Printed in the U.S.A." logo at the bottom right corner. Rear panel is an advertisement for "the Books of Robert Wilder," and shows listings for four books, with two review blurbs for each, beginning with *God Has a Long Face* and ending with *Mr. G. Strings Along.*

FLAMINGO ROAD

MICHAEL CURTIZ

Screenwriter   Robert Wilder, Edmund H. North, Ranald MacDougall (uncredited),
                      Richard Brooks (early treatment, uncredited)
Cinematographer   Ted McCord
Composer   Max Steiner
Cast   Joan Crawford, Zachary Scott, Sydney Greenstreet, David Brian, Gladys George
Studio   Warner Brothers, 1949
Runtime   94 minutes

A literary scout had first brought Wilder's *Flamingo Road* to the attention of Warner Brothers upon its publication in 1942, but no action followed, as its theme of state corruption did not sit well with wartime politics. A stage version written by Wilder and his wife failed badly in New York in March 1946, but nevertheless Jack Warner was eventually persuaded to purchase the screen rights the following October. An early treatment was developed by Richard Brooks and Ranald MacDougall, and author Wilder was finally brought on board to finish the screenplay.

While Joan Crawford and Zachary Taylor are exemplary, the show is stolen by Sydney Greenstreet, whose portrayal of Wilder's corrupt, power-crazed sheriff Titus Semple, tinged with hints of sexual repression, is one of the best of his career. (Robertson)

The last of three contributions by Michael Curtiz, and Edmund North's second of two.

Reference   Selby

Flamingo Road

A NEW NOVEL BY THE AUTHOR OF
"GOD HAS A LONG FACE"

ROBERT WILDER

PUTNAM

LEAVE HER TO HEAVEN

BEN AMES WILLIAMS

Publisher   Boston: Houghton, Mifflin, 1944

Ben Ames Williams' biggest popular success came in 1944 with the publication of *Leave Her to Heaven,* a dark psychological tale that received poor reviews but spent much of the year on the bestseller lists and remained in print for many years after. The film rights were purchased by Twentieth Century-Fox upon publication.

The author's first of two contributions.

Orange-red cloth with titles in black at the front board and spine, no topstain. Binding measures 2.3 centimeters from board to board. Title page shows a date of 1944 (removed for later printings), with book title in orange and a half-title page both before and after the title page. No statement of edition or later printings on the copyright page. Front flap shows a price of $2.50 at the top right corner, followed by a plot summary, ending with "A Literary Guild Selection" and the "Wartime Book" logo at the bottom right corner. Rear flap shows a full-color portrait of the artist with an artist credit for Arthur Pope below it, then a short biographical note. The artwork from the front panel and spine wraps around to the rear panel, overlaid with a quote from the author about the book. A variant binding has been noted, with all book points the same, except that the binding measures three centimeters from board to board, the cloth is a more muted orange, titles on the front board are in blind and spine titles in gilt, the publisher's name ("H. M. / CO.") does not appear at the foot of the spine, there is no half-title page after the title page, book title is in black on the title page, there is no list of the author's previous books opposite the title page, and a red topstain is present. A book club edition and many later printings have been noted, and all are easily identifiable by the lack a date on the title page.

LEAVE HER TO HEAVEN

JOHN M. STAHL

Screenwriter	Jo Swerling
Cinematographer	Leon Shamroy
Composer	Alfred Newman
Cast	Gene Tierney, Cornel Wilde, Jeanne Crain, Vincent Price, Mary Philips, Ray Collins, Gene Lockhart
Studio	Twentieth Century-Fox, 1945
Runtime	110 minutes

A Technicolor melodrama infused with film noir pathology, John M. Stahl's *Leave Her to Heaven* combines vivid visuals with a coldly passionate performance from Gene Tierney to create a memorable femme fatale. Cornel Wilde's Richard is doomed the moment that Tierney's Ellen fixes her icy blue stare on him and mentions his likeness to her beloved, recently deceased father. Stahl suggests the force of that love in Ellen's expressionistic horseback ride to scatter her father's ashes, but the scene in which Ellen impassively puts on her sunglasses and watches Richard's crippled brother drown in an idyllic Maine lake powerfully communicates her utter lack of compassion. (Bozzola)

One of the most popular films of 1945, *Leave Her to Heaven* earned Tierney her sole Best Actress Oscar nomination, while Leon Shamroy won the Oscar for his striking color photography.

Director John M. Stahl's only contribution, and one of only two color films noir from the 1940s with literary sources.

Reference   Selby, Silver and Ward

THE STRANGE WOMAN

BEN AMES WILLIAMS

Publisher   Boston: Houghton, Mifflin, 1944

In a literary career that lasted from the 1910s into the 1950s, Ben Ames Williams became one of the most popular novelists and short story writers in America, his work being the basis for some fourteen movies. He was born in Macon, Mississippi, on March 7, 1889, and was educated in Massachusetts and in Cardiff, Wales, where his father worked as the American Consul. After graduating from Dartmouth, he went to work as a reporter at the *Boston American*, by which time he had sold a few short stories and serials, principally to *All-Story Magazine*. He would continue to write stories for magazines for the rest of his life, notably the *Saturday Evening Post* and *Colliers*. All told, over thirty novels and four hundred short stories were published in his lifetime. His varied output included hunting and fishing stories, historical fiction, mysteries, and sea stories. Much of his fiction was set in Maine, and toward the end of his career he became more interested in sprawling historical novels. *The Strange Woman* combined the author's interest in history and female psychopathology, making it something of a nineteenth-century companion to *Leave Her to Heaven*.

The second of two contributions by Williams.

Gray cloth (mixture of black and white thread, giving a gray effect) with titles in brown at the front board and spine. Maroon topstain. Title page shows a date of 1941 (removed for later printings), with no statement of edition or later printings on the copyright page. Front flap shows a price of $2.75 at the top right corner, followed by a plot summary. Rear flap is an advertisement for *Come Spring* by Ben Ames Williams, followed by five blurbs. Rear panel is devoted to a biography of Ames, with a color photo of the author at the top (design credit at the bottom edge reading, "Kodachrome by Emily Henry Bush"), followed by one paragraph of text.

THE STRANGE WOMAN

EDGAR G. ULMER

Screenwriter	Herb Meadow, Hunt Stromberg, Edgar G. Ulmer
Cinematographer	Lucien Andriot
Composer	Carmen Dragon
Cast	Hedy Lamarr, George Sanders, Louis Hayward, Gene Lockhart, Hillary Brooke, Rhys Williams
Studio	United Artists, 1946
Runtime	100 minutes

The directing experience for *The Strange Woman* was something of a luxury for Edgar G. Ulmer, who was used to low budgets and fast shooting schedules. His childhood friend Hedy Lamarr, who produced the film and played the lead, insisted that he direct her in her first outing away from MGM. This brought him decent actors, a strong script based on a bestselling novel, a fine cameraman (Lucien Andriot), and a reasonable budget and shooting schedule. The result is one of his most engaging works, a wonderfully rich, well-acted noir melodrama. Set in Bangor, Maine, in 1824, Ulmer successfully portrays Lamarr as more than just a sexual temptress—she's an interloper among the rich, an irresistible vixen whose "psychopathology" masks her attempts to subvert the rigid class system of a small New England town. (Gallagher)

Ulmer's fourth of five contributions.

Reference   Selby

The
Strange Woman

*"For the lips of a strange woman drop honey,
And her mouth is smoother than oil."—Proverbs.*

Ben Ames Williams

NONE SO BLIND

MITCHELL A. WILSON

Publisher   New York: Simon and Schuster, 1945

Born on June 17, 1913, Mitchell A. Wilson was an American novelist and nonfiction writer. Prior to becoming an author, he was a research scientist and instructor in physics at the university level. Not surprisingly, invention, and the ethical problems of modern atomic science were the subjects for some of his writing.

At the start of his writing career, Wilson collaborated with screenwriter Abraham Polonsky on a mystery novel titled *The Goose is Cooked*, written under the joint pseudonym of Emmett Grogan. Wilson's first of five subsequent novels was *Footsteps Behind Her*, published by Simon and Schuster in 1941.

Of Wilson's novel, *None So Blind*, filmmaker Jean Renoir remarked: "The theme was that of solitude, one of the great preoccupations of our time. Men sickened by our mass-produced civilization are struggling to escape from the crowd. Solitude is richer for the fact that it does not exist. The void is peopled with ghosts, and they are ghosts from our past. They are very strong; strong enough to shape the present in their image." (Renoir)

The author's only contribution, and only film credit.

Orange cloth with spine titles and rule in gilt against a purple background, navy blue topstain. Title page printed in orange, black and reverse, and shows a date of 1945, with "PUBLISHED BY SIMON AND SCHUSTER, INC." stated on the copyright page. Front flap shows a price of $2.50 at the bottom right corner, and contains a plot summary, which continues to the end of the rear flap. Rear panel is devoted to a short biography of the author.

THE WOMAN ON THE BEACH

JEAN RENOIR

Screenwriter   Frank Davis, Jean Renoir, Michael Hogan
Cinematographer   Leo Tover, Harry Wild
Composer   Hanns Eisler
Cast   Joan Bennett, Robert Ryan, Charles Bickford, Nan Leslie, Walter Sande, Irene Ryan, Glenn Vernon
Studio   RKO, 1947
Alternate Titles   Desirable Woman (working title)
Runtime   71 minutes

In his book, *My Life and My Films*, Jean Renoir eloquently sums up his feelings about *The Woman on the Beach*: "It was the sort of avant-garde film which would have found its niche a quarter of a century earlier, between *Nosferatu the Vampire* and *Caligari*, but it had no success with American audiences. Worse still, it thoroughly displeased the RKO bosses. *The Woman on the Beach* marked the finish of my Hollywood adventure. I never made another film in an American studio. It was not only that particular failure that was held against me. Darryl F. Zanuck, who knew something about directors, summed up my case. 'Renoir,' he said, 'has a lot of talent, but he's not one of us.'"

Renoir's only contribution, and screenwriter Michael Hogan's second of two.

Reference   Selby, Lyons

None
So
Blind

None
So Blind

a novel by

MITCHELL
WILSON

SIMON AND
SCHUSTER

TUCKER'S PEOPLE

IRA WOLFERT

Publisher   New York: L.B. Fischer, 1943

Ira Wolfert studied journalism at Columbia University, and became a newspaper columnist for *The New York Post* upon graduation in 1930. His experience as a sportswriter served him well several years down the road, as he was able to converse easily with soldiers during his years as a war correspondent during World War II, gaining insight into the conflict that eluded many other writers. In 1943, he wrote his first novel, *Tucker's People,* his first novel, based loosely on the life and times of mobster Dutch Schultz, praised as one of the finest and most realistic crime novels of its day. The same year would see the publication of two nonfiction accounts drawn from his wartime experiences, *Torpedo 8* and *The Battle of the Solomons*, the latter winning him the Pulitzer Prize. In 1948, he co-wrote the screenplay for the film adaptation of *Tucker's People* with Abraham Polonsky.

Wolfert's only venture into crime fiction, and his only contribution.

Salmon cloth with a small white leaf decoration at the front board, with the same white titles and decoration on the spine panel. No topstain. Title page shows a date of 1943, with "FIRST EDITION" stated on the copyright page. Front flap shows a price of $3.00 at both the top and bottom right corner (some copies noted only at the top), and contains a plot summary, which continues to the rear flap, ending with the publisher's name and address. Rear panel shows a biography of the author (with no photo), ending with the "Buy Bonds" insignia.

There are two variants of the jacket. The "A" variant, which precedes, is shown at the right. The "B" variant was a cheap edition, with an illustrated jacket and a lowered price on the front flap (see *Appendix A: Secondary Books*).

FORCE OF EVIL

ABRAHAM POLONSKY

Screenwriter   Abraham Polonsky, Ira Wolfert
Cinematographer   George Barnes
Composer   David Raksin
Cast   John Garfield, Beatrice Pearson, Thomas Gomez, Howard Chamberlain, Roy Roberts,
                      Marie Windsor, Paul Fix, Stanley Prager, Barry Kelley, Paul McVey
Studio   MGM, 1948
Alternate Titles   The Numbers Racket, Tucker's People, The Story of Tucker's People (all US working titles)
Runtime   78 minutes

After penning the original screenplay for the highly successful *Body and Soul,* Abraham Polonsky was offered the opportunity to direct. Polonsky and John Garfield, who shared a passion for left-leaning social concerns, decided that *Tucker's People* would make an excellent source for a crime film with a strong radical/socialist element. Though the resulting film, re-titled *Force of Evil,* makes use of only about a third of Wolfert's novel, its strong characters and general spirit were drawn entirely from the original text. The film was a critical success in England, and though it was unsuccessful in the US, it would be incorrect to say that its message was ignored—Polonsky and Garfield were blacklisted in 1951, after both refused to testify before the HUAC. Polonsky did not write or direct again under his own name until 1969.

Polonsky's only contribution as a director, and his second of three as a screenwriter.

Reference   Selby, Silver and Ward

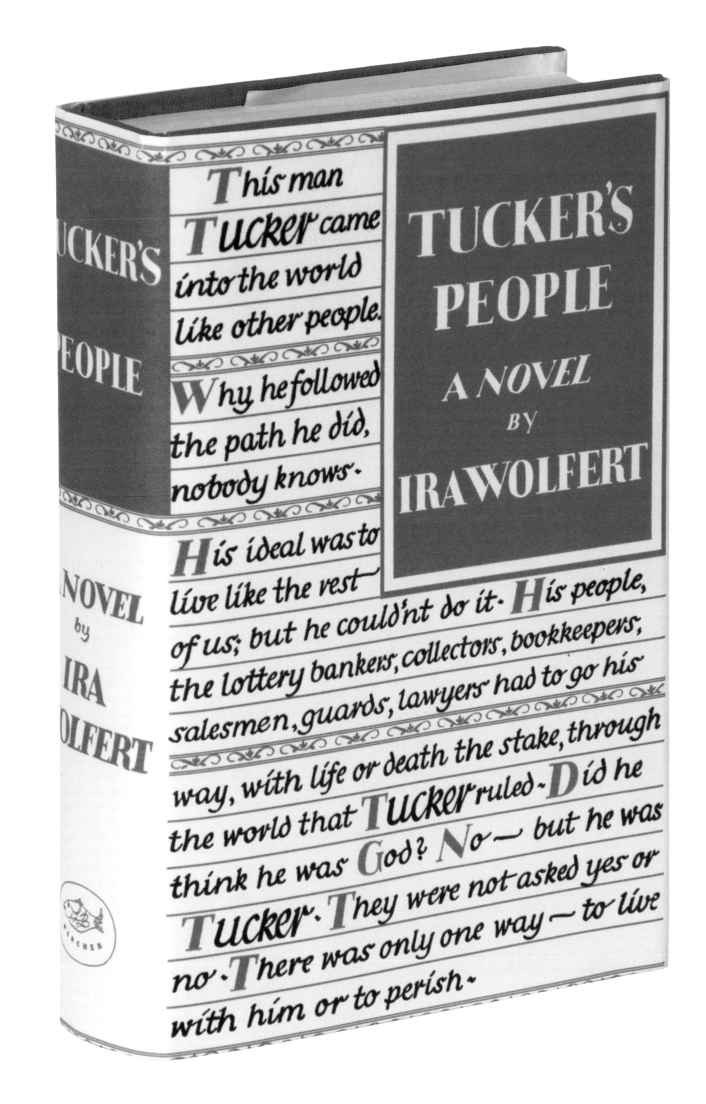

TUCKER'S PEOPLE

A NOVEL

BY

IRA WOLFERT

This man Tucker came into the world like other people. Why he followed the path he did, nobody knows.

His ideal was to live like the rest of us; but he could'nt do it. His people, the lottery bankers, collectors, bookkeepers, salesmen, guards, lawyers had to go his way, with life or death the stake, through the world that Tucker ruled. Did he think he was God? No — but he was Tucker. They were not asked yes or no. There was only one way — to live with him or to perish.

WHISTLE STOP

MARITTA WOLFF

Publisher   New York: Random House, 1941

American author Maritta Wolff was born in 1918 in Grass Lake, Michigan, and her first novel was *Whistle Stop*, written while she was still in college. Her manuscript for the book won the Avery Hopwood Award (a major annual scholarship given by the University of Michigan), gaining the attention of Random House, who published the book in 1941. *Whistle Stop* was called by Sinclair Lewis "The most important novel of the year," and in their 1941 issue on books, TIME magazine placed Wolff in good company, saying, "Two of the most promising of the year's new writers were Maritta M. Wolff and Eudora Welty."

The author's first of two contributions.

Black cloth with red-and-white paper labels at the front board and spine. Red topstain. "FIRST PRINTING" stated at the top of the copyright page, with no mention of later printings. Front flap of the jacket was multi-priced by the publisher, with the only noted price being $2.50 at the top middle. This is followed by a mention of the book being the winner of the Avery Hopwood Award, followed by a plot summary and four quotes from the Hopwood judges. Rear flap is an advertisement for other Random House books , advertising in three sections: American authors, English and Continental authors and "Lifetime" publications (i.e., classics), with a final one-line advertisement for the Modern Library and Modern Library Giant series. Rear panel contains a biography of Wolff, with her photo at the top left.

WHISTLE STOP

LÉONIDE MOGUY

Screenwriter   Philip Yordan
Cinematographer   Russell Metty
Composer   Dimitri Tiomkin
Cast   George Raft, Ava Gardner, Victor McLaglen, Tom Conway, Jorja Curtright, Jane Nigh
Studio   United Artists, 1946
Runtime   85 minutes

Born on April 1, 1914, in Chicago to Polish immigrants, Philip Yordan was an extremely successful Hollywood writer and "script polisher." After completing his higher education at the University of Illinois, and Kent College of Law in Chicago, Yordan made his way to Hollywood and worked as a screenwriter for the rest of his life. During the McCarthy era, he served as a front for many of his blacklisted colleagues, living in Paris much of the time. He reportedly maintained "a basement full of cubicles" there, where he and other writers would turn out screenplays. An example of this work was the 1954 film *Johnny Guitar,* where Yordan's contribution to the screenplay was actually written by Ben Maddow, whom Yordan fronted for.

While considered minor in the pantheon of Ava Gardner films, *Whistle Stop* was actually the turning point for the young actress. On contract to MGM, her career was at a standstill. Sidney Guilaroff, Gardner's hairdresser and longtime friend, said, "MGM didn't even know what they had. They thought nothing of her. She just [played] parts, little things—a girl, a hatcheck girl. Stock shots that didn't matter a thing." In a loanout to United Artists for *Whistle Stop*, where she played opposite George Raft, her luminous presence in the film caught the eye of producers at Universal. She was cast in *The Killers* the same year, and catapulted to stardom. (Hannsberry)

Director Léonide Moguy's only contribution, and Yordan's third of seven.

Reference   Selby, Lyons

MARITTA M. WOLFF

WHISTLE STOP

W

WHISTLE-STOP

WHISTLE-STOP

BY MARITTA M. WOLFF

1941

WINNER OF THE CURRENT AVERY HOPWOOD AWARD.

RANDOM HOUSE

NIGHT SHIFT

MARITTA WOLFF

Publisher   New York: Random House, 1942

The author's second of two contributions.

Navy blue cloth with white and gilt titles at the spine, blue topstain. "FIRST PRINTING" stated at the top of the copyright page. Front flap shows a price of $2.75 at the top right corner, followed by a plot summary. Rear flap contains an author biography, and the rear panel is a "message from the author" about the war effort, ending with a "Buy Bonds" advertisement.

THE MAN I LOVE

RAOUL WALSH

Screenwriter   Catherine Turney, Jo Pagano, W.R. Burnett (uncredited)
Cinematographer   Sid Hickox
Composer   Max Steiner
Cast   Ida Lupino, Robert Alda, Andrea King, Bruce Bennett, Martha Vickers, Dolores Moran, John Ridgley,
                    Don McGuire, Tony Romano, Alan Hale, Warren Douglas, Craig Stevens, William Edmunds
Studio   Warner Brothers, 1947
Alternate Titles   Night Shift (working title), Why Was I Born? (working title)
Runtime   96 minutes

The Man I Love was originally titled Night Shift (after the novel on which it was based), and was set to star Ann Sheridan and Humphrey Bogart. Script rewrites led to a new title, Why Was I Born? before Warner Brothers finally settled on The Man I Love, both of which are names of George and Ira Gershwin songs used in the film. Scheduling conflicts led the producers to recast Ida Lupino and Robert Alda in the lead roles.

The Hays Office wasn't happy with certain elements of the first draft script, objecting to the story's "low moral tone... of adultery and illicit sex" and found many specific things that had to go, including a reference to a slot machine, a suggestion that a cop was crooked, and scenes that "encroach too closely on the intricacies of married life." As a result, the film turned out to be more a matter of atmosphere than plot, with late-night jam sessions, underworld characters, and steamy songs—all making for a memorably moody experience. (Arnold)

Director Martin Scorsese has cited The Man I Love as the principal inspiration for his 1977 melodrama, New York, New York.

Raoul Walsh's third of five contributions, W.R. Burnett's last of five, Catherine Turney's second of three, and Jo Pagano's first of two.

Reference   Selby, Silver and Ward

NIGHT
SHIFT

by MARITTA
WOLFF

NIGHT
SHIFT

MARITTA WOLFF

A NOVEL BY AUTHOR OF · WHISTLE STOP

Salter

RANDOM HOUSE

THE BLACK CURTAIN

CORNELL WOOLRICH

Publisher   New York: Simon and Schuster, 1941

The Black Curtain was the second of the "black books" by Cornell Woolrich, and the second to be published by Simon and Schuster. By far the shortest of his novels, it lacks the episodic structure, formal intricacy, and heavy-handed plot manipulations of *The Bride Wore Black*. But its premise is all but tailor-made for the Woolrich treatment and its atmospherics and coloration are pure noir. In May of 1941, part of a decrepit building collapses on a man walking along the street. He emerges from the rubble with no memory of who he is, and embarks on a dark journey to find out. For most writers doing an amnesia story, the second blow on the head would have been the end, and the protagonist would have begun the slow process of getting to know his wife again and picking up the threads of his former existence. For Woolrich, however this is only the beginning. The falling beam that has restored the man to his original self has also wiped out all memory of who and what he had been since the first blow. (Nevins)

The first of Woolrich's fourteen contributions.

Red cloth with "Inner Sanctum Mystery" logo in white at the center of the front board, with titles in white at the spine, along with a design in black (between the book title and author name) resembling a series of stylized question marks. Black topstain. Title page shows a date of 1941, with no statement of edition or later printings on the copyright page. Front flap shows a price of $2.00 at the bottom right corner, and contains a plot summary that continues to the end of the rear flap. Rear panel advertises two other books by the publisher, *The Trial of Vincent Doon* by Will Oursler and *The Town is Full of Rumors* by Ruth and Alexander Wilson.

STREET OF CHANCE

JACK HIVELY

Screenwriter	Garrett Fort
Cinematographer	Theodor Sparkuhl
Composer	David Buttolph
Cast	Burgess Meredith, Claire Trevor, Louise Platt, Sheldon Leonard, Frieda Inescort, Jerome Cowan, Adeline De Walt Reynolds, Arthur Loft, Clancy Cooper, Paul Phillips, Keith Richards, Ann Doran, Cliff Clark, Edwin Maxwell
Studio	Paramount, 1942
Runtime	74 minutes

Universal bought the rights to *The Black Curtain* for $2225 shortly after publication. *Street of Chance* became the first film noir to be based on a Woolrich mystery, and conversely, it was the earliest Woolrich mystery novel to be made into a film noir. Rich in noir visuals, the film is notable for Theodor Sparkuhl's cinematography—influenced by German Expressionism and French poetic realism—and David Buttolph's moody jazz score. And while amnesia was a relatively well-used plot trick in crime literature by 1942, *Street of Chance* was one of the first films to deal with it.

The story remained a popular one, with a thirty-minute version on the CBS radio series *Suspense,* with Cary Grant and Lurene Tuttle, as well as a one-hour television adaptation on *The Alfred Hitchcock Hour* in 1962.

The only contribution by director Jack Hively, and the third of four by screenwriter Garrett Fort.

Reference   Selby, Silver and Ward, Lyons

THE BLACK CURTAIN

CORNELL WOOLRICH

AUTHOR OF "THE BRIDE WORE BLACK"

AN INNER SANCTUM MYSTERY

AN INNER SANCTUM MYSTERY

SIMON AND SCHUSTER

THE BLACK CURTAIN

CORNELL WOOLRICH

Black Alibi

Cornell Woolrich

Publisher   New York: Simon and Schuster, 1942

In April of 1942, Simon and Schuster published the last of its three Cornell Woolrich novels, *Black Alibi*. It marked the first time the author had set a full-length work of fiction in Latin America since his 1930 autobiographical novel, *A Young Man's Heart*. Plot elements are borrowed from both his 1938 pulp novella, "Mystery in Room 913," and the 1939 short story, "The Street of Jungle Death," with the six-part structure owing a debt to *The Bride Wore Black*. The setting has been moved to Ciudad Real, the third largest city in South America, and the wild animal borrowed from "The Street of Jungle Death" has been changed from a leopard to a jaguar. Press agent Jerry Manning persuades his most important and only client, nightclub entertainer Kiki Walker, that it will give her career a boost if she is seen and photographed strolling placidly along the fashionable Alameda with a jaguar on a leash. The mood changes abruptly when the animal leaps out into the street from the sidewalk café where Kiki has stopped for a Martini Seco and bolts into the Callejon de las Sombras, the labyrinth of alleys between the Alameda and the Plaza. The first part of the novel closes with an unsubtle hint that the vanished animal will return—and return again. (Nevins)

The second of Woolrich's fourteen contributions.

Black cloth with titles in gilt at the spine, ending with the "An Inner Sanctum Mystery" logo. Red topstain. Title page shows a date of 1942, with no statement of edition or later printings on the copyright page. Front flap shows a price of $2.00 at the lower right corner, and contains a plot summary that continues to the middle of the rear flap, ending with "A NOTE ABOUT THE AUTHOR" and three paragraphs of text. Rear panel is devoted to reviews of previous titles titled, "What the Reviewers Say About / CORNELL WOOLRICH," followed by seven reviews for *The Bride Wore Black* and seven reviews for *The Black Curtain*, ending with "INNER SANCTUM MYSTERY."

The Leopard Man

Jacques Tourneur (produced by Val Lewton)

Screenwriter   Ardel Wray, Edward Dein
Cinematographer   Robert de Grasse
Composer   Roy Webb
Cast   Dennis O'Keefe, Margo, Jean Brooks, Isabel Jewell, James Bell, Margaret Landry
Studio   RKO, 1943
Runtime   66 minutes

RKO Radio Pictures bought the screen rights to *Black Alibi* for $5175 and assigned the project to producer Val Lewton, who made a series of remarkably consistent and subtly drawn horror films between 1942 and his death in 1951. *The Leopard Man* was shot in early 1943, in thirty days and on a budget of less than $150,000, with the Spanish actress Margo in the role of castanet dancer Clo-Clo (a cleaned-up version of the near-prostitute in Cornell Woolrich's novel). The film story is faithful to Woolrich's novel, moving the locale from South America to New Mexico, and reversing Woolrich's original substitution of a jaguar back to a black leopard. The story transitions from character-to-character and murder-to-murder in a way that predicts the next Lewton/Tourneur effort, *The Seventh Victim* a film would be much more dreamlike and abstract in its content. Also, two of the victims in *The Leopard Man*, actresses Isabel Jewell and Jean Brooks, would return as the co-stars of *The Seventh Victim*. Lewton and Tourneur both later repudiated *The Leopard Man*, as they saw it as the most explicit and voyeuristic of their efforts, but it remains a triumph of style, and meets the high standard that Lewton set for all his productions.

The third of producer Val Lewton's five contributions, director Tourneur's third of six, and screenwriter Ardel Wray's second of two.

Reference   Selby

Cornell Woolrich

BLACK ALIBI

A NOVEL OF STALKING
TERROR BY THE AUTHOR OF
"THE BLACK CURTAIN"

AN INNER SANCTUM MYSTERY

PHANTOM LADY

CORNELL WOOLRICH WRITING AS WILLIAM IRISH

Publisher   Philadelphia: J.B. Lippincott, 1942

In 1942, Cornell Woolrich met with longtime editor Lee Wright at Simon and Schuster to discuss publication of his novel, *Phantom Lady*, which had just been successfully serialized as *Phantom Alibi* in *Detective Fiction Weekly* magazine. After hearing a criticism over just one paragraph in the manuscript, Woolrich burst into tears (apparently not an unfamiliar response), and exclaimed, "I knew you wouldn't like it, I knew it wasn't good enough for you!" He promptly marched the manuscript around the corner to his former patron Whit Burnett, who by this time helmed *Story* magazine, and had just begun operating an imprint called the "Story Press" under the aegis of J.B. Lippincott. Burnett agreed to publish the book.

Having released three suspense novels under his own name in less than two years, and with more on the way, Woolrich was in danger of glutting the market with his material. If more stories and novels were to be published, a pseudonym would be needed. In a discussion with Burnett and Frederic Dannay (one half of the team that wrote as Ellery Queen), Woolrich suggested a surname based on nationality, "like English, French, Welsh, Irish..." and Burnett broke in and raised his hand, saying, "I'll buy that!" Thus, in two minutes, half the new byline was born. Dannay wrote, "The first name was even more quickly arrived at—a common name, intentionally chosen to keep the emphasis and memory value on the surname."

The third of Woolrich's fourteen contributions, and a Haycraft Queen cornerstone.

Blue cloth with titles in black at the spine, orange-red topstain. No statement of edition or later printings on the copyright page. Front flap shows a price of $2.00 at the bottom right corner, and contains a plot summary. Rear flap is an advertisement for *No Crime for a Lady* by Zelda Popkin. Rear panel advertises four "Recent and Forthcoming Mysteries" by the publisher, beginning with *Death on the Aisle* by Frances and Richard Lockridge and ending with *Death Rings a Bell* by Cortland Fitzimmons, ending with the publisher's name and address.

PHANTOM LADY

ROBERT SIODMAK

Screenwriter   Bernard C. Schoenfeld
Cinematographer   Woody Bredell
Cast   Franchot Tone, Ella Raines, Alan Curtis, Aurora, Thomas Gomez, Elisha Cook, Jr., Fay Helm,
                      Andrew Tombes, Regis Toomey, Joseph Crehan, Doris Lloyd, Virginia Brissac, Milburn Stone
Studio   Universal, 1944
Runtime   87 minutes

Phantom Lady marked the point at which studios stopped thinking of Cornell Woolrich in terms of medium-budget thrillers, and began recognizing the potential of his fiction for "A" pictures. Although Bernard C. Schoenfeld's screen adaptation turns the novel's murderer into a stereotypical Mad Artist, its visual style is very much in harmony with the bleak Woolrich spirit. Robert Porfirio credits Siodmak and cinematropher Woody Bredell with capturing on film "the essential ingredients of Woolrich's world." The film's best-known sequences—the cat-and-mouse between Ella Raines and Andrew Tombes on the Third Avenue elevated platform, and the jam session where orgiastic shots of Cook's drum solo are intercut with Raines' "wordless sexual innuendoes"—are based quite faithfully on scenes in the novel. (Nevins)

The first of Siodmak's ten contributions, and the first of two for screenwriter Bernard C. Schoenfeld.

Reference   Selby, Silver and Ward, Lyons

DEADLINE AT DAWN
CORNELL WOOLRICH WRITING AS WILLIAM IRISH

Publisher   Philadelphia: J.B. Lippincott, 1944

In his posthumously published autobiography, *Blues of a Lifetime*, Cornell Woolrich recalls coming out of a movie theater in 1925, feeling "lonely, standing around at a loss after the crowds started to thin out and go home. But the lights continued to blaze down on the empty, naked-looking sidewalks. I remember how little particles of brightness like mica, fused into the cement of the sidewalk, twinkled under the Paramount Theater marquee." Nineteen years later the clock on top of the Paramount would become virtually a living character in *Deadline at Dawn*. In fact, Woolrich's submitted the earliest version of the story, in 1941, as, "The Clock on the Paramount." (Nevins)

The fifth of Woolrich's fourteen contributions.

Green cloth with titles and design in yellow at the spine (book title is in reverse, author and publisher's names are not). No topstain. No statement of edition or later printings on the copyright page. Front flap shows a price of $2.00 at the bottom right corner, and contains a plot summary. Rear flap is an advertisement for Irish's previous book by the publisher, *Phantom Lady*. Rear flap is devoted to an advertisement for Lippincott's "Main Line Mysteries," with the series' trademark skull-and-crossbones logo at the top of the page, and publisher's information at the bottom.

DEADLINE AT DAWN
HAROLD CLURMAN

Screenwriter   Clifford Odets
Cinematographer   Nicholas Musuraca
Composer   Hanns Eisler
Cast   Paul Lukas, Susan Hayward, Bill Williams, Joseph Calleia, Osa Massen, Lola Lane, Jerome Cowan, Marvin Miller, Roman Bohnen, Steven Geray, Joe Sawyer, Constance Worth, Joseph Crehan
Studio   RKO, 1946
Runtime   83 minutes

Francis Nevins points out that while the film adaptation for *Deadline at Dawn* was straightforward, its creative team came almost entirely from the left-wing theater movement of the 1930s. Director Harold Clurman and screenwriter Clifford Odets were both key figures in New York's Group Theater during the Depression, producer Adrian Scott was blacklisted during the McCarthy trials, and Marxist composer Hanns Eisler was commissioned by RKO on Odets' recommendation to write the musical score. Clurman was a co-founder of the Group Theater, and in 1935 urged Odets to write his first original play, *Awake and Sing!* Ten years later, Odets tabled loftier projects to write this screenplay for Clurman as a return favor.

While Clurman would later dismiss the script for the film as being "of minimal interest," *Deadline at Dawn* remains one of the most fascinating New York City films noir. Odets was at his best writing dialogue, and his transformation of Woolrich's minimalist text into the bizarre intellectual banter of the film (particularly in the case of Susan Hayward's self-possessed character) is strange and unforgettable.

Clurman's only contribution (and only Hollywood credit), and Odets' first of three.

Reference   Selby, Silver and Ward, Lyons

William Irish
Author of "PHANTOM LADY"

Dead-
line
at
Dawn

MYSTERIES
DEADLINE

A
Story
Press
Book

Lippincott

Deadline
at Dawn

P.K.Jackson

THE BLACK ANGEL

CORNELL WOOLRICH

Publisher   Garden City: Doubleday, Doran, 1943

After his break with Simon and Schuster, Cornell Woolrich had begun to publish titles under his new William Irish pseudonym, but needed a new home to continue the "black book" series under his own name. He found it in Doubleday, a well-established publisher of mysteries under its Crime Club imprint. The first of the two Woolrich novels issued by Doubleday was *The Black Angel,* the author's only book narrated throughout in first person by a woman. Borrowing heavily from his own work as he often did, Woolrich combined elements of *Phantom Lady* (a race against the clock), *The Bride Wore Black* (a subtly deranged woman working her way through a "death list" in her address book) and even the basic plot premise of one of his early romances, *Manhattan Love Song.*

Apart from the film version, *Black Angel* was adapted into three separate radio dramas and a one-hour television play. Woolrich's work diary indicates that at one time he was approached about turning the novel into an opera libretto, to have been titled, *The Tape-Recording Angel.* (Nevins)

The sixth of Woolrich's fourteen contributions.

Black cloth with the Crime Club "gun" logo at the center of the front board, and the "ribbon" logo in silver along the top edge. Spine titles and logos in silver and reverse. No topstain. Title page shows a date of 1943, with "FIRST EDITION" stated on the copyright page (removed for later printings). Front flap shows a price of "T.B.A. / Price, $2.00" at the top right corner, followed by a plot summary, ending with a disclaimer about serialization, and a printer's code of 2711-42 at the bottom right corner. Rear flap is an advertisement for War Bonds. Rear panel advertises five "Crime Club" titles, beginning with *Echo of a Bomb* by Van Siller and ending with *Terror by Twilight* by Kathleen Moore Knight.

BLACK ANGEL

ROY WILLIAM NEILL

Screenwriter	Roy Chanslor
Cinematographer	Paul Ivano
Composer	Frank Skinner
Cast	Dan Duryea, June Vincent, Peter Lorre, Broderick Crawford, Constance Dowling, Wallace Ford, Hobart Cavanaugh, Freddie Steele, John Phillips, Ben Bard, Junius Matthews, Marion Martin, Archie Twitchell, Maurice St. Clair, Vilova, Robert Williams
Studio	Universal, 1946
Runtime	83 minutes

Director Roy William Neill's only contribution. An extremely prolific director whose career began in the silent era, Neill was best known for the many *Sherlock Holmes* films he made with Basil Rathbone in the 1940s. *Black Angel* was his last directorial effort, and he died three months after its premiere in New York City.

Novelist-screenwriter Roy Chanslor's second and final contribution. Chanslor was a noted writer of revisionist Westerns, probably best remembered by cinephiles as the author of novels like *Johnny Guitar* and *The Ballad of Cat Ballou,* both of which were made into excellent (and similarly revisionist) technicolor westerns in 1954 and 1965, respectively.

Reference   Selby, Silver and Ward, Lyons

A CRIME CLUB SELECTION

CORNELL
WOOLRICH

The
Black
Angel

BY THE AUTHOR OF
The Bride Wore Black

THE BLACK
PATH OF FEAR

CORNELL WOOLRICH

Publisher   Garden City: Doubleday, Doran, 1944

For his fifth novel in the "black book" series, and second to be published by Doubleday, Cornell Woolrich drew from two earlier short stories, "Annabelle Gets Across" (*Breezy Stories,* 1935) and "Havana Night" (*Flynn's Detective Magazine,* 1942). From the former, he used the idea of a protagonist being drawn into a web of intrigue by wishing to return an item to its rightful owner, and from the latter (the major source), a story about an American lost in the labyrinth of a foreign city's bizarre and dream-like back alleys while attempting to aid a gangster's wife who has fled her confines. (Nevins)

The seventh of Woolrich's fourteen contributions.

Charcoal-gray cloth with the "Crime Club Selection" ribbon logo in black at the top of the front board, and titles in black on the spine, beginning at the top with the "Crime Club Selection" abbreviated ribbon logo, then the title, author, and Crime Club symbol and name. No topstain. "FIRST EDITION" is stated at the bottom of the copyright page. Front flaps shows a price of $2.00 at the top right corner, followed by the Wartime Standards logo and a plot summary. Rear flap shows an advertisement in red and black for War Bonds, with a cut-out address form at the bottom. Rear panel advertises four books, beginning with *Design in Diamonds* by Kathleen Moore Knight and ending with *Jenny Kissed Me* by Ruth Fenisong, then a printer's code 746-44 at the bottom right corner.

THE CHASE

ARTHUR RIPLEY

Screenwriter   Philip Yordan
Cinematographer   Frank F. Planer
Composer   Michel Michelet
Cast   Robert Cummings, Michèle Morgan, Steve Cochran, Lloyd Corrigan, Jack Holt, Don Wilson,
                    Alex Minotis, Nina Koshetz, Yolanda Lacca, James Westerfield, Jimmy Ames, Peter Lorre
Studio   United Artists, 1946
Runtime   86 minutes

Playwright Philip Yordan and director Arthur Ripley elected to take the surreal route in adapting Cornell Woolrich's novel into an "A" picture, casting many of the novel's actual events into a a chaotic dream sequence that commands nearly half of the film, including the protagonist's dream of his own death. Noir critic Robert Porfirio ranks *The Chase* second only to Siodmak's *Phantom Lady* as a "cinematic equivalent of the dark, oppressive atmosphere of Woolrich, especially at the film's conclusion, which collapses the distinction between dream and reality; its eroticism, wherein sexual badgering leads to sexual abuse; its unprecedented elements, including the dreamed death of the hero; and its aspects of cruelty and ambivalence."

Arthur Ripley's second of two contributions, and Philip Yordan's fifth of seven.

Reference   Selby, Silver and Ward, Lyons

THE BLACK PATH OF FEAR

By the
author of
THE BLACK ANGEL

CORNELL WOOLRICH

THE DANCING DETECTIVE

CORNELL WOOLRICH WRITING AS WILLIAM IRISH

Publisher   Philadelphia: J.B. Lippincott, 1946

The Dancing Detective was the fourth "William Irish" book published under Lippincott's "Story Press" imprint, and its second collection of classic Cornell Woolrich stories from the pulps. History does not reveal who chose the eight Woolrich tales contained in the book, but it seems likely that Frederic Dannay was involved, as four of them were reprinted in *Ellery Queen Mystery Magazine*. Another of the stories, "Two Fellows in a Furnished Room," had appeared in *Detective Fiction Weekly* (February 8, 1941) as "He Looked Like Murder." One of Woolrich's most gripping thrillers, the story plays on what Francis Nevins calls the "did he or didn't he" scenario, here played out between two men living together in an apartment, one blaming the other for a dead girlfriend stuffed in the incinerator chute down the hall.

The ninth of Woolrich's fourteen contributions.

Beige cloth with titles and design in black at the spine, no topstain. "FIRST EDITION" stated at the center of the copyright page. Front flap shows a price of $2.00 at the bottom right corner, and contains a plot summary, ending with "A Story Press Book." Rear flap is an advertisement for *Deadline at Dawn*, and begins with three blurbs, followed by a four-paragraph plot summary, ending again with "A Story Press Book." Rear panel is an advertisement for the publisher's "Main Line Mystery" series of titles, ending with the publisher's name and city.

THE GUILTY

JOHN REINHARDT

Screenwriter   Robert R. Presnell, Sr.
Cinematographer   Henry Sharp
Composer   Rudy Schrager, Herschel Burke Gilbert (uncredited)
Cast   Bonita Granville, Don Castle, Wally Cassell, Regis Toomey, John Litel, Thomas E. Jackson,
                      Netta Packer, Oliver Blake, Caroline Andrews
Studio   Monogram, 1947
Runtime   71 minutes

Just after production of the Cornell Woolrich-based film *Fall Guy* was underway at the low-budget film studio Monogram in 1947, producer Jack Wrather began using the same facilities to adapt another "quickie" film version of a Woolrich story, "Two Fellows in a Furnished Room." Directing was German emigre John Reinhardt, from a screenplay by his frequent collaborator, "B" movie stalwart Robert R. Presnell, Sr. The screenplay adds some nice noir touches. The story is structured in flashback, long after the main events have taken place, with one of the characters telling his tale to a local bartender upon his return to town. The murdered girlfriend of Woolrich's story is here split into twin sisters, one good and one evil. The final noir twist, also a departure from the Woolrich story, is that the seemingly innocent narrator turns out to be the killer.

The first of four contributions by director John Reinhardt, and the first of three for screenwriter Robert Presnell, Sr.

Reference   Selby, Silver and Ward, Lyons

THE
DANCING
DETECTIVE

WILLIAM
IRISH

A Story Press Book

THE
DANCING
DETECTIVE

WILLIAM
IRISH

POOR BUTTERFLY

WILLIAM IRISH

AUTHOR OF "DEADLINE AT DAWN"

LIPPINCOTT

I Wouldn't Be in Your Shoes

Cornell Woolrich writing as William Irish

Publisher   Philadelphia: J.B. Lippincott, 1943

Cornell Woolrich's short story from this collection, "Nightmare," was originally published in *Argosy* magazine (March 1, 1941) under the title, "And so to Death." The story became an enduring Woolrich/Irish classic, and appeared once again several years later in another short story collection under the Woolrich name with the book titled after the story, *Nightmare* (Dodd, Mead, 1956).

"Nightmare" is one of many Woolrich/Irish stories that center on a crime committed during a protagonist's blackout, either from alcohol consumption or drug use. In the case of this story, alcohol is the culprit, and the blackout is recalled by the protagonist only in dreams, the details of which eventually lead him to the location and meaning of the original crime.

The tenth of Woolrich's fourteen contributions.

Light blue cloth with "A / STORY / PRESS / BOOK" stamped in pale green at the bottom right corner of the front board. A panel of pale green with the title in reverse at the spine, followed by the author's name and publisher in pale green. No topstain. "First Printing" stated on the lower half of the copyright page. Front flap shows a price of $2.00 at the lower right-hand corner, and contains a plot summary of the stories in the book. Rear flap is an advertisement for the William Irish title, *Phantom Lady,* followed by a plot summary of that book. Rear panel advertises three titles, *Phantom Lady, Hanged for a Sheep* by Frances and Richard Lockridge, and *The Yellow Violet* by Frances Crane," ending with the publisher's name and address.

Fear in the Night

Maxwell Shane

Screenwriter	Maxwell Shane
Cinematographer	Jack Greenhalgh
Composer	Rudy Schrager
Cast	Paul Kelly, DeForest Kelley, Ann Doran, Kay Scott, Robert Emmett Keane, Charles Victor
Studio	Paramount, 1947
Runtime	71 minutes

Cornell Woolrich's short story "Nightmare" was filmed as *Fear in the Night* in 1947, and again later in the American noir cycle as *Nightmare* (1956), with both versions written for the screen and directed by Maxwell Shane. In the first version, Shane reproduces the Woolrich "dream" sequence in an exceptionally stylish and expressionistic manner, where the protagonist is seemingly trapped in a five-sided room where the walls are all made of mirror glass.

Fear in the Night is notable for its location shooting in San Francisco, most notably the Commodore Hotel (then called the New Hotel Commodore) where DeForest Kelley's character lives. The Commodore was an institution in the city for over a hundred years (it was forty years old when the film was made), and converted to condominiums in 2006.

Maxwell Shane's directorial debut, and first of three contributions.

Reference   Selby, Silver and Ward, Lyons

William Irish

I wouldn't be in your shoes

A [...] PRESS BOOK

P. Jackson

AUTHOR OF THE MYSTERY SUCCESS
"PHANTOM LADY"

Lippincott

EYES THAT WATCH YOU

CORNELL WOOLRICH WRITING AS WILLIAM IRISH

Publisher   New York: Rinehart, 1952

Cornell Woolrich's short story, "All at Once, No Alice," was first published in *Argosy* magazine on March 2, 1940. It was one of two classic "annihilation stories" that the author penned within two months, the other being "Finger of Doom." Both have the same premise. A lonely young man has finally found the one right woman, but just prior to the consummation of their relationship, she vanishes into thin air. Everyone who apparently had known and seen the woman denies that she ever existed, and the police and other formal authorities to whom the young man frantically appeals can't find the slightest proof that she ever walked the earth. He is abandoned to maniacal despair by all but one lone-wolf cop who is willing to believe that the young man might just be telling the truth. One of the most powerful premises in noir literature, and one that's been used endlessly since.

This story was not collected until 1952, in the only hardcover publication of Woolrich's short fiction issued by Rinehart (under the William Irish pseudonym), *Eyes that Watch You*.

The eleventh of Woolrich's fourteen contributions.

Black cloth with titles in light blue and the publisher's "Murray Hill Mystery" logo (man in a trenchcoat, walking away) in a slightly deeper blue, both at the spine. No topstain. Publisher's device toward the bottom of the copyright page (removed for later printings). Front flap shows a price of $2.50 at the top right corner, followed by a plot summary, then a jacket design credit for Robert Cato, ending with the publisher's name and city. Rear flap is an advertisement for *The Big Sin* by Jack Webb, and the rear panel is an advertisement for *The Haploids* by Jerry Sohl, ending with the publisher's name and address.

THE RETURN OF THE WHISTLER

ROSS LEDERMAN

Screenwriter   Edward Bock, Maurice Tombragel
Cinematographer   Philip Tannura
Composer   Mischa Bakaleinikoff
Cast   Michael Duane, Lénore Aubert, Richard Lane, James Cardwell, Ann Shoemaker, Sarah Padden
Studio   Columbia, 1948
Runtime   60 minutes

The Whistler ran as a popular radio mystery program from 1942 to 1955, and was first adapted to film in 1945 by director William Castle. *The Whistler* film series was unique in that it was praised by viewers and critics alike. Richard Dix, the star of the first seven *Whistler* films, had been forced to retire after several heart attacks, and Columbia thought it could save the franchise by reworking the format, using obscure actors and stressing story values and suspense. To this end the Cornell Woolrich story, "All at Once, No Alice" was adapted on a "B" picture budget as the eighth (and last) of the films in the series, *The Return of the Whistler*. Only a few parts of the story's premise are retained, and while the translation is a bit on the light side, the noir look that has put all of the *Whistler* films in the noir cycle is nicely preserved. (Nevins)

Director Ross Lederman's second of two contributions, and screenwriter Edward Bock's last of three.

Reference   Selby, Lyons

302

EYES THAT WATCH YOU

William Irish

a murray hill mystery

NIGHT HAS A THOUSAND EYES

CORNELL WOOLRICH WRITING AS GEORGE HOPLEY

Publisher   New York: Farrar and Rinehart, 1945

The only Cornell Woolrich book published in 1945 was a novel titled *Night has a Thousand Eyes*. It was the author's longest and most ambitious work up to that date, and one of his most powerful. For reasons unknown, but probably due to the volume of Woolrich and Irish material on the market, the byline chosen for the book was a new one formed from the author's two middle names, George Hopley. In his 1967 memoir, *The Pulp Jungle,* crime author Frank Gruber wrote, "I asked Stanley [Rinehart] what he thought of Woolrich as a person. He replied that he had never met him, all the negotations had been done by mail—although they both lived in New York City!" (Nevins)

The thirteenth of Woolrich's fourteen contributions.

Blue cloth with titles in silver at the spine only, blue topstain. Farrar and Rinehart logo at the bottom of the copyright page (removed for later printings), and no date on the title page. Front flap shows a price of $2.50 at the top right corner, followed by a plot summary, then a jacket designer credit for Sol Immerman. Rear flap is a continuation of the plot summary, and the rear panel contains an advertisement for three books by the publisher, beginning with *The Wine of San Lorenzo* by Herbert Gorman and ending with *You and I* by Myron Brinig. The front flap, rear flap, and rear panel all end with the publisher's name and city.

NIGHT HAS A THOUSAND EYES

JOHN FARROW

Screenwriter   Jonathan Latimer and Barré Lyndon
Cinematographer   John F. Seitz
Composer   Victor Young
Cast   Edward G. Robinson, Gail Russell, John Lund, Virginia Bruce, William Demarest, Richard Webb
Studio   Paramount, 1948
Runtime   81 minutes

The challenge in adapting Cornell Woolrich's novel to the screen was to somehow evoke the inevitability of its main character's horrific predictions. Screenwriter Jonathan Latimer said in an interview near the end of his life, "What I hoped to establish was a real sense of terror that these things were coming true." Latimer and co-writer Barré Lyndon used a number of new contrivances intended to meet this goal, which, combined with Farrow's stylish direction and Edward G. Robinson's gripping performance, form a sort of surrogate for the "Woolrich atmosphere." The resulting film succeeds on the level of style, if not quite sustaining the level of terror found in the novel. (Nevins)

The third of director John Farrow's four contributions, screenwriter Jonathan Latimer's sixth of seven, and Barré Lyndon's last of four. Also, the first of three films noir on which Farrow and Latimer would collaborate.

Reference   Selby, Silver and Ward

A Novel of a Strange and Terrifying Experience

Night has a thousand eyes

GEORGE HOPLEY

DEAD MAN BLUES
CORNELL WOOLRICH WRITING AS WILLIAM IRISH

Publisher   Philadelphia: J.B. Lippincott, 1948

The first of three Cornell Woolrich titles to appear in hardcover in 1948 was a new collection under the writer's William Irish pseudonym, one of many published by Lippincott (and some, like this one, under the "Story Press" imprint) titled *Dead Man Blues*. Included in the collection was a story titled "Fire Escape," retitled from "The Boy Who Cried Murder," originally published in *Mystery Book Magazine* in March 1947.

The story's third-person protagonist is Buddy, a twelve-year-old with a fertile imagination and a propensity for making up elaborate whoppers—and getting walloped for them by his parents. One night while out on a fire escape, through the narrow strip of window glass beneath an incompletely pulled-down shade, he sees his upstairs neighbors kill a man and prepare to dismember his body with a straight razor.

The last of Woolrich's fourteen contributions.

Teal cloth with titles and design in blue at the spine, no topstain. Title page shows a date of 1948, with "FIRST EDITION—PRINTED IN THE UNITED STATES OF AMERICA" at the top of the copyright page. Front flap shows a price of $2.50 at the bottom right corner, and contains a plot summary, ending with "A Main Line Mystery" in blue. Rear flap with an advertisement for two other William Irish books, *Phantom Lady* and *Deadline at Dawn,* ending with "A Story Press Book" and a diagonally-set, proof-of-purchase coupon at the bottom left corner. Rear panel is an advertisement for the new books in the publisher's "Main Line" mystery series, with five listings, beginning with *Women Are Skin Deep* by Paul Whelton and ending with *Dead Man Blues* by William Irish. then the publisher's name and city.

THE WINDOW
TED TETZLAFF

Screenwriter   Mel Dinelli
Cinematographer   William Steiner, Robert De Grasse
Composer   Roy Webb
Cast   Barbara Hale, Bobby Driscoll, Arthur Kennedy, Paul Stewart, Ruth Roman
Studio   RKO, 1949
Runtime   73 minutes

Until 1949, there had been a clear pattern in Hollywood's use of Cornell Woolrich material. "A" pictures with decent production values had been made out of the novels, and "B" quickies out of the shorter fiction. The next Woolrich-based film may have been intended to stay within the pattern, but in the hands of director (and former Hitchcock cinematographer) Ted Tetzlaff, it was so well made and successful that it broke the tradition, proving that a big hit could indeed be adapted from a Woolrich short story—and thus, in a sense, paving the way for the biggest-budget Woolrich adaptation of them all, Alfred Hitchcock's *Rear Window* in 1954.

Lacking any major stars and running a scant seventy-three minutes, *The Window* transcended its modest beginnings to become a runaway box-office success. Though neither as visually innovative nor as existentially multileveled as the masterpieces of Hitchcock, it stands as a contender in the Hitchcock (and Woolrich) tradition of nonstop, nail-biting terror.

The third of director Ted Tetzlaff's four contributions, and screenwriter Mel Dinelli's second of three.

Reference   Selby, Silver and Ward, Lyons

DEAD
MAN
DEAD MAN BLUES

William Irish

AUTHOR OF "PHANTOM LADY"

LIPPINCOTT

KEEPER OF THE FLAME

I.A.R. WYLIE

Publisher   New York: Random House, 1942

Ida Alexa Ross Wylie was born on March 16, 1885, in Melbourne. She was taken by her parents to London in 1888 and received an education in England, Belgium, and Germany. Her writing career took off while she was still in her teens, and her novel, *The Red Mirage*, was brought to the screen in 1915 as *The Unknown*. This was followed by a string of film adaptations of her work in the silent era and on into the1930s, reaching its peak with *Keeper of the Flame*, a 1942 film noir with Spencer Tracy and Katharine Hepburn. Released by MGM in the midst of World War II, *Keeper of the Flame* is a sophisticated thriller that deals with the investigation of a wealthy and supposedly ultra-patriotic man whose unsavory secrets are revealed after his death. Two more adaptations of Wylie's work would follow in the 1950s.

Wylie was the kind of female public figure that Katharine Hepburn often played onscreen, and remained something of a literary celebrity for most of her career. In 1946, she was one of eleven women cited for her lifetime achievement by the Women's National Press Club.

The author's only contribution.

Black cloth with the Random House logo in red at the front board, and titles in reverse against a red panel at the spine. Red topstain. "FIRST PRINTING" stated at the top of the copyright page. Front flap shows a price of $2.00, followed by a plot summary, ending with "A RANDOM HOUSE BOOK." Rear flap contains an author biography, beginning with a small photo of Wylie, followed by four paragraphs of text. Rear panel is an advertisement for other books by the publisher, with listings for ten titles, beginning with *Storm* by George R. Stewart and ending with *With this Ring* by Mignon Eberhart, then "PUBLISHED UNDER THE RISING STAR OF / RANDOM HOUSE."

KEEPER OF THE FLAME

GEORGE CUKOR

Screenwriter	Donald Ogden Stewart
Cinematographer	William Daniels
Composer	Bronislau Kaper
Cast	Spencer Tracy, Katharine Hepburn, Richard Whorf, Margaret Wycherly, Forrest Tucker
Studio	MGM, 1942
Runtime	100 minutes

Screenwriter Donald Ogden Stewart notes, "*Keeper of the Flame* is the picture that I'm proudest of having been connected with—in terms of saying the most about Fascism that it was possible to say in Hollywood. It was a very good novel, and I didn't change it much. We had to keep it concealed from Mr. Mayer; [as] it wasn't what you'd call a Republican picture. The first time he saw it was in Radio City in New York, and he was so angry at the message of the picture that he got up and walked out. I can't vouch for that story, but I'd be very happy if it was true." (McGilligan, Backstory 1)

The second of four contributions by director George Cukor, and the second of two for Stewart.

Reference   Selby

KEEPER
OF THE
FLAME
·
I. A. R.
WYLIE

Keeper of the Flame

I. A. R. WYLIE

A NOVEL BY THE AUTHOR OF STRANGERS
ARE COMING and MY LIFE WITH GEORGE

RANDOM
HOUSE

NIGHT UNTO NIGHT

PHILIP WYLIE

Publisher   New York: Farrar and Rinehart, 1944

A writer of fiction and nonfiction, Philip Wylie wrote hundreds of short stories, articles, serials, syndicated newspaper columns, novels, and works of social criticism from the 1930s to the 1960s. He also wrote screenplays while in Hollywood, was an editor for Farrar and Rinehart, served on the Dade County (Florida) Defense Council, was a director of the Lerner Marine Laboratory, and at one time was a special advisor to the chairman of the Joint Committee for Atomic Energy. Most of his major writings contain critical, and often philosophical, views on man and society as a result of his studies and interest in psychology, biology, and ethnology.

While today he would be considered a techno-thriller writer in the Tom Clancy vein, Wylie's earliest books exercised great influence in twentieth-century science fiction pulp magazines and comic books. His 1930 character Gladiator, for example, was part of the inspiration for Superman; his 1932 character the Savage Gentleman inspired the pulp-fiction hero Doc Savage; and his 1933 novel *When Worlds Collide* (co-written with Edwin Balmer), was adapted into a notable 1951 film that was a huge influence on science fiction cinema of the 1950s.

Wylie's 1945 novel *The Paradise Crater* was cause for his house arrest by the federal government, as it described a post-World War II 1965 Nazi attempt to rule the world with atomic power.

The author's only contribution.

Light blue cloth with titles in dark blue and gilt rule at the front board and spine, no topstain. Publisher's device appears at the bottom of the copyright page (removed for later printings). Front flap shows a price of $2.75, and is followed by a brief War Production Board compliance statement, then a plot summary that continues to the end of the rear flap. Rear panel is an advertisement for Wylie's book, *Generation of Vipers,* with four review blurbs, the first by Walter Winchell and the last by Thomas Sugrue of *Herald Tribune Books*. Front flap, rear flap, and rear panel all end with the publisher's name and city.

NIGHT UNTO NIGHT

DON SIEGEL

Screenwriter	Kathryn Scola
Cinematographer	Peverell Marley
Composer	Franz Waxman
Cast	Ronald Reagan, Viveca Lindfors, Broderick Crawford, Rosemary DeCamp, Osa Massen, Art Baker
Studio	Warner Brothers, 1949
Runtime	84 minutes

Don Siegel's second feature, *Night Unto Night,* was an assignment from Warner Brothers, and featured extensive location shooting on the beaches of southern California (represented in the film as Florida). In his autobiography, Siegel remembers liking the script very little and finding the book itself incomprehensible, but with a style that became his trademark, he turned a turgid property into an atmospheric, well-paced film. Today it has a brooding quality that makes it stand out even among films noir, with its two heavies playing drastically against type. Ronald Reagan is a psychologically damaged biochemist with epilepsy, and Broderick Crawford is a philosophizing painter who works on giant, abstract murals. Siegel met his first wife, actress Viveca Lindfors, on the set of the film.

The director's second of three contributions, and the last of three for screenwriter Kathryn Scola.

Reference   Selby

NIGHT
UNTO
NIGHT

PHILIP
WYLIE

NIGHT
UNTO
NIGHT

A NOVEL BY

PHILIP WYLIE

FARRAR and
RINEHART

AUTHOR OF "GENERATION OF VIPERS"

THE BIG BOW MYSTERY

ISRAEL ZANGWILL

Publisher   London: Henry, 1892

Israel Zangwill was born in London in 1864, the son of a Russian Jewish refugee who emigrated to London. Raised in a ghetto, the author devoted his life to espousing Jewish causes, Zionism in particular, and gave voice to several unpopular opinions of the time, including woman's suffrage, and used to routinely refer to the League of Nations as the "League of Damnations."

In the eyes of mystery aficionados, Edgar Allan Poe's "The Murders in the Rue Morgue" (1841) is considered the first "locked-room" mystery story, but Zangwill's 1892 novella, *The Big Bow Mystery,* was the first fiction of greater length to use that plot device.

Written as a parody of detective stories, *The Big Bow Mystery* is a tongue-in-cheek story of a man who is discovered with his throat cut in a room that has been locked, sealed, bolted, and "as firmly barred as if besieged."

The story was first published in the London *Star* in 1891, then in book form by London publisher Henry and Company in 1892. The first American edition was published by Rand McNally in 1895, and the last important early appearance was in a 1903 collection of stories by Zangwill published by Heinemann, titled *The Grey Wig.*

The author's only contribution, both a Haycraft Queen Cornerstone and a Queen's Quorum selection.

Published in wrappers, with no known simultaneous hardcover edition. Title page reads: "London: / Henry & Company, 6, Bouverie Street / 1892 / (All Rights Reserved)." The verso of the title page contains an advertisement for the sixth edition of Zangwill's previous book, *The Batchelor's Club.*

THE VERDICT

DON SIEGEL

Screenwriter	Peter Milne
Cinematographer	Ernest Haller, Robert Burks (uncredited)
Composer	Frederick Hollander
Cast	Sydney Greenstreet, Peter Lorre, George Coulouris, Joan Lorring, Rosalind Ivan, Paul Cavanagh
Studio	Warner Brothers, 1946
Runtime	86 minutes

Israel Zangwill's classic crime novel was first filmed in 1928 as *The Perfect Crime,* then in 1934 as *The Crime Doctor.* Twelve years later, Warner Brothers purchased the property from RKO, and Don Siegel, a film technician who specialized in montage work, was tapped to direct. In Siegel's film noir version, Sydney Greenstreet portrays a corrupt police official who frames another man for a murder he has committed.

After completion of the principal shooting, Siegel and his producer William Jacobs drove to Jack Warner's house to screen the picture for him. The director remembers: "The picture ended. The lights went on as the screen was covered with a heavy curtain. Warner looked at us, puzzled, and said 'Greenstreet can't be a murderer.' Jacobs said, 'But Jack, you bought the book. In the book, the Inspector of Scotland Yard committed the murder.' Getting uptight, Warner replied, 'What if, instead of finding out at the end of the film that Greenstreet killed somebody, we show the audience some clues that Greenstreet might be the guilty man? That way, it won't be such a shock to the audience.' I said, 'Will it improve the picture? He's still the murderer.' Warner said, 'It will improve the picture. Do it as soon as you can. Be sure to let me know when I can see the new version. Good night, boys.'" (Siegel)

Don Siegel's first feature film as a director, and first of three contributions.

Reference   Selby, Lyons

PRICE ONE SHILLING.

The Big Bow Mystery.

BY

I. ZANGWILL.

AUTHOR OF

THE Bachelors' Club.

LONDON: HENRY & Co.

THE BIG BOW MYSTERY.

APPENDIX A
SECONDARY BOOK SOURCES

REBECCA

DAPHNE DU MAURIER

Publisher   London: Victor Gollancz, 1938

Presentation Edition, issued by the publisher prior to the trade edition. Two hundred copies were printed. The binding is the same as that of the trade edition, except that the title page and spine panel state "Special Presentation Edition." The only differences in the jacket are visible in the photo at the right.

REBECCA

ALFRED HITCHCOCK

Screenwriter   Robert E. Sherwood, Joan Harrison, Philip MacDonald, Michael Hogan
Cinematographer   George Barnes
Composer   Franz Waxman
Cast   Laurence Olivier, Joan Fontaine, George Sanders, Judith Anderson, Nigel Bruce
Studio   United Artists, 1940
Runtime   130 minutes

Reference   Selby

REBECCA

BY

DAPHNE DU MAURIER

SPECIAL PRESENTATION EDITION

SHED NO TEARS

DON MARTIN

Publisher   New York: Murray and Gee-Robert Frost, 1948

Variant "B" of the jacket, with binding the same as Variant "A." Front flap shows a price of $2.75 at the top right corner, followed by a plot summary, then a publisher's name (different than the publisher shown on the title page) of Robert Frost at the bottom. Rear flap has a single blurb at the center, stating that "Eagle-Lion films has purchased the screen rights... direct from the galley proofs," followed by a mention of the upcoming motion picture and its stars, Wallace Ford and June Vincent. Rear panel shows a lengthy direct quote from the book, framed in the same orange and white found on the front panel.

Robert Frost was the producer of the film version, and the presence of his name as the "publisher" of the book on the variant jacket, indicates that he likely made a "quick" attempt to capitalize on book sales by purchasing the rights just prior to the film's release.

SHED NO TEARS

JEAN YARBROUGH

Screenwriter   Brown Holmes, Virginia Cook
Cinematographer   Frank Redman
Cast   Wallace Ford, June Vincent, Robert Scott, Johnstone White, Dick Hogan
Studio   Eagle-Lion, 1948
Runtime   70 minutes

Reference   Selby, Lyons

Shed no tears

.... a brutal love story

with a haunting impact by

don martin~

DRAGONWYCK
ANYA SETON

Publisher   Boston: Houghton, Mifflin, 1944

Binding "B" is the same as Binding "A" (see Main Bibliography), with the following exceptions: cloth color is turquoise (titles are still burgundy), binding from board to board measures two centimeters, and Lexington Press is the printer noted on the title page and copyright page (instead of Riverside Press). The jacket art is the same except that the author's name on the front panel is in a different font, and the subtitle, "A Novel of America's Feudal Age" is added just below the author name. At least eight later printings have been noted; some state the later printing on the copyright page, and all lack a date on the title page.

DRAGONWYCK
JOSEPH L. MANKIEWICZ

Screenwriter	Joseph L. Mankiewicz
Cinematographer	Arthur Miller
Composer	Alfred Newman
Cast	Gene Tierney, Walter Huston, Vincent Price, Glenn Langan, Anne Revere, Spring Byington
Studio	Twentieth Century-Fox, 1946
Runtime	103 minutes

Reference   Selby

Dragonwyck
ANYA SETON
A NOVEL OF AMERICA'S FEUDAL AGE
Dragonwyck
ANYA SETON
M.CO.

MOONRISE
THEODORE STRAUSS

Publisher   New York: Viking, 1946

There are two variants for both the book and jacket on this title, with no priority. Following is the description of Variant "B." Green cloth with yellow titles at the front board and spine, yellow topstain, and blank endpapers. Title page shows a date of 1946 and the statement, "Published by the Viking Press in October 1946" at the top of the copyright page. Jacket has a man's face present in the front panel illustration (and is on close inspection an entirely different painting than the one found on Variant "A"), shows a price of "Moonrise $2.50" at the top right corner of the front flap, followed by a photo of the author and a biography, ending with the publisher's name and city and a jacket design credit for H. Lawrence Hoffman. Rear flap advertises "Recent and Forthcoming Viking Fiction," followed by four listings, beginning with *End Over End* by Nelson Gidding, ending with *An Afternoon* by Elizabeth Parsons. Rear flap ends with a statement reading, "Descriptive list of other current books / sent on request," followed by the publisher's name and address, ending with a "Printed in the U.S.A." statement. Rear panel is devoted to a plot summary, beginning with the book title, the author name, then three paragraphs of text, ending with the publisher's name and city (with no "Printed in the U.S.A." statement present).

MOONRISE
FRANK BORZAGE

Screenwriter   Charles Haas
Cinematographer   John L. Russell
Composer   Walter Kent, William Lava
Cast   Dane Clark, Gail Russell, Ethel Barrymore, Rex Ingram, Harry Morgan (as Henry Morgan)
Studio   Republic, 1948
Runtime   90 minutes

Reference   Selby, Silver and Ward

THEODORE STRAUSS

Moonrise

THE TREASURE OF THE SIERRA MADRE

B. TRAVEN

Publisher   New York: Alfred A. Knopf, 1935

This is the American edition of *Treasure of the Sierra Madre*, preceded by the UK edition, but the first edition to be translated by Traven. Black cloth with titles in blind at the front board, and titles in gilt at the spine panel. Brown topstain. Title page shows a date of 1935, with "FIRST AMERICAN EDITION" stated on the copyright page. Front flap contains a brief summary of the plot, with a price of $2.50 net at the top right corner. Rear flap reads, "BOOKS BY / B. TRAVEN / In Preparation / THE CARRETA / GOVERNMENT." Rear panel has a large advertisement for Traven's book, *The Death Ship*, with a list of fifteen different countries that have published the book as of January 1, 1935.

THE TREASURE OF THE SIERRA MADRE

JOHN HUSTON

Screenwriter   John Huston
Cinematographer   Ted McCord
Composer   Max Steiner, Buddy Kaye (title song)
Cast   Humphrey Bogart, Walter Huston, Tim Holt, Bruce Bennett, Barton MacLane, Alfonso Bedoya, A. Soto Rangel, Manuel Dondé, José Torvay, Margarito Luna
Studio   Warner Brothers, 1948
Runtime   126 minutes

Reference   Selby

THE
TREASURE
OF THE
SIERRA
MADRE
—
B. TRAVEN

BORZOI
BOOKS

LFRED A.
KNOPF

THE

TREASURE

OF THE

SIERRA MADRE

—

B. TRAVEN

TUCKER'S PEOPLE
IRA WOLFERT

Publisher   New York: L.B. Fischer, 1943

This is the "B" variant of the jacket, preceded by the "A" variant in the Main Bibliography (the binding for both variants is the same). Two points distinguish the "B" variant as being later issue: (1) the price has been lowered drastically, indicating that it was manufactured as a "cheap edition" produced for wartime sale, and (2) a third printing in the "B" jacket has been noted. Front flap shows a price of $1.49 at the top right corner, followed by a plot summary, which continues to the top half of the rear flap. The lower half of the rear flap shows four review blurbs for the book, in this order: *The New York Times*, *The New York Herald-Tribune*, *The Hartford Courant*, and *The Boston Globe*. Rear panel is devoted to a "Buy War Bonds" advertisement.

FORCE OF EVIL
ABRAHAM POLONSKY

Screenwriter	Abraham Polonsky, Ira Wolfert
Cinematographer	George Barnes
Composer	David Raksin
Cast	John Garfield, Beatrice Pearson, Thomas Gomez, Howard Chamberlain, Roy Roberts, Marie Windsor, Paul Fix, Stanley Prager, Barry Kelley, Paul McVey
Studio	MGM, 1948
Alternate Titles	The Numbers Racket, Tucker's People, The Story of Tucker's People (all US working titles)
Runtime	78 minutes
Reference	Selby, Silver and Ward

TUCKER'S
PEOPLE

A Novel by

IRA WOLFERT

APPENDIX B

Secondary Film Sources

I Wouldn't Be in Your Shoes

Cornell Woolrich writing as William Irish

Publisher   Philadelphia: J.B. Lippincott, 1943

First collected in the March 12, 1938 issue of *Detective Fiction*, title novella of this Cornell Woolrich collection, "I Wouldn't Be in Your Shoes," centers on a man sentenced to the electric chair because, on a stifling night, he throws a pair of shoes out of his window at a yowling cat—only to learn later that his shoe prints have been found at a murder scene.

The twelfth of Woolrich's fourteen contributions. One of two short stories from this collection used as a 1940s film noir source. The other is "Nightmare" (see Main Bibliography).

I Wouldn't Be in Your Shoes

William Nigh

Screenwriter	Steve Fisher
Cinematographer	Mack Stengler
Composer	Edward J. Kay
Cast	Don Castle, Elyse Knox, Regis Toomey, Charles D. Brown, Rory Mallinson, Robert Lowell
Studio	Monogram, 1948
Runtime	70 minutes

Steve Fisher: "Now Cornell Woolrich did now and then have one fault as a storyteller. Sitting in that hotel room he wrote at night, continuing through until morning, or whenever the story was finally completed. He did not revise, polish, and I suspect did not even read the story over once it was committed to paper. For that reason (he admitted to me) by the time he was near the end he was almost exhausted and often closed them off abruptly, with little or no hint as to the final fate of his characters. But a screenwriter is obliged to have a climactic understandable ending for his picture. *I Wouldn't be in Your Shoes* didn't have one. So I went to New York to persuade Woolrich to give me an ending that we could film. The closest I could get to him was the telephone. His mother would not permit him to leave the hotel room to meet me in person. What he said was, "Use the ending you had on *I Wake Up Screaming*. I did it, and it worked." (Nevins)

Director William Nigh's only contribution, and Steve Fisher's last of five.

Reference   Selby, Silver and Ward, Lyons

APPENDIX C
RECONSTRUCTED BOOK SOURCES

THE MILLS OF GOD

ERNST LOTHAR

Publisher   London: Secker and Warburg, 1935

Ernst Lothar was born Ernst Lothar Müller on October 25, 1890, in Brunn, Austria-Hungary (now Brno in the Czech Republic). He was a novelist, theatre director, producer, and is best known for his novel, *The Angel with the Trumpet.*

Three of Lothar's novels were made into well-known films, including *The Clairvoyant,* a 1934 thriller starring Claude Rains and Fay Wray, and *The Angel with the Trumpet,* a 1950 film adapted to the screen by Clemence Dane.

The author's only contribution.

Light blue-green cloth with dark blue titles at the spine, no topstain. Title page shows a date of 1935, with no statement of edition or later impressions on the copyright page. Front flap shows a price of "7s. 6d. / net" at the bottom right corner, and contains a plot summary, ending with a translation credit for Mr. and Mrs. Muir. Rear flap not seen. The rear panel advertises five books by the publisher, beginning with *Young Joseph* by Thomas Mann and ending with *Little Tales* by Lion Feuchtwanger. Upper and lower portions of the spine in the photo at right have been reconstructed, and may not be completely accurate.

AN ACT OF MURDER

MICHAEL GORDON

Screenwriter	Michael Blankfort, Robert Thoeren
Cinematographer	Hal Mohr
Composer	Daniele Amfitheatrof
Cast	Fredric March, Edmond O'Brien, Florence Eldridge, Geraldine Brooks, Stanley Ridges, John McIntire, Frederic Tozere, Will Wright, Virginia Brissac, Francis McDonald, Mary Servoss, Don Beddoe, Clarence Muse
Studio	Universal, 1948
Alternate Titles	The Judge's Wife (working title), Live Today for Tomorrow (US re-release title)
Runtime	91 minutes

An Act of Murder is probably the ultimate example of a 1940s film that spends nearly all its running time evading the Hays Code, only to submit in the end. In the story, a stern by-the-book judge commits euthanasia to save his terminally ill wife from further suffering. Eventually, he determines to kill her by driving the both of them off a cliff. His wife is killed according to his plan, but he unfortunately survives and ends up turning himself in with a full confession. Enter the judge's brilliant lawyer, who not only justifies the old judge's actions, but also proves that the wife took a fatal dose of poison before getting in the car, therefore committing suicide. The judge is freed and returns to his courtroom where he oversees his cases with a renewed sense of compassion.

Director Michael Gordon's third of four contributions, Michael Blankfort's first of two, and screenwriter Robert Thoeren's last of four.

Reference   Selby

THE
MILLS
OF GOD

Ernst
Lothar

ERNST
LOTHAR'S
New novel

THE MILLS
OF GOD

Author of
LITTLE
FRIEND

MARTIN
SECKER

FREQUENTLY USED TERMS

American film noir cycle or **noir cycle**

Term used to indicate the period from 1940-1965, when American films were made in what is today called "the noir style." Films made after 1965 in the noir style are generally referred to as **neo-noir** or **post-noir.**

House Un-American Activities Committee (HUAC)

The House Un-American Activities Committee (HUAC) was originally established by the US Congress in 1937 under the chairmanship of Martin Dies. The main objective of the HUAC was to investigate un-American and subversive activities, and its original targets were both left-wing and right-wing political groups. Eventually, however, the HUAC focused its investigation on the possibility that the American Communist Party had infiltrated the Federal Writers Project and other New Deal projects. This led to a more specific investigation into the Hollywood motion picture industry, and in September 1947, the HUAC interviewed forty-one individuals who were working in Hollywood. These individuals attended voluntarily and became known as "friendly witnesses." During interviews several people accused of holding left-wing views were named by the interviewees. Ten of those named, including Herbert Biberman, Lester Cole, Albert Maltz, Adrian Scott, Samuel Ornitz, Dalton Trumbo, Edward Dmytryk, Ring Lardner Jr., John Howard Lawson and Alvah Bessie refused to answer any questions. This group claimed the Fifth Amendment of the United States Constitution as their grounds for silence, and became known as the **Hollywood Ten**. The members of this group were found guilty of contempt of Congress and sentenced to between six and twelve months in prison.

After the jailing of the **Hollywood Ten**, other actors, producers, and directors such as Larry Parks, Leo Townsend, Isobel Lennart, Roy Huggins, Richard Collins, Lee J. Cobb, Budd Schulberg, and Elia Kazan, fearful that they would go to prison, came before the HUAC and named people who had been members of left-wing groups. Edward Dmytryk, who had originally refused to talk, changed his mind in order to save his career. Those identified as communists or socialists were then ordered to testify before the HUAC, and those who refused to name names were added to a growing "blacklist." The 320 people on this list were effectively kept from working legally in the entertainment industry. Among those blacklisted were Lillian Hellman, Dashiell Hammett, Clifford Odets, Larry Parks, Michael Wilson, Paul Jarrico, Louis Untermeyer, Anne Revere, Jeff Corey, Arthur Miller, Pete Seeger, Yip Harburg, John Garfield, Howard Da Silva, Joseph Losey, Richard Wright, and Abraham Polonsky. Many of the writers continued to work under assumed names, or under the name of an existing, non-blacklisted person. The writers who allowed their names to be used in such substitutions were known as "fronts."

After losing credibility during hearings held against Abbie Hoffman and Jerry Rubin in 1967, and again during the 1968 Democratic National Convention, the HUAC was renamed the Internal Security Committee. Six years later it was abolished and its few remaining functions were transferred to the House Judiciary Committee.

The Production Code (also known as **Hays Code**)

A set of industry guidelines governing the production of American motion pictures. The Motion Pictures Producers and Distributors Association (MPPDA), which later became the Motion Picture Association of America (MPAA), adopted the Code in 1930, began effectively enforcing it in 1934, and abandoned it in 1967 in favor of the subsequent MPAA film rating system. The Production Code spelled out what was and was not considered morally acceptable in the production of motion pictures for a public audience. The Code's most adamant enforcer was **Joseph I. Breen**, who was its chief 1934 to 1954.

Haycraft Queen Cornerstone (1748-1952)

Howard Haycraft was a historian of the detective story who in 1942 chose the books he believed formed "cornerstones" in detective fiction. This list was originally published in a volume by Haycraft titled *Murder for Pleasure* in 1942, and covered crime fiction published between 1748 and 1942. Mystery writer Ellery Queen (a collaboration of Frederic Dannay and Manfred B. Lee) later added titles also be included, bringing the end date for books considered up to 1952.

Queen's Quorum (1845-1967)

Ellery Queen made a selection of crime fiction separate from the titles found on the Haycraft Queen list, and later updated this list with nineteen additional titles. The complete list is referred to as the **Queen's Quorum**, and its range of considered titles is from 1845 to 1967.

Connolly 100 (1888-1950)

Cyril Connolly defined the Modern Movement in literature as a "revolt against the borgeois in France, the Victorians in England, the puritanism and materialism of America," and chose one hundred books written in France, England, and America that reflected this spirit. (Ahearn)

The Pulitzer Prize for Literature and Drama

Joseph Pulitzer, publisher of the *New York Globe*, established the Pulitzer Prize through an endowment to Columbia University in 1911. The Awards for Literature and Drama are given annually for a book by an American author, preferably dealing with American life.

Hubin

Used to refer to Allen J. Hubin's seminal guide, *Crime Fiction, 1749-1980: A Comprehensive Bibliography*, an exhaustive list of crime fiction authors, titles, first edition publishers, series characters, and locations that has come to be a standard for readers and collectors.

SELECTED FILMOGRAPHY

Adams, Gerald Drayson	*Dead Reckoning*	1947	Screenwriter
	The Big Steal	1949	Screenwriter
Allen, Lewis	*The Unseen*	1945	Director
	Desert Fury	1947	Director
	So Evil My Love	1948	Director
	Chicago Deadline	1949	Director
Altman, Robert	*Bodyguard*	1948	Screenwriter
Ambler, Eric	*Journey into Fear*	1943	Author
	The Mask of Dimitrios	1944	Author
Anderson, Edward	*They Live by Night*	1948	Author
Anderson, Maxwell	*Key Largo*	1948	Author
Armstrong, Charlotte	*The Unsuspected*	1947	Author
Atlas, Leopold	*Her Kind of Man*	1946	Screenwriter
	Raw Deal	1948	Screenwriter
Auer, John H.	*The Flame*	1947	Director
	I, Jane Doe	1948	Director
Avery, Stephen Morehouse	*Deep Valley*	1947	Screenwriter
	The Woman in White	1947	Screenwriter
Babcock, Dwight V.	*So Dark the Night*	1946	Screenwriter
	Bury Me Dead	1947	Screenwriter
Bachmann, Lawrence P.	*Fingers at the Window*	1942	Screenwriter
Baker, C. Graham	*Danger Signal*	1945	Screenwriter
	Shadow of a Woman	1946	Screenwriter
Bare, Richard	*Smart Girls Don't Talk*	1948	Director
	Flaxy Martin	1949	Director
Baum, Vicki	*The Great Flamarion*	1945	Screenwriter
	A Woman's Secret	1949	Author
Beaudine, William	*Below the Deadline*	1946	Director
	Don't Gamble with Strangers	1946	Director
	Incident	1949	Director
Beeding, Francis	*Spellbound*	1945	Author
Belgard, Arnold	*The Invisible Wall*	1947	Screenwriter
	Second Chance	1947	Screenwriter
Belloc Lowndes, Marie	*The Lodger*	1944	Author
	Ivy	1947	Author
Benedek, László	*Port of New York*	1949	Director
Bengal, Ben	*Crack-up*	1946	Screenwriter
	Illegal Entry	1949	Screenwriter
Bennett, Charles	*Ivy*	1947	Screenwriter
	The Sign of the Ram	1948	Screenwriter
	Black Magic	1949	Screenwriter
Benson, Sally	*Shadow of a Doubt*	1943	Screenwriter
Bercovici, Leonardo	*The Lost Moment*	1947	Screenwriter
	Kiss the Blood Off My Hands	1948	Screenwriter
Berke, William	*Shoot to Kill*	1947	Director
	Treasure of Monte Cristo	1949	Director
Berkeley, Anthony	*Suspicion*	1941	Author
Berkeley, Martin	*Shock*	1946	Screenwriter
	So Dark the Night	1946	Screenwriter

Bernhard, Jack	*Decoy*	1946	Director
	Violence	1947	Director
	The Hunted	1948	Director
	Blonde Ice	1948	Director
Bernhardt, Curtis	*Conflict*	1945	Director
	High Wall	1947	Director
	Possessed	1947	Director
Bezzerides, A.I.	*They Drive by Night*	1940	Author
	Desert Fury	1947	Screenwriter
	Thieves' Highway	1949	Author, Screenwriter
Blair, George	*End of the Road*	1944	Director
Blankfort, Michael	*An Act of Murder*	1948	Screenwriter
	The Dark Past	1948	Screenwriter
Block, Libbie	*Caught*	1949	Author
Bock, Edward	*Key Witness*	1947	Screenwriter
	The Thirteenth Hour	1947	Screenwriter
	The Return of the Whistler	1948	Screenwriter
Bodeen, DeWitt	*Cat People*	1942	Screenwriter
	The Seventh Victim	1943	Screenwriter
Boehm, Sydney	*High Wall*	1947	Screenwriter
	The Undercover Man	1949	Screenwriter
Boetticher, Budd	*Behind Locked Doors*	1948	Director
	Assigned to Danger	1948	Director
	The Missing Juror	1944	Director
	Escape in the Fog	1945	Director
Bolton, Muriel Roy	*My Name is Julia Ross*	1945	Screenwriter
	The Amazing Mr. X	1948	Screenwriter
	Mystery in Mexico	1948	Screenwriter
Booth, Charles Gordon	*The House on 92nd Street*	1945	Screenwriter
	Johnny Angel	1945	Author
	Behind Green Lights	1946	Screenwriter
	Strange Triangle	1946	Screenwriter
Borzage, Frank	*Moonrise*	1948	Director
Bottome, Phyllis	*Danger Signal*	1945	Author
Bowers, William	*The Web*	1947	Screenwriter
	Pitfall	1948	Screenwriter
	Larceny	1948	Screenwriter
	Abandoned	1949	Screenwriter
Brackett, Charles	*The Lost Weekend*	1945	Screenwriter
Brackett, Leigh	*The Big Sleep*	1946	Screenwriter
Brahm, John	*The Lodger*	1944	Director
	Guest in the House	1944	Director
	Hangover Square	1945	Director
	The Locket	1946	Director
	The Brasher Doubloon	1947	Director
	Singapore	1947	Director
Brecht, Bertolt	*Hangmen Also Die!*	1943	Screenwriter
Brentano, Lowell	*The Spider*	1945	Author
Bretherton, Howard	*Whispering Footsteps*	1943	Director
Bricker, George	*Inside Job*	1944	Screenwriter
	Mark of the Whistler	1946	Screenwriter
Bright, John	*I Walk Alone*	1948	Screenwriter
	Open Secret	1948	Screenwriter
Bristow, Gwen	*Tomorrow is Forever*	1946	Author, Screenwriter

Brooks, Richard	The Killers	1946	Screenwriter
	Brute Force	1947	Screenwriter
	Crossfire	1947	Author
	Key Largo	1948	Screenwriter
	Flamingo Road	1949	Screenwriter
Brower, Otto	Behind Green Lights	1946	Director
Brown, Fredric	Crack-Up	1946	Screenwriter (story)
Brown, George Carleton	The Tiger Woman	1945	Screenwriter
	The Big Punch	1948	Screenwriter
Browning, Tod	Inside Job	1944	Screenwriter
Burgess, Gelett	Two O'Clock Courage	1945	Author
Burnett, W.R.	High Sierra	1941	Author, Screenwriter
	The Get-Away	1941	Screenwriter
	This Gun for Hire	1942	Screenwriter
	Nobody Lives Forever	1946	Author, Screenwriter
	The Man I Love	1947	Screenwriter
Busch, Niven	The Postman Always Rings Twice	1946	Screenwriter
	Pursued	1947	Screenwriter
	Moss Rose	1947	Screenwriter
Butler, Gerald	Kiss the Blood Off My Hands	1948	Author
Buzzell, Edward	The Get-Away	1941	Director
Cain, James M.	Double Indemnity	1944	Author
	Mildred Pierce	1945	Author
	Postman Always Rings Twice	1946	Author
	Out of the Past	1947	Screenwriter
Carleton, Marjorie	Cry Wolf	1947	Author
Carpenter, Margaret	Experiment Perilous	1945	Author
Caspary, Vera	Laura	1944	Author
Castle, William	The Whistler	1944	Director
	When Strangers Marry	1944	Director
	Mark of the Whistler	1944	Director
	Dillinger	1945	Screenwriter
	The Voice of the Whistler	1945	Director
	Mysterious Intruder	1946	Director
	The Lady from Shanghai	1947	Screenwriter
	Johnny Stool Pigeon	1949	Director
	Undertow	1949	Director
Chamberlain, George Agnew	The Red House	1947	Author
Chambers, Whitman	Shadow of a Woman	1946	Screenwriter
	Big Town After Dark	1947	Screenwriter
	Manhandled	1949	Screenwriter
Chandler, Raymond	Double Indemnity	1944	Screenwriter
	Murder, My Sweet	1944	Author
	The Unseen	1945	Screenwriter
	The Blue Dahlia	1946	Screenwriter
	The Big Sleep	1946	Author
	Lady in the Lake	1947	Author, Screenwriter
	Brasher Doubloon	1947	Author
Chanslor, Roy	Destiny	1944	Screenwriter
	Black Angel	1946	Screenwriter
Charteris, Leslie	Lady on a Train	1945	Screenwriter
	Two Smart People	1946	Screenwriter

Chodorov, Edward	Rage in Heaven	1941	Screenwriter
	Undercurrent	1946	Screenwriter
	Road House	1948	Screenwriter
Clark, Alan R.	High Wall	1947	Author
Clemens, William	Night in New Orleans	1942	Director
	The Thirteenth Hour	1947	Director
Clifton, Elmer	The Judge	1949	Director
Clurman, Harold	Deadline at Dawn	1946	Director
Coffee, Lenore J.	Tomorrow is Forever	1946	Screenwriter
	Beyond the Forest	1949	Screenwriter
Cohn, Art	The Set-Up	1949	Screenwriter
	Illegal Entry	1949	Screenwriter
Cole, Royal K.	Blackmail	1947	Screenwriter
	Parole, Inc.	1948	Screenwriter
Collier, John	Deception	1946	Screenwriter
	The Unfaithful	1947	Screenwriter
Collins, Wilkie	The Woman in White	1947	Author
Colmes, Walter S.	Accomplice	1946	Director
	Road to the Big House	1947	Director
Colton, John	The Shanghai Gesture	1941	Author
Comandini, Adele	Strange Illusion	1945	Screenwriter
	Danger Signal	1945	Screenwriter
Connolly, Myles	The House Across the Bay	1940	Screenwriter
	The Great Mystic	1945	Screenwriter
Conway, Jack	Crossroads	1942	Director
Cooper, Dennis J.	When Strangers Marry	1944	Screenwriter
	Fear	1946	Screenwriter
	City Across the River	1949	Screenwriter
Cortez, Ricardo	Girl in 313	1940	Director
Cotten, Joseph	Journey into Fear	1943	Screenwriter
Cromwell, John	Dead Reckoning	1947	Director
Cukor, George	A Woman's Face	1941	Director
	Keeper of the Flame	1942	Director
	Gaslight	1944	Director
	A Double Life	1947	Director
Curtiz, Michael	Mildred Pierce	1945	Director
	The Unsuspected	1947	Director
	Flamingo Road	1949	Director
Darling, W. Scott	Behind Green Lights	1945	Screenwriter
	The Spider	1945	Screenwriter
Dassin, Jules	Two Smart People	1946	Director
	Brute Force	1947	Director
	Naked City	1948	Director
	Thieves' Highway	1949	Director
Davenport, Marcia	East Side, West Side	1949	Author
Daves, Delmer	The Red House	1947	Director
	Dark Passage	1947	Director
David, Charles	Lady on a Train	1945	Director
De Cordova, Frederick	Her Kind of Man	1946	Director
	Illegal Entry	1949	Director
de la Fouchardiere, Georges	Scarlet Street	1945	Author

De Toth, André	*Dark Waters*	1944	Director
	Guest in the House	1944	Director
	Dishonored Lady	1947	Screenwriter
	Pitfall	1948	Director
Del Ruth, Roy	*Red Light*	1949	Director
DeMond, Albert	*Shock*	1946	Screenwriter
	Blackmail	1947	Screenwriter
	Red Menace	1949	Screenwriter
Denham, Reginald	*Ladies in Retirement*	1941	Author
Dieterle, William	*Love Letters*	1945	Director
	The Accused	1949	Director
	Rope of Sand	1949	Director
Dinelli, Mel	*The Spiral Staircase*	1945	Screenwriter
	The Window	1949	Screenwriter
	Reckless Moment	1949	Screenwriter
Dmytryk, Edward	*Murder, My Sweet*	1944	Director
	Cornered	1945	Director
	Crossfire	1947	Director
Dostoyevsky, Fyodor	*Fear*	1946	Screenwriter (story)
Douglas, Gordon	*Walk a Crooked Mile*	1948	Director
Dratler, Jay	*Laura*	1944	Screenwriter
	The Dark Corner	1946	Screenwriter
	Call Northside 777	1948	Screenwriter
	Pitfall	1948	Author
	Impact	1949	Screenwriter
Du Maurier, Daphne	*Rebecca*	1940	Author
Du Soe, Robert C.	*The Devil Thumbs a Ride*	1947	Author
Duff, Warren	*The Fallen Sparrow*	1943	Screenwriter
	Experiment Perilous	1945	Screenwriter
	Chicago Deadline	1949	Screenwriter
	A Dangerous Profession	1949	Screenwriter
Duncan, Sam	*A Tragedy at Midnight*	1942	Screenwriter
	Circumstantial Evidence	1945	Screenwriter
Dunning, Decla	*The Stranger*	1946	Screenwriter
	I, Jane Doe	1948	Screenwriter
	Sleep, My Love	1948	Screenwriter
Duvivier, Julien	*Flesh and Fantasy*	1943	Director
	Destiny	1944	Director
Eberhart, Mignon	*Three's a Crowd*	1945	Author
Eby, Lois	*Larceny*	1948	Author
Eisinger, Jo	*The Spider*	1945	Screenwriter
	Gilda	1946	Screenwriter
	The Walls Came Tumbling Down	1946	Author
Elman, Irving	*Accomplice*	1946	Screenwriter
	Backlash	1947	Screenwriter
	Roses are Red	1947	Screenwriter
Endfield, Cy	*Argyle Secrets*	1948	Director
	Sleep, My Love	1948	Screenwriter
Endore, Guy	*Vicious Circle*	1948	Screenwriter
	Whirlpool	1949	Author
English, John	*Port of 40 Thieves*	1944	Director
Englund, Ken	*The Unseen*	1945	Screenwriter

Engstrand, Stuart	*Beyond the Forest*	1949	Author
Erskine, Chester	*All My Sons*	1948	Screenwriter
	Take One False Step	1949	Director
Essex, Harry	*Desperate*	1947	Screenwriter
	Bodyguard	1948	Screenwriter
	He Walked By Night	1948	Screenwriter
Eunson, Dale	*Guest in the House*	1944	Author
Farrow, John	*Calcutta*	1947	Director
	The Big Clock	1948	Director
	Night Has a Thousand Eyes	1948	Director
	Alias Nick Beal	1949	Director
Faulkner, William	*Mildred Pierce*	1945	Screenwriter
	The Big Sleep	1946	Screenwriter
	Deep Valley	1947	Screenwriter
Fearing, Kenneth	*The Big Clock*	1948	Author
Feist, Felix E.	*The Devil Thumbs a Ride*	1947	Director
	The Threat	1949	Director
Felton, Earl	*Criminal Court*	1946	Screenwriter
	Trapped	1949	Screenwriter
Fenton, Frank	*Nocturne*	1946	Screenwriter
	Out of the Past	1947	Screenwriter
Ferguson, Margaret	*The Sign of the Ram*	1948	Author
Fisher, Steve	*I Wake Up Screaming*	1941	Author
	Johnny Angel	1945	Screenwriter
	Dead Reckoning	1947	Screenwriter
	Lady in the Lake	1947	Screenwriter
	The Hunted	1948	Screenwriter
	I Wouldn't Be in Your Shoes	1948	Screenwriter
Fitzgerald, F. Scott	*The Great Gatsby*	1949	Author
Fleischer, Richard	*Bodyguard*	1948	Director
	Trapped	1949	Director
	The Clay Pigeon	1949	Director
	Follow Me Quietly	1949	Director
Fletcher, Lucille	*Sorry, Wrong Number*	1948	Author
Fleming, John	*Larceny*	1948	Author
Florey, Robert	*The Face Behind the Mask*	1941	Director
	Danger Signal	1945	Director
	The Beast with Five Fingers	1946	Director
	The Crooked Way	1949	Director
Foote, John Taintor	*Notorious*	1946	Author
Forbes, Murray	*Hollow Triumph*	1948	Author
Ford, Philip	*The Tiger Woman*	1945	Director
	The Last Crooked Mile	1946	Director
	The Mysterious Mr. Valentine	1946	Director
Forde, Eugene	*Backlash*	1947	Director
	The Invisible Wall	1947	Director
Foreman, Carl	*Champion*	1949	Screenwriter
	The Clay Pigeon	1949	Screenwriter
Fort, Garrett	*Ladies in Retirement*	1941	Screenwriter
	Among the Living	1941	Screenwriter
	Street of Chance	1942	Screenwriter
	Inside Job	1944	Screenwriter

Foster, Lewis R.	*The Lucky Stiff*	1949	Director
	Manhandled	1949	Director
Foster, Norman	*Journey into Fear*	1943	Director
	Kiss the Blood Off My Hands	1948	Director
Friedman, Seymour	*Chinatown at Midnight*	1949	Director
Frings, Ketti	*Guest in the House*	1944	Screenwriter
	The Accused	1949	Screenwriter
Fuchs, Daniel	*The Big Shot*	1942	Screenwriter
	The Gangster	1947	Author, Screenwriter
	Hollow Triumph	1948	Screenwriter
	Criss Cross	1949	Screenwriter
Fuller, Samuel	*Shockproof*	1949	Screenwriter
Furthman, Jules	*The Shanghai Gesture*	1941	Screenwriter
	The Big Sleep	1946	Screenwriter
	Moss Rose	1947	Screenwriter
	Nightmare Alley	1947	Screenwriter
Gabel, Martin	*The Lost Moment*	1947	Director
Gage, John	*The Velvet Touch*	1948	Director
Garmes, Lee	*Angels Over Broadway*	1940	Director
Garnett, Tay	*The Postman Always Rings Twice*	1946	Director
Gates, Harvey	*Below the Deadline*	1946	Screenwriter
	Don't Gamble with Strangers	1946	Screenwriter
George, George W.	*Bodyguard*	1948	Screenwriter
	I Married a Communist	1949	Screenwriter
Gilbert, Anthony	*My Name is Julia Ross*	1945	Author
Godfrey, Peter	*The Two Mrs. Carrolls*	1947	Director
	Cry Wolf	1947	Director
	The Woman in White	1948	Director
Goldsmith, Martin	*Dangerous Intruder*	1945	Screenwriter
	Detour	1945	Author, Screenwriter
	Blind Spot	1947	Screenwriter
Goodis, David	*Lady in the Lake*	1947	Screenwriter
	The Unfaithful	1947	Screenwriter
	Dark Passage	1947	Author
Gordon, Michael	*Woman in Hiding*	1940	Director
	The Web	1947	Director
	An Act of Murder	1948	Director
	The Lady Gambles	1949	Director
Gordon, Robert	*Blind Spot*	1947	Director
Goulding, Edmund	*Nightmare Alley*	1947	Director
Grayson, Charles	*I Married a Communist*	1949	Screenwriter
	Red Light	1949	Screenwriter
Greene, Graham	*This Gun for Hire*	1942	Author
	Ministry of Fear	1944	Author
	The Confidential Agent	1945	Author
Gresham, William Lindsay	*Nightmare Alley*	1947	Author
Gruber, Frank	*The Mask of Dimitrios*	1944	Screenwriter
	Johnny Angel	1945	Screenwriter
	Accomplice	1946	Author, Screenwriter
Gunn, James	*Born to Kill*	1947	Author
Hamilton, Patrick	*Gaslight*	1944	Author
	Hangover Square	1945	Author

Hammett, Dashiell	*The Maltese Falcon*	1941	Author
	The Glass Key	1942	Author
Harrison, Joan	*Rebecca*	1940	Screenwriter
	Suspicion	1941	Screenwriter
	Dark Waters	1944	Screenwriter
	Nocturne	1946	Screenwriter
	Ride the Pink Horse	1947	Screenwriter
Harvey, William Fryer	*The Beast with Five Fingers*	1946	Author
Haskin, Byron	*I Walk Alone*	1948	Director
	Too Late for Tears	1949	Director
Hathaway, Henry	*The House on 92nd Street*	1945	Director
	The Dark Corner	1946	Director
	Kiss of Death	1947	Director
	Call Northside 777	1948	Director
Hawks, Howard	*The Big Sleep*	1946	Director
Hayward, Lillie	*Blood on the Moon*	1948	Screenwriter
	Follow Me Quietly	1949	Screenwriter
	Strange Bargain	1949	Screenwriter
Hecht, Ben	*Angels Over Broadway*	1940	Director
	Journey into Fear	1943	Screenwriter
	Spellbound	1945	Screenwriter
	Cornered	1945	Screenwriter
	Gilda	1946	Screenwriter
	Specter of the Rose	1946	Author, Director
	Notorious	1946	Screenwriter
	Dishonored Lady	1947	Screenwriter
	Kiss of Death	1947	Screenwriter
	Ride the Pink Horse	1947	Screenwriter
	Cry of the City	1948	Screenwriter
	Whirlpool	1949	Screenwriter
Heisler, Stuart	*Among the Living*	1941	Director
	The Glass Key	1942	Director
	Smash-Up: The Story of a	1947	Director
Helseth, Henry Edward	*Cry of the City*	1948	Author
Hemingway, Ernest	*The Killers*	1946	Author
	The Macomber Affair	1947	Author
Herald, Heinz	*Vicious Circle*	1948	Author, Screenwriter
Herczeg, Geza	*The Shanghai Gesture*	1941	Screenwriter
	Vicious Circle	1948	Author
Hichens, Robert	*Temptation*	1946	Author
Higgins, John C.	*Railroaded!*	1947	Screenwriter
	T-Men	1947	Screenwriter
	He Walked By Night	1948	Screenwriter
	Raw Deal	1948	Screenwriter
	Border Incident	1949	Screenwriter
Hilton, James	*Rage in Heaven*	1941	Author
Hitchcock, Alfred	*Rebecca*	1940	Director
	Suspicion	1941	Director
	Shadow of a Doubt	1943	Director
	Spellbound	1945	Director
	Notorious	1946	Director

Hively, Jack	Street of Chance	1942	Director
Hoffenstein, Samuel	Flesh and Fantasy	1943	Screenwriter
	Laura	1944	Screenwriter
Hogan, Michael	Rebecca	1940	Screenwriter
	The Woman on the Beach	1947	Screenwriter
Holding, Elisabeth Sanxay	The Reckless Moment	1949	Author
Holland, Marty	Fallen Angel	1945	Author
Horman, Arthur T.	Conflict	1945	Screenwriter
	Dark Waters	1944	Screenwriter
	The Suspect	1944	Screenwriter
	Undertow	1949	Screenwriter
Huggins, Roy	Woman in Hiding	1940	Screenwriter
	I Love Trouble	1947	Author, Screenwriter
	The Lady Gambles	1949	Screenwriter
	Too Late for Tears	1949	Screenwriter
Hughes, Dorothy B.	The Fallen Sparrow	1943	Author
	Ride the Pink Horse	1947	Author
Humberstone, H. Bruce	I Wake Up Screaming	1941	Director
Hume, Cyril	The Great Gatsby	1949	Screenwriter, Producer
Hunter, Ian McLellan	Mr. District Attorney	1947	Screenwriter
	The Amazing Mr. X	1948	Screenwriter
Hurst, Fannie	Humoresque	1946	Author
Huston, John	High Sierra	1941	Screenwriter
	The Maltese Falcon	1941	Director
	Dark Waters	1944	Screenwriter
	Three Strangers	1946	Screenwriter
	The Stranger	1946	Screenwriter
	The Killers	1946	Screenwriter
	The Treasure of the Sierra Madre	1948	Director
	Key Largo	1948	Director
	We Were Strangers	1949	Director
Huxley, Aldous	Woman's Vengeance	1948	Author, Screenwriter
Ingster, Boris	The Stranger on the Third Floor	1940	Director
Isherwood, Christopher	Rage in Heaven	1941	Screenwriter
Jackson, Charles	The Lost Weekend	1945	Author
James, Henry	The Lost Moment	1947	Author
Job, Thomas	The Strange Affair of Uncle Harry	1945	Author
	The Two Mrs. Carrolls	1947	Screenwriter
Johnson, Nunnally	Moontide	1942	Screenwriter
	The Woman in the Window	1945	Screenwriter
	The Dark Mirror	1946	Screenwriter
Kahn, Gordon	Two O'Clock Courage	1945	Screenwriter
	Her Kind of Man	1946	Screenwriter
	Ruthless	1948	Screenwriter
	Whiplash	1948	Screenwriter
Kanin, Garson	A Double Life	1947	Screenwriter
Kazan, Elia	Boomerang!	1947	Director
Keighley, William	The Street With No Name	1948	Director
Kellogg, Virginia	T-Men	1947	Screenwriter
	White Heat	1949	Screenwriter
Kent, Robert E.	Two O'Clock Courage	1945	Screenwriter
	Assigned to Danger	1948	Screenwriter
	The Reckless Moment	1949	Screenwriter
Kimble, Lawrence	Criminal Court	1946	Screenwriter

	The Flame	1947	Screenwriter
	I, Jane Doe	1948	Screenwriter
	Mystery in Mexico	1948	Screenwriter
King, Rufus	*Secret Beyond the Door*	1948	Author
King, Sherwood	*The Lady from Shanghai*	1947	Author
Kleiner, Harry	*Fallen Angel*	1945	Screenwriter
	The Street With No Name	1948	Screenwriter
Koch, Howard	*The Letter*	1940	Screenwriter
	Three Strangers	1946	Screenwriter
Korda, Zoltan	*The Macomber Affair*	1947	Director
	A Woman's Vengeance	1948	Director
Landau, Richard H.	*Secret of the Whistler*	1946	Screenwriter
	The Crooked Way	1949	Screenwriter
Landers, Lew	*The Power of the Whistler*	1945	Director
	The Mask of Diijon	1946	Director
	Inner Sanctum	1948	Director
Lang, Fritz	*Moontide*	1942	Director
	Hangmen Also Die!	1943	Director
	Ministry of Fear	1944	Director
	The Woman in the Window	1945	Director
	Scarlet Street	1945	Director
	Secret Beyond the Door	1948	Director
Langham, James R.	*Night in New Orleans*	1942	Author
Lardner, Ring W.	*Champion*	1949	Author
Lardner, Ring, Jr.	*Laura*	1944	Screenwriter
Larkin, John	*Circumstantial Evidence*	1945	Director
Latimer, Jonathan	*Night in New Orleans*	1942	Screenwriter
	The Glass Key	1942	Screenwriter
	Nocturne	1946	Screenwriter
	They Won't Believe Me	1947	Screenwriter
	The Big Clock	1948	Screenwriter
	Night Has a Thousand Eyes	1948	Screenwriter
	Alias Nick Beal	1949	Screenwriter
Laurents, Arthur	*The Snake Pit*	1948	Screenwriter
	Caught	1949	Screenwriter
Le Borg, Reginald	*Destiny*	1944	Director
	Fall Guy	1947	Director
Le May, Alan	*The Walking Hills*	1949	Author, Screenwriter
Lederman, Ross	*Key Witness*	1947	Director
	The Return of the Whistler	1948	Director
Lederer, Charles	*Fingers at the Window*	1942	Director
	Kiss of Death	1947	Screenwriter
	Ride the Pink Horse	1947	Screenwriter
	The Lady from Shanghai	1947	Screenwriter
	Cry of the City	1948	Screenwriter
Leonard, Robert Z.	*The Bribe*	1949	Director
Lerner, Joseph	*C-Man*	1949	Director
LeRoy, Mervyn	*Johnny Eager*	1942	Director
	East Side, West Side	1949	Director
Levin, Henry	*Night Editor*	1946	Director
Lewin, Albert	*The Picture of Dorian Gray*	1945	Director

Lewis, Joseph H.	*My Name is Julia Ross*	1945	Director
	So Dark the Night	1946	Director
	The Undercover Man	1949	Director
Lewton, Val	*Cat People*	1942	Producer
	I Walked with a Zombie	1943	Producer
	The Leopard Man	1943	Producer
	The Seventh Victim	1943	Producer
	The Body Snatcher	1945	Producer
Ling, Eugene	*Shock*	1946	Screenwriter
	Assigned to Danger	1948	Screenwriter
	Behind Locked Doors	1948	Screenwriter
	Port of New York	1949	Screenwriter
Lipsky, Eleazar	*Kiss of Death*	1947	Author
Litvak, Anatole	*Out of the Fog*	1941	Director
	Blues in the Night	1941	Director
	The Long Night	1947	Director
	Sorry, Wrong Number	1948	Director
	The Snake Pit	1948	Director
Lord, Mindret	*Glass Alibi*	1946	Screenwriter
	Strange Impersonation	1946	Screenwriter
	Alias Nick Beal	1949	Screenwriter
Lothar, Ernst	*An Act of Murder*	1948	Author
Lubin, Arthur	*Impact*	1949	Director
Lussier, Dane	*Whispering Footsteps*	1943	Screenwriter
	Port of 40 Thieves	1944	Screenwriter
	Three's a Crowd	1945	Screenwriter
Lyndon, Barré	*The Lodger*	1944	Screenwriter
	Hangover Square	1945	Screenwriter
	The House on 92nd Street	1945	Screenwriter
	Night Has a Thousand Eyes	1948	Screenwriter
Macaulay, Richard	*They Drive by Night*	1940	Screenwriter
	Out of the Fog	1941	Screenwriter
	Born to Kill	1947	Screenwriter
MacDonald, Philip	*Rebecca*	1940	Screenwriter
	Strangers in the Night	1944	Screenwriter
	The Body Snatcher	1945	Screenwriter
	Love from a Stranger	1947	Screenwriter
	The Dark Past	1948	Screenwriter
MacDougall, Ranald	*Mildred Pierce*	1945	Screenwriter
	Possessed	1947	Screenwriter
	The Unsuspected	1947	Screenwriter
	Flamingo Road	1949	Screenwriter
Machaty, Gustav	*Jealousy*	1945	Director
Maddow, Ben	*Framed*	1947	Screenwriter
	Kiss the Blood Off My Hands	1948	Screenwriter
Maibaum, Richard	*The Great Gatsby*	1949	Screenwriter, Producer
Mainwaring, Daniel	*Big Town After Dark*	1947	Screenwriter
	Out of the Past	1947	Screenwriter
	They Made Me a Killer	1946	Screenwriter
	The Big Steal	1949	Screenwriter
	Out of the Past	1947	Author
Maltz, Albert	*This Gun for Hire*	1942	Screenwriter

	The Red House	1947	Screenwriter
	Naked City	1948	Screenwriter
Mamoulian, Rouben	Laura	1944	Director
Mankiewicz, Herman J.	Christmas Holiday	1944	Screenwriter
	A Woman's Secret	1949	Screenwriter
Mankiewicz, Joseph L.	Dragonwyck	1946	Director
	Somewhere in the Night	1946	Director
	House of Strangers	1949	Director
Mann, Anthony	Strangers in the Night	1944	Director
	The Great Flamarion	1945	Director
	Two O'Clock Courage	1945	Director
	Strange Impersonation	1946	Director
	Desperate	1947	Director
	Railroaded!	1947	Director
	T-Men	1947	Director
	He Walked By Night	1948	Director
	Raw Deal	1948	Director
	Follow Me Quietly	1949	Director
	Reign of Terror	1949	Director
	Border Incident	1949	Director
March, Joseph Moncure	The Set-Up	1949	Author
Marin, Edwin L.	Johnny Angel	1945	Director
	Nocturne	1946	Director
	Race Street	1948	Director
Markle, Fletcher	The Lady from Shanghai	1947	Screenwriter
	Jigsaw	1949	Director
Marshall, George	The Blue Dahlia	1946	Director
Martin, Don	The Pretender	1947	Screenwriter
	Shed No Tears	1948	Author, Screenwriter
Massie, Chris	Love Letters	1945	Author
Maté, Rudolph	The Dark Past	1948	Director
Maugham, W. Somerset	The Letter	1940	Author
	Christmas Holiday	1944	Author
Mayo, Archie	The House Across the Bay	1940	Director
	Moontide	1942	Director
McCarey, Ray	Strange Triangle	1946	Director
McDonell, Gordon	Shadow of a Doubt	1943	Screenwriter
	They Won't Believe Me	1947	Author
McGann, William C.	Highway West	1941	Director
McPhail, Angus	Spellbound	1945	Screenwriter
Mendes, Lothar	The Walls Came Tumbling Down	1946	Director
Milestone, Lewis	Guest in the House	1944	Director
	The Strange Love of Martha Ivers	1946	Director
	Arch of Triumph	1948	Director
Miller, Arthur	All My Sons	1948	Author
Miller, Seton I.	Ministry of Fear	1944	Screenwriter
	Calcutta	1947	Screenwriter
	Singapore	1947	Screenwriter
Miller, Winston	They Made Me a Killer	1946	Screenwriter
Millhauser, Bertram	The Big Shot	1942	Screenwriter
	The Suspect	1944	Screenwriter
	The Web	1947	Screenwriter

	Walk a Crooked Mile	1948	Screenwriter
Milne, Peter	*The Verdict*	1946	Screenwriter
	High Tide	1947	Screenwriter
Minnelli, Vincente	*Undercurrent*	1946	Director
Moguy, Leonide	*Whistle Stop*	1946	Director
Monks, John, Jr.	*The House on 92nd Street*	1945	Screenwriter
	Cry of the City	1948	Screenwriter
	Knock on Any Door	1949	Screenwriter
Montgomery, Robert	*Lady in the Lake*	1947	Director
	Ride the Pink Horse	1947	Director
Motley, Willard	*Knock on Any Door*	1949	Author
Murphy, Richard	*Boomerang!*	1947	Screenwriter
	Cry of the City	1948	Screenwriter
Nebel, Frederick	*The Bribe*	1949	Screenwriter
Negulesco, Jean	*The Mask of Dimitrios*	1944	Director
	Three Strangers	1946	Director
	Nobody Lives Forever	1946	Director
	Humoresque	1946	Director
	Deep Valley	1947	Director
	Road House	1948	Director
Neill, Roy William	*Black Angel*	1946	Director
Newfield, Sam	*Apology for Murder*	1945	Director
	The Lady Confesses	1945	Director
Newman, Joe	*Abandoned*	1949	Director
Niblo, Fred, Jr.	*Bodyguard*	1948	Screenwriter
	Incident	1949	Screenwriter
Nichols, Dudley	*Scarlet Street*	1945	Screenwriter
Nigh, William	*I Wouldn't Be in Your Shoes*	1948	Director
North, Edmund H.	*Dishonored Lady*	1947	Screenwriter
	Flamingo Road	1949	Screenwriter
Nosseck, Max	*Dillinger*	1945	Director
Nugent, Elliott	*The Great Gatsby*	1949	Director
Oboler, Arch	*Bewitched*	1945	Director
	The Arnelo Affair	1947	Director
Odets, Clifford	*Deadline at Dawn*	1946	Screenwriter
	Notorious	1946	Screenwriter
	Humoresque	1946	Screenwriter
O'Farrell, William	*Repeat Performance*	1947	Author
O'Hara, John	*Moontide*	1942	Screenwriter
O'Neal, Charles	*The Seventh Victim*	1943	Screenwriter
	The Missing Juror	1944	Screenwriter
Ophüls, Max	*Caught*	1949	Director
	The Reckless Moment	1949	Director
Oursler, Charles Fulton	*The Spider*	1945	Author
Ozep, Fedor	*Whispering City*	1947	Director
Pagano, Jo	*The Man I Love*	1947	Screenwriter
	The Unfaithful	1947	Screenwriter
Parker, Dorothy	*Smash-Up: The Story of a*	1947	Screenwriter
Pascal, Ernest	*Flesh and Fantasy*	1943	Screenwriter
	Destiny	1944	Screenwriter
Patrick, John	*Framed*	1947	Screenwriter
	Second Chance	1947	Screenwriter
Paul, Elliot	*A Woman's Face*	1941	Screenwriter
Paxton, John	*Murder, My Sweet*	1944	Screenwriter

	Cornered	1945	Screenwriter
	Crack-up	1946	Screenwriter
	Crossfire	1947	Screenwriter
Paxton, John	*Rope of Sand*	1949	Screenwriter
Percy, Edward	*Ladies in Retirement*	1941	Author
Perdue, Virginia	*Shadow of a Woman*	1946	Author
Petitt, Wilfred H.	*The Voice of the Whistler*	1945	Screenwriter
	The Walls Came Tumbling Down	1946	Screenwriter
Phillips, Arnold	*Bluebeard*	1944	Screenwriter
	Jealousy	1945	Screenwriter
Pichel, Irving	*Tomorrow is Forever*	1946	Director
	Temptation	1946	Director
	They Won't Believe Me	1947	Director
	Without Honor	1949	Director
Polonsky, Abraham	*Body and Soul*	1947	Screenwriter
	Force of Evil	1948	Director
	Caught	1949	Screenwriter
Preminger, Otto	*Laura*	1944	Director
	Fallen Angel	1945	Director
	Whirlpool	1949	Director
Presnell, Robert, Sr.	*The Guilty*	1947	Screenwriter
	High Tide	1947	Screenwriter
	For You I Die	1947	Screenwriter
Price, Will	*Strange Bargain*	1949	Director
Rackin, Martin	*Desperate*	1947	Screenwriter
	Riffraff	1947	Screenwriter
	Race Street	1948	Screenwriter
	A Dangerous Profession	1949	Screenwriter
Rand, Ayn	*Love Letters*	1945	Screenwriter
Raphaelson, Samson	*Suspicion*	1941	Screenwriter
Rapper, Irving	*Deception*	1946	Director
Ratoff, Gregory	*Moss Rose*	1947	Director
	Black Magic	1949	Director
Ray, Nicholas	*They Live by Night*	1948	Director
	A Woman's Secret	1949	Director
	Knock on Any Door	1949	Director
Reinhardt, John	*For You I Die*	1947	Director
	The Guilty	1947	Director
	High Tide	1947	Director
	Open Secret	1948	Director
Reis, Irving	*Crack-up*	1946	Director
	All My Sons	1948	Director
Remarque, Erich Maria	*Arch of Triumph*	1948	Author
Renoir, Jean	*The Woman on the Beach*	1947	Director
Reville, Alma	*Suspicion*	1941	Screenwriter
	Shadow of a Doubt	1943	Screenwriter
Rice, Craig	*The Lucky Stiff*	1949	Author
Richards, Robert L.	*Act of Violence*	1948	Screenwriter
	Johnny Stool Pigeon	1949	Screenwriter
Richards, Silvia	*Possessed*	1947	Screenwriter
	Secret Beyond the Door	1948	Screenwriter

Ripley, Arthur	*A Voice in the Wind*	1944	Director
	The Chase	1946	Director
Rivkin, Allen	*Highway West*	1941	Screenwriter
	Dead Reckoning	1947	Screenwriter
	Border Incident	1949	Screenwriter
Roberts, Florian	*Lady Gangster*	1942	Director
Roberts, Marguerite	*Undercurrent*	1946	Screenwriter
	The Bribe	1949	Screenwriter
Robertson, Willard	*Moontide*	1942	Author
Robson, Mark	*The Seventh Victim*	1943	Director
	Champion	1949	Director
Ronald, James	*The Suspect*	1944	Author
Bachmann, Lawrence P.	*Fingers at the Window*	1942	Screenwriter
Rosen, Phil	*Paper Bullets*	1941	Director
	The Great Mystic	1945	Director
Rossen, Robert	*Out of the Fog*	1941	Screenwriter
	Blues in the Night	1941	Screenwriter
	The Strange Love of Martha Ivers	1946	Screenwriter
	Johnny O'Clock	1947	Director
	Desert Fury	1947	Screenwriter
	Body and Soul	1947	Director
	All the King's Men	1949	Director
Rosson, Richard	*The Get-Away*	1941	Director
Rosten, Leo	*The Dark Corner*	1946	Screenwriter
	Lured	1947	Screenwriter
	Sleep, My Love	1948	Screenwriter
	The Velvet Touch	1948	Screenwriter
Rotter, Fritz	*Strange Illusion*	1945	Screenwriter
Rowland, Roy	*Scene of the Crime*	1949	Director
Rubin, Stanley	*Decoy*	1946	Screenwriter
	Violence	1947	Screenwriter
Santley, Joseph	*A Tragedy at Midnight*	1942	Director
	Shadow of a Woman	1946	Director
Saul, Oscar	*Woman in Hiding*	1940	Screenwriter
	The Dark Past	1948	Screenwriter
	Road House	1948	Screenwriter
	The Lady Gambles	1949	Screenwriter
Schnee, Charles	*I Walk Alone*	1948	Screenwriter
	They Live by Night	1948	Screenwriter
	Scene of the Crime	1949	Screenwriter
Schoenfeld, Bernard C.	*Phantom Lady*	1944	Screenwriter
	The Dark Corner	1946	Screenwriter
Schrock, Raymond L.	*Secret of the Whistler*	1946	Screenwriter
	Key Witness	1947	Screenwriter
	The Thirteenth Hour	1947	Screenwriter
Scola, Kathryn	*The House Across the Bay*	1940	Screenwriter
	Caught	1949	Screenwriter
	Night Unto Night	1949	Screenwriter
Seiler, Lewis	*The Big Shot*	1942	Director
	Whiplash	1948	Director
Sekely, Steve	*The Lady in the Death House*	1944	Director
	Hollow Triumph	1948	Director

Selander, Lesley	Three's a Crowd	1945	Director
	Blackmail	1947	Director
Seton, Anya	Dragonwyck	1946	Author
Shane, Maxwell	Fear in the Night	1947	Director
	Big Town After Dark	1947	Screenwriter
	City Across the River	1949	Director
Shaw, Irwin	Out of the Fog	1941	Author
	Arch of Triumph	1948	Screenwriter
	Take One False Step	1949	Screenwriter
Shearing, Joseph	Moss Rose	1947	Author
	So Evil My Love	1948	Author
Sherman, George	Secret of the Whistler	1946	Director
	Larceny	1948	Director
Sherman, Vincent	Nora Prentiss	1947	Director
	The Unfaithful	1947	Director
Sherwood, Robert E.	Rebecca	1940	Screenwriter
Short, Luke	Blood on the Moon	1948	Author, Screenwriter
Shulman, Irving	City Across the River	1949	Author
	City Across the River	1949	Screenwriter
Shumlin, Herman	The Confidential Agent	1945	Director
Siegel, Don	The Verdict	1946	Director
	Night Unto Night	1949	Director
	The Big Steal	1949	Director
Simon, S. Sylvan	I Love Trouble	1947	Director
	Lust for Gold	1949	Director
Sinclair, Robert B.	Rage in Heaven	1941	Director
	Mr. District Attorney	1947	Director
Siodmak, Curt	I Walked With a Zombie	1943	Screenwriter
	The Beast with Five Fingers	1946	Screenwriter
	Berlin Express	1948	Screenwriter
Siodmak, Robert	Phantom Lady	1944	Director
	Christmas Holiday	1944	Director
	The Suspect	1944	Director
	Conflict	1945	Screenwriter
	The Strange Affair of Uncle Harry	1945	Director
	The Spiral Staircase	1945	Director
	The Killers	1946	Director
	The Dark Mirror	1946	Director
	Cry of the City	1948	Director
	Criss Cross	1949	Director
Sirk, Douglas	Lured	1947	Director
	Sleep, My Love	1948	Director
	Shockproof	1949	Director
Springsteen, R.G.	Red Menace	1949	Director
St. Claire, Arthur	The Mask of Diijon	1946	Screenwriter
	Philo Vance's Gamble	1947	Screenwriter
Stahl, John M.	Leave Her to Heaven	1945	Director
Stevenson, Robert	Dishonored Lady	1947	Director
	To the Ends of the Earth	1948	Director
	I Married a Communist	1949	Director
Stevenson, Robert Louis	The Body Snatcher	1945	Author
Stewart, Donald Ogden	A Woman's Face	1941	Screenwriter
	Keeper of the Flame	1942	Screenwriter

Stewart, Peter	Money Madness	1948	Director
Stewart, Ramona	Desert Fury	1947	Author
Stoddart, Dayton	Ruthless	1948	Author
Storm, Barry	Lust for Gold	1949	Author
Strabel, Thelma	Undercurrent	1946	Author
Strauss, Theodore	Moonrise	1948	Author
Sturges, John	The Sign of the Ram	1948	Director
	The Walking Hills	1949	Director
Sturges, Preston	Unfaithfully Yours	1948	Director
Sylvester, Robert	We Were Strangers	1949	Author
Taylor, Dwight	I Wake Up Screaming	1941	Screenwriter
	Conflict	1945	Screenwriter
Tetzlaff, Ted	Notorious	1946	Cinematographer
	Riffraff	1947	Director
	The Window	1949	Director
	A Dangerous Profession	1949	Director
Thayer, Tiffany	Chicago Deadline	1949	Author
Thoeren, Robert	Rage in Heaven	1941	Screenwriter
	Temptation	1946	Screenwriter
	Singapore	1947	Screenwriter
	An Act of Murder	1948	Screenwriter
Thomas, William C.	They Made Me a Killer	1946	Director
	Big Town After Dark	1947	Director
Thorpe, Richard	Rage in Heaven	1941	Director
Tinling, James S.	Roses are Red	1947	Director
	Second Chance	1947	Director
Totheroh, Dan	Deep Valley	1947	Author
Tourneur, Jacques	Cat People	1942	Director
	I Walked With a Zombie	1943	Director
	The Leopard Man	1943	Director
	Experiment Perilous	1945	Director
	Out of the Past	1947	Director
	Berlin Express	1948	Director
Townsend, Leo	Port of New York	1949	Screenwriter
Tracy, Don	Criss Cross	1949	Author
Traven, B.	The Treasure of the Sierra Madre	1948	Author
Truesdell, June	The Accused	1949	Author
Trumbo, Dalton	Jealousy	1945	Screenwriter (Story)
	The Gangster	1947	Screenwriter
Turney, Catherine	Mildred Pierce	1945	Screenwriter
	The Man I Love	1947	Screenwriter
	Cry Wolf	1947	Screenwriter
Tuttle, Frank	This Gun for Hire	1942	Director
	Suspense	1946	Director
Ullman, Allan	Sorry, Wrong Number	1948	Author
Ulmer, Edgar G.	Bluebeard	1944	Director
	Strange Illusion	1945	Director
	Detour	1945	Director
	The Strange Woman	1946	Director
	Ruthless	1948	Director
Vale, Martin	The Two Mrs. Carrolls	1947	Author
Van Dyke, W.S.	Rage in Heaven	1941	Director

Veiller, Anthony	The Stranger	1946	Screenwriter
	The Killers	1946	Screenwriter
Vidor, Charles	Ladies in Retirement	1941	Director
	Gilda	1946	Director
Vidor, King	Beyond the Forest	1949	Director
Viertel, Peter	We Were Strangers	1949	Screenwriter
von Sternberg, Josef	The Shanghai Gesture	1941	Director
Vorhaus, Bernard	Bury Me Dead	1947	Director
	The Amazing Mr. X	1948	Director
Vosper, Frank	Love from a Stranger	1947	Author
Waggner, George	Sealed Lips	1941	Director
Wald, Jerry	They Drive by Night	1940	Screenwriter
	Out of the Fog	1941	Screenwriter
Wald, Malvin	Behind Locked Doors	1948	Screenwriter
	The Dark Past	1948	Screenwriter
	Naked City	1948	Screenwriter
	The Undercover Man	1949	Screenwriter
Walker, Gertrude	Whispering Footsteps	1943	Screenwriter
	End of the Road	1944	Screenwriter
	Railroaded!	1947	Screenwriter
Wallace, Richard	The Fallen Sparrow	1943	Director
	Framed	1947	Director
Wallis, J.H.	The Woman in the Window	1945	Author
	Strange Bargain	1949	Screenwriter
Walsh, Raoul	They Drive by Night	1940	Director
	High Sierra	1941	Director
	The Man I Love	1947	Director
	Pursued	1947	Director
	White Heat	1949	Director
Ward, Mary Jane	The Snake Pit	1948	Author
Warner, Jerry	Inside Job	1944	Screenwriter
	Fall Guy	1947	Screenwriter
Warren, Robert Penn	All the King's Men	1949	Author
Webb, Robert	The Spider	1945	Director
Weidman, Jerome	House of Strangers	1949	Author
Welles, Orson	Journey into Fear	1943	Director
	The Stranger	1946	Director
	The Lady from Shanghai	1947	Director
	Black Magic	1949	Director
Werker, Alfred	Shock	1946	Director
	Repeat Performance	1947	Director
	He Walked By Night	1948	Director
West, Nathanael	Stranger on the Third Floor	1940	Screenwriter
Wexley, John	Hangmen Also Die!	1943	Screenwriter
	Cornered	1945	Screenwriter
	The Long Night	1947	Screenwriter
White, Ethel Lina	The Unseen	1945	Author
	The Spiral Staircase	1945	Author
Whitfield, Raoul	High Tide	1947	Author
Whorf, Richard	Love from a Stranger	1947	Director

Wigton, Anne	*The Great Flamarion*	1945	Screenwriter
	Strange Impersonation	1946	Screenwriter
Wilbur, Crane	*The Amazing Mr. X*	1948	Screenwriter
	Canon City	1948	Director
	He Walked By Night	1948	Screenwriter
	The Story of Molly X	1949	Director
Wilde, Hagar	*Guest in the House*	1944	Author
	The Unseen	1945	Screenwriter
Wilde, Oscar	*The Picture of Dorian Gray*	1945	Author
Wilder, Billy	*Double Indemnity*	1944	Director
	The Lost Weekend	1945	Director
Wilder, Robert	*Flamingo Road*	1949	Author, Screenwriter
Wilder, Thornton	*Shadow of a Doubt*	1943	Screenwriter
Wilder, W. Lee	*Glass Alibi*	1946	Director
	The Pretender	1947	Director
	Vicious Circle	1948	Director
Wiles, Gordon	*The Gangster*	1947	Director
Williams, Ben Ames	*Leave Her to Heaven*	1945	Author
	The Strange Woman	1946	Author
Wilson, J. Donald	*The Whistler*	1944	Screenwriter
	Key Witness	1947	Screenwriter
Wilson, Mitchell A.	*The Woman on the Beach*	1947	Author
Wisberg, Aubrey	*Escape in the Fog*	1945	Screenwriter
	The Power of the Whistler	1945	Screenwriter
	So Dark the Night	1946	Screenwriter
	Road to the Big House	1947	Screenwriter
	Treasure of Monte Cristo	1949	Screenwriter
Wise, Robert	*The Body Snatcher*	1945	Director
	Criminal Court	1946	Director
	Born to Kill	1947	Director
	Blood on the Moon	1948	Director
	Mystery in Mexico	1948	Director
	The Set-Up	1949	Director
Wolfert, Ira	*Force of Evil*	1948	Author, Screenwriter
Wolff, Maritta	*Whistle Stop*	1946	Author
	The Man I Love	1947	Author
Wood, Sam	*Ivy*	1947	Director
Woolrich, Cornell	*Street of Chance*	1942	Author
	The Leopard Man	1943	Author
	Phantom Lady	1944	Author
	Mark of the Whistler	1944	Author
	Deadline at Dawn	1946	Author
	Black Angel	1946	Author
	The Chase	1946	Author
	Fall Guy	1947	Author
	The Guilty	1947	Author
	Fear in the Night	1947	Author
	The Return of the Whistler	1948	Author
	I Wouldn't Be in Your Shoes	1948	Author
	Night Has a Thousand Eyes	1948	Author
	The Window	1949	Author

Wray, Ardel	*I Walked With a Zombie*	1943	Screenwriter
	The Leopard Man	1943	Screenwriter
Wyler, William	*The Letter*	1940	Director
Wylie, I.A.R.	*Keeper of the Flame*	1942	Author
Wylie, Philip	*Night Unto Night*	1949	Author
Yarbrough, Jean	*Inside Job*	1946	Director
	Shed No Tears	1948	Director
Yordan, Philip	*When Strangers Marry*	1944	Screenwriter
	Dillinger	1945	Screenwriter
	Whistle Stop	1946	Screenwriter
	Suspense	1946	Screenwriter
	The Chase	1946	Screenwriter
	House of Strangers	1949	Screenwriter
	Reign of Terror	1949	Screenwriter
Zangwill, Israel	*The Verdict*	1946	Author
Zeisler, Alfred	*Fear*	1946	Director
	Parole, Inc.	1948	Director
Zinnemann, Fred	*Act of Violence*	1948	Director
Zuckerman, George	*Whispering City*	1947	Screenwriter
	Border Incident	1949	Screenwriter
	Trapped	1949	Screenwriter

Thanks

For editorial assistance, encouragement, support, and advice: Spencer Selby, Greg Gibson, Tom Congalton, John W. Knott, David Ford, Otto Penzler, Francis M. Nevins, Mark Parker Miller and Bob Fleck at Oak Knoll Press, and most of all, my wife Lyn.

For contributing rare books and jackets from their collections to be photographed:
Otto Penzler, Mark Terry, Bill Pronzini, John W. Knott, Between the Covers, Robert Dagg, Richard Thomas, James Hamlen, Ralph Sipper, Martin O'Connell, Barry Zeman, Heritage Bookshop, Bob Adey, Peter L. Stern, Kathleen Manwaring at Syracuse University, Lyndsey Greenslade, Graham Barkham, Jenni Chrisstoffels at the National Library of New Zealand, Verity Orme at the Bodleian Library, and Graham Yearley.

For providing answers to many questions: all of the individuals in the lists above, Barbara Richards, Sidney S. Keywood, Alan Zipkin at Derringer Books, Nicholas J. Certo, Mark Hime, Jackson Bryer, Dan Adams at Waverley Books, Richard Davison, Jeff Maser, Terry Zobeck, Adam Blakeney at Peter Harrington Rare Books, Brian McCaffrey, Jon Gilbert at Adrian Harrington Rare Books, Lew Buckingham at Buckingham Books, John Nash, Mark Kram, Boyd White, James Pepper, Robin Smiley, Bruce Palese, and Howard Prouty at ReadInk.

For contributing untold hours of their time in the making of this book:
John Malloy, Dan Gregory, Steve Erwin, Rebekah Berger, Molly Sacamano, Amber Fricke, Erin Haithcock, Theresa Rothschadl, Graham Yearley, and Faye Levine.

Bibliography

Ahearn, Allen and Patricia. *Book Collecting 2000*. New York: Putnam, 2000.

Ambler, Eric. *Here Lies: An Autobiography*. London: Weidenfeld and Nicholson, 1985.

Arnold, Jeremy. *The Man I Love*. Turner Classic Movies. www.tcm.com.

Bacher, Lutz. *Max Ophüls in the Hollywood Studios*. New Brunswick, New Jersey: Rutgers University Press, 1996.

Barzun, Jacques and Wendell Hertig Taylor. *A Catalogue of Crime*. Revised Edition. New York: Harper and Row, 1989.

Baum, Vicki. *It Was All Quite Different: the Memoirs of Vicki Baum*. New York: Funk & Wagnalls, 1964.

Behlmer, Rudy. *Behind the Scenes*. New York: Samuel French, 1992 (revised edition).

Behlmer, Rudy. *Inside Warner Bros. [1935-1951]*. New York: Viking, 1985.

The BFI Companion to Crime Films. London: Cassell, 1998.

Bishop, Jim. *The Mark Hellinger Story*. New York: Appleton-Century Crofts, 1952.

Bogdanovich, Peter. *Who the Devil Made It*. New York: Knopf, 1997.

Bozzola, Lucia. *Leave Her to Heaven* (Review). www.allmovieguide.com.

Brennan, Paul. *The Gangster* (Review). www.imdb.com

Burgess, Anthony. *99 Novels: The Best in English since 1939*. New York: Summit Books, 1984.

Callow, Simon. *Orson Welles: Hello Americans*. New York: Viking, 2006.

Casty, Alan. *The Films of Robert Rossen*. New York: Museum of Modern Art, 1969.

Chandler, Raymond. *The Selected Letters of Raymond Chandler*. (Frank MacShane, editor). New York: Columbia University Press, 1981.

Crowe, Cameron. *Conversations with Wilder*. New York: Knopf, 1999.

Dumont, Herve. *Frank Borzage*. New York: McFarland, 2006.

Eames, John Douglas. The MGM Story. New York: Crown, 1975.

Eisenschitz, Bernard. *Nicholas Ray: An American Journey*. London: Faber, 1993.

Encyclopedia of World Biography. www.bookrags.com.

Eder, Bruce. *Champion* (Review). All Movie Guide at www.allmovieguide.com.

Erickson, Glenn. *Too Late for Tears* (Review). www.dvdsavant.com.

Erickson, Hal. *Three's a Crowd* (Review). www.allmovieguide.com.

Feuchtwanger Library website at the University of Southern California. www.usc.edu/libraries

Fetherling, Doug. *The Five Lives of Ben Hecht*. New York: Lester and Orpen Limited, 1977.

Fujiwara, Chris. *Jacques Tourneur: The Cinema of Nightfall*. Baltimore: Johns Hopkins Press, 1998.

Fujiwara, Chris. "4 X Otto Preminger." www.filmint.nu.

Fujiwara, Chris. "Senses of Cinema: Otto Preminger." May 2002. www.sensesofcinema.com.

Gallagher, Tag. "All Lost in Wonder: Edgar G. Ulmer." Paris: *Cinemathique 15*, 1999.

Gifford, Barry. *The Devil Thumbs a Ride and Other Great Films* (Grove Press, 1988)

Gottfried, Martin. *Arthur Miller: His Life and Work*. Cambridge, MA: Da Capo Press, 2003.

Greco, J. *The File on Robert Siodmak in Hollywood: 1941-1951*. USA: Dissertation.com, 1999.

Griffin, Alice. *Understanding Arthur Miller*. Columbia: University of South Carolina Press, 1996.

Hannsberry, Karen Burroughs. *Femme Noir: Bad Girls of Film*. Jefferson, NC: McFarland, 1998.

Hauptfleisch, Gordon. "Pulp Pages: Thieves Like Us" (Review). www.blogcritics.org

Haut, Woody. *Heartbreak and Vine*. London and New York: Serpent's Tail, 2002.

Hoder-Salmon, Marilyn. "Biography of Phyllis Forbes-Dennis." The Thomson-Gale Dictionary of Literary Biography, 2006.

Herman, Jan. *A Talent for Trouble: The Life of Hollywood's Most Acclaimed Director, William Wyler*. New York: Putnam, 1995.

Hiney, Tom. *Raymond Chandler: A Biography*. New York: The Atlantic Monthly Press, 1997.

Hoopes, Roy. *Cain*. New York: Holt, Rinehart, Winston, 1982.

Hubin, Allen J. *Crime Fiction III: A Comprehensive Bibliography, 1749-1995*. Locus Press, 1999.

Hudgins, Morgan. "Second Hollywood." New York Times, June 22, 1947.

Huston, John. *An Open Book*. New York: Knopf, 1980.

Johnson, Doris and Ellen Leventhal. *The Letters of Nunnally Johnson*. New York: Knopf, 1981.

Keaney, Michael F. *Film Noir Guide*. Jefferson, NC: McFarland, 2003.

Keating, H.R.F. *Crime and Mystery: The 100 Best Books*. London: Xanadu, 1987.

Lambert, Gavin. *On Cukor*. New York: Putnam, 1972.

Laurents, Arthur. *Original Story By*. New York: Knopf, 2000.

Lee, Kevin. *Shooting Down Pictures: The Blank Wall*. www.alsolikelife.com/shooting.

Leff, Leonard J. *Hitchcock & Selznick*. New York: Weidenfeld and Nicolson, 1987.

Lower, Cheryl Bray & R. Barton Palmer. *Joseph L. Mankiewicz: Critical Essays with an Annotated Bibliography and a Filmography*. Jefferson, NC: McFarland, 2001.

Lowndes, Marie Belloc. *Diaries and Letters of Marie Belloc Lowndes 1911-1947*. London: Chatto & Windus, 1971 (Susan Lowndes, editor).

Luhr, William. *Raymond Chandler and Film*. New York: Frederick Ungar, 1982.

Lyons, Arthur. *Death on the Cheap The Lost B Movies of Film Noir!* New York: Da Capo Press, 2000.

MacAdams, William. *Ben Hecht: A Biography*. New York: Barricade Books, 1990.

MacKethon, Lucinda. "The Setons." University of North Carolina *Traces of Life* Biography Series. www.nhc.rtp.nc.us/biography.

McCoubrey, Carmel. *Dr. Gerard Chrzanowski, Innovative Psychoanalyst, Dies at 87* in *The New York Times*. November 12, 2000.

McGilligan, Patrick (editor and interviews). *Backstory 1: Interviews with Screenwriters of Hollywood's Golden Age*. University of California Press, 1986.

McGilligan, Patrick (editor and interviews). *Backstory 2: Interviews with Screenwriters of the 1940s and 1950s*. University of California Press, 1991.

McGilligan, Patrick. *Fritz Lang: The Nature of the Beast*. New York: St. Martin's Press, 1997.

Meisel, Myron "Edgar G. Ulmer: The Primacy of the Visual" in *Kings of the B's*. New York: E.P. Dutton, 1975 (Todd McCarthy and Charles Flynn, editors).

Meyer, William R. *Warner Brothers Directors*. New Rochelle, New York: Arlington House, 1978.

Miller, Clive T. "Nightmare Alley: Beyond the B's" in *Kings of the B's*. New York: E.P. Dutton, 1975 (Todd McCarthy and Charles Flynn, editors).

Moffat, Ivan; Miriam Gross (editor). "On the Fourth Floor of Paramount: Interview With Billy Wilder," *The World of Raymond Chandler*. New York: A and W Publishers, 1978).

Morgan, Ted. *Maugham: A Biography*. New York: Simon and Schuster, 1980.

Nevins, Francis. *Cornell Woolrich: First You Dream, Then You Die*. New York: Mysterious Press, 1988.

Parish, James Robert. *The RKO Gals*. New Rochelle, New York: Arlington House, 1974.

Parkinson, David (editor). *The Graham Greene Film Reader: Reviews, Essays, Interviews & Film Stories*. London: Carcanet, 1993.

Phillips, Gene D. *Hemingway and Film*. New York: Frederick Ungar, 1980.

Phillips, Gene D. *Graham Greene: The Films of His Fiction*. New York: Teachers College Press, 1974.

Porfirio, Robert. *Film Noir Reader 3: Interviews with the Filmmakers of the Classic Noir Period*. New York: Limelight Editions, 2002.

Pratley, Gerald. *The Cinema of John Huston*. New York: A.S. Barnes, 1977.

Rand, Ayn; Michael S. Berliner (editor). *Letters of Ayn Rand*. New York: E.P. Dutton, 1995.

Reilly, John M. (editor). *Twentieth-Century Crime and Mystery Writers (Second Edition)*. New York: St. Martin's Press, 1985.

Renoir, Jean. *My Life and My Films*. London: Collins, 1974.

Rich, Nathaniel. *San Francisco Noir*. New York: The Little Bookroom, 2005.

Robertson, James C. *The Casablanca Man: The Cinema of Michael Curtiz*. London and New York: Routledge, 1993.

Ryley, Robert M. (editor). *Kenneth Fearing: Complete Poems*. The National Poetry Foundation, 1994.

Sarris, Andrew. *The Films of Josef von Sternberg*. New York: Museum of Modern Art, 1966.

Sarris, Andrew. *The American Cinema: Directors and Directions 1929-1968*. New York: E.P. Dutton, 1968.

Selby, Spencer. *Dark City: The Film Noir*. Jefferson, North Carolina: McFarland, 1984.

Sennett, Ted. *Warner Brothers Presents*. New Rochelle, New York: Arlington House, 1972.

Sherry, Norman. *The Life of Graham Greene: Volume I: 1904-1939*. London: Viking Penguin, 1989.

Sherry, Norman. *The Life of Graham Greene: Volume II: 1939-1955*. London: Viking Penguin, 1994.

Siegel, Don. *A Siegel Film: An Autobiography*. London: Faber, 1993.

Siegel, Joel. *Val Lewton: The Reality of Terror*. London: Secker & Warburg, 1972.

Silver, Alain and Elizabeth Ward. *Film Noir: An Encylopedic Reference to the American Style* (Third Edition). Woodstock, New York: The Overlook Press, 1992.

Silver, Alain. *Film Noir Reader 3: Interviews with the Filmmakers of the Classic Noir Period*. New York: Limelight Editions, 2002.

Smiley, Robin. *Books into Film*. Santa Monica, California: Capra Press, 2003.

Spicer, David. *Film Noir*. London: Longman/Pearson Education Limited, 2002.

Truffaut, Francois. *Hitchcock/Truffaut (Revised Edition)*. New York: Touchstone, 1985.

Ursini, James. *Film Noir Reader 3: Interviews with the Filmmakers of the Classic Noir Period*. New York: Limelight Editions, 2002.

Vallance, Tom. *A.I. Bezzerides*. London: *The Independent*. January 20, 2007.

Wallis, Hal and Charles Higham. *Starmaker: the Autobiography of Hal Wallis*. New York: Macmillan, 1980.

364

INDEX OF BOOKS

INDEX OF FILMS

INDEX OF NAMES